COLUMBUS
AMERICA'S CROSSROADS

by Betty Garrett with Edward R. Lentz

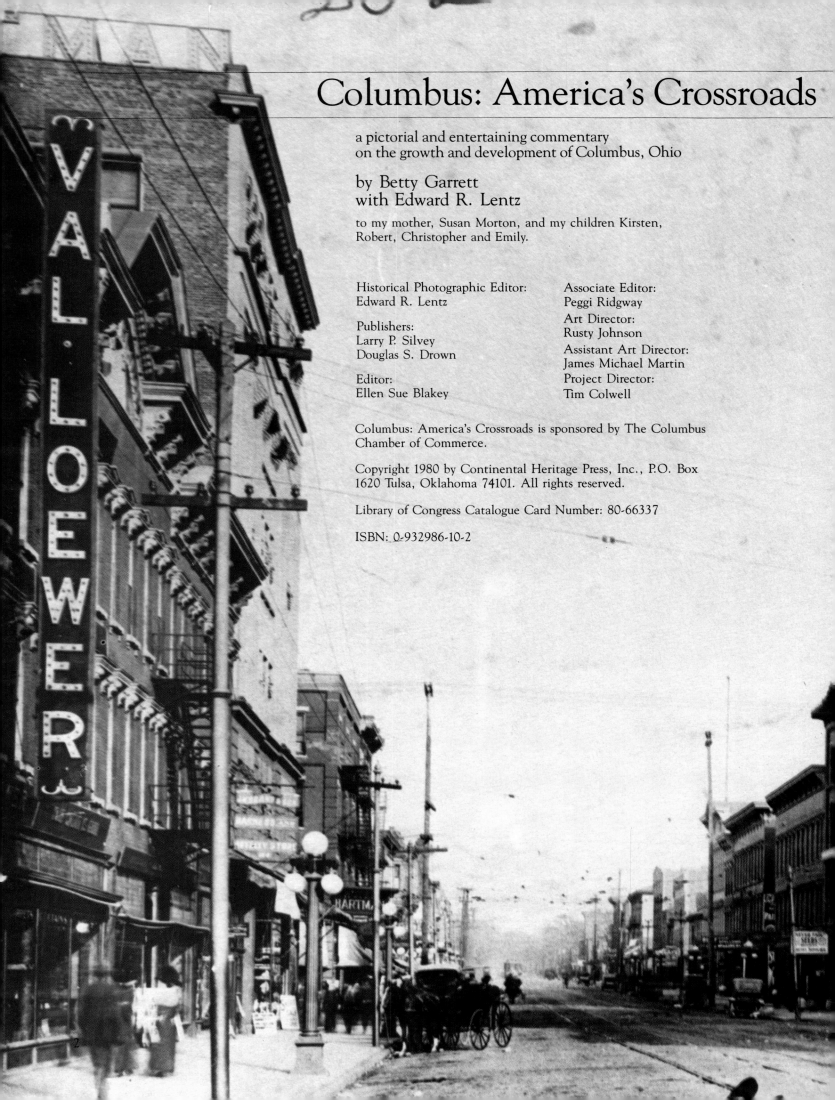

Columbus: America's Crossroads

a pictorial and entertaining commentary
on the growth and development of Columbus, Ohio

by Betty Garrett
with Edward R. Lentz

to my mother, Susan Morton, and my children Kirsten,
Robert, Christopher and Emily.

Historical Photographic Editor:
Edward R. Lentz

Publishers:
Larry P. Silvey
Douglas S. Drown

Editor:
Ellen Sue Blakey

Associate Editor:
Peggi Ridgway

Art Director:
Rusty Johnson

Assistant Art Director:
James Michael Martin

Project Director:
Tim Colwell

Columbus: America's Crossroads is sponsored by The Columbus
Chamber of Commerce.

Library of Congress Catalogue Card Number: 80-66337

ISBN: 0-932986-10-2

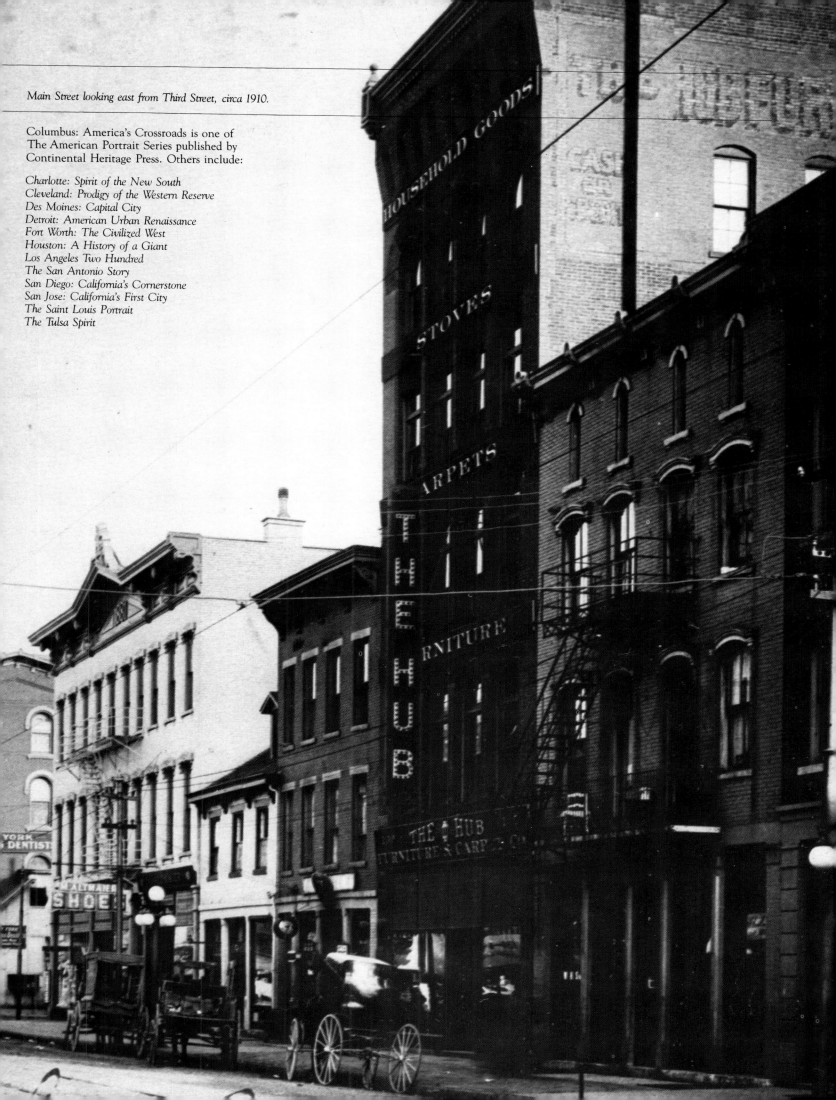

Main Street looking east from Third Street, circa 1910.

Columbus: America's Crossroads is one of
The American Portrait Series published by
Continental Heritage Press. Others include:

Drawn from nature & printed in colors by E. Sachse & C? Baltimore Md.

1. Deaf & Dumb Asylum. 2. Insane Asylum. 3. St Joseph's Cath. Church. 4. Blind Asylum. 5. Starling Medical
College. 6. High School. 7. Holy Cross Cath. Church. 8. Lutheran Church. 9. Heyl's Female Seminary.
10. Universalist Church. 11. 1st Presb. Church. 12. Lutheran Church. 13. Baptist Church. 14. 2d Presb. Church.
15. State Capitol. 16. 2d Meth. Episc. Church. 17. St James' Epis. Church. 18. Platt Block. 19. Statesman Building.

VIEW OF

UMBUS O.

ty.

Published by J.T. Palmatary.

20. County Court House. 21. Meth. Epis. Church. 22. American House. 23. German Refrm. Church. 24. Neil House. 25. Blenners
Brewery. 26. Hoster & Co. Brewery. 27. Hills Foundery. 28. Ridgways Foundery. 29. Gas Works. 30. Wollen Factory. 31. Battles,
Comstock & Co. Planing & Flour Mill. 32. Ohio Tool Co. 33. Howietts Soap Factory. 34. Rolling Mill. 35. Ambos &
Lennox Foundry & Machine Shop. 36. Ridgway & Kimball's Can Factory. 37. Ohio Penitentiary.

Benefactors and Sponsors

The following Columbus area firms, organizations and individuals have invested toward the quality production of this historic book and have thereby expressed their commitment to the future of this great city and to the support of the book's principal sponsor, The Columbus Area Chamber of Commerce.

AccuRay Corporation
Action Energy, Inc.
Adria Laboratories, Inc.
Alban Equipment Co.
Alexander, Ebinger, Fisher, McAlister & Lawrence
American Aggregates Corp.
*Anderson Concrete Corporation
Lenora Andrews
Anheuser-Busch, Inc.
Apco Industries, Inc.
Archer-Meek-Weiler Insurance Agency, Inc.
Arjay Construction Company, Inc.
Armstrong Mortgage Company
Ashland Chemical Company
Associated General Contractors, Central Ohio Division
B & A Paint and Wallcovering
Robert W. Baird & Co., Inc.
Baker & Hostetler
*BancOhio National Bank

*Bank One Corporation
*Banning & Pickett
R. G. Barry Corporation
Bates & Rogers Construction Corporation
*Battelle Memorial Institute
*Big Bear Stores Company
*Big Drum Inc.
Bohl Painting Company
*Borden Inc.
Briscoe Manufacturing Co.
Brown Van & Storage Co.
Brubaker/Brandt, Inc.
Buckeye Boxes, Inc.
Buckeye Business Forms
*Buckeye Federal Savings & Loan Association
*Buckeye International, Inc.
Buckeye Union Ins. Co.
Business/Personal Income Consultants
Byer & Bowman Advertising Agency, Inc.
*Geo. Byer Sons, Inc.
Bob Caldwell Chrysler-Plymouth
Cam Taylor Co., Realtors
Capital University
Cardinal Industries, Inc.
Central Ohio Label Company
Clark Converse Electrical Service
The Clinton Oil Company
*Columbia Gas of Ohio, Inc.
*The Columbus and Southern Ohio Electric Company
The Columbus Bar Association

Columbus Cello-Poly Corp.
*Columbus Citizen-Journal
Columbus Electrical Works Co. Inc.
Columbus Para Professional Institute
*The Columbus Show Case Company
Columbus Steel Drum Co.
Columbus Wood Preserving Co.
Concrete Construction Co.
Connecticut Mutual Life Insurance Company
Connell's Flowers
Copco Papers Inc.
Crane Plastics Manufacturing
Deloitte Haskins & Sells
Ralph Dickson & Company
*The Dispatch Printing Company
Doctors Hospital
*Dollar Savings Association
Dresser Power Transmission Division
Dublin Building Systems
*Ebco Manufacturing Company
Echenrode Furniture Co.
Elford Inc.
Dave Ellies Industrial Design Inc.
T. William Evans, DDS, MD
The Favret Company
Stanley Ferger & Associates
First Community Bank
*Franklin Federal Savings and Loan Association
*Franklin University

Freedom Federal Savings and Loan Association
The Fritz-Rumer-Cooke Co.
Frank Gates Service Co.
Mary Gabel Water Conditioning
*John W. Galbreath & Co.
The Gardner Company
General Electric Company — Specialty Materials Dept.
Genuine Parts Company (NAPA)
The Greater Columbus Arts Council
HER, Realtors
*Hanna Chemical Coatings Corp.
Harper Engraving and Printing Company
*Highlights for Children, Inc.
Hills Company
Holiday Inn Airport
Holzer-Wollam Realtors
*The Huntington National Bank
Ingersoll-Rand
J.P. Sand & Gravel Co.
Jai Lai Restaurant
Janitrol Aero Division
The Jeffrey Company
Jeffrey Mining Machinery Division, Dresser Industries, Inc.
Robert H. Johns Co.
Howard Johnson's North
The Katz Management Group, Incorporated
George B. Kauffman
Melvin Kent & Associates

Bird's eye view of Broad Street from the Harrison Building, circa 1908 with the Board of Trade Building, the Journal building, First Congregational Church, Trinity Episcopal Church and Statehouse Square.

Key Oldsmobile
Kientz & Company
Kight Cowman Abram, Inc.
William W. Kight
John Kincheloe, Architect
Kitchen Kraft, Inc.
Knodt/Maddox Inc.
 Architects-Planners
Kobacker Stores
Scott Krauss News Agency
In Memory of Scott & Venus
 Krauss
*The Kroger Co.
Lambert Sheet Metal, Inc.
*Lane Aviation Corporation
*Lazarus
*Lennox Industries Inc.
R. J. Leukart
W. J. Leukart, Jr.
Walter J. Leukart, III
*Liebert Corporation
Longanbach, Giusti and
 Associates
Marsh & McLennan Real Estate
 Advisors, Inc.
McDonald, Cassell & Bassett, Inc.
 — Architects
*The McElroy-Minister Company
The McNally Lumber Co.
Michael's Finer Meats, Inc.
Mid-Ohio Electric Co.
*The Midland Mutual Life
 Insurance Company
Midland-Ross Corporation
Midwestern Digital Electronics, Inc.

Moling & Associates, Inc.
*Motorists Mutual Insurance
 Company
Muetzel Plumbing and Heating
 Co.
The Murphy Company
*The Nationwide Organization
*Neil House Motor Hotel
OCLC, Inc.
Office Outfitters
*The Ohio Bell Telephone
 Company
*The Ohio Company
Ohio Medical Indemnity Mutual
 Corp.
Ohio Mobile Telephone, Inc.
Ohio State Federal Savings &
 Loan Association
*The Ohio State University
Jim Owen & Co., Inc., Realtors
Palmo Advertising, Inc.
Panic Lighting Co.
*The Palmer-Donavin
 Manufacturing Company
Peat, Marwick, Mitchell & Co.
J. C. Penney Co. Inc.
Pingue Properties, Inc.
Pitney-Bowes, Inc.
Price Waterhouse & Co.
Professional Book Distributors,
 Inc.
The F. L. Purdy Company
*Ranco Incorporated
*RAX Systems, Inc.
Reiner Realty and Consultants Inc.

Remarks, Inc.
 The Robins Beverage Group
*Roman Catholic Diocese of
 Columbus
*Ross Laboratories Division of
 Abbott Laboratories
*The Thomas W. Ruff and
 Company
*Ruscilli Construction Co., Inc.
*SCOA Industries Inc.
SST Inc.
St. Ann's Hospital of Columbus,
 Inc.
Sandefur Companies
Sauer Mechanical, Inc.
*Schoedinger Funeral Service
*M/I Schottenstein Companies, Inc.
Schuler Leukart Incorporated
*The Setterlin Company
 The Sheraton Columbus
*The Sherman R. Smoot
 Company, Inc.
Howard Daniel Smith
Edw. F. Sommer, C.L.U.
The Southgate Development
 Corporation
Julian Speer Company
*State Automobile Mutual
 Insurance/Columbus Mutual Life
 Insurance
*State Savings
Stone Leasing Co.
*Suburban Motor Freight, Inc.
The Superior Die, Tool &
 Machine Co.

Oscar L. Thomas & Co.
The Thompson Company
Timron Inc.
Top of the Center Restaurant
Trott & Bean Architects
Turner and Shepard, Inc.
20th Century Builders, Inc.
*The Union Fork and Hoe
 Company
United McGill Corporation
United Moving & Storage, United
 Van Lines
*United Way of Franklin County
Vercoe & Company Inc.
Vorys, Sater, Seymour and Pease
WBNS-TV Inc.
WCMH-TV
WTVN-TV
Larry Wade & Co., Realtors
Warner Amex "QUBE"
*Wendy's Old Fashioned
 Hamburgers
Paul Werth Associates, Inc.
*White Castle System, Inc.
*The W. W. Williams Company
Wonder Bread-Hostess Cake
*Worthington Industries, Inc.

*Denotes Corporate Sponsors. The histories of
these organizations and individuals appear in a
special section beginning on page 181.

CONTENTS

From a family album, circa 1890.

AMERICA'S CROSSROADS

by Betty Garrett

James Thurber, the Columbus-born humorist whose stories acquainted the world with his hometown, once puzzled over the city's peculiar beginnings.

"In the early years of the nineteenth century," he wrote, "Columbus won out as state capital by only one vote over Lancaster, and ever since then has had the hallucination that it is being followed, a curious municipal state of mind which affects, in some way or other, all those who live there. Columbus is a town in which almost anything is likely to happen and in which almost everything has."

That is true. Something is happening now, also. More and more, when Columbus people look back, they are not hallucinating. What they see following them is their own past. In 168 years of constantly rushing to become as great a city as legislative fiat declared it should be — while struggling defensively with a reputation for being an overgrown cowtown — Ohio's capital has finally acquired a history. Most cities inherit theirs; in Columbus, it was built — like the city itself — from scratch.

America's Crossroads is an attempt to reconstruct something of what that process was like. It is an opportunity to get acquainted with some of the people who have participated in it over the decades . . . all types of people, not just the official builders and shapers who usually make their way into history books and onto the pedestals of statues.

To do that, virtually all major histories written about Columbus in the past were read, and pertinent information either incorporated or used as background material for this volume. But it also involved a search, following a personal bias, through Columbus' "attic" for the things ordinary individuals, not historians, tend to save. Pieces of clothing long out of style or fit, but "too good to throw away" . . . old theater programs . . . broken toys or games once cherished by children long grown . . . mementos from weddings . . . pressed flowers or obituaries from funerals . . . diaries that weren't always finished, as its confidences were . . . letters to and from friends, relatives, lovers, saved for private (if not fully remembered) reasons . . . books, magazines, stacks of newspapers, with ads that picture the merchandise which is the American dream of a given time . . . stilted studio portraits in Daguerrotypes, as well as Kodak snapshots, preserving unidentified moments and faces from the past.

Parlors, like many histories, only showed the way things were *meant* to be kept always in order. The atmosphere in old attics is a little musty, but comfortable. And those nameless faces staring back from 1812 or 1880 or 1915 or 1943 look curiously familiar. In fact, they resemble ourselves.

So think of this book, if you will, as a sort of family album from an attic in Columbus, Ohio. Although some pages here have been used for people and places never known or only vaguely remembered, they are all related to us in the history of this particular family. And there are new pages in the album, waiting to be filled in by Columbus people every day, day after day.

Columbus Division No. 1

Columbus, circa 1860, looking west from the School for the Blind (above) and present-day Columbus.

GETTING AROUND: By 1863, the popular mode of transportation was the horse-drawn streetcar, seen here circa 1890. By the turn of the century, horse-powered streetcars were replaced by electric versions, and a "stop" and "go" umbrella helped direct traffic on the streets of Columbus.

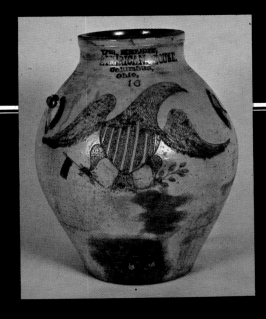

CHAPTER ONE

A CITY IS BORN

1797-1829

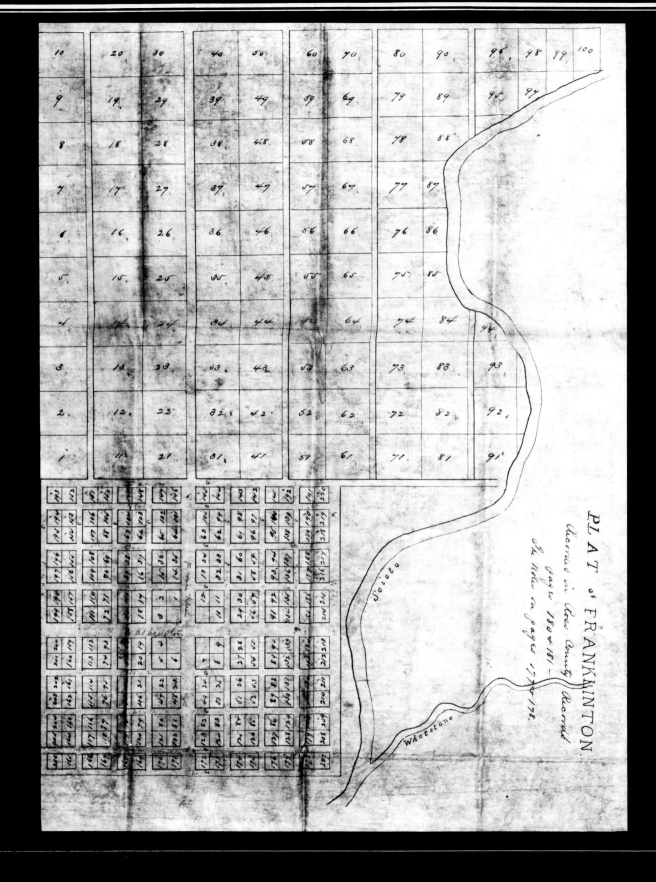

MOUND BUILDERS
AND WARRIORS

Pre-historic Indian tobacco pipe.

When colonial French and English explorers, traders, trappers and settlers arrived in central Ohio in the late 1600s and early 1700s, they encountered several Indian villages where Columbus and Franklin County now stand. Through the period, the Wyandots, Shawnees, Miamis, Delawares, Mingoes and other smaller tribes had been migrating into the Ohio Country, from Lake Erie on the north to the Ohio River on the south.

These tribes (who would claim the Ohio Country as their own in their encounters with white people after 1750) were really latecomers to the area. Since the early 1600s the Shawnees (from the Carolinas), the Delawares (from Pennsylvania) and the Wyandots (from the lake country) had all been pushed westward by the continuing encroachment of French, English, Dutch and other settlements. Until the mid-1700s, these Indian tribes had been kept out of the Ohio Country by the powerful Iroquois confederacy of upstate New York. The confederacy had claimed the Ohio Country as their own private hunting preserve in the 1650s. They had wrested control of the area in 1654 from the Erie Nation who had dominated the Ohio Country since A.D. 1300. The Erie were virtually annihilated in a pitched battle near the lake which bears their name. But with constant European encroachment on their own New York homeland, the Iroquois were no longer able to defend the Ohio Country. By 1750, the great

migration of other tribes began. These tribes were in a constant state of war or armed truce until the threat of white conquest led to partial unity against a common foe — the white man — in the late 1700s. These tribes had little or no knowledge of the people who had preceded them.

As best as can be determined now, the Ohio Country was continuously occupied by human settlement from 6000 B.C. and possibly as early as 10,000 B.C. But evidence of the hunter-gatherer archaic peoples who occupied Ohio until about 1000 B.C. is very limited. They were followed by the more settled agricultural Adena and Hopewell peoples and then the Cole and Fort Ancient peoples (after A.D. 800). These were the so-called Mound Builder cultures. Their construction of elaborate earthen monuments (mounds) were an expression either of religious ritual or reverence for the departed. These cultures disappeared (for reasons still not clear) around A.D. 1600, leaving thousands of mounds throughout the state (50 in Franklin County alone).

The earliest white settlers in the region were not archaeologists or anthropologists. They were a breed interested in building a new civilization, not in preserving monuments to the past. Most of the mounds were promptly leveled. The largest one in Franklin County stretched 40 feet high near the southeast corner of Mound and High streets. (The clay in it was used to make bricks for Columbus' first

statehouse in 1816.) Ironically, it was near that leveled mound site that the old Franklin County Courthouse was later built to store the equivalents of the white settlers' artifacts — written records of domestic arrangements and social behavior. A century later, that courthouse was considered an artifact and demolished — pragmatism taking precedence over history — just as it did when that 40-foot mound was leveled.

Fortunately, some mounds were left intact. (In Columbus, Campbell Mound of McKinley Avenue still stands.) Professionally trained anthropologists were eventually able to examine the remaining meager clues and make some deductions about the Mound Builders.

A few of the mounds were designated as the *effigy* variety. These were probably used for religious ceremonies and rituals. They were impressive — not just for the amount of earth hand-carried to the site but for the primitive aesthetic sense which shaped those mounds into likenesses of animals, birds, snakes and other living creatures. The most famous of these is Serpent Mound in Adams County. Four feet high and two city blocks long, the mound curves in serpentine splendor, with an egg-shaped mound perpetually about to enter the serpent's mouth.

Most mounds were molded into oval or cone shapes and used for burying the dead. A Hopewell or Adena corpse was placed on top of the ground then covered with a generous layer of dirt. Frequently, the same mound was used to bury other

While most mounds are of the oval or cone shape, the Serpent Mound in Adams County snakes over the countryside. It averages four feet in height and is two city blocks long.

bodies, each corpse successively laid on top of the previous one, divided only by a layer of dirt.

Some of the artifacts buried with the people afford clues about their domestic lives. The Mound Builders may have believed (as did the ancient Egyptians) that they would need certain items to recreate their existence in a later life. They were primarily vegetarians who combed the forests for wild fruits, berries, nuts and honey. They fished from dugout canoes in rivers and streams formed after the ice covering the area in the last glacial period melted. Today, these waters amount to three major drainage systems — the Scioto and Olentangy rivers; Big Walnut, Alum and Blacklick creeks; and Big and Little Darby creeks. Food consisted of grain, corn, beans, squash, pumpkins and sunflower seeds. And along with bone and stone tools, mussel shells were also used to dig those mind-boggling amounts of earth which they carried in grass baskets on their heads or shoulders to the sites of the ever-growing ovals, cones and effigies.

They loved jewelry. Combs, necklaces, bracelets and earrings were wrought from mussel shells, animal bones, copper and pearls. They fashioned knives, arrowheads, spearheads, clay pottery, dishes of turtle shells and finely designed pipes.

Aside from the few remaining mounds, nothing is left of the long-vanished Hopewells and Adenas.

Indian tribes of the 1600s, and later, are better documented. By the 1790s, the Ohio tribes of the Wyandots, nominally presided over by a great chief named Tarhe, "the Crane," had one village on Alum Creek, near what is now Livingston Avenue. A second was near what became the Lane Avenue bridge over the Scioto. The Shawnees had a village at the south edge of Columbus on the Scioto. Mingoes lived in three area villages — on the west bank of the Scioto, where Jackson Pike now runs; near where the Scioto and Olentangy join; and on the east bank of the Scioto south of Greenlawn Avenue.

As the explorers, traders and trappers were followed by increasing numbers of white settlers, some of the Indian chiefs and their tribesmen failed to grasp the white man's concept of "manifest destiny". It was becoming clear the uninvited guests had come to stay. Inevitably, some Indians attacked and killed the newcomers as they ventured out alone or in small family groups. As the raids increased, settlers whose homes were burned and whose relatives were killed fought back and killed the Indians with a savagery of their own.

But Chief Logan, a Mingo, saw no reason why the bountiful resources of the Ohio Country could not be shared with the settlers, until after his entire family had been killed in battles with white men. South of what would become Circleville, under an elm (later named for him), Chief Logan spoke to the men fighting his people. He spoke simply and eloquently as he named the relatives he loved and how they had been killed. It was a litany of sorrow but not of bitterness: "I appeal to any white man to say if ever he entered Logan's cabin hungry and he gave him not meat; if ever he came cold and naked and he clothed him not." The speech was widely printed and distributed. Thomas Jefferson, gifted with "felicity of expression" himself, considered it a masterpiece of eloquence and could recite it to the end of his life. It was also inscribed on a plaque at the site. (The tree has finally succumbed to age.)

But one great man's compassion and eloquence was not enough to stop the inevitable. Bloodshed increased between Indians and whites. Indians took sides with both the French and the English during the seven-year French and Indian war. When the bloodletting ended in 1763, the English emerged as victors in control of the Northwest Territory. The Indians, who were still suffering

19

"Treaty of Greenville" by Howard Chandler Christy hangs in the Statehouse rotunda.

under the delusion that it was their land, had won nothing.

After the revolutionary war, the U.S. government either gave the land (sight unseen) as payment to its soldiers or sold it to build up its depleted treasury. Members of the Ohio Company first came to what is now Marietta in the 1780s to survey and stake out settlements. When they steadily moved north, the Indians attacked more fiercely than ever before. Twice the American government tried to drive Indians out of Ohio. Armies led by General Harmor (1790) and by General St. Clair (1792) were defeated by forces led by Miami Chief Little Turtle.

The Indians continued to fight and kill rather than be driven out. At times they spared children, whom they adopted into their tribes. Jeremiah Armstrong was captured at age 9 by the Wyandots and adopted by Chief Tarhe. John Brickell lived with the Delawares for four years. Both often camped with their Indian keepers on sites that were to become Franklinton and Columbus. At the Treaty of Greenville in 1795, General ("Mad") Anthony Wayne negotiated with representatives of twelve tribes. He obtained their promise never to fight again. They gave up most of the Ohio Country for $20,000 in goods. Kidnapped whites such as Armstrong and Brickell were freed. But Armstrong had virtually forgotten his own language, and Brickell retained Indian clothing and customs most of his life. Both became pioneer residents of Franklin County.

For several years, the Indians lived in peace with white settlers. They taught them ancient methods of coping with the harsh wilderness. But as the cities grew, the Indians gradually moved out of Ohio, leaving nothing behind but their customs and names of rivers whose original definitions are rarely known today.

Pioneer house in Franklinton, photograph taken circa 1892.

After Ohio was admitted to the Union in 1803, its legislators met and functioned out of temporary "capitals" in Zanesville and Chillicothe. By 1810, that body decided the government should function from a permanent capital city. Then — in what would become time-honored legislative fashion — they promptly appointed a five-man committee to study the situation.

In brief, they concluded in their study that the new capital should be located near the geographic center of the state, accessible from all main travel routes. It should be equipped with resources necessary to current governmental functions and future growth and development and their choice should offend as few voters as possible.

From the time central Ohio was opened, the entire county was being settled by those who legitimately purchased land as well as squatters who simply moved in and set up housekeeping. Since travel was difficult, people tended to establish their own meeting places which eventually became hamlets or towns. Thus, there were a number of settlements in the area — many of which could have served as the capital.

The leading candidates were Zanesville and Chillicothe — having already served as temporary capitals — and central Ohio's Circleville, Delaware, Dublin, Newark, Worthington and Franklinton (the seat of Franklin County).

Laid out in 1797, by Lucas Sullivant, Franklinton in its earliest years was (according to *We Too Built Columbus*) "just a nameplace in the wilderness." It was a small town directly west of the Capital site on the lower bank of the Scioto, located approximately where today's I-71 first exits off West Broad Street. (Nothing remains of it today but a house just east of the I-71 ramp which may have served as headquarters for General William Henry Harrison during the War of 1812.) Its characteristics were those of most early settlements in the Ohio Country. According to a Mrs. Qualsey Conrad, there was "plenty of mud, plenty of hard times, and plenty of hard work; and we didn't have to go to the circus to see a bear, either." Since early Indian raids had been quieted after the Treaty of Greenville, the chief hazards to survival in Franklinton were frequent outbreaks of fevers only vaguely perceived at that time to be connected to the repeated flooding of the Scioto into the west side "bottoms".

Despite such difficulties, settlers followed the young surveyor Sullivant in building "humble log huts along the river that was part of the main water route between Lake Erie and the Ohio River." Many were lured by a limited number of free plots which Sullivant offered. Among the lucky few were Pennsylvania Germans Katherine and Abraham Deardurff. Their home stood on a street still called Gift Street. Deardurff carried mail and trade items back East, but most of the first Franklinton people were farmers or traders. Many worked on the thousands of acres which Sullivant himself owned and had put under cultivation.

While the town served as county seat until 1824, Sullivant was also Franklin County clerk of courts for some time. Later, while surveying land for supply roads to Lancaster, Newark, Springfield and Worthington, he personally constructed corduroy (flat-sided log) roads in his own settlement. He also built a jail, a log school and a brick courthouse. By 1810, when capital sites were being considered, Franklinton had several stately brick homes. Franklinton was not chosen as the capital — nor were its existing competitors. But the people of Franklinton were about to qualify — along with Ohio's legislators — as the founding fathers, mothers and in-laws of the new capital city.

Chief among them was Lucas Sullivant himself. According to his son Joseph's description, Sullivant was "muscular and well proportioned, quick and active in his movements with an erect carriage and a good walk, a well-balanced head finished off with queue (which he always wore), a broad and high forehead, an aquiline nose, blue-gray eyes, a firm mouth and a square chin. He was firm and positive in his opinions, but courteous in manner and expression, prompt and decisive to act upon his convictions, and altogether a man of forcible character, exercising an influence over those with whom he came in contact."

Sullivant's wife, Sarah Starling Sullivant, bore him three children — William S. (who at the time of his death, in 1873, was America's foremost bryologist), Michael L. (whose interest in agriculture constantly led him to experiment with new implements on the farms his father had under cultivation) and Joseph (an archaeologist and the Starling-Sullivant genealogist/biographer). Although Ohio's constitution forbade slavery, Sarah Sullivant brought with her two "hirelings" — Humphrey and Arthur — former slaves from her family's Kentucky plantation, who served the family all their lives.

To keep Sarah from being lonely during his extended absences, Sullivant induced her sister and her husband, James and Lucy McDowell, to settle in Franklinton in a brick house he built for them across the street from their own home — a three-story brick house with glass windows carried over the Pennsylvania mountains.

LUCAS SULLIVANT

Lucas Sullivant's imprint on Columbus is as indelible as it is invisible. But his visions of the future and his remarkable efforts and achievements did more to shape Columbus than those of any other individual, although little is known of him. In a family genealogy, his son Joseph wrote, "He spoke but seldom of himself or his ancestors." They came into America through North Carolina, from Ireland, but the precise time is not known. The name was originally Sullivan, and "the 't' added at a remote period, to distinguish the family from others of a similar name."

After their arrival in North Carolina, the Sullivants were early immigrants into Virginia. Lucas's father, Michael, married a Miss Lucas. He owned a Mecklenburg, Virginia, plantation and held slaves, but "careless and dissipated [he] wasted his property." He left three children — Lucas, Michael and Ann — and there was dissention between them over what property was left.

An area resident, Colonel William Starling — later his father-in-law — helped Lucas financially and secured him "friends" and a "little patrimony".

Historian Alfred E. Lee elaborated on that sparse family account. "Cast upon his own resources early in life, he [Lucas Sullivant] gained influential friends, one of whom was Colonel William Starling, whose second daughter, Sarah, he later married. By diligent improvement of his time and means, he qualified himself as a Land Surveyor." He had already fought in Indian expeditions in Virginia at the age of 16 and was knowledgeable about the wilderness. After the revolutionary war, Sullivant was one of six appointed to survey the lands ceded to Virginia for residents' wartime services to the national government. He was assigned to the northern portion of the Virginia Military District which extended into the Ohio Country.

In the spring of 1795, Sullivant's surveying party of 20 "appeared in the woods on Deer Creek, within the present confines of Madison County." He and his men entered what is now Franklin County, stopping at a salt lick at one point, where they were attacked by a large wildcat. Just four days before, they had fled from a party of Mingo Indians determined to kill them. As they rowed farther up the Scioto, they encountered an abominable stench. It was so nauseating they could not imagine the origin — until they got closer to the place now worked by the Marble Cliff Quarry Company. There literally hundreds of rattlesnakes were sunning themselves on the cliffs. They had just shed their winter skins, and new snakes were being hatched from eggs. Both the decaying skins and the eggs were the source of the smell. They quickly moved on.

At the confluence of the Scioto and Olentangy rivers, Sullivant found what he had been looking for — the best possible location to make his land claim and build a town. Evidence of an Indian village near the junction of those rivers indicated there was good hunting and rich land for cultivation. The water would provide power. There were abundant trees for building and quantities of limestone, sand and gravel for roads. The rivers could be traveled, and being virtually halfway between the Great Lakes and the Ohio River, the land had potential as a natural trading and transportation center. Sullivant was not just thinking of an important crossroads for the Ohio Country, but the entire Northwest Territory.

He went back to claim his land (it totalled 6,000 acres), and in 1797, he returned, laid out plans for the town and proceeded to build an early version of the city of which he dreamed. Sullivant remained in Franklinton until his death in 1823 at the age of 58. That spring, shortly before his death, he talked with Colonel James Kilbourne of Worthington. He discussed the prospect of a canal system for the Ohio River (by 1831 it would become a reality). Within two months of June 1823, Franklinton was besieged by "a season of unparalleled sickness and deadly fevers." On August 8, 1823, a feverish Sullivant asked his son Joseph to take a walk with him. The son was also feverish but sensed his father's urgency. He followed him to a ridge at the west end of Franklinton where he could "see the spire of the Statehouse and the scattered houses of the new town of Columbus." Sullivant spoke "almost to himself, 'I would like to come back in 50 years and stand on this spot. I would not be surprised to see steam wagons running across those bottoms!'"

Within half that time, "steam wagons" [trains] were running across tracks there. Their arrival — along with the earlier Ohio Canal System and the National Road — accelerated tenfold the development of that natural transportation and trading center Sullivant had envisioned in 1795. Ironically, the site he chose — to stay just within the Virginia Military District for his land grant — was no more than five miles off the mark from the city he had hoped to build. Chronologically, his dreams were a half century ahead of reality. But his vision was uncannily accurate.

NOTICE TO ALL, &C.

It has been my wish, and my practice to suffer people to pass over my bridge gratis, on the Sabbath, if going to or returning from Divine worship. But that indulgence has been very shamefully abused, and it has become a practice for some hundreds of passages to take place, on the Sabbath day, under the pretext of going to, or returning from Divine worship. When, in fact, and in truth, the greater number are going to, or returning from mill, or their grogshops, or are in pursuit of business or amusements, such as visiting, strolling, hunting, fishing, shooting &c. &c. and frequently passing at a very late, and untimely hour of the night. Therefore, be it known unto all, that to avoid such gross impositions, henceforth the gates, will be closed on Sundays, as well as on other days ; and a free passage allowed only to such as appear of record, and I know them to be members of a regular church, and that too, when I know they are actually going to, or returning from Divine service, at proper and suitable hours.

LUCAS SULLIVANT.

November 27, 1818.

23

MAP
of the state of
OHIO
by
Rufus Putnam

Surveyor General of the United States

January 1804   Scale of 20 miles to an inch

References
■ Tracts of land ceded to the United States by the Indian Treaty of 1795
• Towns
▲▲ Indian Villages

NB The river Cayahoga, Tuscarawas Branch, the Indian boundary lines, the Ohio River
    with the rivers and smaller streams running into the Ohio from the North & west
    as far as the Indian boundary with the subdividing lines laid down agreable
    to actual survey except the Ohio from the Scioto river to the little Miami and
    the Virginia reservation, these with the Indian land Detroit &c are taken
    from Huchins's Map corrected by the latest observations

In 1805, he lured Sarah's brother, Lyne Starling, to Franklinton. He placed the young Starling — six feet, six inches tall with red hair and an aristocratic manner — in the county clerk's office. Sullivant also supplied him "with means . . . and entered [him] into partnership in the mercantile business." Starling became a successful merchant and trader. He was one of the few to venture flatboats down the Scioto in 1810 and actually land some of his produce in New Orleans.

Initially he was scornful to Franklinton for its lack of physical and social amenities. But later he allowed that doing without slaves was "not so great a hardship as might be imagined." Starling settled in as he saw the town developing potential (i.e., culture). As his means improved, so did his outlook. In a letter to his sister Jane in Kentucky, dated July 12, 1807, Lyne Starling casually mentioned, "I have lately purchased an elegant site and tract of land opposite town on the other side of the river, which I have an idea of improving." That "elegant" tract was half the land parcel which would become the city of Columbus. Most of Franklinton's earliest residents would eventually relocate to this new site. A few (including Lucas Sullivant) never moved from Franklinton. Among them was Mary Minor Wharton, born in 1810 to Legislator and Supreme Court Judge Isaac Wharton. She died 89 years later in the same bed in the same house where she was born. But sentiments for the past were a luxury to those who realized the future lay across the river on the east bank and in the new capital city. The pragmatists and the optimists transplanted themselves and their resources there.

Dr. Lincoln Goodale, who arrived in Franklinton in 1805, practiced medicine for one year and relinquished the rigors of his profession to own a drugstore and general store which propelled him to wealth. John Brickell and Jeremiah Armstrong, former captives of Indian tribes, returned to their former camping grounds to rejoin white settlers. Dr. James Hoge, Presbyterian minister, and his wife, Jane, operated free schools out of their homes while lobbying for public education. General Joseph Foos, who operated a ferry across the Scioto, became a member of the Ohio Legislature. There were others — Franklintonians such as lawyer Gustavus Swan, James Johnston, Alexander McLaughlin and John Kerr — who purchased land on that undeveloped east river bank. (Although Lucas Sullivant never moved there, he owned substantial acreage himself.)

Lyne Starling (financially subsidized by Lucas) formed a proprietorship with Johnston, McLaughlin and Kerr. They successfully lobbied the undecided legislature to establish a permanent capital city on their land. They offered to lay out the town, donate a ten-acre public square, a ten-acre penitentiary and build the necessary offices a state government would need, including a statehouse. But location remained their chief selling point.

It is difficult to overestimate the strategic location of the site of Franklinton. As Lucas Sullivant noted, the forks of the Scioto was not only the junction of two major waterways from northern Ohio, it was also a major stopover point on the Indian trail to Lake Erie from the

FROM LUCAS SULLIVANT: Founder of the town of Franklinton, which later became Columbus, was Lucas Sullivant. His three sons were (left to right, above) William Starling Sullivant, Joseph Sullivant and Michael Lucas Sullivant. Buildings in settlement included the school (below), Lucas Sullivant's store (center) and the church (bottom), which was a gift to the town from Sullivant in 1811.

FREEMAN'S CHRONICLE.

AMERICAN INDEPENDENCE THIRTY-SEVENTH YEAR.

"HERE SHALL THE PRESS THE PEOPLE'S RIGHTS MAINTAIN,
"UNAW'D BY INFLUENCE, AND UNBRIB'D BY GAIN:
"HERE PATRIOT TRUTH ITS GLORIOUS PRECEPTS DRAW,
"PLEDG'D TO *RELIGION, LIBERTY, AND LAW*."

FEDERAL GOVERNMENT TWENTY-FOURTH YEAR.

PUBLISHED BY JAMES B. GARDINER, AT FRANKLINTON, FRANKLIN COUNTY, STATE OF OHIO.

Volume 1.] SATURDAY, OCTOBER 3, 1812. [Number 14.

THE WAR.

Letter of Col. Cass, of the army late under the command of Brig. General Wm. Hull, to the Secretary of War.

WASHINGTON, Sept. 10th, 1812.

SIR,

Having been ordered on to this place by col. M'Arthur, for the purpose of communicating to the government such particulars respecting the expedition lately commanded by brig. gen. Hull and its disastrous result, as might enable them correctly to appreciate the conduct of the officers and men, and to develope the causes which produced so foul a stain upon the national character, I have the honor to submit to your consideration the following statement:

When the forces landed in Canada, they landed with an ardent zeal and stimulated with the hope of conquest. No enemy appeared within view of us, and had an immediate and vigorous attack been made upon Malden, it would doubtless have fallen an easy victory. I know gen. Hull afterwards declared he regretted this attack had not been made, and he had every reason to believe success would have crowned his efforts. The reason given for delaying our operations, was to mount our heavy cannon and to afford to the Canadian militia time and opportunity to quit an obnoxious service. In the course of two weeks, the number of their militia who were embodied had decreased by desertion from six hundred to one hundred men; and, in the course of three weeks, the cannon were mounted, the ammunition fixed, and every preparation made for an immediate investment of the fort. At a council, at which were present all the field officers, and which was held two days before our preparations were completed, it was unanimously agreed to make an immediate attempt to accomplish the object of the expedition. If by waiting two days we could have the service of our heavy artillery, it was agreed to wait; if not, it was determined to go with out it and to attempt the place by storm. This opinion appeared to correspond with the views of the general, and the day was appointed for commencing our march. He declared to me, that he considered himself pledged to lead the army to Malden. The ammunition was placed in the waggons; the cannon were embarked on board the floating batteries, and every requisite article was prepared. The spirit and zeal, the ardor and animation displayed by the officers and men on learning the near accomplishment of their wishes, was a sure and sacred pledge, that in the hour of trial they would not be found wanting in their duty to their country and themselves. But a change of measures, in opposition to the wishes and opinions of all the officers, was adopted by the general. The plan of attacking Malden was abandoned, and instead of acting offensively, we broke up our camp, evacuated Canada, and re-crossed the river in the night without even the shadow of an enemy to injure us. We left to the tender mercy of the enemy the miserable Canadians who had joined us, and the *protection* we afforded them was but a passport to vengeance. This fatal and unaccountable step dispirited the troops, and destroyed the little confidence which a series of timid, irresolute and indecisive measures had left in the commanding officer.

About the tenth of August, the enemy received a reinforcement of four hundred men. On the twelfth, the commanding officers of three of the regiments (the fourth was absent) were informed through a medium which admitted of no doubt, that the general had stated, that a capitulation would be necessary. They on the same day addressed to gov. Meigs of Ohio a letter, of which the following is an extract:

"Believe all the bearer will tell you. Believe it, however it may astonish you, as much as if told you by one of us. Even a c——is talked of by the . The bearer will fill the vacancy."

The doubtful fate of this letter rendered it necessary to use circumspection in its details, and therefore these blanks were left. The word 'capitulation' will fill the first, and 'commanding general' the other. As no enemy was near us, and as the superiority of our force was manifest, we could see no necessity for capitulating, nor any propriety in aluding to it. We therefore determined in the last resort to incur the responsibility of divesting the general of his command.—— This plan was eventually prevented by two of the commanding officers of regiments being ordered upon detachments.

On the 13th, the British took a position opposite to Detroit, and began to throw up works. During that and the two following days, they pursued their object without interruption and established a battery for two 18-pounders and an 8-inch howitzer. About sun-set on the evening of the 14th, a detachment of 353 men from the regiments commanded by col. M'Arthur and myself was ordered to march to the river Raisin, to escort the provisions, which had some time remained there protected by a party under the command of capt. Brush.

On Saturday, the 15th, about 1 o'clock, a flag of truce arrived from Sandwich, bearing a summons from gen. Brock, for the surrender of the town and fort of Detroit, stating, he could no longer restrain the fury of the savages. To this an immediate and spirited refusal was returned. About 4 o'clock, their batteries began to play upon the town. The fire was returned and continued without interruption and with little effect till dark. Their shells were thrown till eleven o'clock.

At day light, the firing on both sides recommenced; about the same time the enemy began to land troops, at the Springwells, three miles below Detroit, protected by two of their armed vessels. Between 6 and 7 o'clock, they had effected their landing and immediately took up their line of march. They moved in a close column of platoons, twelve in front, upon the bank of the river.

The fourth regiment was stationed in the fort; the Ohio volunteers and a part of the Michigan militia, behind some pickets, in a situation in which the whole flank of the enemy would have been exposed. The residue of the Michigan militia were in the upper part of the town to resist the incursions of the savages. Two 24-pounders loaded with grape-shot were posted upon a commanding eminence, ready to sweep the advancing column. In this situation, the superiority of our position was apparent, and our troops, in the eager expectation of victory, awaited the approach of the enemy. Not a sigh of discontent broke upon the ear; not a look of cowardice met the eye. Every man expected a proud day for his country, and each was anxious that his individual exertion should contributed to the general result.

When the head of their column arrived within about five hundred yards of our line, orders were received from General Hull for the whole to retreat to the Fort, and for the twenty-four pounders not to open upon the enemy. One universal burst of indignation was apparent upon the receipt of this order. Those, whose conviction was the deliberate result of a dispassionate examination of passing events, saw the folly and impropriety of crowding 1100 men into a little work, which 300 could fully man, and into which the shot and shells of the enemy were falling. The Fort was in this manner filled; the men were directed to stack their arms, and scarcely was an opportunity afforded of moving.—— Shortly after a white flag was hung out upon the walls. A British officer rode up to enquire the cause. A communication passed between the commanding generals, which ended in the capitulation submitted to you. In entering into this capitulation, the general took counsel from his own feelings only. Not an officer was consulted. Not one anticipated a surrender, till he saw the white flag displayed. Even the women were indignant at so shameful a degradation of the American character, and all felt as they should have felt, but he who held in his hands the reins of authority.

Our morning report had that morning made our effective men present fit for duty 1060, without including the detachment before alluded to, and without including 500 of the Michigan militia on duty. About dark on Saturday evening the detachment sent to escort the provisions, received orders from gen. Hull to return with as much expedition as possible. About ten oclock the next day they arrived within sight of Detroit. Had a firing been heard, or any resistance visible, they would have immediately advanced and attacked the rear of the enemy. The situation, in which this detachment was placed, although the result of accident, was the best for annoying the enemy, and cutting off his retreat, that could have been selected— With his raw troops enclosed between two fires, and no hopes of succour, it is hazarding little to say, that very few would have escaped.

I have been informed by col. Findley, who saw the return of their quarter-master-general the day after the surrender, that their whole force of every description, white, red & black, was 1030. They had twenty-nine platoons, twelve in a platoon, of men dressed in uniform. Many of these were evidently Canadian militia. The rest of their militia increased their white force to about 700 men. The number of their Indians could not be ascertained with any degree of precision; not many were visible. And in the event of an attack upon the town and fort, it was a species of force which could have afforded no material advantage to the enemy.

In endeavouring to appreciate the motives and to investigate the causes, which led to an event so unexpected and dishonourable, it is impossible to find any solution in the relative strength of the contending parties, or in the measures of resistance in our power. That we were far superior to the enemy; that upon any ordinary principles of calculation we would have defeated them, the wounded and indignant feelings of every man there will testify.

A few days before the surrender, I was informed by general Hull we had 400 rounds of 24 pound shot fixed and about 100,000 cartridges made. We surrendered with the fort 40 barrels of powder and 2500 stand of arms.

The state of our provisions has not been generally understood. On the day of the surrender we had fifteen days of provision of every kind on hand. Of meat there was plenty in the country, and arrangements had been made for purchasing and grinding flour. It was calculated we could readily procure three months' provisions, independent of 150 barrels of flour, and 300 head of cattle, which had been forwarded from the state of Ohio, and which remained at the river Raisin under capt. Brush, within reach of the army.

But had we been totally destitute of provisions, our duty and our interest undoubtedly was to fight. The enemy invited us to meet him in the field.

By defeating him, the whole country would have been open to us, and the object of our expedition gloriously and successfully obtained. If we had been defeated, we had nothing to do but to retreat to the fort, and make the best defence which circumstances and our situation rendered practicable. But basely to surrender without firing a gun—tamely to submit without raising a bayonet—disgracefully to pass in review before an enemy as inferior in the quality as in the number of his forces, were circumstances which excited feelings of indignation more easily felt than described. To see the whole of our men, flushed with the hope of victory, eagerly awaiting the approaching contest,—to see them afterwards dispirited, hopeless and desponding, at least 500 shedding tears because they were not allowed to meet their country's foe, and to fight their country's battles, excited sensations, which no American has ever before had cause to feel, and which I trust in God, will never again be felt, while one man remains to defend the standard of the Union.

I am expressly authorised to state that col. M'Arthur and col. Findlay & lieut. col. Miller viewed this transaction in the light which I do. They know and feel that no circumstance in our situation, none in that of the enemy, can excuse a capitulation so dishonourable and unjustifiable. This too is the universal sentiment among the troops; and I shall be surprised to learn, that there is one man who thinks it was necessary to sheathe his sword or lay down his musket.

I was informed by gen. Hull the morning after the capitulation, that the British forces consisted of 1800 regulars; and that he surrendered to prevent the effusion of human blood.— That he magnified their regular force nearly five fold, there can be no doubt. Whether the philanthropic reason assigned by him, is a sufficient justification for surrendering a fortified town, an army and a territory, is for the government to determine. Confident I am, that had the courage and conduct of the general been equal to the spirit and zeal of the troops, the event would have been brilliant and successful as it is now disastrous and dishonourable.

Very respectfully,
I have the honour to be,
Your most obedient servant,
LEWIS CASS, *Colonel*
3d Regt. Ohio Vol.

The hon. WM. EUSTIS,
Secretary of War.

Ohio River through mid-Ohio. It was also the conjunction of several key land grants made by the U.S. Congress after the American Revolution. The Virginia Military District, surveyed by Sullivant and others, was a pie-shaped wedge of real estate between the Miami and Scioto rivers. The point of the pie was at the fork of the Scioto. Above the fork and east of the Scioto, military lands were for sale, not only to veterans but to anyone with the money to buy from veterans. Sitting in the middle of the wedge were the Refugee Lands. A long narrow tract of land stretched out to the east, starting at the Scioto River from what is now Fifth Avenue to Refugee Road. It extended for dozens of miles. These lands were dedicated to persons who fled British Canada and had their lands confiscated because of loyalty to the Americans in the Revolution. (Most of these refugees, however, never came to Ohio. Instead, they sold their land to brokers who then resold it to the highest bidder.)

All these major land grants came together at the site of what was to be Columbus. The groups of syndicators who controlled the point where they came together were in a strategic position, not only to participate in the sale or resale of several land grant districts, but also to bid for the location of the proposed capital.

Franklinton also offered another advantage. It was located between two major conflicting cultural areas — the Western Reserve area and the southern part of the state. The Western Reserve was largely settled by Yankees. The southern part of the state was mostly settled by persons from below the Ohio River. Franklinton had been settled by persons sympathetic to the Virginia group who dominated the Ohio Legislature. Franklinton is often called the most northern of the Southern settlements, while Worthington — some ten miles north — is the most southern of the Yankee settlements. The clash of southern Ohio Jeffersonianism and New England values was inevitable. (It would continue as late as the Civil War, with Columbus serving as both a bastion of abolitionism and the most northerly Ohio city with strong anti-Lincoln sentiments.)

The location in the central part of the state was ideal — it equalized and eased travel by legislators. And it allowed the city to be custom-built to the specific needs of the government. On February 14, 1812, the state legislature accepted the proposal. They gave the developers five years to make good their promises before planning the first legislative session in the new capital city. The city name was suggested by General Joseph Foos — Columbus — in honor of another boatman, Christopher Columbus.

Joel Wright was chosen as architect. Assisted by Joseph Vance of Franklin County, he set about laying out a town which reflected his New England background. The streets were wide — High Street was 100 feet across and Broad Street 120 feet. All other main streets (initially State and Gay) were 22.5 feet wide. Residential lots went on sale June 18, 1812, the day the United States declared war against England. All lot sizes were generous, and those on Broad and High streets ranged from $200 to $1,000 apiece.

That same day, Franklinton began its period of greatest prosperity. It was selected as a troop center, and 2,000-3,000 soldiers were headquartered there under the command of General William Henry Harrison. But Franklinton's inhabitants were already buying lots in the new capital city. They began building cabins and wood frame homes (only a few brick structures were put up, aside from the public buildings) while the government structures were just starting construction.

By the end of that first year, 300 people had settled in the city near the land laid out for Capitol Square. Jarvis Pike (who was to become Columbus' first mayor in 1816) was busy raising corn and wheat on the ten-acre tract around the foundation of the first statehouse. Seeds were hand-sown. His tools — as those of the other early farmers — were largely limited to shovels, harrows and hoes. Manufactured equipment from the East was not only expensive but difficult to transport into the city. For this reason, it took an entire winter for a lone farmer to thresh and clear the grain crops from ten acres.

There was refreshment for those hardy workers. The flesh was not only willing but hard worked, and the spirits were not weak. Adult Americans of that day drank more than twice as much alcohol per person as they do today. Jug whiskey was usually kept under shade trees for refreshment on the farms as well as in the city. The first tavern in Columbus opened in 1813, under the management of Volney Payne. It was a two-story brick building on the west side of High Street, just south of State Street. (It was a year later before the first church — Presbyterian, at Spring and Third — was built.)

For reading matter, residents had a choice between *The Scioto Gazette* (originated in Chillicothe in 1797 as the "Centinel" [sic] of the Northwest Territory); *Freeman's Chronicle* (established in 1812 in Franklinton) and the *Western Intelligencer* (begun in 1811 in Worthington, it later moved to Columbus where it became the *Ohio State Journal* in the late 1820s, the predecessor of today's *Columbus Citizen-Journal.*)

The only schools available were one-room subscription schools, usually log cabins, where participating parents paid shares of the schoolmaster's fee and took turns providing him room and board.

Occasionally, traveling pitchmen for patent medicines came through with trained animal acts, but the only professional entertainment was provided by occasional touring theatrical companies which followed trade routes of the Ohio and Mississippi rivers.

The population was derived primarily from English stock migrating from New England; Germans, including Amish and Mennonite religious sects (still located around Plain City) who had come over the mountains from Pennsylvania; and Scotch-Irish and English who had come up river routes from Maryland, Virginia and Kentucky. From the start, early lifestyles tended to reflect these diverse cultural backgrounds.

Forty-three "free-coloreds" lived in Franklin County at Columbus' inception. By 1820, there were more than 120 blacks, but aside from the "hirelings" of the Sullivants, they were the nameless waiters at early taverns and hotels. The small area where blacks lived was dubbed "Nigger Heaven".

PIONEER COLUMBUSITES: *John Kerr (top) and his land office on West Broad Street (above); Lyne Starling (right); John Brickell (below); the Rev. James Hoge (center, below); Joel Buttles (right, below).*

Most residents who were not farmers or state lawmakers tended to be (or work for) professionals — lawyers, bankers, ministers, builders, surveyors and small businessmen. There were also shoemakers, hatters, tailors, blacksmiths and cabinetmakers. David Deshler, of German background, worked as a carpenter in the front room of a two-room house he built near Broad and High streets. (A hotel named after him stood at Broad and High streets until the 1960s.) The Deshlers became a prominent banking family. After the first few years, drugstores, hardware stores, dry goods and general stores opened. But large-scale manufacturing was virtually non-existent until well after the middle of the 1830s.

Taverns thrived and multiplied from the first. Jeremiah Armstrong was swift to set up glasses of wine under the sign of the Red Lion, while German-born Christian Heyl operated a superb bakery and served brew in the Swan Tavern. (Heyl was one of the first eighteen men to purchase a lot in Columbus. Later he served ten years as town treasurer.)

By 1816, the town not only had its first bank (Franklin Bank), but the penitentiary and the first Capitol were completed. Legislators moved into Columbus to hold their first session. Columbus, with approximately 700 people in residence, was legally declared a borough. It was a bustling community that welcomed its first American president when James Monroe passed through on a western tour in 1816. On Saturday mornings, farmers brought in meats, maple sugar, wood, flour and feathers, as well as produce, to barter or sell on market day. (Most people bartered — few had cash.) By the 1820s, there were two market days a week.

The town had also acquired a few eccentrics by then. Squire Shields, owner of the market house on State Street, kept rooms on the second floor where he held forth as a justice of the peace and a Methodist minister. Columbus' young men gathered around him often, while he talked religion and temperance over his much-loved "toddys". When asked why he did not practice what he preached, the squire would bellow, "I teach you what is right, and I — well, I do as I please!"

Columbus women, as their sisters in other towns, spent much of their time weaving cloth for homemade clothes (usually linsey-wooley), giving birth to many children (only a fraction of whom lived past infancy) and dying at early ages. Life was aggravated by frequent outbreaks of typhoid and various other fevers. Aside from the exceptional Ann Simpson Davis (who served as a spy for the Continental army during the revolutionary war and lived in Columbus briefly around 1818), women were rarely mentioned in early records except in connection with their husbands since it was considered unladylike, improper and sacriligious to be listed except on the occasions of marriage and death.

Betsy Green Deshler, wife of carpenter David Deshler, wrote frequent letters to her parents from 1817 to 1826. They tell something of domestic life during those years. In 1817, she wrote of the "cheapness" and "plenty" of nearly all foods, "except salt and coffee and a few other grocery articles . . . owing to the distance they are transported . . . from Philadelphia." She and her husband rose early every morning to "have breakfast by candlelight and then work industriously all day" in the 26-foot-wide home he had built. Of their neighbors, she reported, "People here are remarkably kind to strangers."

In 1818, she became ill and was treated by a physician (chiefly with laudanum, an opium derivative). Although she was not expected to live, she survived nearly another decade in the increasingly lively city. In 1821, she wrote, "We have had a number of conspicuous characters in Columbus this winter, among whom [was] Henry Clay of Kentucky, a very genteel man in his appearance, but very plain, indeed." (Clay had come to practice at the federal courthouse which had been completed in 1820.)

During the next few years, most of Betsy Deshler's letters were filled with narratives of the suffering she, her family and the entire town endured. "We have had nothing but sickness and trouble . . . since June [1821]. David . . . was confined to bed for nearly seven weeks, and part of the time entirely deranged. Without help I took care of him 14 nights in succession," Repetitions of the situation throughout 1823, prompted her to write that October, "The sickness of this country does not abate. On a small stream called Darby, about 18 miles from here, there are scarcely enough well people to bury the dead."

The economy was also depressed during those years. The Midwest suffered greatly during the depression of the 1820s. Money was scarce, markets unavailable and the drop in immigration led to a fall in land prices. Things were looking up, however, after the dreadful winter of 1824-25, and Betsy Green Deshler wrote with contentment, "Our town is quite healthy and very lively. Provisions are plenty and cheap." Lawmakers passed regulations about sanitation, attempting to cut down on the diseases, and social life was improving along with the economy. But Betsy Green Deshler did not live to see further progress. She died in 1826, at the age of 30, leaving behind a 10-week-old baby for her husband's next wife to raise.

Joel Buttles was another chronicler of early Columbus. He began writing in his diary of the first days in Columbus when "deer were browsing on the tops of trees which had been felled" for space for the public square and continued writing through several years of "insolence and altercation" between residents of Franklinton and Columbus. For years after Franklinton was passed over as the capital choice, jealousy and hard feelings ran high among the original settlers, those who migrated across the river and newcomers. But that animosity died down in the late 1820s, by the natural course of events. Buttles wrote, "Columbus in a short time overtook Franklinton and the latter began to decline while the former increased rapidly." Yet Franklinton did not disappear then — it literally was absorbed by the new city. And by 1830, Columbus was becoming acutely aware that something more than additional people was needed if it were to become the great state center residents felt it was predestined to be.

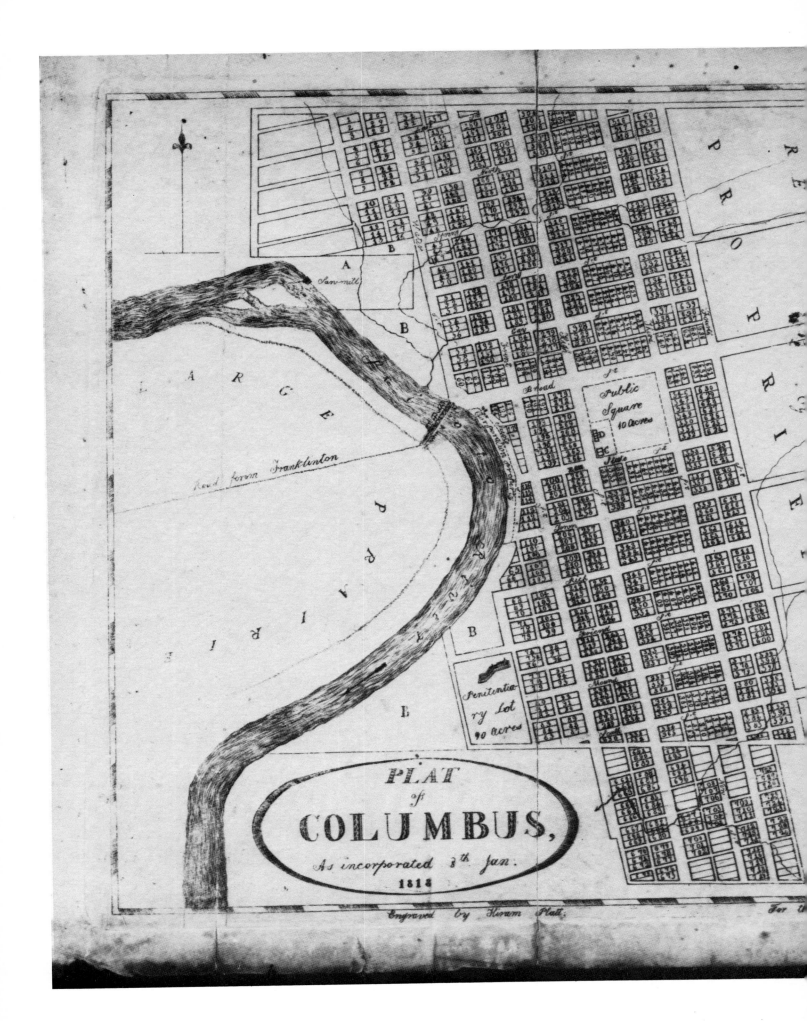

PLAT
of
COLUMBUS,
As incorporated 8th Jan.
1814

Engraved by Hiram Platt.

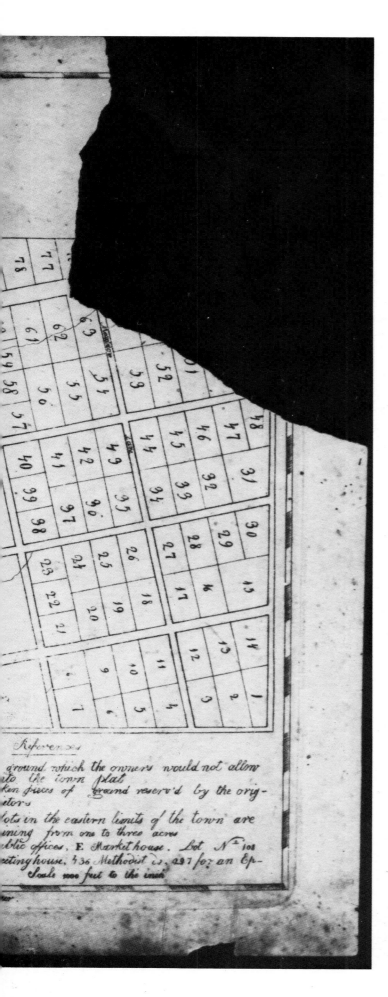

EARLY 1800s: *Plat of Columbus as incorporated January 8, 1818; the first (top) and second (above) city market houses and the Franklinton Courthouse (below).*

National Road marker near
Columbus.

CHAPTER TWO

AMERICA
DISCOVERS
COLUMBUS

1830-1833

National Road from Columbus to Indianapolis, 1827 map.

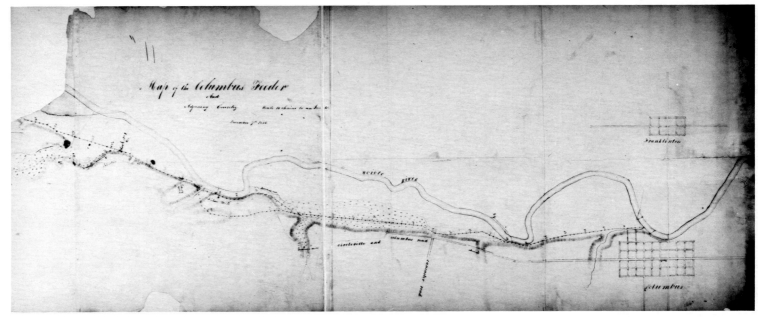

ON THE WATERFRONT:
*Columbus Feeder Canal, 1828
(top); canal boats in Canal Basin
(left center); canal boat warehouse,
1880 (left); flat bottom boat such
as were used on the rivers (right
center).*

The Four Mile House, road house west of Columbus.

In 1830, Columbus had a total population of 2,438 residents and (private census-taker Robert Ware added after the total) "216 males and females of African descent." Although it was already being called "a great place to live," growth was hampered by slow migration of new people. It was not easy to get in or out of the town.

Peter Zinn's stagecoaches pulled up in front of the old National Hotel two or three times a week — if the Good Lord was willing, if the Kinnikinnick Creek or Hargus Creek had not flooded the road or if one of the stagecoaches had not overturned in a race. Weary travelers then fell out of the coaches along with dated mail and newspapers.

Most of the tree stumps had been removed from High Street by that time, although they remained on Third and Long streets for many more years. But even with "corduroyed" streets, High Street was usually a sea of mud. Franklinton had thirteen major floods between its inception and 1883. Nathaniel Hamlin, an early resident of Franklinton was one of the first to leave the swampy bottoms on the west side of the Scioto for Columbus. The new city was laid out on the river's higher — and slightly less swampy — eastern bank. Hamlin prophesied, "The future of our town is on this side of the river. Here we'll be high and dry."

But transportation outside the city was even more difficult. Magnificent stands of nine-foot-tall corn and other produce growing in the rich soil along the Scioto and Whetstone (now Olentangy) rivers provided bounty on Columbus tables but not at the bank. Despite occasional individual successes, there was no reliable way to export produce down the Scioto to the Ohio and Mississippi rivers to New Orleans markets, particularly with Spanish control of the Mississippi River. Neither was there a speedy way to cross the mountains to Pennsylvania and the East before vegetables rotted. As a result, Columbus people could only barter with each other for their respective products and skills. Unable to sell for "cash money," they were also unable to import the manufactured items which geography, geology and lack of skilled labor denied them.

But in 1830, people who settled in the new city doubted the wisdom of their choice. What good was it to be "the Capital" when the "natural transportation center" Lucas Sullivant envisioned could not be reached or left with speed and ease?

While they worried, though, hundreds of anonymous hands were steadily hammering, digging and pounding ways into and out of Columbus. For four years, Irish laborers (many of whom had fled the potato famines and survived "coffin ships" to America) joined 89 convicts from the Ohio Penitentiary in digging a ditch — a ditch designed to serve as a feeder canal to connect Columbus and the Ohio Erie Canal System which stretched from Cleveland's Lake Erie to the Ohio River at Portsmouth. A connection to that canal spelled a first-class ticket to outside civilization and commerce. So in April 1827, when digging began (nearly four years before water could be let into the lock), a crowd of a thousand people gathered at the old Statehouse grounds to celebrate the prospect.

They formed a parade and marched to the banks of the Scioto at the west end of Main Street, led by uniformed militia. Politicians and officeholders carried ceremonial shovels and inspirational speeches for the official groundbreaking. There was a 24-gun salute and a picnic for all the celebrants, donated, prepared and served by Christian Heyl. After finishing Heyl's feast with tortes and other German sweets, everyone danced. After the speechmakers and singers went home, the laborers got down to the real digging.

It was backbreaking labor. The ditch was designed to be eleven miles long, 40 feet wide and four feet deep from Main and Scioto streets to Lockbourne. Brush and trees had to be cleared for trails where horses and oxen could walk as they pulled the boats through the canal berth. The physical toll was heavy. But it represented progress for those who survived malaria and injuries. For the convicts, there were rare pardons. For the predominantly Irish contingent of immigrant laborers on the canal (planned by a man of Irish background named Alfred Kelley), there were full tables, wages and promotions from unskilled labor to professional jobs. Many became operators, maintenance men, contractors and straw bosses of other immigrants who would later lay railroad tracks throughout Columbus.

When the feeder canal was finally completed in 1831, and water was unleashed into it, the first flat-bottom boat arrived from Circleville. The *Governor Brown* — a tidy white vessel with green shuttered windows — was described as a "fairy palace" by people who rushed to

LIDA ROSE McCABE

American House Hotel, established in 1834, one of the National Road stops recollected by Lida Rose McCabe in her writings.

Whenever Columbus writers are mentioned — inside or outside the city — James Thurber's name comes to most minds automatically. Students of American literature are aware of William Dean Howells' newspaper years in the city. And persons familiar with journalism in the past three or four decades are familiar with the names (if not the later work in New York) of John McNulty and Ruth McKenney. But even in Columbus' literary circle, few people have heard the name Lida Rose McCabe. Yet Miss McCabe, the Columbus-born author of *Don't You Remember?*, was a pioneer journalist whose work for Columbus newspapers in the early 1880s led her to New York and Paris and critical acclaim.

Born March 3, 1865, to Mr. and Mrs. Bernard McCabe, she was educated in Columbus schools, then attended the Sorbonne, the Convent rue Notre Dame de Sion in Paris and Columbia University.

Little is known of her personal life. She began as a reporter for *The Ohio State Journal.* She was quite young when she achieved professional publication; she contributed to the *Cincinnati Commercial Gazette* in 1883 when she was 18 years old. At the Ohio Historical Society, one edition of her book is autographed to E. O. Randall (one of Ohio's key early historians and a founder of the society), "with fond affection" for his encouragement of her "early" writing efforts.

At the time the book was printed, Lida Rose McCabe was 19 years old. The stagecoach journey she describes

so vividly occurred 33 years before she was even born.

However, all the major events (such as the 1840 presidential campaign of General William Henry Harrison), local oddities such as the great squirrel hunt of 1822 (when city men and boys killed 19,686 "parasitic" squirrels" in one day) and the people she describes all existed — early governors, legislators and well-known figures like Lyne Starling, lawyer Orris Parrish, gambler John Young and black waiters Jerry Finney and Sam Perkins. They turn up in the works of Columbus historians, but none describe them with anything approaching her skill and style. The technique of transplanting herself into the past to relate things she must have heard from people who lived them, or knew them from their relatives and friends, does not constitute 'traditional' history. But neither is the book fiction. (The book was used for some time as a textbook in Columbus public schools and was endorsed by the Ohio Bar Association because it has the only complete record extant of a famous steamboat trial.)

Lida Rose McCabe went on to the Sorbonne, the Parisian convent and Columbia. When she was 28,

American Girl at College was published in New York. It was the first attempt at a comparative analysis of higher education for women in the United States. Its impact supposedly led the Catholic Church to establish its first college for women in America — Trinity College in Washington, D.C.

For some years, Lida Rose McCabe was an active journalist for foremost Eastern newspapers. She was a correspondent for the *New York Tribune, New York Herald, New York Times, New York Sun* and the *New York Press.* She was the first woman reporter to go to the Klondike (presumably during the gold rush of '98) and stayed several months filing dispatches. Later, in Paris, she was correspondent for the American Press Association. When she returned to New York, she contributed art reviews as well as general articles to newspapers and magazines.

Her most famous book, *Ardent Adrienne* — a biography of the wife of General Lafayette — was published in 1930.

She died in 1938. Her obituary in the *New York Times* noted, "Miss Lida Rose McCabe, author, newspaper correspondent and art critic, died yesterday morning at the Madison Square Hotel, where she had lived for many years." It mentioned that she had completed a biography of the dancer Carmencita, still in manuscript. There was no mention of where or when funeral rites were scheduled.

If burial rites were held in Columbus, the event was very private.

greet the first arrival on the canal. It was luxury of a new kind — mobility. The *Governor Brown* had both a parlor and a large sitting room inside, as well as an outdoor deck where passengers could socialize, partake of food prepared in the boat's kitchen and enjoy the scenery at a leisurely speed of three to four miles per hour.

The captain, two crew members and passengers aboard the vessel were accorded a rousing greeting. Not only was the cannon fired, but church bells all over town tolled as people shouted and cheered all the way to the dock. The Columbus band played, and some people not only danced but strutted onto the boat, then gladly paid the one-cent-per-mile to make the cruise back to Circleville.

Within two months, at least 80 boats made their way to Columbus laden with manufactured goods from other states and departed with crates of Columbus goods to sell to previously inaccessible markets.

For many years, the canal dock and warehouse were the sites of warm weather dances. Canal workers even formed a band. In winter, ice-skating and races on the frozen canal were regular activities.

Never again would commerce, the size and nature of the population and the way people lived in Columbus be as inbred, isolated and insular as it had been prior to 1831.

Marcia Parrish Rhodes, daughter of prominent Columbus attorney Orris Parrish, described the transition vividly. "When the Ohio & Erie Canal was finished and the joy of the West over a new way of communication . . . found public expression . . . the influx of strangers, as a result of Columbus being the capital, and members of the Legislature, made such demands on the hotels that many families received friends . . . for the winter as guests. Our family sometimes numbered twenty. Relatives and friends came to make a visit and . . . [some] remained months and even years. There were many needs to be supplied and my mother was a busy woman. Candles were made in the home [but] our markets were excellently supplied and all food was very cheap. My mother's maids were from Radnor — nice, intelligent Welsh girls. Board could be had for seventy-five cents a week."

Skating on the canal.

Virtually every boat that docked at the Columbus feeder canal not only carried crucial freight but shiploads of immigrants, particularly Germans. Germany in the nineteenth century was a political hodge-podge of kingdoms, duchies, margravates and principalities ruled generally by authoritarian law. The winds of liberalism from the French and American revolutions produced unrest which made the common people yearn to escape. America seemed the best of all possible worlds.

But they were not prepared for urban life as they found it on the Eastern seacoast. They longed for the small town life they had so recently left. And so they moved on west — to Cincinnati, the German melting pot of nineteenth-century America. From there, many went into the Northwest Territory. And as some came through Columbus, they stopped and stayed. Earlier German arrivals (such as David Deshler and Christian Heyl) were already considered Columbusites first and Germans second.

That same year, William B. ("Billy") Neil purchased the stagecoach service that Peter Zinn had started in 1816. Neil was one of those men who were larger than life. He had tried several ventures before he arrived in Columbus in 1818. Columbus agreed with him, and he was almost immediately a success. He set up offices for his Ohio Stage Company next to what would become a later version of his first Neil House hotel. In short order, some 70 coaches were rolling through Columbus every week. Neil — quickly dubbed the "Stagecoach King" — often leaped into drivers' seats and personally cracked the whip to horses when one of his coaches got bogged down in a mud hole. Neil would go on to dabble in hostelry. (The Neil House) — land speculation (at one time he owned most of North Columbus) and railroads. By his death in 1870, he had become immensely rich in land — and although at the end, he was poor in cash, his life had a phenomenal impact on the city.

Traffic in the city multiplied enormously but not in comfort or convenience. Major streets were still corduroy or plank roads, and the planks had a decided tendency to separate in the rain. In 1833, a major event finally validated the hopes and rhetoric about Columbus' potential importance as a transportation capital.

In 1811, the fledgling federal government started construction of a road — then called the Cumberland Road — to ease the arduous journey from the East across the mountains of Pennsylvania into the rugged Northwest Territory. By 1831, renamed the National Road, it finally was extended into Columbus. The route which surveyors had previously plotted through the city was cleared of brush and trees, and workmen spread stone and gravel across wheel-rutted mud. It entered from the east on Main Street, then jogged west out of the city on Broad Street. The old toll bridge William Sullivant had built across the Scioto in 1826 (replacing the first one built in 1816 by his father, the ubiquitous Lucas Sullivant) was replaced with still another larger, stronger covered bridge built by the U.S. government. It had two tracks for wagons and walks on both sides. The public was able to use the new bridge free of charge.

However, there were tollgates every ten miles on the National Road to pay for the wear and tear. A rider on horseback could cross ten miles of the National Road for six cents. A stagecoach, hack or omnibus drawn by two horses was levied twelve cents. The driver of a wagon drawn by one horse or ox paid only five cents, ten cents if two horses or oxen pulled the wagon.

Even in 1833, those tolls were considered bargains. The National Road opened Columbus to traffic that changed it from a borough to a city in more than name. In 1834 formal legislation was enacted declaring it a city.

Farm children sat on fences along the National Road to watch the moving spectacle. Huge Conestoga wagons carried flour from Columbus mills and produce from local farms to Eastern markets. They returned with manufactured products from Eastern markets. Smaller covered wagons brought new families with their belongings, customs and skills. Stagecoaches raced passengers, mail, newspaper packets and each other at speeds they could never achieve on the corduroy and plank roads. Herdsmen on foot headed cattle, sheep, hogs and turkeys to markets. Beggars and tramps, traders and peddlers, traveling musicians and showmen — all passed on the National Road. America was finally able to discover Columbus. In 1833, a cholera epidemic struck the city, wiping out one-third of the residents in Franklinton alone. A Biblical fatalism pervaded the thinking of the time — "The Lord giveth and the Lord taketh away" — reflected on the decorated tombstones with the Tree of Life, the weeping willow

The home of early settler John Otstot was built in 1834 at 318 South Front Street and is a classic example of the homes built in the downtown area in pre-Civil War days.

fronds symbolizing immortality and the epitaphs:

> *Farewell, my friend, but not forever.*
> *You on life's billows toss.*
> *For Jordan's flood, I'm past you see.*
> *And you have yet to cross.*

Despite the harsh reality — or perhaps partially because of it — it was a singularly heady, exciting time for those who lived through the onslaught of disease and natural disasters. The city was still as raw and tasty as fresh produce, as yeasty as bread on the rise and naively as charming as hand-pieced quilts or silhouettes of early residents scissored from paper by traveling limners.

At the same time, some people were already emulating the amenities and sophistication of the overcrowded Eastern cities and the caste-conscious South. Ready-made clothes became available to virtually all classes. And for the most affluent, there were silk dresses and formal frock coats for evenings of Shakespeare and opera at the theater.

In 1884, Lida Rose McCabe, native resident of Columbus and pioneer woman journalist at 19, wrote a remarkable book, *Don't You Remember?* In it, she evoked

Stagecoach lines (below) ran through Columbus along the National Road through the Civil War era; coach passengers might stay at the inn of William Neil (inset).

the atmosphere of her hometown as it was during the 1830s and 1840s, by collecting and recreating sights, sounds and vignettes which made people and places long past spring back to life. She told how in 1832, she had visited Circleville and returned by stagecoach to Columbus. "[I was] more than ready to dash away into the beautiful valley" along the Scioto back to the Capital city, she wrote. "Overflowing of streams caused a number of accidents," delaying the coach, but being on time was unusual then. The driver was "Yank" Cook, "a great, stout muscular fellow skillful with whip or 'ribbon' . . . ready with a song, a joke, a dance or a story and who never was known to hurt the feelings of his fellow men by refusing a draught of 'bitters.' "

Every time her "straggling group of travelers" approached a stagecoach stop, they would hear the cry, 'Here it comes! Here it comes! Here it is!' Four foaming horses and trails of dogs in hot pursuit, mid lashes of whip and flourish of horn, dashed into town and reined up at the tavern door." Coach emptied and mail bag safely delivered, they would be on their way again. Lida McCabe described the scenery, company and conversation during that journey with Dickensian zest. "As the coach rolls along, through the windows steal the odor of pines and fragrance of spring blossoms that grow in wild confusion . . . and over all the fertile valley floats the broad expanse of sky." A stranger in the coach (a typical Englishman visiting the colonies) remarked rhetorically, "A magnificent country." Dick Douglas, familiar to the other passengers as a "lawyer wag," responded proudly, "Not a more fertile valley in the world." Putting aside his copy of *The Scioto Gazette*, Douglas prodded the Englishman, "Do you not see, FEEL, that there is a freedom in the air which every creature breathes alike . . . a freedom that is met within no other land?"

The Englishman smiled and sallied, "Are you not afraid that the boasted freedom will some day grow nauseating? It takes years, you know, to outgrow the customs of one's forefathers."

Douglas cried, "Forefathers? We left them on the other side. It was as much as we could do to get across ourselves, without unnecessary baggage in the shape of hobby horses!" A major who had lost a leg at Fort Detroit in the War of 1812 slapped his wooden peg and hooted. The other Americans chuckled so amiably that even the Englishman saluted the riposte.

And they all laughed at two Irishmen arguing over how early their respective ancestors had migrated to America. One of them snorted, "Shur, then, your great-great grandfather must have come to America before it was discovered!"

Aside from a young girl who wept constantly (her father had been killed recently in a stagecoach that overturned during a race), the passengers did not retreat to solitude for the rest of the trip. The Major explained to the Englishman that they were not passing through "classic ground". When Douglas added that on "still nights . . . you could almost catch a sentence of Logan's eloquent lament," they were all surprised to find that the

Englishman had learned the great Mingo chief's speech "by heart, as a boy" in England.

By that time, torrential rain obscured the scenery. Hargus Creek overflowed its banks, so driver "Yank" Cook reluctantly decided that they would have to "make the best of a night at the tavern" nearby. Such delays were so typical of stagecoach travel that no one but Douglas was disturbed. He was due for the spring term opening of federal court in the Capitol next morning. But once he "sipped a glass or two of hot toddy," Lida McCabe noted, "he was the most contented among us."

Next morning, they forded the stream, with "water at times almost covering the seats of the coach." The river "almost touched the roadside" at points. "A very pretty stream," the Englishman remarked calmly. The Major served as tour guide again, explaining how it came by its name. "The banks of the stream were once skirted . . . by immense parks of deer, which at moulting time came to the water's edge to drink. The surface soon became covered with hairs, and the Indians called the stream Scioto or 'hairy river'."

As the capital grew near, casual conversation gave way to "restlessness and impatience." The haste was shared by "Yank" Cook and another driver from a coach behind them who shouted, "Let's try your mettle, boys. We will make up a purse for the man that first enters the town!" The drivers shrieked as they lashed their horses to greater speed, and mud flew in great heaps as they "galloped into the bustling town of Columbus." "Yank" Cook won the wager and purse, being first to pull up to the old National Hotel.

The hotel was once a noted tavern stand. In 1830 it was the site of a grand banquet for Henry Clay, at which Columbus confectioners Ambos and Edgner introduced the merangue ("meringue").

In 1832, the year of Lida McCabe's travelogue, it was purchased by John Noble. Noble advertised in *The Western Hemisphere* (a Jacksonian Democratic weekly) and *The Ohio State Journal & Columbus Gazette* (its political opposite) that the two-story brick house painted green "located nearly opposite to the Public Buildings and Court House in Columbus and owned by William Neil, Esq. . . . will be furnished and attended to in a style equal to the highest expectations. The stages of the Ohio Stage Company stop at this house, and their office is attached to the establishment."

Noble, later elected to Columbus city council, lived up to his advertising style. It was he who inaugurated legislation which finally cleared Broad Street of all tree stumps, changing that swampy morass into a beautiful thoroughfare which still evokes compliments from visitors a century and a half later.

Staffordshire Blue china Columbus platter, 1832.

CHAPTER THREE

AT WORK AND REST

1833-1849

Franklin County Courthouse (left) and annex, built in 1840.

EARLY BUILDINGS: From Martin's "History of Columbus," the state building (above) included the U.S. Court House, the Public Offices and the Old State House. From artwork solicited in 1929 by Lazarus department store, a watercolor of a home built circa 1835 (below) at Rich and Front Streets, when Columbus was still a small town.

Beginning in 1832 — and certainly after 1833, with the extension of the National Road through Columbus — the next decade in Columbus was "bustling," as Lida McCabe wrote. Lawyer ("wag") Dick Douglas and his conferees tried cases in the United States Courthouse on the northeast corner of Broad and High streets. Built in 1826, the old courthouse had a dome topped with a Liberty statue. (Time, wind and weather treated her somewhat unjustly. Although Liberty stayed aloft with unbalanced scales for years, eventually she was disensconced.)

One of the earliest known photographs of the downtown area, the Tallmadge home on State Street between Third and High Streets.

The presence of a federal court was a distinct asset to Columbus' role as a governmental center. Many complicated land title disputes were tried there, and such noted lawyers as Henry Clay plied their skills before that bar. (Clay also visited the market place and coffeehouses and engaged in public oratory on The Tariff. It was a time when political rhetoric was not only enjoyed as public entertainment but as an art form. People often traveled from small towns into the capital to hear debates.)

By the time Columbus was formally declared a city in 1834, there were no more crops growing in the fields around the Statehouse where pigs and cattle had once roamed freely. The public square was enclosed with a fence of cedar posts, and legislators were discussing the prospect of building a larger, grander statehouse. (It was delayed 20 years due to a bitter political argument.)

Ohio was rapidly growing, with river towns (such as Cincinnati) already metropolises, but the northern area of the state was hampered by transportation problems until the completion of the Erie Canal across New York state in the 1820s. The northwestern area was still undeveloped since several Indian tribes lingered there, and the Great Black Swamp had yet to be drained.

At the very center of Ohio, Franklinton was beginning the slow decline which would eventually lead to its absorption into Columbus. Columbus, on the other hand, was a small town on the verge of impressive growth.

In the mid-1830s and early 1840s, a visitor would have seen, on the surface, a staid, middle-class environment in which government constituted the main source of employment, and shopping was not just a matter of necessity but a leisure pastime.

The business district from 1816 to 1833 took in only a few blocks — from High Street to the river and from Town to Broad streets. But the city of the 1840s was the city now enclosed by the inner belt. There were suburbs with open lots of large sizes, elegant houses and simple cottages near Statehouse Square.

While pointing out the public buildings and grand private homes — such as Salmon P. Chase's residence at State and Sixth streets and Alfred Kelley's Greek Revival mansion on East Broad Street — a native Columbusite would not have mentioned certain other aspects to outsiders.

Only a mere handful of public schools existed, and they were only open three to four months a year. Only one child in eight received an education in 1820. The percentage increased very little from 1830 to 1850. Those who did attend school usually went to private subscription schools.

Numerous fires leveled one building after another because of a lack of water (except when the Scioto flooded). Fire equipment was limited to a few ladders, axes, hooks and a horse-drawn fire engine (nicknamed "The Tub," because it looked like a tub with handles on it) which reposed in the engine house on the State Street side of the public square. When the fire bell clanged, a ladder company (bucket brigade) of twelve men (all volunteers between the ages of 15 and 50) grabbed the horses and "The Tub" and raced to the site. If anything was still standing, they proceeded to hand-pass leather buckets filled with water. Although a safety committee was formed to inspect chimneys, stovepipes and other danger points, it would be another decade before the city invested in efficient fire-fighting equipment.

The city's inordinate amount of sickness and death from influenza, ague, cholera, typhoid and unidentified 'fevers' continued unabated. Due to the poor drainage of area swampland, creeks overflowed after any heavy rain, and large pools of water became breeding pools for flies and mosquitoes. Such insects carried germs to a people who had no knowledge of their existence, no screens for windows and doors, no central water system and no sewage disposal plant. Drinking water from yard wells or underground tanks grew more and more impure as the population grew.

As diseases proliferated, the City Council enacted strong ordinances about removing trash heaps from the streets, but enforcement was limited. Since there were no paid policemen, citizens were called at random to serve

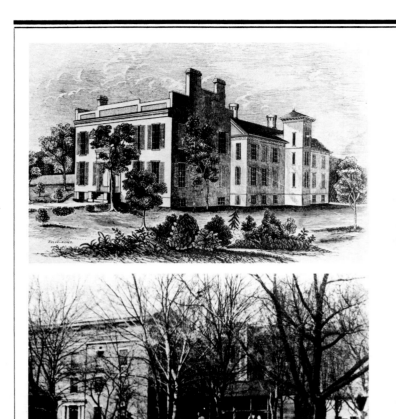

FIRST HOMES: In the state's early years, its institutions were centralized in Columbus — the Ohio Asylum for Imbecilic Youth (top left), the Central Ohio Lunatic Asylum (top right), the Deaf and Dumb Institute (center left), the Institution for the Blind (center right), all mid-1800s.

The Ohio Penitentiary, 1846.

as "watchmen". From ten until five, they performed their solemn civic duty by lighting street lamps and bringing before the major or marshal all lawbreakers. In 1828, that meant "anyone found in a state of intoxication or strolling about with an improper or evil design after 10 in the evening." (Lawmakers soon figured out that evil and improper things sometimes happened before 10 p.m.) An 1829 ordinance, which stood for years, called for "all vagrants, idlers and riotous and lewd persons guilty of disorderly and indecent behavior [or] persons intoxicated" to be taken before the city marshal for unspecified punishment.

The new Ohio Penitentiary — built on approximately 30 acres of land on Spring Street — was first occupied in 1834. It was the third maximum security state prison built in Columbus (on the site of today's Arsenal-Cultural Arts Center). The first two were rapidly overcrowded. (The 1834 penitentiary still stands on the same site and is still in use.) Designed for 700 prisoners, it was built at a cost of $93,370.50, including an estimated $78,428 of inmate labor which, if stretched out, would have equalled 1,113,462 days. The site contained sufficient acreage for many buildings and factories necessary to later growth. By 1837, eleven cells were added for female prisoners. It was a source of city pride that the facility not only confined Ohio prisoners but, by contract with the federal government, served as a territorial institution for federal prisoners.

By and large, social concerns and inadequacies were dealt with in a surprisingly progressive manner. By the 1830s, reformers began to address the problems of American society itself. People such as William Lloyd Garrison (the abolitionist) and Lucretia Mott (the women's rights advocate) were joined by Dorothea Dix in the fight against the awful conditions in prisons and asylums. The movement was extremely strong in Ohio, and during the 1830s, the state constructed a number of major institutions in the Columbus area for the mentally ill, the deaf, and the blind, as well as a new prison. These institutions were built just outside the city. The schools for the blind and for the deaf were located near the east side, the prison just north of the city limits. As the city grew, the institutions were moved out again in an effort to provide clean air and water and space to grow food. But they were always kept close enough to take advantage of the services and opportunities.

After 1838, many charitable activities "for the poor and afflicted" were handled by the Columbus Female Benevolent Society.

From spring through fall the city market was the center of activity. As many as 350 farmers tilling the rich soil around Columbus brought produce, meat and dairy products in white covered wagons to the Statehouse Square, usually parking on the east side of the street. The official market house was at the southwest corner of State and Front streets, on a site purchased by the city council in 1830. It was a long one-story shed-like building with six brick pillars on each side. A wide aisle cut a swath through the center so people could shop on all sides of the numerous stalls. When roads were in good condition and traffic was particularly heavy, market stalls often stretched south to Town Street and north to Broad Street. Depending on the season, shoppers could buy lettuce and "sallet" makings in spring; beets, cabbages, potatoes and succulent sweet corn in summer; and pumpkins and applies in the early fall. During summer months, there were also long strings of perch, bass and suckers from the Scioto hanging out for shoppers' inspection. Butchers sold prime beef at 2.5 cents per pound.

The keen-eyed Lida McCabe viewed market days as "stirring panoramas of western life . . . dutch gardeners and frauleins . . . ragged urchins . . . [wearers of] homemade blue jeans or linsey . . . English traditionalists still wearing the knee breeches, leggings and silver buckles . . . [an individual] clinging to the Emerald Isle . . . jolly face . . . over a great frieze coat, and carrying a black thorn stick."

When the daylight hours and money were spent, farmers' wives usually stopped at a weaver's shop to see the results of their week's spinning. Townswomen might visit local shops to buy some of the first imported ready-made clothes or examples of a milliner's art. They might consult one of the few doctors in town, but more likely they purchased herbs and patent tonics in the drug department of Samuel Crosby's general store across Broad Street from the Ridgeway House.

John French — asked to come from New York to head the drug department for Crosby — later opened his own drugstore at the northeast corner of High and Rich streets. He introduced some new ideas for the first time. The most notable was hiring young women. On the second floor, above the drug store proper, French had his female employees making trusses and other appliances, as well as packaging garden seeds for commercial sale.

Come twilight, unless there was a political debate, most farmers headed home along with their wives. Livelier forms of activity were then taken up, particularly during winter months when the state legislature was in session. "There was a time when there was not a capital in the United States that attracted such a motley throng of wit, talent and depravity as Columbus," noted Lida McCabe. Her aunt Cyntha concurred, swearing that "between the years of [1835 and 1840], the society of Columbus was famous for its beautiful women."

Among them was a mysterious and beautiful Southerner married to her own cousin, a Democratic legislator. Before she married the Ohioan, she was divorced from a Spaniard who attempted to stab her during a fit of jealousy. He killed her intervening mother instead. The divorced spouse threatened to kill her if he ever got out of prison. In the meantime, she was reigning queen at the old National Hotel during the legislative sessions. After dinner, she often led a contingent to the city's first playhouse, the Columbus Theater. Hastily built in 1835, it was on the west side of High Street between Broad and Gay streets. The theater was approximately 50 feet wide and 120 feet long but could accommodate up to 1,500 people — according to Philip Sheridan, a chronicler of city entertainments — which was

MARKET HOUSE: *The old City Market-House, on the southwest corner of Town and Fourth Streets (above), from Martin's "History of Columbus" 1857; Central Market on Rich Street (top), circa 1911-12.*

"remarkable, since the entire population of Columbus then numbered only about 4,000."

"Winter was the best season for theater in Columbus," Sheridan observed, "since the legislature was in session and visiting legislators and lobbyists had more free evening time and fewer restrictions than townsmen. The entire theatrical season lasted from about the end of November into the middle of March." The social and political elite who attended probably occupied three tiers of private boxes with cushioned seat backs. They may have frequented private salons to admire portraits of William Shakespeare and Christopher Columbus. During the four seasons before legitimate theater died, patrons were exposed to lectures, opera recitals, minstrel shows and melodramas. Lida McCabe fondly remembered "Cherry and the Fair Star," someone dancing the Mazurka and the hornpipe, and Mrs. Drake, the "most celebrated Lady Macbeth of the first half of the century."

As transportation improved, Columbus also became a convention center. The most notable one was the Ohio-Whig convention of 1840. General William Henry Harrison was promoted for the presidency. Several thousand people traipsed to town to participate in what

turned out to be a drunken and memorably destructive torchlight parade.

A new and exciting public entertainment made its debut in Columbus on July 4, 1842 — balloon ascensions. Richard Clayton — advertised as "the most daring aeronaut in the world" — decided to make his 30th ascension from Columbus' Capitol Square. A "spacious amphitheatre" was erected for the exhibition, according to historian Alfred E. Lee. "To generate all the necessary quantity of hydrogen gas for the inflation of this stupendous vessel," Clayton claimed he needed "2,800 pounds of oil and vitriol, 3,000 pounds of iron, and 15,000 pounds of water." A "vast concourse of people" occupied streets, windows and tops of buildings to witness the ascension and found it "beautiful." The "intrepid aeronaut waived an adieu" to the congregated thousands. "In return," Clayton wrote, "as I arose, hats and handkerchiefs were waved, and the military gave a salute."

Entertaining at home was another popular pastime. Marcia Parrish Rhodes (daughter of the Columbus attorney Orris Parrish) recalled, "The wine parties have been very numerous during the winter. It is here

A balloon takes off in what is now the middle of downtown Columbus, circa 1890s. In the background is the Welsh Presbyterian Church, built in 1888, now headquarters for the Columbus Metropolitan Area Community Action Organization.

particularly that the 'members' of the Legislature show off. If ladies chance to be present, as is not usually the case, they are too often left to the solitude of their own reflections. The gentlemen are in an adjacent apartment listening to the popular songs of Jim Crow and Clar de Kitchen. . . . As to their morals, they grossly violate in the evening and livelong night the very laws which they were enacting during the day. In this capital of our State are supported two billiard tables [and] two roulette tables expressly for gambling. We have gambling prohibitions, but they are quietly reposing on the shelf . . . the citizens are pleased to have the salaries of members untransferred from the city."

Marcia Parrish also referred to the most popular pastime for male Columbusites — frequenting coffeehouses. "Among the exhilarating drinks dispensed there," Alfred E. Lee pointed out wryly, "coffee was one of the last called for, or thought of." On the east side of High Street, there was Christian Heyl's Swan Tavern, later known as the Franklin House. On the west side of High, just south of State, was Robert Russell's The Globe. Between Rich and Town streets was Jeremiah Armstrong's Columbus Hotel with the Sign of the Red Lion. And north of State, on the west side of High was by far the most popular and important of the

coffeehouses — gambler John Young's The Eagle Coffee House. It was a particularly popular hangout for lawyers and legislators of the Whig persuasion. (Maverick Democrats of the day — nicknamed Loco Focos — held secret caucuses and social pastimes at a rival hostelry called the Tontine on the south side of State just west of High.) However, the Eagle's general popularity was so great that Lee wrote, "It was remarked that 'everybody went there except Dr. Hoge.' " (Dr. Hoge, the prominent Presbyterian minister who first settled in Franklinton, had moved to Columbus with his wife Jane and their large family. They lived where the Athletic Club now stands.)

In pleasant weather, male citizens sat outside the coffeehouses on benches, leisurely sipping mint juleps and discussing the news of the day. Lyne Starling could be seen outside the Eagle virtually every day. (He may have owned the property, although John Young was the proprietor of the building.) When a lady passed, the gentlemen rose to toast her with their minted glasses. They toasted each other, too, in the midst of "gossip, refreshment and gaming . . . for which no excuse can be made except that it was the amusement of a raw frontier town which had scarcely any other." John Young added the billiard table to Columbus along with casino rooms.

47

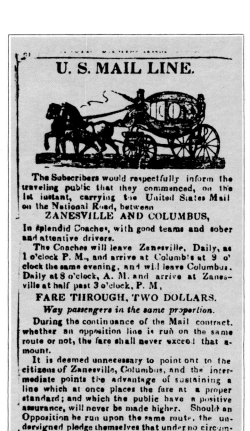

FROM THE EARLY DAYS: *The boyhood home of General Irvin McDowell (above), commander of the Union forces; business place of C.M. Hubbard (below), 1892. The Hubbard establishment was originally the Old Swan Tavern, built in 1813, one of the first taverns in Columbus; it was turned from tavern to commercial business building in the early 1840s.*

Lee wrote that singing was also a favorite pastime. One night in the '30s, passing the door of The Eagle Coffee House, a citizen saw Tom West lying on the counter in an accustomed state of intoxication. Beside him was a group of revelers . . . singing 'Old Rosin the Bow,' closing each stanza with the refrain:

> Now I'm dead and laid on the counter,
> A voice shall be heard from below,
> A little more whiskey and water
> To cheer up Old Rosin the Bow.

"Old Rosin the Bow" had many choruses and certain ribald connotations which Lee did not wish to explore too closely. But he concluded that "after each chorus, a draught of whiskey was administered to the swaying West," who must have sunk into the sunset in a superbly bowed state.

The Eagle had the only public bathhouse in town. Water for it was pumped by a big black bear chained to a treadmill. One day the bear was teased by a bystander until it broke loose. "Among those who broke for a place of safety" was one John M. Kerr. "He leaped upon a table, and in the excitement of the occasion was unconscious for several minutes that the rear part of a dress coat he had on had been torn away by the latch of a door on which he had been leaning." With such free public amusements, small wonder the Columbus Theater had difficulty filling all those seats.

Inside the Eagle, drinks were served by the establishment's most famous waiter, Jerry Finney who had been lured away from the old National Hotel. Finney, a black, was a popular figure with lawyers and members of local military companies and was often taken along on camping trips. (One night in 1857, Finney was lured over to Franklinton, kidnapped and carried back to slavery in Kentucky. A party of Eagle habitués took up his cause. Unable to free him by legal means, they bought him from his owner and freed him. Finney was eventually returned to Columbus, but his captivity broke his spirit. He died shortly after his return.)

Lida McCabe lamented, "The delightful convivial meetings at the coffee-house, sad to relate, often led to confirmed drunkenness." But she wrote with reluctant amusement of the place's popularity among lawyers. "Occasionally, after the decision of an important law case . . . lawyers such as Stanberry of Newark and Orris Parrish of Columbus, would congregate at the Eagle to discuss the fine points of the trial. And over a glass of toddy, mint julep or slice of rare venison, many a . . . complicated case suddenly unraveled.

"Often in the heat of argument a flow of impromptu eloquence silenced the clicking of billard balls or wine glasses. Then would follow the story weaving through the long night." Many of those stories centered on Parrish, who apparently knew how to play a jury. He was known to pack a small pistol in his pocket "to defend himself from any personal assault he might provoke from the defendant," upon whom he "would heap denunciations and abuse in the free vocabulary of the English language . . . . Among the legislative fraternity," Lida McCabe related, "it was a common way to estimate a brother's capacity [for liquor] by saying, 'He knew more law when drunk than any other lawyer knew when sober.' "

Such revelry apparently was missed by English author Charles Dickens when he made his stagecoach journey from Cincinnati to Columbus in 1842 (recorded in his *American Notes*). A decade after Lida McCabe's trip from Circleville, he duplicated that part of her route but not her experiences. Dickens praised the "macadamized road the whole way, and the rate of travelling . . . six miles per hour" through "a beautiful country, richly cultivated, and luxuriant in its promise of an abundant harvest." But he found the stops at roadside inns in central Ohio "always dull and silent. . . . One phrase was repeated over and over again to the most extraordinary extent . . . and adapted to every variety of circumstance and pause in the conversation." While waiting for dinner in a wayside inn, two gentlemen — one wearing a straw hat and the other a brown hat — conversed slowly and without any emotion that Dickens could discern:

Straw Hat: Warm weather, judge.
Brown Hat: Yes, sir.
Straw Hat: There was a snap of cold last week.
Brown Hat: Yes, sir.
Straw Hat: Yes sir.
Brown Hat: This coach is rather behind its time today, I guess.
Straw Hat: Yes, sir.
Brown Hat: Yes, sir . . . nigh upon two hours.
Straw Hat: Yes sir!
All The Other Inside Passengers: Yes, sir.

To compound the taciturnity, Dickens complained, the place did not allow liquor on the premises. It was a "Temperance Hotel, and spirits are not to be had for love or money. We have nothing to drink but tea and coffee. This preposterous forcing of unpleasant drinks down the reluctant throats of travellers is not at all uncommon in America."

By seven the second evening, Dickens reached Columbus and stayed "to refresh, that day and night: having excellent apartments in a very large unfinished hotel called the Neil House, which were richly fitted with the polished wood of the black walnut and opened on a handsome portico and stone veranda, like rooms in some Italian mansion. The town is clean and pretty, and of course is 'going to be' much larger. It is the seat of the state legislature of Ohio, and lays claim, in consequence, to some consideration and importance."

After the war of 1812, the United States was generally at peace until the Civil War. But the militia continued to meet and drill from time to time, in order to be prepared for possible service. Originally, muster day was a very serious affair. (Citizen militia was the real first line of military defense in a society with a miniscule professional army.) As the years passed, the muster became more of a social occasion. Nevertheless, the United States was reasonably prepared when President Polk called for a declaration of war against Mexico on May 11, 1846. While many historians have concluded that the war with Mexico was at least partly contrived, the war was popular in Columbus as well as most of the West and Midwest. Columbus immediately mustered two companies of soldiers for the conflict. Two more companies followed in early 1847. (Ohio contributed more than 3,000 troops to the American Army.) One of the four companies was completely composed of German-Americans. It demonstrated (to the German community and the city) that the newer immigrants were not only loyal enough to fight and die for their new country but that they would do so with a vigor equal to or surpassing their native American comrades.

The war was short and victorious. The most notable Columbus native to emerge from the struggle was Lieutenant Irvin McDowell who received a field promotion to brevet captain for gallantry in the battle of Buena Vista. After the signing of the peace treaty of Guadelupe-Hidalgo in February of 1848, the troops began the long journey home. Their arrival on July 27th, 1848, was marked by a great celebration. A large parade moved through the town, stopping at the Statehouse and ending at a banquet hall where dinner was served and the usual round of speeches and presentations were made. The conflict had a significant impact on Columbus. It renewed and strengthened the citizen militia and provided valuable direct military experience to a new generation of Columbusites. It also guaranteed the opening of the great West to American control, an opening which would provide markets for Columbus produce and manufactured goods in the coming decades.

Lida Rose McCabe mourned and eulogized the loss.

Bill of Fare.

SUPPER Given by Joshua Baldwin, D. Adams, jr., W. G. Deshler, E. F. Drake and M. L. Sullivant, at the Neil House, Thursday Evening, December 27, 1849.

OYSTER SOUP.

ENTREES.

Boned Turkey, Aspic Jelly.
" Geese " "
" Ducks, " "
" Chicken, " "
Chicken Sallad.
French "
Oyster Patties.
Green Tea.
Black Tea.
Coffee.

ENTREES.

Sliced Chickens.
" Turkey.
" Tongue.
" Ham.
" Beef.
Ham Sandwiches.
Fried Oysters.
Warm Rolls.
Bread and Butter.

PICKLES.

Mangoes.
Cucumbers.
Grapes.

Peaches.
Cherries.
Red Peppers.

PASTRY.

Lady Cake.
Snow do.
Sponge do.
Pound do.
Cup do.
Ginger do.
Raspberry Puffs.
Green Goosberry do.

Strawberry Puff.
Jelly Cake.
Fruit do.
Oriental do.
Plum do.
Jumble do.
Almond do.
Matrimonial do.

CREAMS AND JELLIES.

Vanilla Ice Cream.
Lemon " "
Rose Custard.
Lemon "
Peach "
Charlotte de Russe.
Almond Blanc Mange.

Rose Blanc Mange.
Calves Feet Jelly.
Wine " "
Cranberry "
Apple "
Russine "

CONFECTIONERY.

Pyramids of Kisses.
" of Macaroons
Grape Fountains.

Marengoes.
Bonbons.
Kisses.

FRESH FRUITS.

Malaga Grapes.
Isabella "
Malaga Raisins.

Turkey Figs.
Almonds.
Apples.

FRUITS.

Preserved Peaches.
" Pippins.
" Pears.
" Plums.

Preserved Quinces.
Brandied Peaches.
" Cherries.
" Raspberries.

Nick Koerner's grocery, circa 1880s, at Front and Broad Streets, where early-day residents could get food and something to wet the whistle too.

"Primitive simplicity and sturdy yeoman customs . . . gave way to the giant, *Progress*. Turn pikes [sic] and mud roads with many a romance at the old tollgate, gave way to hissing steam, and serpentine tracks of glistening iron. Ingenuity, ran wild along with longings for wealth in the humblest breast."

Numerous forty-niners rushed through Columbus on their way to search for gold, and part of the population moved west with them. Many of the early landmarks were growing old. John Brickell died, still clad in his buckskin clothes.

Lyne Starling died, "an eccentric, wealthy old bachelor, and in apology for not contributing to the population, he bequeathed to Columbus for the relief of other men's descendants, the grand medical college which bears his name." (The medical college would later become Saint Francis Hospital.)

The Eagle Coffee House declined after its initial prosperity, and gambler John Young moved to Cincinnati, where he died in poverty. Columbus friends failed in an effort to collect enough money to "bring his polluted body" back to the city for burial.

The old market place Lida McCabe and her friends loved was demolished. In her old age, she wondered, "Where are they that bartered and higgled with a smile and a song and good will for all? 'In memory, perhaps of some grey-haired pilgrim, they still live; but for the greater part, their graves are scattered.' "

A few members of the first Columbus elite — notably the Sullivants and the Starlings — were literally transplanted from the old Franklinton Cemetery on McKinley Avenue to the statelier Greenlawn Cemetery. But most passed into posterity nameless.

In Franklinton Cemetery and in the small unmarked graveyard (once Kempton Cemetery) are the wind-wasted markers of such people as Betsy Skeels, Cyrus Partridge, Tracy Wilcox, Catherine Preston and "Her Infant Children". Now they lie toppled on a hill above the North Freeway, next to a development of condominiums.

51

Capital University at Goodale and High Streets, 1850.

CHAPTER FOUR

RAILROADS AND RIDERS

1850-1861

The first Wesley Chapel, important early-day center for Methodists.

Columbus not only "entered the meridian of the century" in 1850, as historian Alfred E. Lee observed, "it entered a new sphere of existence."

A new charter for the city of 17,822 residents was passed by the Ohio General Assembly. The Columbus and Xenia Railroad had just been built, while other lines were already under construction. Increasing numbers of steam engines rolled into a new depot which resembled an elongated barn, replete with cupolas, at the corner of Naghten and High streets.

By 1849, the prospect of railroads loomed over the horizon. Men like Lucas Sullivant had dreamed of rail transportation since the early part of the century. The idea of self-propelled rail transportation was even older. As early as the 1820s, experimental tracks had been tried in the East. By the 1840s, scheduled lines were operating. There were two problems of western rail travel — technical and fiscal. The technical problems involved finding materials strong enough for rails and ties and engines durable enough to handle the mountains and rough terrain of the West.

By the 1840s these problems were largely on the way to being solved by the advent of steel rails and a new generation of powerful engines. The more difficult problem was financing. Enormous amounts of capital were needed to construct railroads. And while it was felt that the railroad would generate massive amounts of immigration and trade, financiers were not fully convinced that the rural Midwest was as yet well-enough developed to support this form of transportation. Fortunately men like Alfred Kelley (who had been instrumental in financing the canal system) and William Neil (who had forged the hugely successful Ohio Stage Company) saw railroads as the wave of the future.

The first railroad to enter Columbus was constructed with the help of Kelley and Neil. They also helped support several early short lines. After the first train on the Columbus and Xenia Railroad entered Columbus in 1850, it was quickly followed by others. In a few short years, the state was becoming covered with a spiderweb of railroad lines. They linked the major cities with smaller villages and towns. The battles over the construction of these lines was every bit as competitive and vicious as had been the struggle for dominance in the stagecoach

F. and R. Lazarus & Company was founded in 1851; the store was built in 1895.

business. But because of the amounts of capital required, the railroad business was not for the small entrepreneur. It was for that newly emerging breed of American businessman — the capitalist, the financier and broker who could muster large sums of loaned and invested money to advance enterprise. The stakes were quite high. Control of the railroads for an area meant a strong say in the destiny of a region. As the main commercial center in central Ohio, Columbus money was determined to insure that management — if not the control — of midwestern railroads stayed with midwestern interests (preferably, Columbus interests). With the coming of the railroad, the canal and stagecoach systems were doomed to oblivion.

A wave of prosperity and a building boom began in the late 1840s and continued unabated. By 1852, the assessed value of real estate and personal property in the city totaled more than six million dollars — prosperous for just under 18,000 residents, although the wealth was not equally divided.

The city began to spread out. While most of the land beyond the present innerbelt was still open and mostly farmland, the large spaces within the innerbelt began to be platted and settled. As late as 1840, a house such as Alfred Kelley's mansion (where the Christopher Inn now sits) was considered out of town. But in the decade before the Civil War, people moved out from the old downtown area as it filled up. Fashionable districts emerged along High, State and Town streets. At the same time, the areas north and south of downtown continued to fill up with recent immigrants, largely the Irish to the north and the Germans to the south. On the west side, the land between the Broad Street bridge and the heart of Franklinton (I-71 and Broad Street) filled up with commercial buildings and working class homes. This was the original factory district. Although the city was not yet a manufacturing metropolis, it developed a number of notable small industries.

Men like Peter Hayden, Joseph Ridgway and John Gill began producing machine parts, specialized foundry work and leather goods. These provided a small but significant component of the city's economic well-being. Such companies generally were located near the river since they usually needed water. Transportation

GERMAN COMMUNITY: *No. 1 of the first volume of a German newspaper (left), published October 1843. By the 1860s, the German community had grown to include many houses near the mid-central business district, such as the home of Johanna Meyer (above). The Liederkranz Band (top), a singing society, was founded in August 1866.*

was also important — for both receiving and sending goods. Thus they located near downtown to be close to the canal, the National Road and the railroads. As factory and commercial establishments dominated the area around the river, it became a less desirable area for settlement and fashionable residence. Instead, the poor and the working classes occupied the area. (This pattern can still be seen today in German Village. The houses adjacent and just east of the breweries by the river are less prepossessing than the mansions which are south, away from the noise, bustle and the noxious factory odors.)

The German Central School Building, on the northeast corner of South and Fourth Streets, 1863.

It was a small but bustling Midwestern town, growing because of its central location and the growing commercial efforts. There was commercial and — generally — personal prosperity. Yet cultural and civic beneficence accompanied conspicuous consumption in architecture, fashion and society.

In 1851, the same year that a former Rabbinical student from Bavaria, Simon Lazarus, established a department store empire in one 20-by-40-foot room at Town and High streets, Jenny Lind appeared in Columbus. Prominent resident Mrs. William A. Platt described Lind as "an angel lacking only the wings. Poetry has no language that will describe her music."

Further emphasis on the spiritual reached Columbus in 1851 by the Misses Fox of Hydeville, New York. They were the original mediums of American spiritualism, "as manifested by rapping and knockings and mysterious seances." According to Lee (confirmed by other area skeptics), the Fox sisters gave sittings at a private residence on Third Street near Broad. Later, "a little knot of spirit rappers [continued] their orgies near Peter's Run in the south end of town" on Sunday mornings and afternoons. "At night, by the way of variety, they were held in a dark room occasionally." However, "interest in spiritualism waned considerably when the editor of the *Ohio State Journal* visited a seance in a hall at the corner of High and Rich streets, and at the height of the 'manifestations' lighted the candles which he had brought with him and showed up the performance as a complete humbug!"

Columbus women — at the ethereal Jenny Lind's arias or the Fox sisters' auras — succumbed frequently to fainting spells which may have been brought on by the latest fashion — corsets. In *We Too Built Columbus*, area women of the 1930s recounted the fashion foibles of their mid-nineteenth century sisters. "As prosperity came . . . dress became more elegant and . . . silk dresses stood alone because of their excellent quality. By the fifties, an 'outfit' was thought to be essential, including afternoon, going-away and evening gowns. Tight lacing was so accepted a practice that 'hygenic instructors' gave discourses on its evil."

Those lectures were not nearly so popular early in the '50s as the "wholesome pastime [of] horseback riding, or

equestrianism, as it was called then. Merry parties of cavaliers and their fair companions were dashing through the streets and along the suburban thoroughfares, as many as 50 couples riding out together."

A perfect fashion came along for women who tired of riding sidesaddle and for modish females struggling to "bestride velocipedes," the newest sport. "In 1851 came a furor of discussion about the beauty and suitability of women's dress that was caused by the invention of a costume called bloomers. They received their name from Mrs. Amelia Bloomer of Mt. Vernon [Ohio], a forward-thinking woman who edited a paper, *The Lily*, devoted to dress reform. She made some converts in Battle Creek, Michigan. On July 4, 1851, 31 young women paraded in . . . the abbreviated skirts. Almost immediately, several bloomers appeared on the streets of Columbus. Writers to the newspaper took both front and back viewpoints on them. Opponents said they were inconvenient and undignified and 'not consistent with the modest apparel enjoyed by the Apostles.' Others thought they [were] decidedly elegant and neat." One earnest female advocate of the pantaloons ("full and flowing and fastened at the ankle with bands of velvet") chided other Capital City ladies for their backwardness in not adopting "this new and decided improvement in dress." She could not "imagine what immodesty the most fastidious [could] possibly see in . . . dress . . . so simple and beautiful."

Despite the attention to dress and decorum, commerce flourished apace. Most of the development—private and commercial — flourished downtown. In 1852, Mr. and Mrs. William Neil Sr. resided in a large home "with white stone front" on Third Street near Broad, near general store owner Otis Crosby's "substantil [sic] and commodious home" on the northeast corner of Broad and Third. Refined young lady students attended Heyl's Seminary School for Girls, administrated by Lewis Heyl (son of Columbus pioneer Christian Heyl) near today's Athletic Club. Trinity Church at the corner of Pearl Street and Broad attracted the elite of the non-German Protestant worshippers.

High Street shops, such as Jonas Rudisil's, catered to those who could afford the finest furs, but "public" marketing for all classes was done at the new city markethouse on Fourth Street. It opened for business June 1, 1850. The two-story building was 388 feet long and 37 feet wide in the center.

By 1852, the Neil House was improved to give better light and ventilation. The *Ohio Statesman*, in 1854, carried recurring notices of downtown development. "William Neil is excavating for three new stores on the east side of High Street, between Broad and Gay . . . . D.W. Deshler is preparing to build on the site of the City Hotel, southeast corner of High and Town streets . . . . Iron fronts are coming into vogue . . . . D.W. Deshler is using them in his splendid block on the corner

A BREATH OF FRESH AIR: Out for a stroll and enjoying new freedoms near the turn of the century are the ladies of Columbus (above) identified as being from "John's household." An outing along Ohio State University's Mirror Lake (below), circa 1890s.

of High and Town."

Just the year before, *The Ohio State Journal* had editorialized on the domestic attractiveness of Columbus. "Our city just now looks enticing, even to one who has arrived from the rural districts. The neat yard plots, with their profusion of flowers, give a rural freshness to Columbus which cannot but render it attractive." Block after block of new three-story brick homes were being built out by Town Street. The first steps were taken in 1854 for a systematic water supply and home delivery of ice. A city express was established for "people wishing to send packages to different parts of the city" by horsedrawn omnibus.

The Esther Institute, an exclusive private school pictured in Martin's "History of Columbus," 1857.

By the mid-nineteenth century, approximately one-third of Columbus' population was from Germany. According to LaVern J. Rippley, in *Columbus Germans*, most of the older immigrants had fled from the revolutions of 1830 and 1848 in their homelands. They tended to be Democratic; in fact, "it was considered heretical to be Whig." They were zealous about preserving their native language and traditions through German language newspapers, such as the outspokenly Democratic *Westbote*. (Editor and part-owner Jacob Reinhard arrived as an engineer on the National Road and stayed to set up the newspaper at East Main Street.)

The German immigrants founded Capital University, begun in 1831 as a theological seminary for German Lutherans. In 1850, Capital University was located at the northwest corner of Goodale and High streets, where it remained until 1876. The German community also developed their own grade schools. It was in one of those German grade schools, in 1858, that the first kindergarten (a concept developed in Germany) in the United States was opened.

Although the German immigrants expanded into all parts of the city, a majority of them settled in the 233-acre tract of 1,600 homes, now designated German Village. Those homes, built primarily in the mid-1800s, were attempts by the newcomers to reconstruct the atmosphere of the homes they had left behind.

The simplest style was dubbed the shotgun house — because an individual could literally stand at the front door and fire a shotgun straight through and out the back door. Most houses, though, were one-and-a-half-story brick structures with gray slate roofs, peaking gables and cut stone on the sills and lintels. Interiors tended to have tiny bedrooms and big kitchens. Virtually all had narrow, dark cellars for storing food and wine. Exteriors were often surrounded by wrought iron fences. In back, tiny gardens were graced with grape arbors and a profusion of flowers. The transplanted *hausfraus* ("housewives") were so proud of these homes that on many mornings they could be seen scrubbing the patterned brick sidewalks and streets with soap and water.

Social consciousness and progessivism marked other aspects of their lives. As early as 1843, many German Protestants rejected the traditional rites of the Lutheran Church. They introduced an independent Protestant German church which gave female members an equal voice in the church's affairs and also taught evolutionary creation. By the 1850s, virtually all their Protestant churches organized Beneficial Societies for charitable activities. These were predecessors of an organization called *Arbeiter-Verein*, designed to aid the working class.

German Catholics had to content themselves with traveling priests for several years until Holy Cross Church was built at Rich and Fifth streets. The "Mother of all Catholic life in Columbus," it had pastors exclusively of German birth until 1877. Columbus did not gain a second Catholic church until 1852, when construction was begun (completed in 1855) on Saint Patrick's Church at Grant and Naghton streets. It became known as "The Irish Church of Columbus." Eventually, about one-fourth the original German membership of Holy Cross joined the town's Irish sector in worshipping at Saint Patrick's.

German Jews had been in Columbus since 1838 but had no congregation — for lack of a Rabbi — until 1851. Young Simon Lazarus arrived in Columbus determined to open a clothing store rather than pursue his former rabbinical studies. But he found himself doing both. The Orthodox society, B'Nai Jeshuren, was soon organized. Although services were conducted in Hebrew, all records for the Jewish community (The Protokoll Buch) were kept in German at least three decades before English was adopted.

For the most part, the German, Irish and native communities lived in harmony, although separately. This separation may have been due to tolerance or it may have been due to contempt. In the 1850s, however, native reaction to the swelling western European immigration grew until it erupted in the Know-Nothing or nativist movement throughout the country. Many Americans felt their whole way of life was being threatened. The Know-Nothing party gathered great strength in rural America, supporting anti-Catholicism, immigration restriction and opposition to social change. The movement aroused extraordinary resentment within the ethnic groups. The showdown in Columbus came on July 4, 1855.

The German community had traditionally marched on that day to celebrate the nation's independence. But there had been several recent small but violent clashes between Germans and non-Germans over the propriety of the Germans' flaunting their culture in public. Determined to march at all costs, the German athletic groups, military companies and singing societies formed

GOODALE GIFTS: Lincoln Goodale (above), original settler and physician in Franklinton, gave the city its first park (left) to preserve green space in the downtown area. The park (above, circa 1900) was named for him, as was the street running along the edge of the park.

Ohio's Underground Trails

by

Wilbur H. Siebert

up as usual. As the column moved east on Town Street up the hill toward Broad, the crowd began to jeer and throw rocks. The heavily armed Germans endured the insults and assault until the column was split as it turned north on High to march to the Statehouse. No one knows exactly what happened. But the Germans apparently thought they were being fired on and began to fire in return. The crowd claimed that the Germans simply started shooting in the confusion. One person in the crowd was killed by gunfire and sixteen Germans

were arrested, all but one released quickly. That person was indicted but never tried. Both sides made every effort to forgive and forget the incident. (There would never again be a confrontation of this sort — with a killing — between Columbus Germans and their adopted home, although hostility toward the Germans in World War I would disrupt the cultural identity which they had kept intact for decades.

But the early community did remain largely separate until after the First world war. In the mid-nineteenth century (since the Germans "made distinctive contributions only in . . . organizations exclusively German"), they were viewed simply as "that fraction of an amorphous population in a typical midwestern city which was much more interested in building for its future than in chronicling the past."

Some quiet glimpses of life among the "amorphous population" of the middle and upper middle-classes in the 1850s were recorded many years later (1930) in a hand-written memoir by Alice Strickler Keyes (1851-1935). Her recollections of Columbus — "including the things my mother told me" — dated back 96 years to 1834. At that time, her mother was a young woman living at the Buckeye House, an "old tavern standing on a site at the corner of East Broad Street and Pearl Alley," near the old National Hotel.

Alice Keyes' recollections are most vivid when she describes that prosperous but quiet decade before the Civil War. In 1850, her father, Joseph Strickler, was a marble dealer. He "bought the full lot from Gay Street to Elm Street in . . . 1847. There was a story-and-a-half cottage facing Gay Street on the lot, built entirely of black walnut. The rest of the lot was well-kept garden. A large two-story shop was then built on the corner facing Gay Street. On the north side of the yard, Strickler decided to build a row of cottages "for small families of moderate income." No one had thought previously of building houses for that class. By 1851, "there were six of these cottages and they were well patronized." So was "an old dingy brick building" across Gay Street — formerly the first Columbus jail, by then divided into tenements for "very poor people" (a group noted from a distance but not publicly described in those days).

For themselves, the Stricklers built a home on "the most beautiful spot near Columbus . . . in the country two miles north on High Street, then known as the Columbus and Worthington plank road." They bought ten and one-half acres from the owner, William Neil, "across from the beautiful ground now known as Indianola. The front line of this plot extended on High street from the entrance lane to the 'Old Ohio Field,' " where generations of Ohio State University students would play football from the 1890s to the 1920s. At the time, it was a pasture with "a fine woods full of large trees" where young Alice Strickler could swing on strong

A programme from the Fourth of July celebration in 1859.

grapevines. To reach the field, she crossed a little bridge over a ditch "leading west to the residence of William Neil Jr., near the lake . . . now part of the Ohio State University campus." Generations of young people since have called it Mirror Lake.

Living "so far in the country," well away from the downtown horse-drawn omnibuses, the way to town seemed very long indeed. "We passed under a toll gate. Just before coming to the numerous railroad tracks, which stretched across High Street on the street level, we passed the old North Graveyard, which extended quite a distance along the west side of High Street, enclosed in a high picket fence and planted thickly with shrubbery. . . . It was a rather dismal place to pass at night. The burying ground extended to Park Street on the west. The North Market House now occupies part of this ground." (It still does. It is just slightly closer to town than Goodale Park, which Dr. Lincoln Goodale, owner of much of the "near north side" in the 1850s, bequeathed to the city in 1851.) Aside from cemeteries and public squares, Goodale Park was the city's first real park. It attracted many people who, because of it, felt the city was a desirable place to live.

Alice Keyes had both cheerful and painful memories of the home her father "designed, supervised and built with loving care." (It would be the residence of Ohio State University presidents in later decades.) Her mother was its first mistress. In it, her little sister Ida was born in 1856, and her next little sister was the first person who died there. The first woman physician in Columbus officiated at these births. She was Mahala Pike Senter, the mother of Orestes Senter and Mrs. F.F.D. Albery who became well known Columbus citizens.

Mahala Pike Senter moved to Columbus from Vermont when a young married woman. Although a graduate physician and a woman advanced in liberal thought, she was not able to practice, so great was the prejudice against women doctors. Since she was the mother of three children and responsible for their support and education, she became a strong advocate of women's rights before her death in 1879. Apparently, she delivered the Strickler daughters in the mid-1850s as a midwife rather than an accredited physician.

But if Columbus was not greatly interested in women's rights in the mid-1800s, it was well known as a stronghold for abolitionists. The Underground Railroad

SEAT OF GOVERNMENT: *The Old State Office building (above left) with the Statehouse at right, under construction in the background, circa 1857. The Senate chambers (below), circa 1910; the Ohio Statehouse (above), circa 1870s.*

had operated in the city for nearly two decades. Alice Keyes explained: "One of the interesting things about the old 'Buckeye House' is that it was a station of the so-called 'Underground Railroad.' The kitchen staff was all colored. From time to time, new faces would appear among these colored people. After a few days, they might be gone, and after a while, others come and later disappear.

"Long afterward, Mother learned that these fugitive slaves, who had succeeded in crossing the Ohio River, had been quietly forwarded to Columbus when opportunity offered, and so under the cover of night and various disguises, were slipped from point to point until they reached Lake Erie, were smuggled into boats, and sent to Canada, where they were free by English law." Although the location of some of these stops were well known, others were kept secret or not discussed openly in those last years preceding the Civil War. Even in an abolitionist stronghold, there were Southern sympathizers such as Keyes' neighbor, Samuel Medary, who was to start a pacifist newspaper, *The Crisis*, in 1861.

This mixture of abolitionist tendencies and Southern feelings was the result of the city's location, background and mixed people. It was one of the southernmost areas settled by New England immigrants — but it sat geographically on the edge of more than half of a state that retained Southern ties of sympathy and blood.

In 1856, *The Ohio State Journal* had a compositor named William Dean Howells. The son of a Martins Ferry, Ohio, journalist with itchy feet, Howells learned to set type in Cincinnati at the age of nine. By twelve, he was a compositor for a German newspaper in Dayton. He was a full-fledged writer on the Columbus paper from 1856 to 1860. In 1914, after 38 novels and a stream of critical essays and reviews for *The Atlantic Monthly* and *Harper's Magazine*, Howells ("The Dean of American Letters") wrote "In An Old-Time Capital," a recollection of his days in pre-Civil War Columbus. He eulogized its people as "very charming . . . and [having] a pleasant refinement [and] certain fixed ideals which were none the less graceful and becoming because they were simple old American ideals now vanished."

Howells was both a sentimentalist and a realist. In 1855, while Colonel Alfred E. Lee — later to become Columbus' most assiduous historian — was fuming that "great hooped skirts were among the contrivances adopted by the fair sex for keeping men at a distance," he conceded that "they were not always effectual in this respect." Howells, obviously not intimidated, found that to his "fond young taste women dressed beautifully . . . floated in airy hoops and were as silken balloons sailing in the streets."

Howells frequented homes where "charming people . . . were readers and lovers of books," some of them no doubt purchased at McClelland's Bookstore downtown. In one of those homes, he met a visitor from Vermont, Miss Elinor Mead. They married a few years later. He may have had her in mind when he wrote, with amusement, of "a visiting young lady from New England [who] screamed at the sight of *The Atlantic Monthly*. 'Why, have you *The Atlantic Monthly* out here?'" The response was — with cold superiority — "There are several subscribers to *The Atlantic Monthly* in Columbus!"

One of them may have been Tod Galloway, youngest son of Samuel Galloway, a lawyer and politician who had served as secretary of state and commissioner of schools for Ohio. A nationally known orator, the senior

Neil House bill of fare, pre-1860.

Galloway was a close friend of Abraham Lincoln, with whom he had an extensive correspondence. During the great building boom of 1852, Galloway built one of those stately brick mansions on East Town Street. Tod described it fondly as a place with "high ceilings, broad hallways and spacious rooms, big windows with old-fashioned outside shutters and a broad winding stairway . . . to an attic which covered the entire third story . . . an attic where were numerous bound volumes of old newspapers. . . ."

Another "place of delight" was the "big, cool cellar" whose walls were lined with "barrels of apples, potatoes, molasses, vinegar and cider; while a generous winding shelf held hams, tongue and fresh vegetables from the farm. . . . In one part was a sunken place in the floor lined with stone slabs where, with fresh water, the milk and cream would be kept cool and sweet. . . .Ice packed in sawdust was always kept in an icehouse."

In later years, Galloway provided nostalgia for generations of Yale alumni as the composer of "The Whiffenpoof Song." But he never lost his own nostalgia for that home's "plentious supply of provender which was indicative of the open-handed hospitality of the home through [which] passed a constant stream of guests — one day, the most distinguished; the next, bland and humble. . .a United States senator, often; and often visiting politicians, a stump speaker or a county chairman."

Politics was becoming an important topic in the city. On January 23, 1854, the Kansas-Nebraska Act advocated admission of territories with or without slavery ("popular sovereignty"), a Congressional doctrine of nonintervention in the territories and repeal of the Missouri Compromise. On January 24, an "Appeal of the Independent Democrats" was published, condemning the measure as a "gross violation of a sacred pledge" and a "slaveholders' plot." Signers included Ohio Senator Salmon P. Chase, long an implacable opponent of the extension of slavery and a leader in the anti-Nebraska "fusionist" movement.

Nominally a Whig some years before, Chase's convictions led him into the Liberty Party and then into the Free Soil party. A coalition of Free Soilers and Democrats in the Ohio Assembly were considered responsible for his election to the Senate in 1849. Chase had already won national recognition for his vigorous opposition to the Compromise of 1850. And although the Kansas-Nebraska bill passed after a bitter three-month fight, the "Appeal" Chase signed was widely reprinted.

On February 28, 1854, a coalition of Whigs, Free-Soilers and antislavery Democrats meeting at Ripon, Wisconsin, recommended organizing a new party based on the single principle of opposing extension of slavery into the territories. The name Republican was suggested.

Preston Wolfe, retired publisher of *The Columbus Dispatch,* a noted Columbus Republican and ardent history buff, points out, "The Republican Party had their first meeting here [on July 13, 1855]. Whigs, Free Soilers, anti-Nebraskans and abolitionist groups all got together and prevailed upon Salmon Chase to run for governor. And that was really the beginning of the Republican Party."

The fusionists did formally organize the party on that occasion; Chase did run as their candidate for governor and after an exceptionally bitter campaign, won. The outcome of that election was not only considered a victory for the Republican party in Ohio but for the new party nationally.

Despite serious politics, there was plenty of time for social parties in that era. Virtually anything would serve as an excuse for throwing a "gala." (Tod Galloway's departure for a musical career in the East actually prompted a number of parties where ladies "wore mourning" to lament his absence.)

By all odds, though, the greatest social wing-ding of the 1850s took place in 1857—the opening of the new Statehouse—the structure authorized by the Ohio Legislature in 1838. There had even been a cornerstone laying on July 4, 1839, but a bitter political feud led to repeal of the authorization. Work was stopped totally until 1848. Out of 50 plans submitted by architects from across the country, three were selected for consideration. Finally, construction commenced under the supervision of architect Henry Walter of Cincinnati, who blended all three plans.

Basically, the plans called for a classic Doric style, with eight stone columns on the east and west sides and four each on the north and south. It was 304 feet long and 184 feet wide. The height from the rotunda floor to the dome was 136 feet — the dome truncated rather than traditionally round.

The legislative halls were first to be ready for occupancy in 1857. There was much rejoicing, particularly since the old Statehouse had burned down in 1852. The entire structure would not be completed until 1859 — 20 years after the start of the project. With gray limestone from an area quarry and omnipresent convict labor, the total cost was only $1.35 million for what authorities then proclaimed "the greatest state Capitol building in the United States." It is still one of the largest Capitol buildings outside Washington, D.C. and easily one of the most impressive.

In 1857, Frederick Fay, a Columbus resident, wrote his sister that since the major portions were completed, "the people here thought it was appropriate to have a house-warming. So a committee was appointed to superintend the affair. Tickets were issued to the inhabitants of the county at five dollars each, ladies free. Out-of-the-county tickets were sent all over the state admitting the person to whom sent, free of charge."

When time for the ball came, "railroads reduced their fare to one-half price. There were over 20,000 tickets issued and. . .differing estimates on the number present. . .from five to ten thousand persons . . I did not attend," Fay added nonchalantly, "as I thought I could put my spare five to better use." But then, he noted, "such a crowd I never saw!" There was only one open door to get in "through such a great squeeze. The ladies' whalebones suffered to an alarming extent. I heard of one lady that had the whalebones in the waist of her dress all broken, and then she fainted under the belief that it was her ribs."

Governor Salmon P. Chase — first occupant of the Statehouse — was supposed to open the affair with a speech. But it took him "about 1½ hours to get in." By 10 p.m., though, everyone was in, or so it seemed. Somehow, people found room in those crowded chambers to dance to the music of two bands. "The dance was was kept up until daylight, for it was impossible to clear the building, as the greater part were strangers and the hotels being full, they had no place to stay. . .and so they danced the night away." Fay confessed that it was "such a great affair that if I had supposed it would have been so large a gathering, I would have attended."

The atmosphere at the Statehouse was considerably quieter on September 16, 1850, when Abraham Lincoln stood on the steps to make his first important address in the state.

In that year, black faces appeared and disappeared with increasing frequency on the Underground Railroad in Columbus. Meanwhile, Daniel Decatur Emmett (a caucasian) was in New York City enjoying fame as the originator of minstrel shows. The son of a Mount Vernon, Ohio, blacksmith, Emmett had already earned plaudits for such hits as "Old Dan Tucker" before turning out a catchy new walk-around song for the Bryant Minstrels. It was called "Dixie." Even Abraham Lincoln allowed later that the song was one of his favorites. But when he left Columbus on that September day in 1859, "de land ob cotton" (The Confederacy of seceded southern states adopted "Dixie" as its battle hymn) was not an object of romance. It was a breeding ground for rebellion.

By December 1859, a convention of the entire Ohio militia asked the General Assembly for appropriations to encourage militia organization. Ohio's capital was about to become a focal point for Union Army activities. The quiet times in that old capital Howells cherished were over.

Abraham Lincoln visited Columbus — by railroad — twice before his body joined the bodies of the young men of Columbus, and of America. That casualty was commemorated by American poet Walt Whitman:

> *When lilacs last in the dooryard bloom'd,*
> *And the great star early droop'd in the western sky in the night,*
> *I mourned, and yet shall mourn with ever-returning spring.*

Turn Hall at High and Beck Streets, looking west, 1879.

CHAPTER FIVE

BODY COUNTS AND PROFIT MARGINS

1861-1878

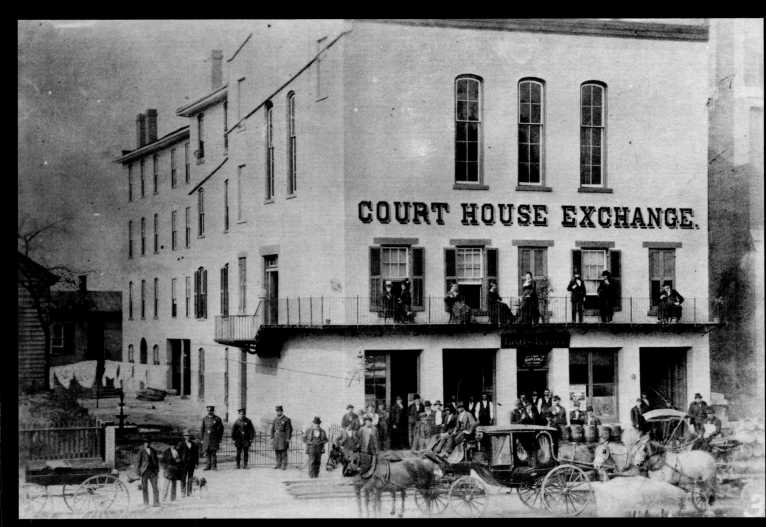

The Court House Exchange, the old Sehrimer Building, 1875.

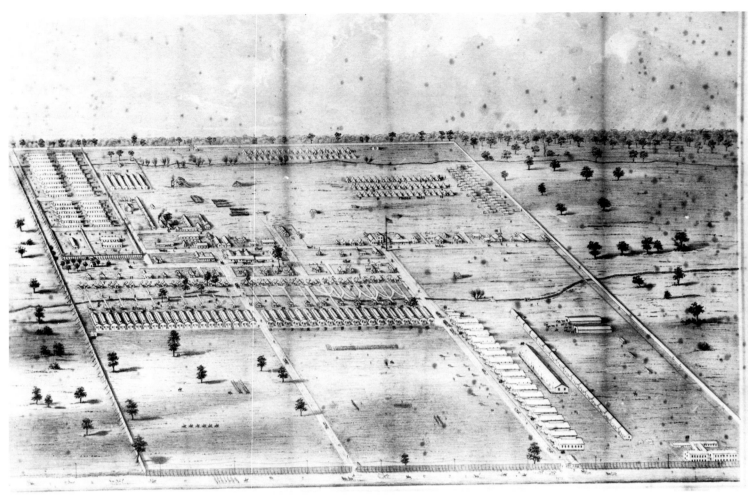

Camp Chase, Confederate prisoner of war camp.

Morgan's Raiders escape from the Ohio State Penitentiary during the Civil War.

W**ar is hell.** The phrase has been repeated by survivors and observers of war ever since the Civil War. It is credited to General William Tecumseh Sherman of Lancaster, Ohio, a quiet, comely and prosperous town just east of Columbus. Presumably, Sherman said it while burning his way through Georgia. Actually, the phrase originated in Columbus about two decades after the war. Sherman — "Uncle Billy" to the men who served under him — attended a national convention of G.A.R. veterans at Franklin Park on August 11, 1888. He had not planned to make a speech but was finally urged onto the platform. Longer on action than words, he stood up and said (roughly paraphrased), "Boys, they say that war is glory, but you and I know, war is all hell." In repetition later, it was condensed to these three immortal words.

Ironically, there were published rumors during the war that Sherman was literally insane, but they rose out of his fellow officers' distaste for his crude techniques and language. (War was, then, still supposed to be a "gentleman's" exercise in courtesy as well as courage.)

In 1861, certainly, righteous fervor and belief in freedom for all men still prevailed over Sherman's grim truth.

When President Lincoln declared on April 15, 1861, that "insurrection existed," Columbus' response to Lincoln's call for men was "instantaneous," "splendid" and "a prodigious outburst of patriotic fervor."

Before the 36-hour firing on Sumter was even finished, 20 full companies had reported to Ohio's Governor Dennison, anticipating a call for immediate service. The governor had yet to send the summons to the state at large.

Ohio provided an inordinately large number of leaders in both Lincoln's Cabinet and his Army. The state contributed Secretary of War Edwin Stanton; Secretary of the Treasury (and former Ohio Governor) Salmon P. Chase and Generals W. T. Sherman, James A. Garfield, Rutherford B. Hayes, Philip P. Sheridan and Ulysses S. Grant. All are now represented in a statue on the Statehouse lawn titled *These Are My Jewels.* It certainly would have been much more difficult than it was to win the war without them. Without Grant and Sherman, it was even possible the Union Army might have lost.

But then, they might also have lost without the individuals and collective groups from all over the state who literally showered the capital with telegrams —

Capt. G.B. Bailey, Portsmouth; "Will leave for Cincinnati with company on first boat; thence by railroad." R.F. Day, Plymouth; "We are ready." G.B. Mason, Circleville; "We will be on hand tomorrow at noon, seventy-five strong."

Because of its location, Columbus became a center of activity for the entire Union Army. Every train brought full loads of volunteer soldiers, along with office seekers, contractors and (inevitably) profiteers. The streets were crowded with strangers, and hotels and boarding houses were full within hours. The town — grown to more than 18,000 residents — was simply not equipped to accommodate the newcomers.

Neither was the state government. Although the possibility of war had been anticipated for months, officials and legislators (as those in many other states) were almost wholly unprepared in terms of resources or arrangements for the rapidly arriving volunteer soldiers. The state arsenal (now the Cultural Arts Center) had exactly 2,767 muskets and 197 sabers with which to arm the 23 regiments Ohio promptly assembled. Governor Dennison immediately asked the General Assembly to appropriate $450,000 for arms and equipment. Legislators (who had been delaying action on a bill appropriating $100,000 for the anticipated war) unanimously passed a bill authorizing a million dollars. Terms of that grand legislative appropriation authorized a Sinking Fund Commission to borrow the million dollars at six percent interest on certificates exempt from state taxation. D.W. Deshler of the National Exchange Bank of Columbus personally offered the governor whatever money he needed until the certificates could be negotiated. His bank provided $100,000, and other banks around the state responded so quickly that the entire million-dollar loan was negotiated almost as soon as the volunteers began to pour into Columbus.

Aside from lacking arms, no provisions had been made to feed or shelter an army. Individuals came in civilian dress, "some even wearing high silk hats," Alfred E. Lee observed. They had expected to find uniforms ready. Volunteer militia organizations which had been in existence for years, such as Zouaves, already had their own outfits, replete with exotic ballooning trousers and sashes at the waists. Others simply uniformed themselves with what they figured was the most military combination of ordinary clothing, such as red shirts with blue trousers.

OF FRANCIS SESSIONS: *Columbus banker and businessman, Francis Sessions (above) took packages to General Grant's troops in the western campaign. From these trips, he sent first-person accounts of the battlefields and news to the homefront in Columbus. Sessions' home (left) was built in the Romantic Revival style of pre-Victorian architecture popular in the 1850s and 1860s.*

Those first several hundred men could wait for uniforms, but not food or housing. The state commissary-general was authorized to put them in various hotels at rates ranging from 75 cents to $1.25 per day "and up." This was so expensive that, within 48 hours, a few sheds were contracted to house men until camp grounds could be selected, barracks built and tents bought. Sleeping bunks and long dining tables were acquired whenever possible, but they could fill only a fraction of the needs.

As the number of volunteers increased with each day's train arrivals, many were temporarily lodged in such places as Starling Hospital, the Ohio Penitentiary and the Capitol building itself. Sleeping bodies were scattered all over the terraces, the rotunda and the hallways.

Ordered to send the earliest organized troups to Washington for possible defense of the Union capital, Governor Dennison pleaded unpreparedness, but the telegraph message returned, "Send them on instantly and we will equip them here."

While Ohio officials negotiated in both eastern and midwestern states to buy, trade or beg war implements, profiteers were not whistling "Dixie" or even the noble strains of the "Battle Hymn of the Republic." Messrs. J. & H. Miller of Columbus quickly sold 4,000 overcoats at $6.65 each. Merchants from other towns came in with quick supplies of other uniform clothing priced, according to Lee, "in proportion to direct need."

By April 19, another 20 companies were dispatched to Washington, but new volunteers quickly took their place in Columbus. Goodale Park was pressed into use. As sheds were thrown up on the lawn, it was renamed Camp Jackson and officially designated rendezvous for all troops north of Hamilton County and south of the Western Reserve.

Reporters from the *Ohio State Journal* — undaunted by guards posted to keep back curious crowds — managed to look over or get through high picket fences to describe some of the occupants. They were "splendid looking fellows," many "fresh from the country . . . .They are of all ages, from the man whose head is gray to the boy on whose cheeks the down has not yet obscured the bloom." All those faces, miraculously, were visibly "resolute," "determined," with "fight in them." They were also physically "of . . . good condition." Popular assessment — a week's drilling would render them ready not only for battle but victory.

On Monday, April 22, a hand-signed call was circulated: "Mothers! Wives! Sisters! Let us do our part in our country's cause!" Area women responded by meeting in the basement of the First Presbyterian Church. While setting to the immediate work of repairing clothes for the soldiers and contributing everything from cash to wool socks, they formalized their activities by organizing the city's first Soldiers' Aid Society. Within a month, they were put to work at a military hospital set up at 208 South High Street. Later in the war, Saint Francis Hospital was pressed into service, and Lewis Heyl's school for young women was converted into an additional hospital for the duration of the war.

With all those young men stranded in Columbus, away from their homes and loved ones, there were other needs to consider. While Columbus' benevolent ladies were organizing their energies for the cause of freedom, pragmatic madams were also swift on getting off their feet

OF THE DESHLER FAMILY: *David Deshler (above) was the first generation of the Columbus family that built the Deshler Block (right) at Broad and High Streets. The row of businesses was torn down in 1915 to build the fashionable Deshler Hotel, which stood until 1969.*

— particularly one Madam Metcalfe.

That spring of 1861, the state government was building an arsenal (later Fort Hayes). More quickly, overcrowded and impatient troops from the makeshift arrangements at Goodale Park were transferred to a site four miles west of the city on the National Road (Broad Street). The name Camp Jackson was transferred from Goodale Park along with the men at first, but the new location was soon designated Camp Chase. (Other small camps were later built in Franklin County, but Camp Chase remained the center of activity throughout most of the war.)

While the state was completing these facilities, Madam Metcalfe was the first woman in Columbus to establish a house away from home in the war years. According to the *Ohio State Journal*, she "held sway" in a large, three-story brick house on Seventh Street, near Rich. Madam Metcalfe had a nosy attorney who lived just around the corner and who frequently found ways to annoy his flamboyant neighbor. Knowing the antagonism between the two, some soldiers and town pranksters smeared tar on the front of Madam Metcalfe's newly painted house, then dripped the tar in a tell-tale path to the lawyer's woodshed. Next morning, following the obvious clues to the allegedly guilty gent, "her wrath knew no bounds." She went to his office with a horsewhip and lashed him down every step and out onto the street.

Within a short time, the impatient men at Camp Chase were dispatched to various battlefields in the South. From the earliest days of battle, dreadful numbers of lives were lost on both sides. But the majority of victories went to the Confederates. They believed their fervor and fighting skills would enable them to whip the Yankees back to the north in a month or two. Union leaders were equally unrealistic. Alfred Lee, Columbus historian, wrote, "The popular impression, encouraged from Washington, had been that the war would be brief. Mr. Seward had inferentially assured . . . the trouble would be a matter of sixty days."

But after the battle of Bull Run (July 21, 1861) resulted in "disastrous defeat, panic and flight of northern soldiers . . . consternation which can hardly now be adequately conceived" set in. In Columbus, as news on the battle was awaited, the *Ohio State Journal* reported, "An immense, surging crowd assembled in front of our office. All expected the enemy would soon be ours . . . but at noon came dispatches announcing a disaster, and a most despondent gloom spread over faces . . . and a pall seemed to settle upon their spirits. By the evening, though, revengeful resistance was aroused . . . 'I feel like going myself!' was the exclamation of everyone who spoke."

Columbus was particularly upset at the outcome of the battle since the commanding general was General Irvin McDowell, son of prominent Columbus citizen Abram McDowell. McDowell was a competent, if not heroic soldier, who had the exceptional bad luck to be commander of an unprepared army in a battle his opponents had to win. However, he did go on to provide important service during and after the war as a high-ranking soldier.

Franklin County men — as others in the country — saw that the initial three-month call for volunteers was totally inadequate. More volunteered. Finally the government foresaw the grim possibility of a longer war.

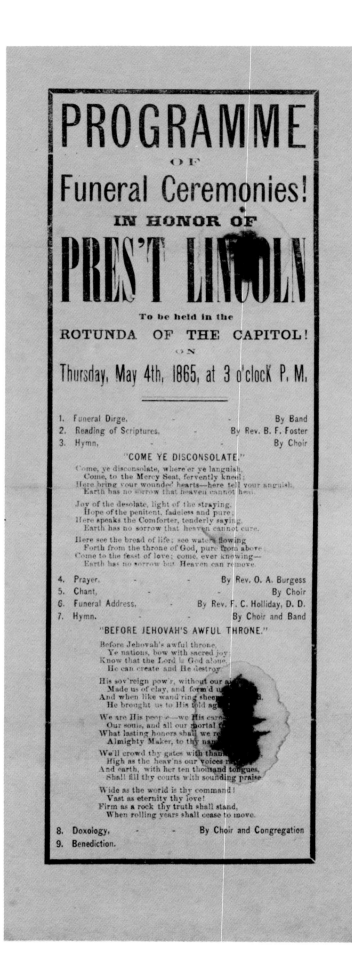

PROGRAMME
OF
Funeral Ceremonies!
IN HONOR OF
PRES'T LINCOLN
To be held in the
ROTUNDA OF THE CAPITOL!
ON
Thursday, May 4th, 1865, at 3 o'clock P. M.

1. Funeral Dirge, - - By Band
2. Reading of Scriptures, - By Rev. B. F. Foster
3. Hymn, - - By Choir

"COME YE DISCONSOLATE."
Come, ye disconsolate, where'er ye languish,
Come, to the Mercy Seat, fervently kneel;
Here bring your wounded hearts—here tell your anguish,
Earth has no sorrow that heaven cannot heal.

Joy of the desolate, light of the straying,
Hope of the penitent, fadeless and pure;
Here speaks the Comforter, tenderly saying,
Earth has no sorrow that heaven cannot cure.

Here see the bread of life; see waters flowing
Forth from the throne of God, pure from above;
Come to the feast of love; come, ever knowing—
Earth has no sorrow but Heaven can remove.

4. Prayer, - - By Rev. O. A. Burgess
5. Chant, - - By Choir
6. Funeral Address, - By Rev. F. C. Holliday, D. D.
7. Hymn, - - By Choir and Band

"BEFORE JEHOVAH'S AWFUL THRONE."
Before Jehovah's awful throne,
Ye nations, bow with sacred joy;
Know that the Lord is God alone,
He can create and He destroy.

His sov'reign pow'r, without our aid,
Made us of clay, and form'd us men;
And when like wand'ring sheep we stray'd,
He brought us to His fold again.

We are His people—we His care,
Our souls, and all our mortal frame;
What lasting honors shall we rear,
Almighty Maker, to thy name?

We'll crowd thy gates with thankful songs,
High as the heav'ns our voices raise;
And earth, with her ten thousand tongues,
Shall fill thy courts with sounding praise.

Wide as the world is thy command!
Vast as eternity thy love!
Firm as a rock thy truth shall stand,
When rolling years shall cease to move.

8. Doxology, - - By Choir and Congregation
9. Benediction.

A CITY MOURNS: *Funeral ceremonies were conducted in honor of a slain president, Abraham Lincoln, on May 4, 1865 in Columbus (programme, left). The Sehrimer Building (above) and the Capitol (below) were draped in solemn blacks as the funeral cortege (bottom) proceeded through the city.*

Recruiting commenced with President Lincoln's July 1, 1861, call for 300,000 three-year men. Several new companies were organized and promptly put into service. Despite a few minor triumphs, the early defeats of 1861 continued throughout 1862 for the Union Army.

Crates of supplies from the Soldiers' Aid Society were frequently carried to battlefields in the South by prominent Columbus merchant Francis C. Sessions. Within hours of the April 1862 battle at Shiloh, Tennessee, he took fifteen boxes of hospital stores from the Society by steamboat to the battlefield. Sessions visited the sick and wounded from the area, as well as those from other Ohio regiments. They were, he telegraphed back, being "cut to pieces." He spent two weeks (often without sleep for several days) conferring with Ohio military leaders and medical personnel. He also wired or wrote daily reports back home about further supplies needed for "soldiers who seem grateful enough that they are not left to die."

As those men — and more from other battles — arrived in Columbus, they were often in need of more than nursing care. Virtually all were hungry and had no money. Women marshalled contributions of food and carried them to the trains, feeding men from other towns who were passing through, as well as local soldiers being moved to hospitals.

In ways as various as their personalities and beliefs, women all over the country proved themselves capable of bravery. Lucy Webb Hayes, wife of Rutherford B. Hayes, is described in *Women in Ohio* as an "exceptional hostess" who dispensed "democratic hospitality" both in her home and, after the war, as First Lady of the state (in Columbus), then in the White House during her husband's presidency. But during the years when Hayes was in the field, she not only visited him between campaigns but personally "nursed him after he was severely wounded at South Mountain, Maryland."

Frances Dana Gage — a remarkable woman who spent 25 years mothering six sons and two daughters while "participating in unpopular social movements" (primarily women's rights) — was always more interested in dispensing justice than hospitality. For many years prior to the war, she was a contributor to, then editor of, the *Ohio Cultivator* in Columbus. She also traveled to other cities for lectures. And in 1851, she "presided over a large history-making women's rights convention in Akron. Her opening speech "received wide acclaim."

When four of her sons went off to war, though, "Fanny" Gage immediately headed south herself where she "ministered to the wounded." After the war, she taught freedmen and superintended a refuge for them in South Carolina. She was crippled in a carriage accident in 1864 but continued her work through lectures until a stroke paralyzed her in 1867. She was a prime example of the women's rights activists who set aside that work to devote their energies to the abolitionist cause before and

A reminder of Camp Chase is the monument built at the turn of the century by the Daughters of the Confederacy.

after the war. There are no statues of these women on the Statehouse lawn, but they are cause for pride in Columbus' history.

Despite all the adversity of 1861-1862, courage was still demonstrated. Courtly (even cavalier) attitudes of hospitality prevailed. If city "guests" happened to be captured Confederates, they were referred to in the newspaper accounts as "distinguished Sesech captives." Although housed in Camp Chase, they were often allowed to roam about the city freely. As Americans, the two factions were as inextricably related as they were at odds.

By 1863, though, there were no delusions left that the Civil War was just the equivalent of a family dispute where two brothers quarrel, get it out of their systems with a good fistfight, and then sit down to Sunday dinner and forget it ever happened. Feelings grew resentful, then bitter. With the two overlapping factions in the area, there was strained relations intensified among residents. Anti-abolition sentiments ran high in the area settled by Southern sympathizers. Most of them felt the war was a needless attack on individual and state's rights. The clash of cultures within the state and city brought the conflict into the very hearts and everyday lives of the people.

In February 1863, the offices of *The Crisis* were mobbed by Union soldiers and angry Columbus residents. The premises were literally torn apart, but by some quirk, the presses remained intact.

In the spring of 1863, General John Hunt Morgan mounted a 2,500-man cavalry raid deep into Ohio. Its purpose was to link up with General Lee's army which was advancing into Pennsylvania. The campaign, which ended at Gettysburg, was a dangerous gamble. It was hoped that Morgan's raid would draw off a sizeable number of Union troops and thus aid Lee. And it did — but Morgan's force was cornered in Columbiana County and forced to surrender. Most of the captured cavalrymen were confined in Camp Chase prison. Morgan and several of his officers were housed in the Ohio Penitentiary — then considered escape-proof. According to penitentiary history, they were not given prison numbers and were "treated a bit better than the run-of-the-mill convicted felon." They responded to this courtesy by using tablespoons to break into an airshaft and escape over the walls. They had only been in prison two months.

On the way out of town, some of the Raiders decided to shop at F&R Lazarus department stores. "Lazarus," an in-store history, notes that some of the "famous Morgan's Raiders . . . stole clothing from the Lazarus store." Owner Simon Lazarus' sons, Fred and Ralph, obtained guns from the store and went to Camp Chase where the thieves were hiding in the quarters for captured Rebels and "got the goods back." Afterwards, captives were housed at Camp Chase. It became one of the largest

THE MID-1860s: *The first streetcar (above left) on the streets of Columbus, 1863; the flood of 1865 (above right), looking west from State and Front Streets; the Clinton Bank (below) on the corner of High Street.*

Confederate prisoner-of-war camp in the North. That did not prevent other soldiers escaping from the city as surely as Morgan's Raiders did. Unfortunately, many of them happened to be Union soldiers. Desertions, according to Lee, had become an "enormous evil." In March of that year, an "authentic estimate" of deserters from 33 Ohio regiments in the field totaled about 5,000. The *Ohio State Journal* of January 14, 1863, carried the headline: "700 Deserters from Camp Chase." (These were resident Union troops not captives.) Subsequent May editions of the *Journal* indicated desertions from Columbus averaged no less than fifteen to seventeen per day. (The newspapers were also filled with advertisements of "recruits for hire.")

When Grant took Vicksburg on July 4, 1863, after a six-week siege, 40,000 troops were surrendered to him along with the city. There were hopes throughout the North that the battle would convince the Confederates to surrender, but the carnage was to drag on nearly two more years.

The problem of housing Confederate prisoners became increasingly difficult. In August 1864, there were as many as 3,500 prisoners at one time in Camp Chase. Some were processed out to other camps in other cities, but new ones arrived daily in batches of several hundred. Crowded unsanitary conditions led to widespread disease, and many prisoners died.

At the time, city residents were busy scanning extended lists of the dead and wounded in the battle at Chickamauga, and the battles that followed, before General Lee surrendered to Grant on April 9, 1865.

The body of Abraham Lincoln — the war's ultimate casualty — was returned to Columbus by train April 29, 1865. Thousands of people from all over the state poured into the capital to stand in silent lines and wait for a chance to pay their respects at his coffin. It was placed on a catafalque in the Statehouse rotunda. Between the allotted hours of nine and four, more than 50,000 people viewed the remains of a face more sorrowful still than theirs.

Outside, on the cornice above the Statehouse columns, was a quotation from his inaugural address: "With Malice toward none, with Charity for All."

Over 500 Franklin County men died in that war. On Memorial Day, some people still visit the small tombstones in Greenlawn and other cemeteries which bear the long-forgotten names and death-dates from battles which must be looked up in history books. The graves are decorated with small American flags with stars for all the states in the Union, including those they fought. In the cemetery on Sullivant Avenue are the graves of the 2,260 Confederate soldiers who died at Camp Chase. A small committee, formed long ago, places American flags there on Memorial Day.

The population of Columbus grew nearly 70 percent during those years. And at the end of them, there was furious building activity as commerce and industry seemed unable to build new and larger facilities fast enough to accommodate profits.

Columbus at the end of the Civil War was bustling.

Early shop owners on the southeast corner of Spring and High Streets.

The improved rail system — developed to move men and supplies in the war with speed — and the construction of the Columbus barracks (Fort Hayes) and Camp Chase had provided jobs and economic growth for the city. New homes, restaurants, saloons and retail stores had grown up to meet the needs of the influx of troops. By 1863, Columbus even had its first streetcar on High Street. It replaced the horsedrawn omnibuses of an earlier day. Many persons riding that early horsedrawn car and a carriage noticed little difference between them, except the ride was smoother and cheaper. But that car — and the ones following it did much in the next 30 years to change the physical face of Columbus.

In the two decades after the Civil War, the city was still pretty much a walking city. Because of inadequate and slow public transportation and because only the streets near the center of the city were paved, people of all classes still needed to live close to their work. The downtown area around the Statehouse still contained numerous private residences. The most exclusive of these was located around Capitol Square and down Broad Street. The alleys of the central city were crammed with smaller homes of working-class people and tradesmen. Some of the worst slums in the city were along the Scioto River near the factories and canal wharves. The bottoms across the river from the city were still almost empty except for factories and railroad yards because the river still flooded frequently and forcefully. The flood of 1865 heavily damaged buildings and property in the

BUGGIES, BUGGIES, BUGGIES: By the 1880s, twenty operating companies made Columbus the buggy capital of the world, including the Buckeye and the Columbus Buggy Companies.

Hoster Beer Truck, from one of four German family breweries which had brewed beer in Columbus since the 1830s.

lowlands.

Most of Columbus still lived within the area now contained by the inner belt except for the emerging ethnic communities. By 1850, more than a third of the city's population was German and located in the southern half of the city. But as the German population grew, it moved farther south. By 1870, homes were added in what is now German Village. The Catholic church erected Saint Mary's in 1871 at the corner of Third and Sycamore streets. The German community flourished during the 1870s. They unofficially appropriated the city park at the south end of the city as their own and renamed it Schiller Park. There were singing societies, service organizations, independent military companies, schools and churches to serve the German people. Their political power was consolidated in the wards of the near south side.

The Irish were also coming into their own as an independent community. In Columbus, they were never as tightly knit as the Germans. Many of the Irish immigrants had come to work on the canals and railroads and had staked out the area just below the railroad station as their own. Naghten Street was affectionately called "Irish Broadway". The Irish community was anchored by Saint Patricks Church on the east and the Irish hotels, saloons and shops on High Street near the train station. This neighborhood had been well-entrenched since the 1850s. But it began to split up by the 1870s, as many second- and third-generation members of Irish families moved north of the railyards and across the river to old Franklinton to escape the noise and squalor of the Naghten Street "gateway" neighborhood. (With the expansion of both the railyards and the downtown business district, much of the original Irish community would be gone to other areas by 1900. The most important of these new areas was the Franklintown bottoms, which came to be called Middletown.) Franklinton itself changed after the Civil War. As it became absorbed into the city, it developed into more of an industrial and commercial suburb.

By 1870, Columbus was the third largest city in the state. Franklin County had 53,217 residents; Columbus, 31,274. The Legislature authorized the building of a state university. Located within the expanding street boundaries were 31 churches, more than 100 saloons, 24 hotels, thirteen livery stables, 45 physicians, eleven restaurants, 56 attorneys, seven book stores, seven tanneries, thirteen drug stores, 122 groceries and the City Market. Real estate between Gay and Broad streets was valued at $500 per frontage foot. Sidewalks were paved on both sides of Capitol Square and double rows of trees planted along Broad Street, despite complaints that

OHIO STATE UNIVERSITY

Higher education for the masses

Within a year after the Civil War began, Abraham Lincoln's administration — which could only pay cash pittances to Union soldiers — rewarded all citizens in "each loyal state" with a gift that proved to be of incalculable value to their children and their descendants.

On July 2, 1862, Congress approved the Lincoln-sponsored Morrill Act, granting each state in the Union 30,000 acres for each senator and representative then in the U.S. Congress (thus aligning the grant size with population). The purpose of the grants was to establish agricultural colleges.

Each state legislature was to sell its land grant scrip at the best available profit, then devote the proceeds to "the endowment, support and maintenance of at least one college where the leading subject shall be, without excluding other scientific and classical studies, and including military tactics, to teach such branches of learning as are related to agriculture and the mechanical arts, and in such a manner as the legislatures of the states may respectively prescribe in order to promote the liberal and practical education of the industrial classes." That act democratized higher education. The ensuing financing from public pockets made college available to the working classes for the first time.

In Franklin County, Capital University, established by the Evangelical Lutheran Synod, had been in existence since 1831. And in 1868 — the year the Pope sent a letter creating the First Catholic Diocese of Columbus — St. Mary's of Spring's College (established in 1866 on Johnstown Road by Dominican Sisters) was incorporated. However, tuition fees put such education beyond the reach of the working classes.

According to James E. Pollard's *History of the Ohio State University's First 75 Years,* eleven years passed before state legislators completed selling Ohio's scrip (at considerably less profit than they had hoped), exacted matching funds from competing counties and obtained a site. The place settled upon was four miles north of downtown Columbus, "out in the country." A 327-acre "respectable German farm" formerly owned by William Neil, it had "a good spring . . . and fences all in good repair." This led to Ohio State's early (and persistent) designation as a "college in a cornfield."

With the location finally settled, lawmakers and the board of trustees, which they appointed, were at odds on whether they should cultivate minds by "narrow gauge or broad gauge" interpretations of the Morrill Act. "Narrow-gaugers" clung to a literal reading of such branches of "learning . . . related to agriculture and the mechanical arts." "Broad-gaugers" wanted liberal arts included in the cirriculum and cited the phrase "without excluding . . . scientific and classical studies." "Broad-gaugers" won out by exactly one vote, but treasurer Joseph Sullivant proclaimed it was a great victory that "classical studies have not lost all efficacy." However, when he designed the institution's official seal, it was in the shape of a pyramid symbolizing art, science, philosophy and letters rising, in that order, on the foundation of agriculture.

When the Ohio Agriculture and Mechanical College opened the doors of its one building (University Hall) on September 17, 1873, nine departments were devoted to agricultural and mechanical arts and one to classical languages. Twenty-four students were on hand to begin their studies.

At its inception, Pollard noted, the public showed "suspicion" and "antagonism" toward the college. There were charges that it was a "godless" place. In 1878, O.S.U.'s first president, Edward Orton, remarked, "The order and discipline of this university is excellent. We have been happily free during our short history from the relics of that barbarism which still survives in so many colleges in the shape of hazing and the reckless destruction of property.

"During the six years in which the college building has been occupied, it is safe to say that $6 would cover all the wanton injury it has received. Not a single exercise has been interrupted by college tricks."

When the university opened, *The Columbus Dispatch* noted, "They say a small beginning makes a good ending." The more than 50,000 students who a century later comprise the population of that massive, sprawling campus have borne that out.

OHIO STATE UNIVERSITY: One of the first buildings on campus was Orton Hall (top), built by 1893 and named after the university's first president, Edward Orton; it still stands on The Oval of the main campus. Two years later, the McMillan Observatory (above) was built and was named after science professor Emerson McMillan while he was still living; the observatory was one of the few on state university campuses then. Three years later, The Armory (right) was built to house the ROTC as well as the gymnasium; it was destroyed by fire in 1958. OSU lived up to its description as "the college in the corn field" when Ohio Stadium was dedicated in 1922, in the middle of agricultural crop land.

"a noble rage for improvement seems to have possessed city council like a spend-thrift devil."

The industrial heart of the city was also beginning to grow. Columbus had virtually little or no industry in the first 50 years of settlement. Its isolation in the center of the state away from easy access to markets was eased by the canal, the National Road and railroads. But the town still viewed itself primarily as a commercial and government city. A few men had done quite well for themselves.

Capital University in 1876.

Peter Hayden made a career out of using prison labor on contract to run a variety of businesses — a foundry, saddle works and a tool factory. The very low wages paid to prisoners gave Hayden an economic advantage. When he left Columbus for New York in 1850, his sons managed his Columbus enterprises well.

Joseph Ridgway had also done well for himself. Ridgway — often considered the pioneer industrialist of Columbus — was active from the 1830s in a variety of businesses. By the Civil War, he settled on foundries and tool-making as his major enterprises.

The German brewery families of Hoster, Schlee, Born and Blenkner had been brewing beer since the 1830s, but since there was no refrigeration, it was largely consumed locally. Most of the factories were located in the middle of downtown on both sides of the river in order that workers could be close to their work, water could be obtained for use in the plants and finished goods could be shipped on nearby rail lines.

The total impact of these entrepreneurs on the city in 1870 was not large. The enterprises employed only a few hundred workers and little heavy machinery. The great fortunes of Columbus up to the end of the Civil War were not in industry. They were in banking (David Deshler), transportation (William Neil and Alfred Kelley) and land speculation (Neil, Kelley, Deshler and a host of others). Nevertheless, it was the beginning of the industrial revolution that would eventually transform Columbus. With improved access to Eastern markets and available natural resources, small companies like the Columbus Buggy Company grew rapidly. With success came imitation, and by the 1880s, 20 operating companies would make Columbus the buggy capital of the world. Still, most citizens thought the city little more than a small and picturesque capital.

According to *We Too Built Columbus*, "all that emphasis on commerce was not the only preoccupation of a very delightful society." Ladies drove out on Broad Street in carriages beneath their small silk sunshades. Opera troupes were well received, and "women as well as men, when invited to any social gathering, prepared themselves for days in advance in order to take part in the various topics of conversation, including evolution, astronomy, science and politics." A group of wealthy citizens sponsored a free circulating library and reading room for the public. It was extremely popular.

The most important additions to the city in the post-war period were governmental. Ohio had decided to centralize most major state institutions for the afflicted and the criminal. After the Civil War, a new series of decisions were made regarding the future of these institutions. In 1861, major additions had been made to the Ohio Penitentiary. In 1864, construction was begun on a new Deaf Asylum to replace the woefully inadequate original one. Completed in 1866, the new structure was one of the most modern in the country. The old asylum for the insane — which had been crowded and disease-ridden — burned in 1868. Construction began in the Hilltop area west of the city in the early 1870s.

(These organizations had been centralized early by tireless volunteer efforts of a small group of non-professional philanthropists. In the 1870s, a new group of professionals took over, but both groups agreed. Because many of the treatments for the mentally ill, the deaf and the blind were similar, it was useful to have them near each other.

The construction of these institutions was a godsend. In 1873, economic panic set in across the country (largely induced by the collapse of Ohio banker Jay Cooke's financial empire). Columbus entered a four-year depression. Because money and work were scarce, social unrest began to flare. The money and work involved in building these institutions helped Columbus ride out the depression more easily than many Eastern cities.

The real trouble came in 1877. By that time, the railroad industry had become one of the largest businesses in America. Hundreds of small lines had been bought up by a few large rail lines based on Eastern capital. These lines had a stranglehold on the Midwest. They were the only way to ship Midwest products to Eastern markets. Most of the lines were notoriously unconcerned about the welfare of their workers. In 1877, the fledging railway workers unions — unrecognized by the companies — called a nationwide strike. Such a move was unprecedented in American history. The Great Railroad Strike of 1877 was the first real indication that organized labor was, indeed, organized. Baltimore, Saint Louis, Chicago and a dozen other cities broke out with pitched battles among strikers, railway workers and state and federal troops. Columbus was one of those cities. As a major railhead, it was imperative to local striking workers that the railyards be closed. If they were, more than half the rail traffic north of the Ohio River would have to be delayed or re-routed. The strikers met in Goodale Park, then marched to the railway station where they met head-on with a mixed force of company and city police, railroad workers loyal to the company, and elements of federal and local military forces.

The confrontation was hostile but mercifully short. No one was killed, and both sides fell back to find a way to resolve the situation. The result was a compromise —

Second railway station, Union Depot, 1877.

trains would run but only carry essential materials. There were random incidents of violence the next few days but no full-scale battles such as raged in the East. The strike failed for two reasons — the national leadership was unable to sustain a continuous strike by all local branches, and federal cavalry were introduced (President Hayes intervened to insure continued mail delivery). But the strike was a harbinger of the labor violence that would follow later in the nineteenth century.

There was another noticeable change in the city by the late 1870s. The factories were bigger, and there were more of them. Their smoke cast a pall over downtown. And there was the stench — even with county jail convicts cleaning the streets, the horses were always a few steps ahead. Still, it was not as bad as it had been. The remnants of everyday life once left in open gutters at the side of the road were now carried away in a series of intercepting sewers built in the downtown area.

There were more streetcars on High Street — and there were more police officers. The force had been reorganized and its size increased in the late 1870s.

The corner of Long and High streets was now the hub of black business. Business, in general, was moving up the street toward the train station. At Broad and High, the covered bridge across the river still existed, but the Neil House was replaced by another structure. The Statehouse was now the main attraction. (The outside had been completed in 1857, but the interior had not been finished until the mid-1860s. The Square was not fully planted until the 1870s.)

Still, Columbus was the same city — a little larger, a little dirtier, but still the capital. Life was still easy — not too hectic, and progress was being made — but not too quickly.

GRAND CELEBRATION

LAYING THE CORNER STONE
OF THE
Central Lunatic Asylum
AT
COLUMBUS, OHIO,
Monday, July 4, '70.

PROGRAMME.

President of the Day, - - - - - - Gov. R. B. HAYES.
Orator of the Day, - Hon. BELLAMY STORER, of Cincinnati.

THE GRAND PROCESSION

will form precisely at 1 o'clock P. M.

Knights Templars, in full costume, will form on High, right resting on State street.

I. O. O. F. will form on East State street, right resting on High.

Workingmen's Association will form on West State street, right resting on High.

(All other Societies reporting will be assigned proper places.)

Master Masons will form on East Town street, right resting on High.

Grand Lodge of Ohio, F. & A. M., Governor, Orator, State Officers, Trustees of Asylum, Mayor and City Council, on West Town.

Fire Department of the City.

LINE OF MARCH.

South on High to South street; returning on High to Depot; thence by cars to Asylum grounds.

ORDER OF EXERCISES ON THE GROUNDS.

Music by the Band.

Prayer.

Opening Address, by the President of the Day.

Origin of the Modern Reform in the Management of the Insane—By the President of the Board of Trustees, Dr. S. M. Smith.

History of the Care of the Insane by the State of Ohio—By Dr. Wm. L. Peck, Superintendent.

NATIONAL AIR—"AMERICA."

My country, 'tis of thee,
Sweet land of liberty,
Of thee I sing!
Land where my fathers died—
Land of the pilgrim's pride—
From every mountain side
Let freedom ring!

My native country, thee,
Land of the noble free,
Thy name I love;
I love thy rocks and rills;

Thy woods and templed hills;—
My heart with rapture thrills,
Like that above!

Let music swell the breeze,
And sing from all the trees
Sweet Freedom's song;
Let mortal tongues awake—
Let all that breathe partake—
Let rocks their silence break—
The sound prolong!

Oration—By the Orator of the Day.

MUSIC BY THE BAND.

The presentation of the Corner-Stone and Records of Deposits, by the Trustees of the Asylum.

MASONIC ODE.

Placed in form the corner stone,
True and trusty, brothers own,
Come and bring, in thought sincere,
Hands to help, and hearts to cheer.
Come and bring, in thought sincere,
Hands to help, and hearts to cheer.

Mark'd with love the Masters will
Kindly proved the work of skill;
Beauteous forms in grace shall rise,
'Neath the arch of favoring skies,
Beauteous forms, &c.

Join we now our offering tone,
While our homage we renew;
Bear to him whose praise we sing,
Thanks that from each bosom spring.
Bear to him, &c.

When on earth our work is o'er,
Be a dearer life in store;
Each in form, in heart upright,
Taught by truth's unerring light.
Each in form, &c.

Raising of the Stone.

Prayer by the Grand Chaplain, Rev. A. H. Washburn, of Cleveland.

Depositing of the Records by the Grand Treasurer, Flavius J. Phillips, Georgetown.

Reading of the Records by the Grand Secretary, John D. Caldwell, of Cincinnati.

Lowering of the Stone, and placing it in position by Alexander H. Newcomb, M. W. G. M., assisted by Phillip M. Wagenhals, R. W. Dep. Gr. M., and the other officers of the Grand Lodge of Ohio, of F. & A. M.

(Band playing while lowering the Stone.)

Benediction.

Inspection and Review of Knights Templars.

Form Procession and return to the city.

Chief Marshal, Sir Knight Jos. M. Stuart.

Jones & Sons Druggists and Chemists.

CHAPTER SIX

GILDED BARONS AND KNIGHTS OF LABOR

1879-1909

Reinhard Bank of the 1880s.

ON THE STREET: *The Von Gerichten Art Glass Company's float (above) toured the streets of Columbus in 1902. Another family business, Bauer's Bakery, got its start at Fourth and Rich Streets (below) in the 1880s.*

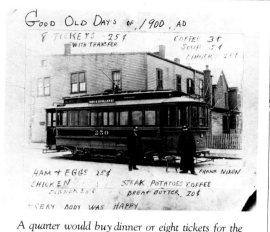

A quarter would buy dinner or eight tickets for the trolley at the turn of the century.

Around 1880, coal oil lamps lit the Columbus streets. People were also known to knock on those lamp posts with rocks if they needed a policeman, and that form of call was usually answered very quickly. That was efficient, indeed, considering the city had 51,647 residents by that time. The Franklin County count stood at 86,797.

The pace of post-Civil War living was still somewhat pastoral. Almost every yard in town still had hitching posts, according to Carlos B. Shedd, who wrote local historical anecdotes for the *Columbus Citizen*. "Some were designed as a little colored jockey," he recalled, "with an arm stretching up, holding an iron ring in his hand."

Milk was delivered to homes by one of three town milkmen. Shedd's supplier was named Purcell, and he lived on the northwest corner of Parsons and Franklin avenues, with his cow barns and pasture located nearby, "just south of Whiting's Pond on the southeast corner of State and Parsons." Purcell conducted business in a one-horse, four-wheel covered wagon carrying two large twelve-gallon tins filled with cold milk. He made two trips a day — one in the morning, one in the afternoon. When he drove up to a home, he immediately rang the doorbell. Customers were expected to be punctual in answering, with their milk pitchers in hand, ready for filling so as not to delay his next stops.

And national heroes were still figures of respect in those post-war decades. Shedd held fond memories of the time General U.S. Grant stopped for a reception in the State rotunda. City kids had a favorite game then. They would visit the Statehouse to try walking forward and stopping on the exact center of the rotunda floor (marked by a small piece of marble centered under the great seal of Ohio) while looking up at the rotunda dome. It was not easy. The game was forsaken, however, when Grant visited the Statehouse. Instead, "all the school children in the city passed by a reviewing stand located in the center of the rotunda and shook hands with him."

A rawer side of existence was crowding to the surface, though. Perhaps it was best expressed in a popular poem of the time:

'Tis a nice world to live in
To buy, or sell, or give in
But to borrow, beg, or hold a man's own
'Tis the very worst world that ever was known.

There was a growing gap between the haves and have-nots throughout America. Although the working and middle classes constituted a majority of Columbus' population, there was a wide gap between the upper and lower classes.

It was a period of rapid growth. There were more people because manufacturing in the city was growing and drew in more workers. Many of these migrated from the farms. Still Columbus remained basically a commercial and governmental center.

The real key to growth — particularly the spreading of the city — was the streetcar. Before its advent, people had to be close enough to walk to work (particularly the working classes who often worked exhausting 10-12 hour days). The horsedrawn car and the electric streetcar, after 1893, changed that pattern. People could live farther from work and commute to work cheaply.

As a result, the southern tier of the city expanded. The "streetcar suburbs" of the near north side (today's Victorian and Italian villages) and the Main Street and Livingston Avenue districts blossomed. This expansion created another side effect. People could not only choose where to live but whom to live near. They began to sort themselves more by social and economic classes.

The emerging middle class supplanted the wealthy in the older desirable districts near Goodale, Schiller and Franklin parks. The rich moved out further — to the areas around Capital University, Ohio State University and a new district, Grandview, beyond the river. The working class flowered, like hollyhocks in back alleys, in Old Franklinton, in what is now German Village and Flytown.

Flytown was part of a sub-culture never known to average Columbusites. It was a distinctive neighborhood, home of the city's ethnic working lower classes. Although still remembered with affection by older residents, it has now vanished, a victim of slum clearance projects in the 1950s and '60s. Former residents interviewed in the Dispatch Sunday Magazine in 1980 claim the district "stretched from Dennison Avenue on the east to the Olentangy River on the west, and from Spruce Street on the south to Buttles Avenue on the north." However, the Franklin County Historical Society market on Goodale Boulevard sets the northern boundary at Goodale Street. In either event, Flytown was crowded with immigrants, many of them Irish, many of whom worked in local industries and factories related to the buggy industry.

Other residents operated small grocery stores, barber shops, shoe repair stores and a number of well-populated saloons within the neighborhood. "Those who

IN THE SAME CITY: *Hickory Alley, a Columbus slum that existed from 1860 to the turn of the century. In 1895, Smith's European Hotel was just beginning to enjoy its heyday in Columbus. The New York Oyster House, notable restaurant on the first floor of the hotel, was near the corner of Broad and High Streets. Later, the building was used as a business college; a variety of retail shops are now housed there.*

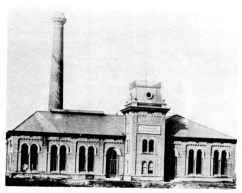

remembered Flytown," Betty Daft wrote, "still talk of the streets and alleys teeming with people, houses crowded shoulder-to-shoulder and hawkers selling fruits and vegetables. And they talk of how people would gather in the saloons, play cards there and visit." Others gathered around store barrels which held pickles and pigs feet. Kids bought hokey pokeys (ice cream cones). Storekeepers kept little books to mark down the amounts people charged during lean times. Credit was practiced strictly on a personal basis with trust as collateral. Further, those large families, whose kids played around the railroad tracks as well as in Goodale Park, had enormous cameraderie. "Everybody knew each other, were friends . . . Their doors were always open to each other."

In certain parts of the city, funerals, as well as weddings, were held in family living rooms. The late Monsignor Edmund Burkley, pastor of St. Mary's Church on South Third Street for more than half a century, recalled nearly dying of typhoid fever and pneumonia in 1894. "Typhoid was pretty common here," he told the *Citizen-Journal* in 1969. "Anyway, they had ordered my coffin. Not a casket, mind you. Those cost $600; a coffin was about $60. The funeral business wasn't always what it is today. There weren't even many funeral parlors in those days. People were laid out in their living rooms. We figured if a house was good enough to live in, it was good enough to be carried out of."

During this time, the location and nature of working

places underwent a drastic shift. Downtown real estate in the area around Broad and High streets had become too expensive for factories. Industrialists followed the river north and the lines of the railroad tracks in all directions for building sites. In the late 1890s, industrial districts emerged around First Avenue and Fourth Street and also off South Parsons Avenue (Steelton). By 1900, little heavy industry was left in the downtown area. Even light industries, such as the breweries, were moving. Downtown space was at a premium, not only for expanding governmental and retail services, but also for warehouses and office space near the major rail depots.

The result was a skyscraper. In 1897, the Wyandotte Building was erected. It was the first major skyscraper in the city — but not the last. No longer did Gothic religious buildings spiral skyward alone. Suddenly busines and profit margins leaped vertically, and monuments to them appeared on the horizon.

Politically, Columbus never had the equivalent of a Tammany Hall or a Boss Tweed — nothing on that scale — but some of the national cynicism and graft in the political process crept into what Mayor George J. Karb (1891-1894) dubbed "Good Old Columbus Town." Carlos Shedd wrote about the "old election days" — those last two decades of the nineteenth century:

About 5 o'clock in the morning, there would be someone knocking or ringing our door bell, arousing my father, to be sure to hurry down to the voting place to help open up the polls. Seems that the party having the most representation

The Wyandotte Building, built by 1897, an example of the Chicago "skyscraper school" of architecture.

would be entitled to choose the judge who would manage that poll all day. Then they would select two assistants from each party to help him. These voting booths were almost always located in the back room of some neighborhood drugstore or barbershop or what have you.

At each voting place they always had a horse and carriage all day long to go after delinquent voters. Things went along very smoothly until about 10 minutes or more before closing time, when the party having the most representatives at that time, would gather in front of the poll window. If you were not of their class (i.e., party), you couldn't get to the window to vote, and even if you did get through, they would challenge your vote and by the time that would be settled, it would be too late. The poll would be closed and your vote lost.

After supper everybody gathered downtown or at the City Hall . . . where the election returns were received and read. Saloons were opened all day and night. When the successful candidates were pretty well assured, the real celebration was started, ending up with a huge bonfire at the corner of Broad and High. . . . A good time was had by all except the defeated candidates.

At the same time, social reforms of all sorts were being preached by Washington Gladden in his First Congregational Church on East Broad Street. Gladden was one of the most remarkable men ever produced by Columbus. He was leader in what came to be known as the Social Gospel movement. His Sunday evening sermons or discourses covered such topics as the rights of labor, the despicable survival of poverty in a land of plenty, the evils of big business and the advantages of municipal ownership. Gladden had a probing mind and

Washington Gladden, from the pulpit.

steadfast integrity. Although he was widely recognized and respected in the community for 30 years, as many people opposed him as supported him. (And if they supported him on one issue, they might oppose him on another.) However, he not only made people think but prodded them to action. And he was pragmatic. Since he was willing to compromise to achieve the possible, many concrete reforms were made in city government and social services.

From 1882 until the building was razed in 1905, Gladden's sermons not only made a tremendous impact on his hometown but were printed and distributed nationally. At the end of his life, it was truly said that few ever really disliked him.

The reform spirit Gladden reflected was in the air all across America. Historian Richard Hofstadter called it "The Age of Reform." Women's rights, prohibition of alcohol, reformation of local government — such issues were debated vigorously everywhere. But Columbus was still basically traditional. Many ideas were rejected as laws by voters. Change came slowly and only when beneficial value could be proven. Columbus hesitated to enlarge its size (moderate) and its population (largely homogeneous, closely linked to the rural countryside). Its laboring classes were small. Its middle and upper classes were still largely non-existent. It was still a midwestern community representative of the state from which it sprang, not yet like the larger American cities, many of which had become seething cauldrons of discontent.

Technology, however, drew public interest in pragmatic Columbus as it carried into private homes. In 1880, the first public telephone was in use in the area. It was the result of experiments conducted in 1877 by the

The first balloon ascension took place in Columbus in 1842, and ballooning continued to be a popular pastime through the century. In 1910, Knabenschue's balloon, operated by a skillful aeronaut and showman, sailed about Columbus skies; Knabenschue controlled the aircraft from a rig below the balloon.

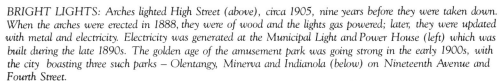

BRIGHT LIGHTS: Arches lighted High Street (above), circa 1905, nine years before they were taken down. When the arches were erected in 1888, they were of wood and the lights gas powered; later, they were updated with metal and electricity. Electricity was generated at the Municipal Light and Power House (left) which was built during the late 1890s. The golden age of the amusement park was going strong in the early 1900s, with the city boasting three such parks – Olentangy, Minerva and Indianola (below) on Nineteenth Avenue and Fourth Street.

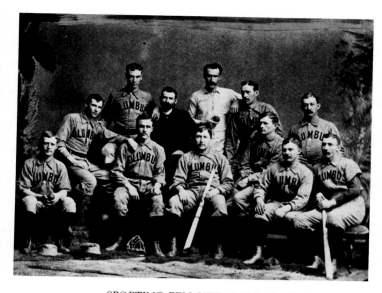

SPORTING FELLOWS: A Columbus baseball team (left), 1884; and the Ohio State University football team (right), 1890.

Brown Brothers, local title abstractors. On July 12, one of the brothers picked up a little gadget in his office at 37 North Third Street and yelled into it. A mile away, in his brother's branch office near the courthouse, a clerk put a similar gadget to his ear and had the first telephone conversation in Columbus.

That private device consisted of only two crude receivers connected by a wire. The line used was put into operation just three months after the first telephone line in the world was strong, and it was the beginning of telephone leasing on an annual basis.

By January 1, 1879, the Columbus Telephone Exchange (owned by partners Colonel Orlando Smith, T. J. Janney, George H. Twiss and Francis Sessions) opened its circuits with two lines. Headquarters were set up in the Sessions Block, which that gentleman had built after his missions for the Union during the Civil War. (Sessions himself lived in a grand home where the art gallery now stands.)

The first operators employed by the Columbus Telephone Exchange were males. Unfortunately, they had a habit of cursing at disgruntled customers who called to complain about service. So in October 1879, a 16-year-old girl named Alice Belle Hodgkins became the first woman telephone operator in Columbus and the third in Ohio.

Since there was no tone signal on the phones, the exchange employed a young Ohio State University student, Dudley Fisher (father of cartoonist Dudley Fisher), to play a flute into the telephone at 50 cents an hour, from 4 p.m. to midnight. If people heard the flute, they knew the line was on. In the meantime, Alice Hodgkins utilized daytime hours to train men not to curse at customers. One of them, William Bresnahan, learned the lessons so well he reputedly stood up and tipped his hat when ladies phoned in.

One of the few surviving photographs from the Milo-Grogan district northeast of the city rail yards.

Mark Twain visited the city on February 9, 1885, to speak at the Comstock Opera House. Admission price to hear the world-famous humorist was costly, "up to $1" per ticket, but "the best people of the city" paid the price. That same year, on March 3, the Ohio Historical Society was chartered and headquartered in Columbus. It began to assemble materials relating to the history of the 82-year-old state.

A majority of the populace then was still more interested in new ways to shed light on the present and future. In 1887, the Columbus Electric Light Company was incorporated. From about 1890 to 1914, arches of electric light framed city streets. As a result, Columbus was titled "The City of Arches."

In 1888, the Buckeye Buggy Company was destroyed by fire. Other buggy companies continued to operate, though, and business in general prospered in accordance with national trends. In January 1891, The Deshler National Bank was formed, and seven years later, William G. Deshler executed a trust fund to provide money for a hotel at the corner of Broad and High streets.

For recreation, people often whiled away the golden hours at Neil Park or Indianola Park. Roller skating was particularly popular at a rink located next to the Park Hotel at North High and Goodale streets. The activities of the Anti-Saloon League, founded in 1893 in Oberlin, Ohio, but headquartered in Columbus until it moved to Westerville in 1909, were not yet an organized annoyance to the enjoyment of spirits and brew. As in other cities, there was in Columbus an expanding population of saloons — one for about every 400 men, women and children.

A number of dedicated do-gooders were also busy cleaning up the notorious vice district centered around Seventh Street. The area first rose to prominence, with Madam

91

CURE-ALLS
The Peruna Empire

The turn of the century was a great era for the buying and selling of hope in various liquid forms. In Columbus, it usually came in bottles. In *Tales of Old Columbus*, Carlos B. Shedd affectionately recalled the patent medicine men ("certainly . . . characters") who sold their wares on city street corners. "What a thrill we kids would get out of watching them. They would arrive in town usually in a four-wheeled buggy, driven by two fine horses and locate most of the time on Broad and High, or on our market street corners, where it would be easy to draw a crowd. Generally they had a couple of colored comedians with them to start attracting the crowd, which didn't take long. Of course, this medicine would cure almost any disturbances the human body could possibly be victim of and you would be surprised how many victims he would get at a dollar a bottle. I don't suppose it cost them 20 cents to concoct it, so the profits were great. They would have a wonderful line of talk and if you were not sick [they] made you feel you were . . . . We all enjoyed listening to them."

It was in Columbus that the patent medicine gambit was elevated from street corner to national prominence in what reformer Samuel Hopkins Adams called one of "the most conspicuous of all medical frauds." One of the giants in the field was a product called Peruna.

Peruna was made in Columbus by Dr. S.B. (Samuel Brubaker) Hartman. It catapulted into the national consciousness, innards and pocketbooks through the early advertising genius of Frederick W. Schumacher whose promotional methods made it a "household word all over America." Little is known of Schumacher except that he was from Waco, Texas and supposedly "in oil" before he showed up in Columbus.

An "almanac" by Hartman showed a log cabin where he allegedly first developed and began making Peruna sometime during the early 1890s and progressed to a tremendous plant covering two solid blocks of Columbus with a "towered and crenelated Hartman Sanitarium beyond it."

Hartman contended that all the troubles of the human race coul be traced to *catarrh*, a malady which afflicted every portion inside or outside the human body, from the head to the lungs to the stomach, through the liver, kidneys and bladder, down to the pelvic region and — in case anything was missed on the way down or up — there was the all-encompassing "systemic" catarrh. Naturally, Peruna cured all catarrhs. (Peruna happened to be at least 25 percent alcohol, with a few herbs thrown in to disguise the taste of cheap whiskey. A few nips were guaranteed to while away the golden hours in the hazy battle with catarrh.)

Schumacher originated the advertising testimonials. In the days when Peruna was just one of hundreds of cure-alls, letters began to appear in newspapers, magazines and periodicals signed by Mr. and Mrs. S. W. of Coshocton, Ohio or Mrs. I. M. Johns of Pittsfield, Massachusetts, testifying to the rosy glow of health produced by Peruna.

The letters were originally the products of F. W. Schumacher's fertile imagination. Eventually, he garnered testimonials from real — even famous — people, from governors and congressmen to national heroes. Peruna began to outsell the previous national bottled favorite, Lydia Pinkham's Compound. For 25 years, Peruna used more newspaper advertising space than any other patent medicine in the United States.

Business flourished at both the Peruna Laboratories and the Hartman Sanitarium (which also offered, advertisements noted, "all the great Water Cure Facilities of Karlsbad, Nauheim, Kissinger, and Vichy," along with the "treatment of heart disease, rheumatism, anemia, rickets, erysipelas, nervous prostration and paralysis" for anyone who might have escaped catarrh.

Hartman built a palatial home, farms and the Hartman Theater — home of legitimate theater in Columbus for many decades.

Schumacher, who married Hartman's daughter, built a veritable castle, replete with Gothic towers, finials and false faces. Inside, he hung works of art (gathered during his European travels) by some of the finest artists the world has produced.

Trouble first appeared in September 1905, when Edward Bok, editor of *Ladies' Home Journal* (which had long refused to accept advertising for patent medicines) ran an exposé of Peruna. The magazine had an experiment conducted by a doctor to test the alcoholic content of various patent medicines. Four metal containers, holding three big-selling patent medicines and one of beer, were attached by rubber tubes to a gas burner and mantle. Heat was applied to the solutions. Peruna's vapor "gave a bright illumination" that came in second only to something called Hostetter's Celebrated Stomach Bitters. Beer came in fourth out of four.

In *Collier's Weekly*, Samuel Hopkins Adams added in 1906 that "the Internal Revenue authorities bade old Doc Hartman either to put some real medicine into his drink or open a bar." (It was already barred on Indian reservations.)

From then on, Peruna bottles were openly labeled "25 percent of alcohol by volume." But to maintain the medical illusion of respectability, some different herbs were added and a slight laxative. Sales continued at a high volume until at least 1927, long after most patent medicines of its time had gone by.

THE 1890s: Mobs were immobilized during the streetcar strike of 1890 (above left); Olentangy Park (above right); troops trained for the Spanish American War mobilization at Camp Bushnell (lower left) and marched in the city streets (lower right) in 1898.

Metcalfe, during the Civil War. It flourished long after the soldiers left, until ministers and civic-minded women saw to it "the houses" were evacuated.

A real recreational landmark occurred on May 3, 1890 — a Sunday. Ohio State University played its first football game against Ohio Wesleyan University. Ohio State won. At the time, professional baseball still ranked as Columbus' favorite sport. The city had supported a number of professional teams since the mid-nineteenth century.

In 1896, the Southern Theater was completed. "Diamond Lil" was among the many well-known celebrities who stopped to perform briefly along with the regular denizens.

Buildings of all sorts were beginning to spiral skywards — the Chittenden Hotel at the northwest corner of Spring and High streets had several levels of residential rooms, and the Wyandotte Building on West Broad Street, opened in 1897, was the first steel-framed skyscraper built in Columbus. (It is one of the few downtown buildings preserved from that era and has been given National Register status.)

The American Federation of Labor (later AFL-CIO) was founded in Columbus on December 9, 1886; and the United Mine Workers Union originated here January 25, 1890.

The central reason both groups organized here seems to have been location rather than motivation.

Both the AFL and UMW were a convergence of several similar labor groups from across the country with common goals. In the case of the AFL, Columbus did have a particularly strong unit of a national group called the Knights of Labor, which originated in 1871 in Philadelphia. Nationally, it was an industrial union, open to all gainfully employed persons, regardless of sex, race or color, although "¾ of each assembly were required to be wage earners." In the West, farmers dominated; in the East, trade unionists. In the Columbus assembly, which met in the old International Order of Odd Fellows (IOOF) Building, most members were trade unionists of German origin. The Knights supported demands for an eight-hour day, boycotts and arbitration (rather than strikes) and various political reforms, including adoption of a graduated income tax and consumer and producers cooperatives, more than 100 of which were formed nationally.

O. HENRY
Surprise beginnings and endings

William Sidney Porter, also known as O. Henry.

It has been nearly a century and a half since the "old" Ohio Penitentiary was built on Spring Street 1834. Although the state's new maximum security facility is located in Lucasville, in southern Ohio, the Gothic stone-walled prison in Columbus is still in use. Behind those closed doors, from the bullpen back through the halls where tiers of metal cages are stacked like rabbit hutches, are stories more fascinating than fiction.

During the Gilded Age (from the late 1870s to just after the turn of the century), newspapers chronicled the feats and fortunes of "robber barons" who knew how to steal legally. But two inmates at the Ohio Penitentiary were also getting ahead in different ways.

On April 25, 1898, William Sidney Porter, an unknown 33-year-old alcoholic bookkeeper, went inside the federal penitentiary to serve five years for embezzlement at a Texas bank.

Born in Greensboro, North Carolina, in 1862, Porter lived his childhood with a maiden aunt who ran a private school. He studied with her five years. At the age of 15, he began work in his uncle's drugstore where he became a registered pharmacist. Bored, he ran away and landed in Texas. Porter worked at a variety of jobs while trying to write (with little success) for newspapers and humor magazines. Then, while working in an Austin bank, he embezzled an unknown amount of funds.

Once inside the Ohio penitentiary, Inmate #30664 worked in the prison hospital. During the lonely night hours, he proceeded to write numerous short stories.

Penitentiary histories say they were smuggled outside mysteriously (i.e., probably through a friendly or greedy guard). They were published nationally, always under the pseudonym O. Henry. Unlike his previous efforts as William Sidney Porter, O. Henry's stories were greeted with great popular acclaim. The Christmas classic, "The Gift of the Magi," was just one of many popular stories O. Henry wrote while doing time.

Critically, he is credited with a facile invention, an exhaustless fund of comic situations and a vivid sense of portraiture, but he has also been faulted for sacrificing realism in order to achieve the "double twist" surprise endings of his stories.

On July 21, 1901, W. S. Porter was discharged from the penitentiary. He emerged, according to *Heritage of American Literature,* "a craftsman in the art of short fiction," and went to New York to practice his craft. Whether he took with him all the stories he had written during his three years inside is unknown. To this day, rumors persist that some of his stories are hidden in a rooming house somewhere in Columbus.

At any rate, he went on to publish successful stories in New York, usually on a weekly basis for the *New York World.* But he was always in debt to his editors for advances on unwritten stories. Porter had returned to the bottle. On June 5, 1910, less than nine years after his release, he was found dead on Skid Row with 23 cents in his pockets.

His heritage to the literary world was "so powerful a force . . . as to have influenced the course [of the short story], almost without the aid of other workers. In only eleven years of actual creative activity, he rose to a height of popularity that was rivaled only by the . . . vogue of Mark Twain."

From 1885 to 1896, those sentenced to die in Ohio — 28 in all — were hanged. The proceedings, which required from five to 28 minutes to bring about death, took place in earlier years in public view. Crowds sometimes threw vegetables at the victims.

In 1896, according to Richard Barrett in the *Columbus Dispatch Sunday* Magazine, an electric chair was installed in the Ohio Penitentiary to "provide a more humane form of execution . . . in a few seconds." The electric chair was supposedly installed by an inmate with a special knowledge of electricity, one Charles Justice, also known as Charles Jackson. Justice was paroled in 1908, but in 1910, he returned under sentence of first degree murder. He was executed in his own chair October 27, 1911. It was a double twist ending O. Henry would have appreciated.

The chair is now installed in the Lucasville facility, and it has been used 315 times since 1897. It has been strictly "on charge" since 1963.

OHIO PEN: The Ohio Penitentiary's annex (top), cell blocks (left) and electric chair (above).

AUTO AGE: Columbusite Perry Okey (left) figured if Henry Ford could build one, he could too. So, Okey tinkered about in his garage for about five years and built himself a car; it rolled off his "assembly line" in 1910. Columbus claims America's first structure built specifically for nothing other than pumping gasoline – the Standard Oil of Ohio station (right) opened about 1910.

The Camel Engine, B&O No. 181 on May 29, 1887.

When representatives from the Knights of Labor and 25 other labor groups, representing about 150,000 members, met in Columbus December 8, 1886, the Federations of Trades and Labor Assemblies absorbed many of the Knights by accepting members and locals into a larger body being organized as the AFL. Greatest gains were made in coal mining, railroad and construction industries. Samuel Gompers, one of the founders of the union, was elected president. But when Gompers tried to speak on the steps outside the meeting hall, the alleged agitator was not so gently led away by policemen. "It was a very reform-minded era," recalled *Dispatch* publisher Preston Wolfe. "Sometimes things got very tough."

Tensions between management and workers emerged during a street railway strike the summer of 1890. However, the climate calmed when workers had their wages increased, and their hours decreased from sixteen to twelve hours.

After the beginning of 1893, things got extremely tough in Columbus and across the United States. The country entered the worst depression it had ever encountered. Not until the Great Depression of the 1930s would times be as hard and prospects as grim for the great majority of American people. That depression had many causes. There were droughts and terrible winters in the late 1880s in the grain belt. Monetary policies of both Republic and Democratic administrations were deliberately restrictive. But the primary cause was the cyclical nature of economic growth. The American economy had boomed after the Civil War at a rate unprecedented before (or since) in world history. There had been several severe but manageable depressions after the Civil War, but the time had come for a major retrenchment. The economy plunged into a deep trough which took nearly four years to correct.

On the whole, Columbus weathered the period reasonably well. Like the rest of the country, the city suffered massive layoffs which resulted in dire poverty for many. But the diversified economy of government, commerce and industry rode out the depression far better than great industrial cities. And even with the grimness of the times, people still found ways to relax.

In 1899, Olentangy Park was built just west of High Street and north of Kelso Avenue. Amusement parks were one of the newer ventures of the times. Built for the public's enjoyment, they were also a shrewd investment on the part of streetcar companies which financed a large share of the construction cost. By offering the public special inducements to travel in their off-hours (weekends and evenings), the streetcar companies increased patronage and, thus, profits. In their 40-year heyday before the automobile and motion pictures, the amusement parks were one of the joys of life.

Highly innovative for its day, Olentangy Park featured numerous thrill-and-chill rides, such as the roller coaster, along with the best of the touring stock companies, which occasionally trotted out *Uncle Tom's Cabin*. A Columbus woman, Mary Howard (later wife of Kinnis Fritter, who built Greystone Court Apartments, and sister-in-law to Lincoln Fritter, builder of the Lincoln-LeVeque Tower) played *Little Eva* from the 1880s until both she and the play were "simply too old for it." She turned in her long golden curls, sent to Paris for marcelling irons and set to work as a hairdresser about 1895. "I was very good," she claimed proudly in a *Citizen-Journal* interview, "so good that the only Columbus women who could afford my services were the very wealthy and the ladies from the sporting houses."

Her most important client during that era was Mrs. William McKinley, wife of the Ohio governor who later became United States president. Twice a week, Mary Howard Fritter visited their suite in the Neil House. She recalled Mrs. McKinley as a "kindly woman" with "a devoted husband."

A later client was Alice Roosevelt Longworth who visited Columbus with her congressman husband, Ohioan Nicholas Longworth. "Everyone thought Alice was eccentric and naughty because she smoked cigarets, which was terrible in that day and age," Mary Fritter noted, "but don't you believe all that, she was a *lovely* girl." A lifelong Republican, Mary Fritter visited her friend Alice at the White House and met Teddy Roosevelt. He was "a wonderful man, but I never liked that *other* one, you know his cousin Franklin. And they wouldn't have anything to do with him, either."

A brief military interlude was provided by the mercifully short Spanish-American War of 1898. The war — over in 90 days — provided the first real trial at arms for the American Army since the Civil War, other than the Indian wars. It provided a testing ground for a generation of young Americans who had only heard of, but never seen, combat. Many Columbus volunteers never saw action but suffered the privation and disease of the campaign. Camp Bushnell was established east of Columbus as a temporary mobilization center. (It would later become the suburb of Bexley.)

As the century turned, Columbus and the nation experienced another transportation revolution. The railroads had expanded in the late nineteenth century until they were the most reliable method of transportation known. America's rail system had few peers in the world. It could rapidly and efficiently move large numbers of people and great quantities of goods. The problem was that they moved only in a very limited number of places. Streetcars and omnibus service were available within the cities. But for people in small towns, transportation was limited to foot, train or horse. What was desperately needed in a society linked more closely than ever by telephone and rapid train travel was a means to link the smaller midwestern cities and the major rail networks. Some people felt that the horseless carriage or automobile might be the answer. But the latter vehicles were still fragile and expensive, and there were few good roads. For the average citizen, the answer to the dream was something else — the interurban.

The interurban was a high-speed passenger train with only a few cars that could whisk people from town to town on a regular schedule. Theoretically, because of its high speed and frequent use, it could afford to stop at many small towns avoided by main line railroads and still keep fares low. It was a grand idea, given every opportunity to succeed. Unfortunately its economic theory did not work. After enormous investments of capital, interurban owners discovered that the system was simply not used sufficiently or efficiently enough to keep the fares low. And without low fares, the interurban could not draw large numbers of working and lower class people necessary to its success.

For 20 years after the turn of the century, the interurbans made a valiant effort to succeed — and did in some parts of the state. They borrowed techniques pioneered by the urban streetcar companies — group fares, Sunday fares and the subsidization of amusement

THE FAIR: A highlight of the year, the Ohio State Fair brought in the money (above) — $30,000 in sight — and offered excitement on the Ferris Wheel (right). Buildings on the fairgrounds included the Administration Building (facing page, bottom), along with the Women's Building and a Press Club (facing page, top).

A CENTURY IN PROGRESS: Ground-breaking ceremonies (facing page, top) for the American Insurance Union Citadel, completed in 1927 and later known as the Leveque-Lincoln Tower; the Toledo & Ohio Central railroad depot (facing page, bottom) and the library's reading room, both circa 1900.

parks, such as Buckeye Lake near Newark. But like the amusement parks, the interurban was doomed by the ever increasing acceptance of the automobile.

Still their significance should not be overlooked. They contributed to the beginning of the end for the isolated smalltown dominance of Ohio life. The interurban also permitted small towns such as Westerville, Hilliard, Grove City and Canal Wichester to be easily linked to the big cities like Columbus. These small towns (which had been languishing) now became more a part of the city proper as they were linked by the "traction line".

Fords — and other early autos — were already America's future. In 1901, sixteen horseless carriage owners banded together to form the Columbus Automobile Club. And in 1903, daredevil Barney Oldfield broke the world automobile speed record before a crowd of 10,000 at the Columbus Driving Park. Oldfield hit 60 miles per hour.

In that same year, Columbus acquired another college; Franklin University was founded in 1903. Originally an educational branch of the YMCA, Franklin soon achieved a deserved reputation as an excellent business and professional school.

Even with the depressions of the 1870s and 1890s, the Columbus economy — and prospects for its future — continued to grow by leaps and bounds. Much of this was due to the railroads, nearly 20 years after the Civil War, when the city realized their full potential. Railways eased movement of goods and produce between established farming areas and Eastern cities and opened up whole new areas of the state.

For years, the southeastern quarter of the state was known to be extremely rich in natural resources — timber, iron ore, natural gas and coal. But there was no

inexpensive way to tap them. In the 1880s, Columbus banking and financial interests began to invest in coal mines, timber development and iron ore extraction at a phenomenal rate. By controlling many of the railroads, mines and other major extractive companies in the region, Columbus was in a power position.

In 1870, the Hocking Valley Railroad reached Athens in the heart of southeastern Ohio. By 1877, what came to be the Scioto Valley New England Railroad reached Chillecothe and Portsmouth. The Toledo and Ohio Central was completed between Columbus and Lake Erie. These roads — largely financed and controlled by Columbus interests — were critical in forming the industrial Columbus.

Buggy companies found Columbus ideal because the site allowed easy access to the timber of the Hocking Valley on one hand and easy access to major rail lines for shipping finished goods on the other. The Columbus Buggy Company employed 1,100 men, produced a buggy every eight minutes and sold more than $2 million in goods in 1890 alone.

Iron and steel industries became important since iron ore and coal were close by. The glass industry moved in when natural gas was discovered in the 1880s and thus provided large quantities of fuel. The shoe industry — particularly H.C. Godman Company — was attracted because of the central location and good transportation.

The soft coal mining industry grew as the southeastern Ohio coal fields were linked by rail with the Great Lakes shipping basin.

Within three decades, more than fifteen rail lines entered the city, and more freight tonnage was moved in Columbus than any other city of its size.

Between 1880 and 1910, area population increased more than 300 percent. Numerous people were employed in the Hoster and Gambrinus breweries. While brothers Edgar and Charles Wolfe owned the C.&E. Shoe Store on Fulton Street, Robert F. Wolfe purchased the *Columbus Dispatch* from William Brickell, launching a new era in journalism in Columbus.

More than 50 magazines and papers from across the country were available in the city — and all could be read (free) at the Carnegie Public Library opened on Grant Avenue.

Over 140 daily trains moved through Union Station and the Toledo, Ohio Central railroad depots. Residents and visitors could tour 160 acres of city parks or take advantage of such spectator sports as OSU football or Columbus professional baseball games. And if they wished to participate in a sport, there was golf, polo, trap shooting and bowling.

Enrico Caruso thrilled crowds at the new Memorial Hall on Broad Street (now Center of Science and Industry) in 1908. That same year, William Jennings Bryan, "The Great Commoner" — whose ideals were fading nationally — spoke there to a packed house. Socially, technologically, economically and, in some ideologies, the city and its inhabitants had come a long way in 30 years — but it was still "Good Old Columbus Town."

CHAPTER SEVEN

OVER HERE, OVER THERE

1910-1920

The Southern Theater, built in 1895, home to touring repertory companies at
the turn of the century.

IN PRINT: Home of "Ohio's greatest home daily," The Dispatch, circa 1925 (above). Former paperboys (below) for The Ohio Sun get together once a year to sell a special edition for charity; the men's group, the "Charity Newsies," was founded shortly after the turn of the century. Theater broadside, 1891, from Odeon Hall heralds the Ethiopian Serenaders and Harlequin, also known as the Black Ghost.

All was quiet on the midwestern front in 1910 — well, almost all. Although Columbus had 181,511 of Franklin County's 222,567 residents, there was still a small-town ambience.

More men were buying horseless carriages, and the Columbus Buggy Company manufactured an electric car. Women shopping at Lazarus were buying, for dress occasions, Princess silhouette suits — $25 — with long puffed-sleeve coats cut away below the buttons as is a man's tuxedo. Hats were almost as wide as parasols, but their shade value was outweighed by moulting plumage, fruit and other paraphernalia perched atop them. The "shirtwaist" dress, dating back to the Gibson Girl look, was already becoming a virtual uniform for the first women to work in offices and stores.

A popular refreshment in warm weather months for parents and children alike was the ice cream soda. Lazarus also installed a tea room where ladies might meet in the afternoons, starting a tradition which is still perpetuated — although males have crashed the bastions in the past few years.

Concert bands played the equivalent of Boston Pops programs at the Chamber of Commerce auditorium and at Olentangy Park, while people with a taste for vaudeville went to B. F. Keith's theater on the northeast corner of Gay and Pearl. Numerous nickelodeons — particularly Max Stearn's The Exhibit, at 155 North High — were popular with early fans of the flicking pictures. Columbus theater historian Phil Sheridan describes Stearn's as seating 200, with a marble lobby and a numbered shelf where male patrons parked their expensive cigars until after the show.

Aside from Memorial Hall, the city contained eight downtown theaters by 1911, including the Great Southern, the Hartman, the Grand, the Colonial (where the Palace is now), Keith's Exhibit and the High Street Theater between Spring and Chestnut streets. However, by 1910, admission for even the nickelodeons had risen to a dime. Audiences gladly continued to pay the price.

And by 1910, Columbus was feeling growing pains again. As industry and its needs grew, more people were moving to the city from country towns. The downtown

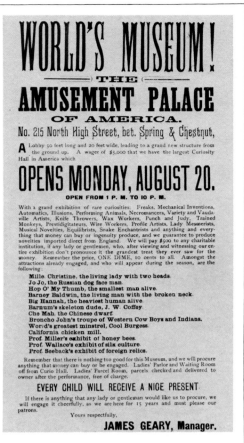

The World's Museum, which opened in 1888, advertised "a grand exhibition of rare curiosities" for the admission of – "10 cents to all."

business district expanded, and industry moved toward the northern and southern edges of the town. The streetcar allowed the working class and poorer districts to also make the move. The Goodale Park district which had once been the realm of only the rich began the slow conversion to a middle-and working class district. Similarly, the fashionable residences along town — Main, Rich and State street were abandoned by the rich and occupied by the middle class. The entire southern end of the city below Main Street was still the German district. The black community which had been clustered predominantly on the near north side near the corner of Long and High streets began to shift east.

The real growth was in the new working and middle class suburbs. Older established upper-middle class areas, such as the University district, the south end of the German village area and the east side beyond Parsons Avenue to Franklin Park began to emerge as middle-class suburbs. The west side was being developed, particularly out toward the centralized Hilltop institutions and away from the flood plain.

What emerged was the segregation of the population into areas more clearly defined by economic class, race and ethnicity. Naghten Street was still "Irish Broadway", but many of its original residents had already moved north of the tracks and beyond. The south end was still a German stronghold, but even the Germans were beginning to move out into the greater city. The clearly identifiable laboring class neighborhoods included the Steelton district (on the far south side), the Milo-Grogan district near Cleveland Avenue (north of the rail yards), the Flytown ghetto (near Goodale Park) and the so-called Middletown district (the old Franklinton area across the Scioto from downtown) and further out, the Sellsville area (across the Olentangy from the Ohio State University) which then served as winter quarters of the Sells Bros. Circus.

Even the rich were moving out. While many of the wealthy maintained both city and country homes, others simply moved beyond the city limits and/or the streetcar lines to newer areas. These included Clintonville (north of the city). It was a small crossroads village near East North Broadway and High Street that formed an

FRANKLIN COUNTY SUFFRAGISTS

Suffragists parade, July 30, 1914.

Clara Geer Reynolds was a Franklin County Republican Committeewoman for many years, the very essence of establishment, respectability and decorum on the surface. Not everyone who knew her in recent decades was aware that she was one of the fieriest of the city women who fought for women's right to vote.

"When I was a girl, I remember my mother getting my father his good shirt and a razor strop out, to get ready to go vote" she said in an unpublished interview, conducted not long before her death in the latter 1970s. "I said, 'Mother, why don't *you* go to vote?' She just said, 'Hush, I'm busy,' then whispered, 'Women don't vote. . . .' So I said, "When I'm big, I'll change the law. I couldn't have been over four or five then. It was the contest between McKinley and Bryan for president, I walked with my father to the polling place. 'What do you do to vote?' I remember asking him. And he said, 'Put marks on a paper.'

"Men were passing by on horses, tipping their hats at each other, and saying to my father, 'Howdy do, Mr. Geer,' and I was thinking that I could put marks on a paper. When we got to the gate, he said, 'You can't go in now, Clara.' And I asked him, 'Why not?' And he said, too, 'Women and girls don't.' "

Clara rebelled against "feminine restrictions" from that election day. She played ball, climbed trees and indulged in horseback riding ("I could ride with the best of 'em"). She heard a lot about suffragette Elizabeth Cady Stanton in her home because Stanton's family had intermarried with her father's family generations before.

"In those days, women . . . even suffragists, were very timid. Even those who rang doorbells asking other women if they wanted to vote were timid. I said, 'I'm all for it!' and started passing out literature and marched."

She married in 1914, but "I told him I would not have children, I would not go through what my mother and other women went through, and anyway, when I could get a Phi Beta Key, why should I do so just to later have children whimpering and [have to change] diapers? I knew that wasn't for me, and my husband knew what he was getting when he married me. He knew I expected equal rights."

In 1917, municipal suffrage was granted to Columbus women. National suffrage came through in 1920. Clara Geer Reynolds went to the graveside of Elizabeth Cady Stanton and "just stood there for awhile."

Lucille Atcherson (Mrs. George) Curtis, was born in Columbus, educated at the Columbus School for Girls and graduated from Smith College in 1913 at the age of 18. When she returned home she realized she didn't want to be a secretary or a school teacher, "and those were about the only jobs open to women back then."

She became a part of the women's movement. "It was better than sitting in the front porch swing," she told *Columbus Monthly* in 1978. She was one of the first Columbus recruits to the National Woman's Party (NWP). The others were Mrs. Julius Stone, Dr. Alice M. Johnston, Harriet Bradbury and Mary Senter (daughter of the female doctor who was not allowed to practice in Columbus in the 1850s). Lucille Atcherson also served as executive secretary of the Franklin County Woman's Suffrage Association. She issued a special invitation to the black women of the community who were reluctant to push suffrage. As a result of her efforts, the Sojourner Truth Woman's Suffrage Association "federated with the Franklin County Woman's Suffrage Association." With Nannie B. Goode as president, the black suffragists distributed thousands of leaflets of various kinds, including one making a special appeal "to the colored men to vote 'Yes' for the proposal to strike [the words] "white" and "male" from the constitution of the state of Ohio." The group changed their name to the National Woman's Party in 1916 and kept up their campaigns until victory in 1920.

Lucille Atcherson went on to become, (over stiff male opposition in Congress) the first woman in the United States to receive an appointment in the diplomatic service. In 1921, when "women's clubs deluged Washington with appeals to appoint a woman to this service, [they emphasized] that Lucille Atcherson was well fitted by education and character for such a post." In addition to local and national service for the NWP, Lucille Atcherson had gone to France and organized efforts to aid the wounded there during World War I.

She "passed the examination with a high grade, and President Harding appointed her to the Latin-American division." She was then transferred to the Legation in Berne, Switzerland, and in 1927, to the Legation at Panama. She resigned in 1928 to marry Dr. George Morris Curtis, whom she had met abroad. They returned to Columbus in 1932 when the late Dr. Curtis was appointed professor of medical and surgical research at OSU.

Their daughter, Charlotte Curtis, a former reporter and society editor on the *Citizens-Journal*, has been, for some years now, editor of the *New York Times* Op-Ed page, and is considered one of the two or three most influential women in contemporary American journalism.

amalgam of distinct neighborhoods. Out East Broadway was the exclusive residential suburb of Evanston. Farther north near the Stop Eight station (now Morse Road and High Street), the Jeffrey family established a summer estate called Beechwold; several other wealthy families also built there. To the east, the area that is now the city of Bexley was developing as an exclusive suburb near and around Capital University. And north and west of the city, the suburb of Grandview was expanding and being joined by the equally elegant suburb of Marble Cliff. In 1917, King Thompson and his brother Ben embarked on what was probably the most famous single real-estate venture in the city's history — the creation of an entirely planned and very exclusive residential community at the end of the northwest Columbus streetcar lines — Upper Arlington.

Downtown, the electric arches were replaced in 1914 by more traditional fixtures. The three and four-story cast-iron-front brick commercial buildings which had dominated the streets for 50 years vanished rapidly. New five- ten- and fifteen-story steelframe skyscrapers rose in their place. The brick streets were replaced by macadam.

By 1900, the physical shape of the city was more of a truncated cross centered on Broad and High streets. By the early twentieth century, the streetcars had performed their magic. By the end of World War I, Columbus resembled an elongated cross — the basic shape it would retain for a generation.

The economy had rebounded well following a serious depression in 1907. On the east side of town, the Ralston Steel Car Company was operating the equivalent of a "company town," supplying homes to keep its employees close to the 40-acre plant. Several hundred German, Italian, Polish and Hungarian employees and their families, and eight black families, lived in the neighborhood, roughly in a triangle between James Road, Cassady Avenue, East Fourth Avenue and Delmar Drive. Most of Ralston's workers (some of whom stayed with the company throughout World War II) had little cause to leave. A former resident said, "Everything we needed was in the neighborhood." Betty Daft wrote in the *Dispatch Sunday Magazine* that the Ralston company town had handy "grocery stores, barber shops, a theater and other small businesses along East Fifth Avenue," and "even a small emergency clinic on East Fourth Avenue."

Company camaraderie was easier in those days, because of size as much as spirit. In a *Dispatch Sunday Magazine* article of February 10, 1980, "The Glory Days of the Second Regiment Marching Band," 76-year-old Peter France recalled how his father organized a company band for his employer, Ohio Malleable, Inc., about 1900. The elder France played trumpet. When he changed jobs, joining the Columbus waterworks, "the band went with him. It became the Citizens Band." By 1914, the growing band joined the Knights of Pythias, organized into military ranks and became the Second Regiment Marching Band. They became a "Columbus institution, a fixture in every parade" for many years, only encountering trouble at segregated events or places. The existence of that black company band, as well as the

Streetcar strike of 1910.

few black families in Ralston's company town, indicated that at least some of Columbus' "colored" workers were moving out of the strictly waiter/domestic ranks into private industry.

Not all labor relations were as harmonious as the Second Regiment Marching Band's tunes. On July 3, 1910, troops were called in to stop violence after a three-month-long streetcar strike. For the most part, craft unions dominated the small labor movement for many years. But as the nineteenth century ended and Columbus increased its industrialization, there was severe labor unrest (as there was across America). While the pace and tempo of labor organization and activity increased, most of this activity generally was non-violent — and unsuccessful. With the exception of the rather raucous streetcar strike in 1890 and a modestly violent

brewery worker's strike in 1907, the city had not seen severe labor agitation since the 1877 railroad strike.

But the calm was shattered in 1910 by what would be the longest, most bitter, violent and bloody strike in Columbus' history. It was the longest period of sustained civil disorder in the city's history.

The reasons for the strike were not particularly unique. Most of the car lines had been electrified and consolidated under the ownership of the Columbus Railway and Light Company in the mid-1890s. Workers had been agitating regularly against low pay, long hours, wretched working conditions and little job security. They had not had much success. But by 1910, the progressive political spirit of the times and increased activity by labor organizers caused the car workers to organize a fledgling union which — although repudiated by the company —

at least had modest public support.

After several earlier minor confrontations, the union went on strike on July 24. The general public, and even the business community recognized their legitimate complaints and the company's unwillingness to negotiate. As the strike dragged on, the public became impatient with the workers as well as the company. Frustrations pent up for so long exploded. Carmen and strike breakers clashed repeatedly, exchanging barrages of rocks, bricks, rotten eggs and gunfire. Car barns, streetcars and tracks were dynamited. The rioting exhausted the undermanned and overworked police force. The National Guard — equipped with machine guns mounted on automobiles — were twice called and remained on duty for two months. Eventually, the workers gave up as the strike wore on with no conclusion, and the strike failed. But the city felt the impact for a long time. Columbus labor proved they were determined to struggle indefinitely if need be. There was one indication of the extent of public outrage. In the election of 1908, the fledgling and unpopular Socialist Party got only 1,000 votes. In the 1910 election (after the strike), the Socialists received 12,000 of the 40,000 votes cast — not in support of socialism but as a public protest against the strikers, the Company and the civic and community leadership that permitted the strike to go on so long.

Aside from being teachers, the few women in the job market tended to be store clerks or forerunners of today's clerk-secretaries. There were exceptions. The late Millicent Easter — a familiar figure in Columbus before her death a few years ago at 97 — was a pioneer news woman at the turn of the century. Millicent Easter wandered into "the old *Press Post,* a newspaper that used to be where the Hartman is now." In an interview with the *Citizen-Journal* not long before her death, she recalled how one of the short stories she'd been writing came to the attention of that paper's city editor. He took a look at the carrot-topped Easter, waved the story around and offered her a job as reporter at $5 a week, "though I didn't make any bones of the fact that I hadn't gone to college. So when he asked, 'Can you type?' I just said, I think I can by tomorrow morning. I went down to the newspaper building that night. I had a quarter in my pocket, tapped it on the window and got the janitor to let me in. I worked on a blessed Underwood all night

until I got the hang of it. That served me many years." In addition to doing features and interviews, Millicent Easter was dramatic editor. The quality of that work led her to become press agent for Keith's Theater in 1910. She remained there until 1930 and the collapse of vaudeville.

Harry Houdini asked her to write his publicity releases. They became such good friends that "at one time he offered to tell me some of those great secrets . . . but I wouldn't let him. That was too big a secret to keep," she explained. "You see, I was also a friend of Howard Thurston, the great Columbus magician, and I was afraid he might ask me about them."

Tessa Sweazy Webb, a schoolteacher from New Pittsburg, Ohio, came to Columbus in 1911 to seek treatment for her ailing husband, Reuben H. Webb. When it became obvious he would need a long convalescence, Tessa Webb felt it "behooved me to work and carry on. I got a newspaper, looked at ads, saw one that said 'Wanted Girl Friday for Light Office work,' and went to work next day." She enrolled in Columbus Business College and "went to school mornings, worked afternoons and studied nights." She also sent out poems which she had been writing since she was 17. In the next several decades, her poems were printed in countless national magazines. For years, she importuned legislators to establish an official Ohio Poetry Day. It is now observed each October.

The Ohio Constitutional Convention of 1851 had specified in a burst of Jeffersonian spirit that a Constitutional Convention would be mandatorily requested of the people every 20 years. The Convention of 1873-4 had had no substantial effect on Ohio government since it had been dominated by conservatives who favored the constitution as it was and saw no reason to tinker with it. By 1912, the situation had changed. Since the turn of the century, men like Tom Johnson in Cleveland and Samuel Jones in Toledo, and Washington Gladden in Columbus had been advocating major reforms of Ohio government. These men were reformers — and not radical revolutionaries as their enemies claimed. They felt that the conservative response to massive change espoused by socialist and other radical forces was illogical and counterproductive. By 1912, the progressive movement had developed a national following.

In the summer of 1912, 5,000 women marched in Columbus in support of woman suffrage, hoping to sway public opinion to support the constitutional amendment. Undaunted, the suffragists continued their campaign seeking major referenda again in 1914 and 1917. In each case they failed, although modest gains had been made in Columbus by the end of World War I when women were permitted to vote in school elections. Some of the opposition was purely cultural — the attitude of the male population that women had no place in the voting booth. Many women held the same attitude. But the suffrage movement had formed alliances early in the twentieth century with several other reform movements, including the prohibitionists. Ethnic and minority urban dwellers who generally opposed prohibition often viewed suffrage as another means of accomplishing that end. Many traditionalist and conservative voters viewed the movement with distrust because of its alliance with the reformers. But actually, suffrage failed the first time for the same reason it ultimately triumphed—its spirited, uncompromising, unshakable determination to accomplish its objective as soon as possible by every means possible.

THE FLOOD OF 1913

THE RAINS CAME: *Looking south from State Street, the river front (above) before the flood of 1913; the factory district seen looking north from the Broad Street bridge (left) was lost in the flood. Water was everywhere by March 26, 1913 — McKinley Avenue (facing page, top), West Town Street (facing page, bottom left) and at Broad and Levee Streets (facing page, far right) — and the fire department came to the rescue (facing page, center left) many times.*

COLUMBUS O. FLOO
NEAR McKINLEY AV,

BROAD & LEVEE STS-
COL. O. FLOOD-3-26-13

Old Central High School at Broad and Fourth Streets in 1915.

The call for the Convention was also supported by the Ohio State Board of Commerce (who wished an adjustment of Ohio tax law more beneficial to business), the liquor interests (who hoped several amendments would blunt the impact of the growing and powerful prohibition movement exemplified by the Westerville-based Anti-saloon League of America), and the public who voted 10-1 in favor of the convention.

The convention itself was loud, long and bitterly contested. It was dominated by Herbert Bigelow, the radical Cincinnati Congregationalist minister and by the heavy representation of conservative members from both rural and urban areas. The general tone of the final set of proposals submitted for a vote was decidedly liberal by the standards of the day. In addition to the abolition of convict labor (passed) and woman suffrage (vetoed), there were other measures initiated — recall and referendum, municipal home rule for cities and major reforms in the electoral and regulatory process (all passed). In all, 42 amendments were proposed, and 34 passed. Among those defeated were a call for the abolition of capital punishment, elimination of the word white from the Ohio Constitution, the adoption of voting machines and a constitutional mandate to maintain the state road system. In all the forces of progressivism had every reason to be happy and optimistic.

The most important amendment was probably the passing of municipal home rule. Columbus was the second city in the state (Cleveland was first) to adopt home rule and it changed the city in many important ways. Until 1912, the cities were literally creatures of the Ohio General Assembly. The legislature could (and often did) adopt special legislation which influenced only one city or a small group of cities. It could set the political boundaries and insure the control of the dominant party in the legislature. With this sort of power, the door had been open for a century to the worst excesses of political bossism, official corruption (especially in public service and police departments), urban deterioration and social decay.

Municipal home rule permitted the city to determine its own destiny in local matters. In 1913, Columbus voters approved the formation of a Charter Commission to write a home rule charter. Heavily influenced by persons like the Reverend Washington Gladden, and his parishioner, George Knight, Ohio State University professor of history, the commission pondered many alternatives and finally adopted a modified federal plan which imposed power in a strong mayor and an almost equally strong council. The new charter implemented civil service, provided for the initiative, referendum and recall of legislation by the public, lengthened terms of office from two to four years, removed party names from the ballot and eliminated ward lines. This last provision meant that the seven members of the new city council would be elected city-wide as would other elected officials. This innovation was supposed to eliminate political corruption and ensure that every council person would be responsible to every voter. But it also eliminated entire classes of persons from the opportunity to hold office. Many of the poorer ethnic and minority neighborhoods had had representation on the old council simply because candidates could afford to run in a small area like a ward. Now without independent means or the support of a political party, a candidate from one of these segments of the population simply could not get elected. (From the passage of the charter until the 1960s, no black person served on the city council. Still it did break the back of the old ethnic and minority political machines and permitted new talent to enter public service.

"The Ohio Constitution Convention in 1912 was the most famous ever held in the city," said Preston Wolfe. "The Workmen's Compensation Act, [which] passed at the convention, was the first in the country and served as a model" for similar acts in many states.

Ohio also became one of the first states to get rid of convict labor. Previously, convicts had been "hired out" to local businesses. The practice remained common in other states for many years.

On March 25, 1913, Columbus was hit with the most disastrous flood in its history. Three to 22 feet of water covered land from the Scioto River to the hilltop. Four bridges were torn out, and nearly $6 million in property was destroyed. Many parts of the city that had never flooded were hit by high water. The old Middletown or bottoms area — gateway community for the poor — was hardest hit by the flood. (The river had been rising for several days before the flood, however, and many persons were able to move away from low ground.) The west side was completely isolated without power, water or easy escape. Even with private boats assisting in the rescue effort and the help of numerous volunteers, the city was virtually incapacitated for weeks. Fifteen years later civic leaders worked to dredge out and widen the river channel, built new bridges, acquired land and constructed the new Central High School, City Hall, the Safety Building and the State Office Building. But those efforts, too, were diverted by America's entry into World War I in 1917.

The single group most affected by the entry of the United States into World War I was the German community of South Columbus. Although German citizens had endured some criticism since the war began in 1914, most of the community tended to treat the war as distant until April 1917 when America joined the fray. Then a wave of hysteria overtook citizens. The Germans were exhorted to be 100-percent American throughout the war. There was little reaction because the native German population was now only two percent of the population. The Germans no longer possessed the political and social force they had held for three generations.

Columbus industry and labor cooperated under state and federal regulations to meet war production quotas. The Red Cross and other volunteer organizations were

"CAPTAIN EDDIE" RICKENBACKER

World War I flying ace Eddie Rickenbacker was the sort of larger-than-life character about which movies are made. (One was made in the 1940s, but it was a syrupy imitation of the gutsy, crusty character.)

Born in Columbus in 1889, he was from a Swiss-German family named Riechenbecher. (The name did not become Rickenbacker until the war, when he "took the Hun out of the name" by changing "Reich" to Rick.)

About the turn of the century, his family — used to "hard times" — lived in a house at 1334 Livingston Avenue. It is still standing.

In a 1970 interview with the *Columbus Citizen-Journal* conducted when he was 81, Rickenbacker recalled that his father died when he was 16 and "some fellow came out to sell my mother a tombstone. I was intrigued. Next morning, I went to the monument place and got a job." Rickenbacker carved the headstone for his father's grave (which is in Greenlawn Cemetery) himself. He made sure it was Vermont marble.

Rickenbacker was so fascinated by cars that he got a job sweeping out an early car factory, Frayer and Miller Corporation at Fourth and Chestnut. Rickenbacker soon began practicing driving at the Columbus Driving Park. By 1915, he was considered America's foremost race car driver and had won an estimated $80,000 in prizes. "Actually," he admitted, "I earned more than that, but I never told the truth about it because I was afraid promoters would cut the prizes."

That devil-may-care attitude was invaluable to those first American pilots trying out a new craft against Germany's crack 'Flying Circus' during World War I.

Young Reichenbecher/Rickenbacker joined the Signal Corps, intending to learn to fly and went about preaching "men, money and munitions, while everyone else was preaching peace and all that hokum." That outlook ingratiated him with Billy Mitchell, chief of the Army Air Services, who saw that Rickenbacker was given a chance to learn to fly. In three weeks, he was off for the front. Rickenbacker downed 26 German planes in just four months. Those air contests, he explained, were a direct "competition between a machine and a man, and you and your machine . . . and they weren't too strong in those days. Either you killed or got killed. No ifs, ands or buts."

At the end of the war, "Captain Eddie" Rickenbacker — winner of the Croix de Guerre, Legion of Honor, Distinguished Service Cross and Medal of Honor — came home not only as Columbus' favorite son but also as America's hero. He was greeted in his hometown with an incredible parade in 1919.

Later he participated in World War II as a special consultant to the secretary of war. He was once lost at sea, adrift in a rubber raft, for many weeks. Rickenbacker estimated, he cheated the Grim Reaper "at least seven times in my lifetime. I felt my toes inside the pearly gates so far it pinched . . . but I always fought my way out."

Columbus reacts to the First World War.

extremely popular, and everyone responded well to food, tin, glass and other drives.

Johnny went marching away from Columbus to join America in keeping the world safe for democracy. Often those young men did not come home, and more military white grave markers in Greenlawn Cemetery joined the ranks of the dead from other wars.

Domestically, people seemed most affected by fuel-less Mondays and the closing of stores. But sacrifices had to be made. The fuel was needed in Europe, where Columbus' Eddie Rickenbacker was busy becoming America's foremost Flying Ace.

When the war broke out, Columbus-born Elsie Janis was gracing music halls in New York and London with her "lanky, lovely" presence. A Broadway star since she was 17, Janis was in her mid-20s when she became the first woman entertainer permitted by the government to perform close to the battlefield on the western front. She did nine 45-minute shows a day, "at the very threshhold of danger," singing, dancing and giving comic impersonations.

There was still entertainment at home as well. In New York City, Circleville-born but Columbus-adopted Ted Lewis, who'd been wowing them since "before the Palace was even built, added a prop — a battered old top hat he won on a dice roll from a hansom cab driver in 1917 — to his saxophone and clarinet act. "A gent named W. C. Fields taught me a lot of tricks to do with that hat," he told the Citizen-Journal in 1970. From then on, Lewis never sang "Me and My Shadow" without tilting and twirling the battered top hat.

Lewis may be remembered best for his slogan, "Is everybody happy?" "I was cutting up with a five-piece jazz band in New York during World War I," Lewis recalled. "After we'd done a number, I just turned to the audience and asked . . . kind of spontaneously, 'Is everybody happy?' and they applauded wildly. So I kept it up."

Certainly Columbus people were happy when hometown soldiers came marching home. During the Armistice parade in 1918, Lazarus clerks got so excited they ran out into the streets to dance leaving the cash registers unlocked.

It was a time for goodwill. Columbus chalked up another first that year by becoming the first city in the United States to organize community fund-raising under one umbrella. It was called the Community War Chest and was the predecessor of today's United Way. The civic leaders who originated the project included Robert Jeffrey, Robert F. Wolfe and Simon Lazarus.

But even though Johnny had come marching home, having made the world safe for democracy, everything was different somehow.

Young people were restless. A February 15, 1919, City Bulletin (official publication of the city) published a vice commission report which indicated prostitution and venereal diseases in the general populace were on the increase at an alarming pace. (In fact, if the report were to be taken at face value, it is conceivable that half the city had some form of social disease. It certainly was not that bad but it was increasing.)

The Prohibition Amendment drove restless young people to the speak-easies. When women obtained the vote in 1920, their elders swore everything had finally gone to hell — obviously, all democracy meant to this Jazz Age generation was the freedom to eat, drink plenty, make lots of money and lots of whoopee — all of which the young people proceeded to do.

Local artist John Barsotti depicted life during the depression.

CHAPTER EIGHT

ALL THAT JAZZ AND THE BIG BUST

1920-1939

Laying of the city hall cornerstone, 1926.

TWO LIFESTYLES: *Life was bleak for some Columbusites, as evidenced by a downtown street scene (above) with "money to loan" shops for everything from diamonds to overcoats. However, Bobby Jones (below) golfed his way to world-wide prominence and a more comfortable way of life.*

The 1920s and 1930s were, as Charles Dickens remarked of the French Revolution, the best of times and the worst of times. But people rarely remember what goes up must come down. For every action, there is an equal and opposite reaction.

The 20 years between 1920 and 1940 saw the city continue to expand. But because of depressed economic conditions at the beginning and end of the period, the growth was slower and more selective. Downtown was massively redeveloped by the construction of the Civic Center. The Army Corps of Engineers worked out flood control measures, and downtown began to assume the appearance of other modern American cities.

The suburbs did not grow as rapidly. Clintonville was annexed to the city in 1928 as was the community of Linden in the northeast quadrant. Bexley emerged as an independent exclusive suburban city in the '20s. The independent communities of Grandview and Upper Arlington continued to grow. The poor and underprivileged increased although their opportunities did not. Flytown was still the worst slum in the city, while the middle-class neighborhoods of German Village and the western part of old Franklinton housed the working class and poor. The black community, more and more centralized in the near northeast quadrant of the city, began to move out Long Street and Mount Vernon Avenue. They established themselves as a strong multi-class and independent community of their own, with their own network of social, religious and cultural self-help organizations.

It was a city of automobile and streetcar suburbs but still tightly linked to public transportation. Except for the upper middle class, the automobile was still a luxury for anything other than business or occasional use.

As America entered the twentieth century, it was clear that the transportation of the future was road and air. Columbus was as impressed as the rest of the country with the Ohio-born Wright Brothers achievement in air travel. In 1910, a bolt of silk was delivered from a Dayton department store to a Columbus store in the first commercial flight in history. More sophisticated aircraft in the 1920s carried passengers and freight. Civic leaders recognized that Columbus' strategic position could be enhanced once again if suitable terminals were available for emerging airlines. Largely through the efforts of Edgar Wolfe and other civic leaders, Port Columbus Airport came into being in 1929 and served as a way station for

Old City Hall.

one of the early efforts in transcontinental air travel. Transcontinental Air Transport used Columbus as one of its terminals for combined air-rail continental service in 1929. With the addition of a Naval Air Station, Columbus early established itself as a center for the nation's air services in the Midwest.

The automobile brought about another transportation revolution. Originally it was a toy of the rich. But when Henry Ford introduced the Model T in 1926, it was suddenly available to the average person.

But fuel for the auto was not widely available in some parts of the country. Ohioans were lucky. Standard Oil Company of Ohio and others had storage tanks and oil fields around the state. (Until the massive oil fields of the West opened up in the '20s, Ohio along with the Midwest was one of the major oil producing regions in the world.) The first gasoline station in America opened in Columbus in 1910.

Roads were a different problem. The main federal highways had been surfaced with macadam as early as 1913. The old National Road (which had become U.S. Route 40) was also paved. But they were expensive to build and maintain. Many rural Americans saw no need for them — and could not have afforded them if they had. The state began a program of major road resurfacing back in 1908, but highway construction in the state lagged until well after World War I. It was well into the '20s before Ohio could boast a state highway system. However, once it got underway it would eventually lead to the integrated system of state highways which mean so much to the city's prosperity. Once again — because of its central location and because so many roads passed through the city — Columbus established itself as a transportation center for highway traffic. From this time forward the great trucking firms of America used the city as a major depot for storage and transfer of goods and services.

The economy was boosted when Columbus was chosen one of the three U.S. sites for a major military supply depot during World War I. The $7-million facility provided jobs and income. Between World War I and World War II, economic development was uneven. There was a depression after World War I, and investors were slow to capitalize on the good times of the '20s.

Although the shoe industry, the mining machine business and a few others expanded during the '20s and '30s, it was not a period of massive growth. Two major

WILD BLUE YONDER: The early days of the airport, known as Port Columbus, brought out Ford tri-motors (right) and dapper folk (left) ready to fly.

companies were built — The Timken Company plant (1,300 workers) and the Ford Motor Company assembly plant. But they did not alter the general trend.

With improved transportation, close proximity to natural products and increased factory size, other towns were becoming centers of particular industries.

Detroit emerged as the automobile capital; Pittsburgh, Gary, Indiana and Cleveland were steel capitals and Akron was the rubber capital. Columbus had no such title — and yet, when the Great Depression came and single-industry towns were decimated, Columbus — with its fingers in so many pies — fared much better.

It is perhaps typical of Columbus that both extremes — the boom of the '20s and the bust of the '30s — were experienced on a more 'moderate' scale than in many other American cities. Still, Columbus could never retreat to the halcyon period prior to World War I, when it was still so very much like Wilder's *Our Town*, despite its size and overgrown cast.

The city had changed, the town commentator had his role taken over by reporters, columnists and editorial writers for *The Columbus Dispatch, The Columbus Citizen, The Ohio State Journal,* and (by 1931), the *Columbus Star,* along with national media reporters and radio commentators and entertainers. And the yeasty, non-stop action of those decades was reflected in the content and style of the stories, from the giddy to the grimy and gory.

Sports and sports heroes; movies and movie stars; crime and its perpetrators (from isolated domestic violence to organized mayhem usually tied to Prohibition); social trends and fashions; and the comings of the old and *nouveau riche* — anything or anyone glamorous, held a particular fascination for the public during the 1920s. In the first years of what was to become today's nationally venerated phenomenon — The Miss America Pageant — Columbus' own Mary Catherine Campbell won the first year's title, then succeeded herself the second year.

In 1922, a peculiar horseshoe-shaped structure was built on the OSU campus and began drawing football crowds which increased in size and fervor, forcing an addition of seats over the years.

By 1932, Red Bird's stadium was built to accommodate Columbus' popular hometown baseball team. But as early as 1923, the local sporting set acquired a warm weather distraction — Beulah Park, still considered one of the country's finest medium-sized horse racing tracks. At its inception, the stands were filled with men wearing double-breasted *Great Gatsby* suits and fedoras, while their flapper ladies wore short fringed skirts and covered their bobbed hair with cloche hats at rakish right angles. *Dispatch* cartoonist Billy Ireland captioned one drawing of the fashion: "This summer the right eye has gone completely out of style." But Ireland did not just tackle mass frivolity in his "Passing Parade." His gentle drawing style frequently lent itself to biting social commentary. In the early '20s, Ireland regularly pilloried the Ku Klux Klan. The Klan had acquired an alarmingly large membership and an amazing amount of political clout nationally, with one million members in Ohio. Nowhere (except in Indiana) was its membership larger than in Ohio. However, Governor ("Honest") Vic Donahey vowed to drive the Klan out of the state. His efforts — along with those of such commentators as Ireland — gradually forced the Klan to keep its public rallies out of Columbus. As its operators were reduced to disreputable secrecy and its affairs scrutinized with regard to moral corruption and venal dishonesty; so, too, did the group's membership dwindle.

That was serious stuff, though, and most people preferred not to think about such matters when they could dance the tango or practice the new knee-slapper, the Charleston. In April 1923, silent screen heartthrob Rudolph Valentino and his wife, Natasha Rambova, danced at Memorial Hall, prompting unsilent sighs from at least the female half of the audience. In 1924, dancers headed for the "new' Valley Dale on Sunbury Road to practice the latest steps. The former stagecoach-stop-turned-dance-hall — the Dale — had been home in various reincarnations to Columbus lovers of ballroom dancing from the waltz era of the early 1900's through the tangos and Charlestons of the '20s. Later, it would jitterbug through the '30s; slow-dance through the Big Band Era of the '40s and rock through the '50s. (During the following two decades, as dance halls declined, so did the Dale. However, a reprieve has been granted. The old ballroom will be renovated and given a new lease on life.)

In the mid-1920s, commerce was flourishing in a seemingly endless climb. The present Neil House was built in 1924, and in the next year the *Columbus Dispatch* moved to its present location at 34 South Third Street. In 1926, a new insurance company, Farm Bureau Mutual Auto Insurance Company (now known as Nationwide Insurance) was founded. "The company didn't own an automobile for at least a year after I came on the job," said retired Senior Vice President Charles Leftwich. "The first company automobile was a 1926 Nash coach, as two-doors were called then. We acquired it through a collision claim. A policyholder had driven it into a ditch, rolling it over a time or two. By today's standards, it would have been junked, but we had it repaired at the Nash Agency in Cincinnati. Our policy holder wouldn't accept delivery and I can't say that I blamed him. So we settled the claim for cash, kept the car and used it for quite a few years. When you started out on a trip in that automobile, you never knew what would happen."

That same year, a grander monument to the insurance industry was erected — the American Insurance Union building, also known as the LeVecque-Lincoln Tower. It is still a landmark on the city's changing physical and business horizon, as more and more insurance firms move their national headquarters to Columbus.

The Ohio premiere of Vitaphone ("talking pictures") took place at J. Real Neth's Grand Theater. Once Jolson sang "Mammy," that was it for the silents. Growing audience interest in the movies — along with a national prosperity which led to a preoccupation with exotic decor — led to the building of two of Columbus' greatest movie emporiums, the Ohio and Palace theaters. (In an era when most major cities have lost all their period baroque film houses, Columbus has managed to retain and renovate both theaters as monuments from a time when fantasy films were showcased in luxurious surroundings.)

An interest in culture via ballet was manifested by Columbus society during the mid-'20s, according to ballet master Jorg Fasting, now 84. In the early '20s, the Norwegian was premiere dancer with the Metropolitan Opera Ballet Company and the Chicago Grand Opera Company. The son of a famous Norwegian writer and the piano student of a "neighbor" named Edvard Grieg, Jorg Fasting — who readily admits to being an "unmitigated snob" — hobnobbed with the likes of George Bernard Shaw, Anna Pavlova, Clarence Darrow and simply "everyone who was anyone" on either side of the Atlantic.

In 1925 Fasting was at the height of his career with the Chicago Grand Opera Company. Mrs. Graham B. Huntington — attended one of his performances. "Absolutely *the* top person [in Columbus] socially," "Fasting recalled in a memoir for *Columbus Monthly* magazine. Afterwards, in a backstage conversation, she informed Fasting that she wanted to "assemble some sort of religious pageant in Columbus." She convinced him to come to her hometown and stage it.

Taking a three-month leave of absence, Fasting staged the event in a building used as a civic auditorium for such cultural occasions (where the Lazarus Annex now

BEFORE AND AFTER: A broadside from a Woman's Vigilant Committee (left) warns of the dangers of "a strictly Temperance Eating-House," where the profits of the establishment are from the sale of liquors "to be drank on the premises." After the repeal of prohibition (right), beer flowed freer in Columbus.

Beware! Beware!!
THERE is DANGER
To the Unwary!
Listen to our Warning!

Two squares from the Columbus Depot, on the corner of Spring and High streets, you will see in bold letters, and in full view as you cross Spring street, coming from the Depot, "HOLLY TREE COFFEE AND LUNCH ROOM." It is well known to all intelligent persons that "Holly Coffee House," or "Holly Tree Inn," means a *strictly Temperance Eating-House*, where at any hour of the day a traveller or other persons can have a cup of hot tea, coffee or soup, for *half the price of bad whisky*. This, which we herein describe, is in *no sense* of the words a "Holly Tree Coffee Room." The *real profits* of the establishment are from the *sale of liquors* to be drank on the premises, and the sign "Holly Tree Coffee and Lunch Room," is an evil *device to catch* the weary traveller. Young men entering the city, after a long journey, would naturally drop in at the first *respectable-looking* place to get a hot meal.

With a desire to save *them* and help *all* in the path of sobriety and peace, and subserve the highest moral welfare of our city, we feel it our duty solemnly and fearlessly to brand the aforesaid "Coffee and Lunch Room" herein described as a disgrace to the city of Columbus, and a dangerous place and a deadly snare to the unwary.

By Order of

A WOMANS' VIGILANT COMMITTEE.

THREE AREA ARTISTS

George Bellows, Emerson Burkhart, Elijah Pierce

Unlike harmoniously composed pieces of ripe pears and apples in sculpted bowls or flowers caught in vases at the peak of their blossom in still lifes, artists are not always enjoyed while they are alive and yielding up their best. But that honor has been bestowed upon three Columbus artists, all of whom were working in the 1920s or 1930s.

George Bellows

George Bellows was born in Columbus in 1882. He went to New York in 1904 to study with another Ohioan, Robert Henri. During that first decade of the century, Henri and such pupils as Bellows were breaking away from post-Impressionism and adopting vivid new colors and techniques to reflect social realism. They startled the art world with such work in the New York Armory Show of 1913.

By the 1920s, Bellows' general zest for life was manifested in paintings and lithographs about sports (*Dempsey and Firpo,* a 1924 lithograph), religious revivals (*Billy Sunday,* a 1923 litho) and canvases reflecting the teeming life of the big city, from slum children jumping off the docks to swim in the Hudson, to gaslight parks populated with shadowy night walkers. At the age of 27, Bellows was elected an associate of the

National Academy of Art, the youngest man ever so honored.

Although he died in 1925, leaving behind only two decades of work, Bellows' fame seems securely rested on such pictures as *Both Members of This Club* (1909) at the Washington National Gallery and *Polo at Lakewood* (1910), part of a rich and representative collection of his work at the Columbus Gallery of Fine Arts. (Retired Columbus banker Everett Reese also maintains a superb private collection of Bellows' work.)

Emerson Burkhart was born on a Kalida (Putnam County), Ohio, farm in 1905, of Swiss-Dutch and Pennsylvania Mennonite parents. His father, Albert Burkhart, wanted him to be a lawyer. But Burkhart, who had been drawing since first grade, left Ohio Wesleyan University in Delaware and headed for Provincetown, Massachusetts. In the 1920s, he studied art with Charles Hawthorne and became acquainted with an artists' colony which included such writers as Eugene O'Neill. Burkhart spent four years at the Art Students League and the National Academy of Design in New York but skipped classes in favor of the Metropolitan Museum of Art, where he "sat in front of the masters and studied different styles for [himself]."

He moved to Columbus in 1931, settled into a brick house on Woodland Avenue and stayed the rest of his life, only traveling for occasional painting expeditions abroad with his friend and patron, Columbus industrialist Karl Jaeger.

In his obituary in the *Citizen-Journal,* it was observed that he *made* Columbus his home-base, and that his roots were always those of a man who did not have to be

anywhere, who stakes out one portion of geography for his own, then devotes his life to extracting everything it has to offer and giving it everything in return.

Burkhart always claimed he'd "need a hundred lives just to paint the drama, beauty and suffering in Franklin County alone. If it were done truthfully, it'd make

Emerson Burkhart

Michaelangelo, Shakespeare and Beethoven curl up in their graves with envy."

Burkhart maintained hand-written journals in which he argued out his own notions about art and life with himself, his contemporaries and those defenseless souls who were already dead. "I am free," Burkhart claimed. "I punch no time clock. I see, discover, enjoy and paint in my own way. I like Bellows, Giotto and Francesca, and the kids' sketches at Kenny's grocery store. In short, I like life . . . and if I can paint just what *appears to my eye,* it can surpass any masterpiece ever done. Nature itself . . . provides bigness. You cannot neglect it if you would render yourself great."

He painted the "heightened realism" of car engines in the shapes of sarcophagi, with the entrails of Jesus Christ twisting where carburetors normally rested; WPA-sponsored Depression murals in OSU's School of Sociology and at Central School. Burkhart broke with the Columbus Art League after an exhibit of his works were criticized for "a lack of progress."

For the next three decades, he held his own annual showings. He loved to seduce gullible tour goers with tales of his amorous conquests. (He boasted that he kept a mirror under a canopy so he could "study the expressions.")

His spoof of the Babbits who bought his professional public costume of French beret, artist's cravat and ebony cigaret holder included masterful spiels about being an artist. People would ask, "What does it take to be an artist, Mr. Burkhart! Besides talent, I mean!" And Burkhart would grin wickedly, put aside his cigaret holder and allow, "It takes sensitivity, of course . . . and talent . . . and the strength of a blacksmith don't hurt nothing either!"

"Then why do artists die so young?" one person responded.

With practiced skill, Burkhart answered, "Who says artists die young? That image of artists as frail little aesthetes won't hold. Once I took a pencil and jotted down the life span of all the great artists. Figured it out. Well, they last as long as anybody else. They just suffer louder, is all."

Although his works had been on exhibit at the Whitney Museum, Carnegie Institute, the Art Institute of Chicago and the Corcoran Gallery in Philadelphia, and purchased for the private collections of Walter Chrysler Jr., Burkhart considered that modest recognition. Anyone who says he doesn't want to be famous is a liar. But I know I've done some really great paintings. I will just have to believe now that everything has its day and that my paintings will find their right place, in time."

At present, several hang in the Columbus Gallery of Fine Arts. Former Columbus Gallery of Fine Arts curator Mahonri Sharp Young, now living in New England, is writing a biography and critical appraisal of Burkhart and his work.

During the Depression, an East Long Street barber named Elijah Pierce spent his time between customers carving his vision of America out of odd pieces of wood. Pierce used a pocket knife, a chisel, a piece of broken glass to cut things down, sandpaper and bright lacquers to paint the finished objects. What he carved were his own straightforward images (now dubbed "naive," and "truly primitive folk art" by critics) of Joe Louis and Marian Anderson; his first car, a 1930 Willys-Knight coupe and his own version of Alexander Hamilton's mansion, which enchanted him

Elijah Pierce

during a visit. In Pierce's miniature version, the rooms were filled with carved chandeliers, mantels and rocking chairs, and populated with such wooden figures as a black lady with one shoe off, "under the influence, you might say." He also carved "little animals," which he carried around to street fairs and carnivals and tried to sell. Most wound up as gifts, "little souvenirs," given away to customers and friends.

In a 1972 interview for the *Citizen-Journal*, Pierce said he was born on a Mississippi Delta cotton farm in 1892. "My father was a thoroughbred farmer, [and] my two brothers liked to farm, but I didn't. Guess I was peculiar. I liked the woods . . . I'd go there with my dogs and pocket knives. When I'd find a smooth-bark tree, I'd carve on it — Indians or an arrow and heart . . . whatever I thought of."

He had always wanted to travel, so he got a job on a railroad. About 1912, he recalled getting off a train and seeing a straight hickory stick by the side of the road. "I liked it, cut it down and carved a cane. It's the first thing I can remember carving besides the trees."

In the 1920s, he fell in love with a Columbus woman, decided to settle in the city in 1924. That year, he opened his barber shop on East Long Street, where it is still located. Next door to the shop is a room filled with specimens from a half-century of his carvings. His major work during the Depression, inspired by a religious calling that dated back to his childhood, is a remarkable work called *The Book of Wood*. It is Pierce's personal vision of the New Testament, seven enormous pages with 33 carved pictures "representing highlights from the 33 years of Jesus' life." There are free-floating roses of Sharon above Jesus, whose skin is black from "the grain of the wood." Pierce was in his seventies before he achieved any critical recognition. Friends pressed him to exhibit some of his "little things" at a *Citizen-Journal* Golden Age Hobby Show. An Ohio State University sculptor named Boris Gruenwald came across them there and placed Pierce's works in a campus exhibition. Famed sculptor Frank Gallo was deeply moved by the "naivete, but the deep understanding of his subjects" and arranged an exhibit at the University of Illinois.

Since then — over the past eight years — Pierce has had a one-man show at the Museum of Modern Art in New York City, received an award at Zagreb, Yugoslavia, at an exhibit of international folk artists and was exhibited at the Columbus Gallery of Fine Arts, just around the corner from his shop. Most recently, the 88-year-old artist's work was included in the famed Abby Aldrich Rockefeller Folk Art Center in Williamsburg, Virginia and featured in *Life* magazine.

Elijah Pierce's answer to those who asked how he developed his art is as modest but as straightforward as he is: "God just guides the hands."

stands). Fasting does not remember what that "tremendously successful" pageant was about now. "What the hell do I know about the Bible? Nothing! I know *dance*."

When Mrs. Huntington asked him if he would consider moving to Columbus to set up a professional ballet school, he decided to take the chance. Fasting opened his first school at 111½ South High Street (the ½ meaning it was upstairs).

Although he continued to tour periodically for the Ruth Page Company for a number of years, Fasting's school prospered. (Comedienne Dody Goodman, a 1930 North High School graduate, was a prized student.) Fasting is *still* teaching. From that first performance in 1925 until he stopped dancing seventeen years ago, he always "threw tremendous bashes after performances for as many as 400 people" In the '20s and early '30s, they would come in limousines, the ladies with long trains on their gowns, and the men in top hats.

There were only "twelve to 20 people, perhaps, you might call the top families in Columbus. The rest were what you'd call the ones who came to supper. It was very snooty . . . *very* snooty. Oh, no, not based on blue blood, but money," Fasting said. People were truly "genteel. . . . There were definite rules then about one's public behavior, no matter how one behaved privately. Perhaps they did do the same things people do now . . . but they had good window blinds, and they pulled them down too, and knew enough not to pull them back up until they were through."

The free-wheeling fun and "blind-pulling" of the 1920s was enjoyed and not only by the upper class. During Prohibition, Columbus, as most cities, had "speakeasies" for persons of all classes. In the Flytown area, Salvatore ("Papa") Presutti — who arrived from Italy sometime around 1910 — became proprietor of a saloon called "The First and Last Chance." In a biography of the restauranteur, *Passage to America*, writer Michael Harden recounted Presutti's method for "obtaining the hooch." The compliant farmer "hid the cache of booze in exchange for a cut of the booty," but Presutti had to exercise extreme caution in knocking on the right farmhouse door since the sheriff lived next door. "Selling it was often a greater woe. A rented warehouse on Goodale served as the marketplace. All of the supply for sale was kept upstairs in a fifteen-gallon container with a sink nearby for hasty disposal. A hidden trap door in the ceiling opened each time a customer came seeking a half-pint of whiskey, and the bottle was lowered by a string to Salvatore. The man upstairs always listened careful to the footsteps below him. He knew that if he ever heard the word *buto* shouted up from below, it was time to dump the stuff and run."

Eluding the police was not as bothersome as earlier encounters with the "Black Hand" gang. Composed primarily of Italian/Sicilian immigrants perpetuating homeland traditions, "the young extortionists . . . plagued the Flytown area . . . extorting money from local merchants who, fearing revenge, did nothing. They were often able to walk into a business, push the proprietor away from the cash register, help themselve to a healthy portion of the day's receipts, and leave without ever showing a weapon."

As Presutti's First and Last Chance saloon flourished, it became a target for contributions to the group's cause. Presutti was "standing near the end of the bar one evening when a gang member walked through the door . . . and looking defiantly at Salvatore, opened the cash register. Grabbing a handful of bills, he returned to the door and was climbing onto the back of a motorcycle, which his partner had kept running outside . . . when he felt the stiff grip of a hand on his neck. 'Don't you sons of bitches move,' Presutti warned, 'or I'll shoot your damn heads off.' Presutti had a cocked .38 against the robber's skull."

The crowd gathered in the doorway and silently watched while Salvatore Presutti continued his remarks with one hand on the gun and the other held out, open. "That money is mine," he said. "I've got to buy beer and whiskey and pay my bills. Give it to me." The Black Hand member "put the bills into his hand, and the motorcycle roared away." (Organized crime never really got a strong foothold in Columbus because of strong police action and the individual efforts of men like Presutti. The Black Hand thugs were also the target for another campaign of social commentary cartoons by the *Dispatch*'s Billy Ireland.)

That is one of the bases of the success of this city, according to retired *Dispatch* publisher Preston Wolfe, "We never had a situation in which you've had a dominant political organization, a vicious underground or a badly led [labor] union. When you have those things combined, that's when a city gets in trouble. The underworld gets the money, the politicians get the graft, and unions become wicked." Without the convergence of those elements, he believes, "Columbus has always had a good, clean city government . . . [It has had] a few weak mayors from time to time, but always clean government, as clean as anyplace in the country. And I attribute that to the newspapers here during this century — from 1910 to the present."

The sort of no-holds-barred sensational journalism of that era — eulogized in the play "The Front Page" — also took place in Columbus and area cities, according to longtime Scripps-Howard reporter Ed Heinke, 78. A Coshocton, Ohio, native who graduated from Ohio State University's School of Journalism in 1921, Heinke recalls that he and his colleagues during those decades "didn't really operate any different than reporters in Chicago. We were all a bunch of 'Hildy Johnsons' from *The Front Page*. The big accomplishment was getting things *first* . . . any way you could. You learned to become resourceful. Some reporters who went on fires had their own fire helmets and raincoats. And as a police reporter, I covered a lot of murders and got into places by knocking on doors and saying, 'Police officer, ma'am.' Then I'd ask them for a picture of the dead man. I'd say, 'we need this for our records down at headquarters.' Well, I'd get the picture . . . but one time I saw the real detective coming up the walk and turned into Superman

WORK AND LEISURE: The Ralston Steel Car Company (top) was a WPA project from 1937 to 1942. The Columbus Gallery of Fine Arts opened in 1932 (above), located on the northwest corner of Broad Street and Washington Avenue.

JAMES GROVER THURBER

On an otherwise uneventful night in Columbus, Ohio, the eighth of December, 1894 — later described as "a night of wild portent and high wind" — James Grover Thurber was born to Charles Leander Thurber and Mary Agnes Fisher Thurber.

By the time the doctor arrived at 147 Parsons Avenue, "Young Jamie" had already made his entrance into Columbus and the world. "You might have spared your horse," Mary Agnes Thurber told the physician, "We managed all right without you."

It was from the latter parent, Thurber and other relatives were to claim, that he inherited a sense of humor (indeed, a sense of the absurd) which was always second to his mother's. Thurber's own daughter (and only child), Rosemary Thurber Sauers, loved to repeat family stories about how her grandmother, Mary Agnes, would store a basement full of dogs to sic on wary neighbors or come down to a formal dinner "with her hair all wild, saying she'd escaped from the attic."

According to Thurber's own farcical account, "My Fifty Years With James Thurber," (the preface to *My Life and Hard Times*) he did not walk until age two but formed complete sentences at four. His childhood was "pretty well devoid of significance." Thurber characterized himself as someone who "fell down a great deal during this period, because of a trick he had of walking into himself. His gold-rimmed glasses forever needed straightening, which gave him the appearance of a person who hears somebody calling, but can't make out where the sound is coming from."

In truth, he had been shot in one eye with a bow-and-arrow during a childhood accident. His vision was destroyed in that eye; sight in the other diminished as he grew older, and he was almost totally blind at the time of his death.

Thurber described himself as one of those persons who have a

James Thurber.

"twitchiness at once cosmic and mundane . . . [who have] a genius for getting into minor difficulties . . . [such as walking] into the wrong apartments, [drinking] furniture polish for stomach bitters, [driving] cars into the tulip beds of haughty neighbors."

His own "old school friends" at Ohio State University recalled him as the editor of the humor magazine. But it is his recollections of Ohio State University, and his subsequent attempts to be a newspaper reporter on *The Columbus Dispatch* that the world remembers from *The Thurber Album*. In that volume, Thurber's unforgettable profiles included those of the late OSU English professor Joseph Russell Taylor (who had a formidable influence on Thurber's disciplined style) and *Dispatch* City Editor Gus Kuehner whose tough professionalism Thurber feared, admired and realized he could never really emulate. Critic John K. Hutchens (and a fellow *New Yorker* contributor) said, "The historian who wants to know in A.D. 2000, what university and newspaper life were like in an Ohio city in the second and third decades of the century cannot possibly overlook [*The Thurber Album*]."

Preston Wolfe, did not know Thurber until years later when he was on *The New Yorker,* but confirms some of the legendary anecdotes

about Thurber's ineptitude in the newsroom. He had gotten that job through the influence of his father, "Charlie," then secretary to Columbus' mayor. But to the despair of *Dispatch* editors, James Thurber was "a lousy reporter. He was a scribbler, a *writer . . .* not a working journalist. He could get entrée to anyone, but he'd be talking to some guy and putting him on at the same time.

"They'd send him to cover things like fires, but when he called in, he didn't know the numbers of the buildings that had burnt." Then, in 1921, "there was the night that City Hall burned." For some reason fathomable only to the writer, he emerged "carrying out the blueprints" to the building.

"They couldn't do anything with him," Wolfe said, "so they put him on the telephones. In those days, people felt closer to their newspapers and called all the time. Usually they were women who were upset about something or wanted to get something in the paper. As he talked to these women, Thurber would make sketches based on how they sounded. Then he'd just crumple them up and put them in the wastebasket. I can't count the number of times I've heard people say they wished they could empty those wastebaskets now." Wolfe laughs.

After his brief eighteen-month stint at the *Dispatch,* Thurber joined other American writers in Paris during the early '20s. He wrote for that city's editions of the *Chicago Tribune* and *New York Evening Post.* But he found his true spiritual and literary home at the age of 33 when he returned to America and became a contributor to, and staff member of, *The New Yorker.*

In his brief, whimsical, half-sad humorous sketches and his bemused and bemusing line-drawings, Thurber constantly refined his own definition of humor — "a kind of emotional chaos told about calmly and quietly in retrospect."

Broad Street looking east from Third Street, in the late 1920s.

*GRAND STANDS: Seating for spectators at Neil Park (top)
and Driving Park (above).*

— just threw on my cloak and ran — with the pictures
and story, though."

Heinke recalled, for *Columbus Monthly*, that those
antics took place while he and "all the other reporters
during those days worked 15-16 hours a day and put our
hearts and souls into it." And while those newsmen were
covering such sensational stories as the Theo Hix murder
in the '20s (a pretty OSU coed murdered by her lover, a
highly respected OSU professor), they were also writing
stories that crusaded — as Ireland's cartoons did —
against such social ills as the Klan, the Black Hand,
gangsters and political corruption.

Frank Packard, local architect and civic leader, gave
literally years of his time until his death in 1924, to
bring about a real Civic Center for the city. His dream
was a rebuilt river front — built out of the ruins of the
riverfront slums swept away by the flood. Working with
community leaders, he willed the Civic Center to life.
Though he never lived to see it completed, the
Columbus Civic Center is his monument.

The mid-'20s and the following decade also saw the
banding together of several civic and commercial leaders
to repair and restructure the form of downtown
Columbus, which had still not fully recovered from the
devastating 1913 flood. Special committees and groups
worked with the Chamber of Commerce to improve the
city. Preston Wolfe, who had relatives serving on several
civic committees at one time or another, described the
people as "drawn together to protect the future of the city
and its best interests." The bond issues the groups
supported to rebuild the downtown in the '20s and '30s
"pioneered the incredible growth" Columbus was to make
in successive decades.

At the time, Wolfe recalls, "My father was the one
who got the federal government building built by Herbert
Hoover. That was one of the last pieces of legislation
that he signed. In fact, one version has it that he signed
it while F.D.R. was outside waiting [to take office]."

Outside, of course, was also the Depression. That
national trauma — which began October 29, 1929, with
the collapse of the stock market and did not end until
1939 and the advent of World War II — was not felt as
keenly in Columbus as in many other American cities.
Nonetheless, the impact was deep and sustained, never
to be forgotten by those who survived it.

More than one-third of the population was out of
work. In the early days of the Great Depression, before
massive governmental assistance programs began, the
private charities and social service movement labored
unselfishly and untiringly. These social service groups
included the settlement houses, the religious institutions
and dozens of other agencies which provided assistance to

PEN BURNS: Fire at the Ohio Penitentiary
(top) and its aftermath (above and right), 1930.

129

LAND USE: Sewage disposal (above) and pristine stock farm (below).

an overworked and underfunded local welfare department.

Among the most important of these groups was the Columbus Urban League. It was founded in 1917 as a local chapter in a national organization pledged to ease the plight of the thousands of poor and underprivileged rural southerners (many from Appalachia) who came north to find work in war industries during World War I. The League continued to provide services when industry drew in after the war and thousands of these people were laid off. These newcomers — members of what came to be called the Great Migration — swelled the inner cities of the north. They were ill-equipped to handle the problems of day-to-day survival in the city. They were accustomed to rural living. The inner city was hit hard. Entire neighborhoods decayed rapidly as sewer, water, gas and lighting systems were overburdened by this influx of people. Disease was rampant; families and family life deteriorated. The Urban League and similar organizations acted aggressively to meet these problems. Their board was composed equally of white and black civic leaders. They focused on three areas — jobs, housing and education. The concept of the league was to teach survival skills as well as the skills necessary to lift whole populations out of poverty and into decent livelihoods. By current standards of social service, it may have been patronizing. The League was bitterly criticized in the 1960s as being a tool of the establishment to oppress the poor. But the criticism is shortsighted. At this time, blacks were still not permitted in anything but the balcony of cheaper movie theaters; they were not permitted in some restaurants or clubs at all. They were obliged to attend segregated schools and were relegated (except in their own communities) to largely non-professional jobs. Even though their lot in the North was better than in the South, the period between the wars was not a time to confront the establishment. The leaders of the League realized this and worked for "racial reconciliation," attempting to interest the entire community — especially its leadership — in assisting in the improvement of the lot of the poor and underprivileged. And it worked.

In a half-century retrospective written for the *Columbus Citizen-Journal* in 1979, veteran reporter Ed Heinke interviewed financial authorities who confirmed that 'Good Old Columbus Town' "perhaps weathered the Depression better than any city of similar size in the nation." The unemployed sold apples on the street for five cents here, too; there were food lines for the hungry, but the food always seemed to hold out; and there was script to pay state and federal workers in the city, but the script never had to be used in Columbus.

Longtime resident Theodore ("Buster") James, 69, recalls feeling lucky to get onto a WPA project and bring home $36 every two weeks. He, his wife and three children were "barely living then. Sometimes there was food, sometimes there wasn't. Sometimes there was coal to heat our rooms, but most of the time there wasn't. To me, that was the worst part of the Depression — cold."

Margaret Patten, 85, mainly remembers "living on corn meal. We ate it three times a day. First we made mush, then took what was left and poured it into pans and let it jell and then fried it. I cried because the kids . . . couldn't stomach that cornmeal all the time, and they didn't want to go to school because they didn't have enough to wear."

Another city resident, Catherine Fifer, now 87, says she took care of six persons on $105 a month during the Depression. "We lost our home," she says, "because we couldn't pay the $69 a month, but we got a [double] room for $25. Somehow we held together, and we didn't go into debt."

In that era when crime multiplied and was glamorized by the movie industry, the crowded Ohio Penitentiary suffered a disastrous fire in 1930. The cause was arson perpetrated by three inmates. It resulted in the death of 320 prisoners.

As individual and collective horror stories of the Depression were chronicled, Columbus "went through terrible bank runs without a single closing except on executive order," according to Preston Wolfe, whose family founded and maintains an interest in Bancohio, Inc. "That was a pretty severe test, we [the city] passed it."

An in-store history of F. & R. Lazarus relates a little-known story of a singularly ingenious move for both customers and business. When the surprise announcement of the March 4, 1933, bank holiday was made by F.D.R., Lazarus management "held an impromptu morning meeting on the first floor with the late Ed Neese of the old *Columbus Citizen,* and asked him if the papers could change the ads to include a charge account offer in the home editions. They could and did." That was "the first Lazarus advertising of this form of credit-opener for aggressive promotion since." Columbus also experienced another "first" in 1934 — the first supermarket. Big Bear was founded by the late Wayne Brown in an old skating rink near Ohio State University.

As the Depression dragged on, there were moments to lighten the public mood. Jesse Owens' heroic feats at the 1936 Berlin Olympics in Germany was certainly one. His steadfastness in the face of Nazi ridicule and ultimate triumph over the "master race" won him the admiration of the town he called his home.

For the most part, people turned to movies for diversion. Clark Gable and Claudette Colbert in *It Happened One Night* were good for a laugh, and there was always a chance to win a free dish at the movies, too. There was hope. One fellow storing up on that commodity in Columbus was named James A. Rhodes, a born promoter working his way up from a school board post in the late '30s. Rhodes had his eye on the mayorship and his head full of ideas about jobs.

By 1939, the Lazarus store was displaying early forms of automatic washing machines and demonstrating television sets — harbingers of the affluence and luxuries that American technology could and would provide in the future — but not until technology and ordinary human lives were diverted and intensified by World War II.

World War II tank in front of the Neil House.

CHAPTER NINE

WHITE COLLAR HEAVEN

1940-1960

Fifth Avenue motor bus brings suburban dwellers downtown in the 1920s.

The Scioto River winds through Columbus, 1936.

The census of 1940 made it quite clear — Columbus had virtually become Franklin County. Its population comprised 306,087 of the 388,712 county residents. The capital finally joined the statistical ranks of cities designated metropolitan. Columbus had

The view, 1936, flying into Columbus.

indeed survived the Depression and better than virtually any American city its size. But now it faced — as Americans everywhere — the country's probable entry into another world war. Everyone expected the worst — and had been doing so ever since Hitler invaded Poland in 1939 and then moved against England and France. But no one was really preparing for the inevitable clash, least of all Columbus. The late Robert Lazarus Sr. told the *Citizen-Journal* in a 1970 profile, he deeply regretted "Columbus' insular attitude prior to World War II. The Chamber of Commerce feared bringing in any industries that would also bring unions."

The result was a slower economic recovery from the Depression than might have been possible if additional industries had moved in before the War.

However, Governor John Bricker had already seen to the provision of many state and local facilities for anticipated defense purposes. *The Governors of Ohio* credits Bricker for "advance planning . . . [which] enabled Ohio to slip into wartime gear with a minimum of strain and confusion."

Some private industries were also looking ahead. In 1940, 12,000 people began work on military aircraft at the new Curtiss-Wright plant (later renamed North American Aviation, then Rockwell International). Near Port Columbus and the Defense Construction Supply Center, the factory produced and worked on a wide variety of aircraft.

The significance of the Curtiss-Wright plant is hard to underestimate. As a federally financed industry, it had to be a union plant. The introduction of a plant employing 12,000 unionized workers into a city which valued non-union labor was extraordinary. From this point on, fully unionized industry in Columbus would be a fact of life.

As Hitler's troops made further inroads into Europe, existing industries adopted an industrial defense posture. More defense jobs became available, but commercial construction came to a complete standstill and remained so until after the war.

The late industrial developer Don M. Casto Sr. acquired acreage on the eastern fringe of Columbus near the village of Whitehall, hoping to pursue a radical extension of the concept of small neighborhood shopping centers he had pioneered in 1928. But the project was put on hold again.

Even those who considered America's participation in the war inevitable, were surprised by the suddenness and ferocity of the Japanese attack on Pearl Harbor, December 7, 1941. Virtually everyone in Columbus on that Sunday morning — when news of the attack was broadcast by radio — remembered where they were, whom they were with, what was said and how little could be said. Newsmen described the collective public reaction as stunned amazement. There was no hysteria or running into the streets to talk about the attack; everyone was quiet and solemn.

After December 8, 1941, blue stars began to appear in the window of one home after another. Each one signified a son or husband in service.

All too soon, there were windows with gold stars, a ritual salute to a life lost in that war. Many windows had more than one star. It was happening in other American cities also, but patriotism in that era was expressed as much in terms of our town as our country. People still considered them synonymous.

Unlike World War I, there was no real anti-German agitation against the local German community. Such reactions had become almost negligible, for one thing, and the Germans were so well integrated into the city that they felt themselves Americans — and so did everyone else.

Since America had not really equipped itself for the war, it started out short on armaments, as well as manpower. Those men who were too young or not qualified to fight worked in Columbus industries. They were joined by thousands of women who became an important part of the labor force. Hundreds of industries geared up and revamped for wartime purposes, including Timken Roller Bearing, Jeffrey Manufacturing and the old Ralston Steel Car Company. All existing resources and skills that could be converted into immediate use were moved out at a pace that finally matched Hitler's blitzkrieg techniques.

The conversion to war-time goods meant sacrifices for the home front. "Grave shortages of consumer goods, the rationing of shoes, the rationing of restaurant foods, young men and women going off to join the armed forces, and price controls, were among the occurrences that complicated retailing in the first half of the 1940s," according to Lazarus. "Buyers of those years remember the frantic search for merchandise to sell, and the instant consumer response when it was advertised. Nylon stockings, or any-fiber stockings, were in such short

VJ Day is celebrated in Columbus, Broad and High Streets.

supply that the rare new shipment always caused a riot."

It became common practice for women to stop stocking runs with their nail polish, which tended to be highly-visible flame red or fuschia. More inventive women just drew stocking seams down the backs of their bare legs with eyebrow pencils. Daytime frocks, peplum suits and occasional formals (for females who still had escorts to take them dancing to Chuck Selby's Big Band music at Valley Dale — long or short, daytime or nighttime, no early '40s garment was "chic" without padded shoulders à la Joan Crawford. The net effect resembled a hybrid cross between an OSU fullback and a Warner Brothers femme fatale.

Movies were popular during the stressful times. It was comforting to watch John Wayne fight the enemy onscreen since he always lived to win the next battle. Area actress Agnes Moorehead was repeatedly cast as a German spy or Oriental villainess. There was even easy-going, professional nice-guy mumbler Fred

MacMurray playing the film role of Columbus' World War I flying ace Captain Eddie Rickenbacker. (The real Captain Eddie was fighting the current war along with men half his age.)

Movie fan magazines were popular reading, particularly with women and teenagers. Homemakers' magazines such as *Ladies' Home Journal*, as well as such general interest magazines as Collier's, were often half-filled with illustrations by OSU's Jon Whitcomb during the '40s (and for many years later). A surprising number of Columbus-born writers who graduated from OSU's journalism school in the '20s and '30s or worked on local newspapers then, became famous in New York. James Thurber and former *Columbus Citizen* rewrite man John McNulty were on the staff of The New Yorker. McNulty's characters and materials were virtually all drawn from his years in Columbus, but he transplanted them to a New York bar he frequented called Costello's. The characters seemed so real that readers would often go into the bar asking for them by name. (Few hometown readers followed the *New Yorker* stories of feisty, hard-drinking Eileen McKenney, but she also delighted New Yorkers.)

John Barcroft, a popular public relations man from the 1930s to the 1960s, worked on the *Ohio State Lantern* in 1931, along with another news editor named Earl Wilson. "Earl was always serious about journalism," Barcroft recalled with a grin, "but he was well adapted for what he was doing." (Wilson's "Ohioan on Broadway" gossip column still runs in the *Columbus Dispatch*.) "We also had Ruth McKenney in that class," Barcroft told the *Citizens'-Journal* in a 1967 profile. "I remember once there was a big explosion at the chemistry building. I had a Ford with a rumble seat at that time. I roared down to the fire, jumped out, looked around and there was Ruth in my rumble seat. Boy, she was a tough Irishman."

McKenney went on to New York accompanied by her pretty younger sister Eileen who was a spray of baby's breath in the concrete garden of the universe. The hardhearted New Yorkers (particularly males) fell over themselves "protecting" Eileen, while tough Big Sister collected heel prints across her face. McKenney chronicled their misadventures in a series of funny stories that were turned into a Broadway play in the '40s, "My Sister Eileen." A popular film version (Betty Garrett played McKenney and Janet Leigh played Eileen) came out after the war. Hometown people vicariously enjoyed seeing local girls with good solid Columbus values (Ruth McKenney's boozing was omitted) triumph over all those crazy people in New York City. (By the 1950s, the stories were put back onto Broadway again, this time as a musical called "Wonderful Town.")

Milt Caniff, one of OSU's prize art students, drew a nationally syndicated cartoon strip called "Terry and the Pirates." Lucy Caswell, curator of the Caniff Research Room at OSU's School of Journalism, confirmed in a *Columbus Dispatch* interview that Caniff modeled the Dragon Lady after the ubiquitous Joan Crawford. Other characters were modeled after OSU friends. Frank Higgs became Terry's friend Dude Hennick, so named because he was a flashy dresser, and Columbus friend Philip Cochran became popular ace flyboy Flip Corkin. The World War II adventure strip was so popular, Caswell has inventoried more than 14,000 fan letters to Caniff. Many came from such diverse celebrities as Bing Crosby and John Steinbeck. The *Columbus Dispatch* still carries the "Steve Canyon" strip Caniff began "when Terry and the Pirates" ended.

All those diversions were needed. As the war dragged on, the toll in lives grew beyond emotional comprehension.

One visible cost to Columbus was the physical deterioration of the city. During those years, all available materials, labor and money were diverted into the war effort. James Allen Rhodes, the Jackson County, Ohio, coal miner's son who adopted Columbus as his hometown in 1931, had served as city auditor since 1939. By 1943, when he decided to campaign for the mayor's office, he said, "We [Columbus] were going downhill." Aside from

the war itself, "the morale of the people [was] given up [to] racketeering . . . . The city had 1200 slot machines, prostitution, pocket-picking, open tracks betting, you name it." The *Columbus Citizen* confirmed the assessment in similar terms. "Wide open gambling, prostitution, and a $1 million debt were hanging over the city."

Rhodes also noted, "the people hadn't passed any bond issues in so many years, at least 10 or 12, that the streets were in rotten shape. There were alleys where there'd been no trash or rubbish heap pickups for at least sixteen years. They had such bad morale, they just let things go . . .but the secret of Columbus was always being clean, so I said, 'We're gonna clean it up.' "

Rhodes did not have the backing of the Republican party in that primary, and contrary to longtime stories that the Wolfe family put Rhodes into office, he did not have their backing in that race. The *Columbus Citizen* said, "Rhodes was everywhere. He shook hands, spoke at smokers' and ladies' club meetings, school gatherings and to anyone who would listen. It paid off. He won the nomination by a two to one margin." After winning the general election, he took office in January 1944, at the age of 34, then the youngest mayor of a major city in the nation.

The *Columbus Citizen* (never perceived editorially to be as Republican as the *Dispatch*) rated Rhodes' performance favorably. "He began by cracking down on gambling and vice and putting the city on a pay-as-you-go basis. He expanded the police and fire departments, began watch-dog tactics on city departments and expenditures." Rhodes literally sent out a vice squad armed with fire axes (among other things) to knock down certain doors. There were threats of reprisals from people who did not make such threats idly.

In a 1953 *Columbus Dispatch Sunday Magazine* retrospective of Rhodes' three terms as mayor, political writer Dean Jauchius analyzed the situation as it had been in 1944. "[Rhodes] had two immediate problems. He had to catch up on $44 million of deferred maintenance. And he had $3.7 million in outstanding city debts to pay off. Those included $1.8 million in back pay debts, $800,000 in sewage pollution suits and $1 million in current expenses . . . [Rhodes'] answer to the multi-million dollar deferred maintenance problem was to bring together, within the year, divergent and influential interests — labor, business, mercantile, industrial and property [leaders] . . . a kind of blue ribbon sale force for a huge improvement bond issue." That group included representatives from the Wolfe, Lazarus and Jeffrey families, utility company executives, leading real estate brokers and officers of the Chamber of Commerce.

Despite any commercial, political or personal differences or conflicts, the group displayed one common interest — salvaging and improving the ailing city. It was called the Metropolitan Committee. Bailing out the city was a matter of self-interest for committee members. But it would also benefit the city they genuinely cared about. Individually, even the most powerful member could not have solved the problems alone. By collaring such a divergent group, the task became easier. When long-reluctant voters were asked to pass a $24.5 million bond issue (at a time when it took at least a 60 percent majority vote to get it through the primary), Rhodes and the committee saw the voters approve it.

George De DeNucci, a Columbus cloth cutter, became active as a labor organizer in the 1930s and '40s. He was a founder of the Columbus and Ohio Industrial Union Council and did national work for the AFL-CIO, United Mine Workers and United Steel Workers. He was active in organizing a drive at the Timken plant. With the advent of more labor, labor organizations moved into Columbus. It was supported by Columbus authorities.

"The first couple strikes we had at Timkens, we had a lot of our people arrested by the police," said DeNucci in an interview for the Ohio Historical Society in 1976.

And then we had the scabs in there. I remember the last strike, they got an injunction against us. We were only allowed just a few pickets at the gates and . . . only one of them . . . showed up, and he was a fellow that was servicing and he didn't care whether he was breaking the injunction, so I took over. [The company] had organized a non-union, a scab group . . . and they called them the Blue Column; we called them Bluebirds because they wore blue buttons.

They said the next day they were going into the plant, so they were down on Second Avenue or . . . Third Avenue, on Cleveland. They formed a line, parade . . . a line of [the Bluebirds]. And the mayor says, 'What are you going to do?' I says, We're going to ignore the thing, we're going to have to or we're going to lose out, we're just going to be beat. He didn't say anything more to me, he says, 'That's all I wanted to know.' So these Bluebirds, company union, came up on the opposite side of the street . . . to the main gate. [The] chief of police was there . . . . I noticed they had a cruiser parked in an empty lot right across from there . . . and they came to the gate. We had maybe a couple hundred pickets there. I says, 'Don't move, hold strong, firm.' They [the Bluebirds] came up to the chief of police and says, 'We want to go to work, we demand that you open the picket line and let us get in and work.' So he read the riot act to us and we didn't flinch . . . didn't pay any attention. He read it to us the second time and we wouldn't move. He held up . . . his hand, and the guy in the cruiser, over the loudspeakers says, 'Everybody disperse and go home.' That broke up the company union and that was it. And after that the company didn't try anything anymore.

Two personalities popular in the first decade of area television are still going strong. "Spook" Beckman, who emceed a show for WLW-C, is spinning platters as a radio disc jockey. Bob Marvin, also known as "Flippo the Clown" on WBNS-TV for nearly two decades, has an entirely new career with Warner-QUBE two-way cable television.

V-J Day — August 15, 1945 — was an end to blue stars and gold stars for windows. Those banners and memories of men who died were folded away. It was time to get on with living — and living never looked better to any generation.

Commercial construction resumed on all fronts. The Curtiss-Wright plant had produced a trained and unionized force of more than 25,000 workers available for Columbus work. Don M. Casto Sr. felt it was "time to try for the big one," — the first regional drive-in shopping center in the world. According to an informal history of his organization, Casto erected a huge billboard on his vacant land in Whitehall. It showed an artist's conception of the proposed Town & Country Shopping Center. "Most other real estate men in Columbus and in other cities . . . thought I was going off the deep end," Casto said. The project was referred to as "Castos's Folly." Bankers, insurance company executives and retail chain store owners shared that view. In 1945, Casto began pitching the untested virtues of building a complete variety of shopping facilities in a one-stop location. But Casto's location was in a sparsely populated suburb — and it was well past the end of the city bus lines. Despite such drawbacks, Casto was convinced that if he lined up a real "powerhouse of tenants, with great diversification, people would come from as far as 30 miles around [and] thousands of cars could be funneled into Town & Country from all directions every day."

His first breakthrough was a promise from the president of the company controlling public transportation to establish a bus line to Town & Country if it succeeded in attracting immense numbers of shoppers. All Casto had to do then was line up the tenants, who were assured bus service would be available for consumers. But it would take four years before Casto's efforts paid off.

In 1946, Harry Truman — accompanied by Winston Churchill — spoke at the Deshler-Wallick Hotel to ask for support in a city where moderation had been so essential to electability that it was difficult to tell the Republicans from Democrats. Historically, Franklin County tended to back Republicans for the presidency. And if Ohio's governors and Columbus' mayors were preponderantly Republican, it was more or less evened out by the number of Democrats who held lesser offices.

James A. Rhodes once said, "Profit is not a dirty word in Ohio." But in Columbus — unlike Cleveland, Akron and other industrial cities — it was considered *de rigueur* to refer to growth and progress when discussing profits.

In November of that year, something old was new again to the entertainment scene downtown. The old Knickerbocker Theater on South High Street near the Southern Hotel, was repainted and opened as the Gayety, a burlesque house.

There was a new show each Friday at the Gayety. Each traditionally included a star stripper, three or four supporting strutters, a singer-emcee, some baggy-pants comics, a dancing chorus and a small pit band. Popular performers included Ann ("Bang Bang") Arbor, Tempest Storm, Blaze Fury, Zola ("Queen of the Jungle") and her

MELTING POT: *Columbus embraces many ethnic communities. A group of Italian-born immigrants (above) are students in a citizenship class. A black family (below) pauses for a photograph at their home.*

JAMES ALLEN RHODES

Mayor James A. Rhodes

For 43 years, one man has been more synonymous with politics in Columbus (and Ohio) than any other individual — James Allen Rhodes.

From 1937 to 1939, he was a member of the Columbus Board of Education. In November 1939, he was elected auditor of the city and re-elected to that office in 1941 with twice the number of votes of his opponent. And in November 1943, at the age of 34, he was elected mayor of Columbus, the youngest mayor then of any metropolitan area in the country. He was re-elected twice, serving from 1944 to 1953, during which time he wiped out a $4 million deficit in the city treasury. He was elected state auditor in November 1953 and was twice re-elected, serving ten years with efficiency and economy.

Rhodes won the Republican nomination for governor in 1954, but was unable to beat the popular Democrat Frank Lausche. In 1962, he became governor, defeating Michael V. DiSalle by nearly 556,000 votes. Rhodes was the first governor to be re-elected for two consecutive four-year terms. In 1970, he sat out one term to comply with the law but came back in 1974 to defeat John J. Gilligan and is now serving his fourth term.

At 71, the workhorse governor still exhausts aides as he runs three or four meetings at once, trying to "get some folks together" for a compromise on some tie-up, stopping occasionally on his way through a room to slap someone on the back and say "stick with me" as he rushes to yet another meeting. Long after everyone else has collapsed in bed at night, aides may get calls at 10 p.m. or 2 a.m. to go through a brainstorming session or be at the airport by 5 or 6 a.m. to make an unplanned trip. The only thing Jim Rhodes likes better than his family and working (or getting jobs for others) is fairs and carnivals. At the state fair every year, he blitzkriegs the rides and livestock exhibits while wolfing down hot dogs, Slurpees and cotton candy. He's not *just* politicking, he's in his element. Jim Rhodes loves the Midway; he was born for it. "I've always been a promoter," he understates. "I've always been able to line up ways to make money, even as a kid — get turtle races going, you name it."

Rhodes was born September 13, 1909, in Coalton (Jackson County), Ohio — hilly Appalachian coal country. The family background was Welsh. Rhodes was eight years old when his coal miner father died. He took on all kinds of odd jobs to help provide for his mother (Susan) and two sisters. "My mother was a real disciplinarian," he says, "and I think that makes the yardstick of a boy. She taught me right from wrong."

Rhodes was "inclined to athletics" when he went to Springfield High School (Ohio) and always dribbled a ball to school. He entered journalism school at Ohio State University in 1930, lived on campus and was active in the un-fraternity fraternity full of jokesters called Si-U. Financially pressed, Rhodes had to spend much of his time raising money. One day, in a geography class, Rhodes was staring pensively out the window. One of his band bookings had fallen through the night before. The instructor "asked me to describe the atmosphere outside . . . said it must be pretty nice. I said, "It may look sunny to you, but it doesn't look so sunny to me. I just lost $1200. They threw me out of school . . . said I was a troublemaker." (Rhodes has gone back periodically and audited classes in everything from law to political science.)

Rhodes loved Columbus when he first encountered it. "It was the most friendly place I ever met." He opened a restaurant, called Jim's Restaurant, at 17th and High in the campus area. "I've always been in the catbird seat," he allows, sitting back in his favorite chair (the one reserved for the governor of Ohio).

From the "catbird seat," he has accomplished an enormous amount of what he set out to do, despite the fact that he's usually had to work with a Democratic majority in the Assembly.

Asked how he's been able to promote the legislators into passing bills and programs when they've balked, the governor says he uses a fairly simple formula:

"One, I never allow myself to get so mad about anything that I can't still cut a deal the next morning.

"Two, I always ask for at least twice as much as I need. Then, when they give me the other half [and] walk out the door, they can wave the victory banner and enjoy what they just won."

Another great asset as a politician and as a governor is Rhodes' acute sense of public wants, needs and preferences. He calls it "a happy faculty" that most people like him. "Oh, yeah, there's some would like to take a rifle to me, but even most people who dislike me, they respect me. We're a fixation with some people," he says. Asked why he tends to use the royal "We" rather than "I," Rhodes looked genuinely perplexed. "What do you mean, who's 'we'? Why, it's me and the people!"

James Rhodes' high school graduating class. (Rhodes is third from right, third row.)

one-foot python, Evelyn "$50,000 Treasure Chest" West, Fabulous Fanny and — the undisputed queen of the Gayety — Miss Rose La Rose. La Rose always played to a full house.

And there were other full houses. Those closing months of 1946 saw full maternity wards in all Columbus hospitals. The post-war baby boom had begun, along with the *Ladies' Home Journal* picture of the ideal family (four breast-fed children). Rosie the Riveter was bounced back to earth mother. Within ten years, the 40,675 pupil enrollment in Columbus public schools doubled as did the school district area.

James A. Rhodes was re-elected mayor in 1947. Having taken care of the previous deficit with that first bond issue, he wanted to get on with capital improvements. After setting up a jobs and progress project, he signed into law an amusement tax which other Ohio cities promptly emulated. In 1948 voters passed a 1.5 percent city income tax — the first in the country. "Most other cities didn't get around to it until later in the '50s," Rhodes said. With the help of the Metropolitan Committee, Rhodes persuaded Columbus to pass a $23.1 million bond issue in 1949. That qualified the city for $15 million in federal grants. It was the springboard for the city's freeway system.

The Ohio Legislature carried the picture one step further. They floated a bond issue to connect Ohio with the Pennsylvania Turnpike. The bond issues comprised the first numerous local and state follow-up issues promoting highway systems.

The state and federal highway projects of the previous 50 years had kept Columbus in the foreground as a transportation center. But by the mid-1950s, it was clear that something new was needed. The problem was the highways, the trucking industry and the automobile.

By 1960, one of every six workers in the United States owed his job directly or indirectly to the automobile industry. More cars were being manufactured — and more people were buying them. Private automobiles were crowding the highways. Trucking had become as big an industry as the railroads had been in the past years — and it was suffering as a result of the increased competition with auto traffic.

The answer was the federally-sponsored National Defense Highway System — interstates. Beginning in the '50s, the federal government began a massive grant program to aid the cities. With state and local government, Columbus began construction of the Inner-belt, Outerbelt, I-70 and I-71 through the city. Entire neighborhoods were eliminated and roadbeds substituted to bring high-speed traffic into town. By the early 1970s, the system was complete, and the city was transformed.

But this also sparked a reaction — an exodus to the suburbs that resulted in a change in the face of communities and business.

It was the boom that Don Casto needed. In the spring of 1949, the Town & Country Shopping Center opened. "Casto's Folly" became "Casto's Coup." That fall, the second and third sections were completed. The J.C. Penney chain, which had leased 40,000 square feet,

141

opened a new department store. Founder J.C. Penney was on hand for the event. Other tenants included Kroger and Albers supermarkets, Kresge's, and firms that for the first time in 50 or more years of business had left the downtown area of a major metropolitan city. Casto's instincts were right. He had developed the first truly regional shopping center in the world.

More and more residents were moving to the suburbs. By 1950, the city had a population of 375,901, while Franklin County's total was 503,410 people. Those suburbs represented the American dream in the early '50s — modern ranch-style or split-level homes surrounded by big yards, meticulously free of crabgrass; barbeque grills in the back yards for cookouts — and a television set for watching WLW-C (now WCMH) — the first commercial TV station on the air in 1947, closely followed by WBNS-TV and WTVN-TV. (In 1950, those pioneers braving the manicured wilds of suburbia watched

Frank J. Lausche was elected governor of Ohio in 1945 — the only governor who served five terms and twelve years in office. Lausche was a man with dignified bearing, soft-spoken but articulate. But he was also considered down-to-earth by voters. He moved around among "the people," but at what seemed a leisurely pace. He often carried a toothbrush in the handkerchief pocket of his jackets — as if he had neither the time nor inclination to stop long enough to pack a suitcase. But he was a man of utter integrity in voting his convictions. A veteran political reporter who covered his entire tenure noted that Lausche often was driven in a chauffeured state limousine to within a few blocks of his office, then walked the rest of the way so he could be seen going through the gates on foot. Lausche resigned from the governor's office in January 1957 to take a seat in the U.S. Senate. He was succeeded by Republican C. William O'Neill, who served as governor until 1959.

all the wrestling matches that had a hammerlock on early television programming. But they still had to go downtown to old Vets Memorial on Broad Street to see Don Eagle or Georgeous George in live, glistening armlocked flesh.)

Bob Lazarus Jr. graduated from college and returned to Columbus in 1950. The Lazarus store was making plans to celebrate their 100th anniversary (1851-1951). "We were also rebuilding our downtown building," he recalled, "because after considerable discussion we decided we weren't going to build any branches."

At the time, logic figured into Lazarus' decision as strongly as instinct triggered Casto's. Although the array of stores in Town & Country was obviously appealing to some shoppers, Lazarus was still the city's "only real department store," offering everything from furniture, household appliances and auto equipment to clothing for both sexes of all ages and income levels. (Morehouse-Martens across the street — later called The Fashion,

The Union, and now Halle's — was considered only a durable "specialty store" for higher priced clothing.)

The family and key staff were aware that the freeway system was just getting started. "Columbus [was] really early with [the freeway system]," said Lazarus. "All the same, it was a completely downtown-centered city. There was no real development on East Broad Street, not even any talk of moving past Nelson Road." Streetcar trolleys had just been pulled into the barn for the last time, but bus lines still had a long way to go past Columbus School for Girls, almost a cut-off point for the metropolitan Columbusite.

Downtown was still the important place. "Everybody came downtown to the movies then," said Lazarus; "the Palace, the Ohio, the Grand, the Majestic. And hotels! We had the Deshler-Wallick, the Fort Hayes, the Chittenden.

"North High Street was in fairly good shape, overall, between Broad and Union Station," as was South High to at least the Southern Hotel. "And we had three newspapers — The *Dispatch*, the *Columbus Citizen* and the *Ohio State Journal*." (The latter two merged in 1959.) "And Saturday afternoons had always been a big day for us, particularly during a big football season. There'd be the games, and shopping and going out. Because of all that, we were just slow in branching out in the '50s. We figured even people coming in from Newark wanted to come downtown. Now they go to [Lazarus] Eastland." (Today, Lazarus — a Federated store — has gone well beyond the suburbs and built stores in such towns as Mansfield. Previously people drove the 40 to 50 miles to Columbus to go to the Lazarus store.)

Many Columbus residents, such as Bob Lazarus, look back on the '50s with nostalgia. And many of them recall those football Saturdays — especially the November 25, 1950, Snow Bowl/Blizzard Bowl. More than 50,000 rabid OSU fans braved their way through outrageous weather into the stadium that day, not knowing until the last minute — as the players did not — whether OSU and Michigan officials would okay the game or cancel it. Admiral Peary might have sat that one out, but what did logic have to do with the annual OSU-Michigan battle! Mush! To hear it told now, at least half of Columbus was inside the stadium that day. Apocryphal stories abound, but some facts emerge. It was snowing so hard that people on the 50-yard line could not see the players. The players couldn't always see each other either, unless they slid and fell on each other. It was a new form of tackling. Neither Vic Janowicz — OSU's dazzling left half-back who won the Heisman Trophy that year — nor his teammates, nor their opponents, could see even the goalposts during most of that game — least of all the ball! And when they did get the ball, their hands were so frozen they kept dropping it anyway. Officials kept bringing out new balls; there was no use to look for the lost ones in a field that had been accumulating inches of snow ever since the ground crew had peeled the frozen tarpaulin off the field to start the game.

Janowicz borrowed Ernie Godfrey's gloves, "but they

Shoppers spend an August afternoon at Central Market, 1939.

were lined with rabbit fur or something inside, and the stuff froze and stuck all over my hands." Janowicz managed at least one touchdown. But he won the game for Michigan by two points when he fell back to punt near his own goal line; he couldn't see, slid on the kick, and a Michigan player fell on him hard enough to land them both in OSU's end zone, giving Michigan a safety. Aside from the snow, the sub-zero temperatures were not alleviated by all the flasks of booze consumed by those fans, virtually all of whom stayed to the bitter end — and past it. Some were so drunk they passed out there or stayed in the stadium restrooms

because they couldn't drive back to their hometowns in the blizzard. Romanticists claim that Janowicz and other players had frozen tears on their faces at the end of that game. "Naw, we didn't cry," says Janowicz. "I didn't anyway. We all went downtown later to Marzetti's Restaurant and got to feeling real good."

By the 1951 season, that brand of "feeling real good" was out for OSU football players. Wayne Woodrow Hayes arrived as the new candidate for the "graveyard of coaches" as OSU had been called. Pressure to win games at OSU was so intense it had allegedly driven previous coach Wes Fesler to a nervous breakdown. For the next

143

28 years, Hayes proceeded to give other people nervous breakdowns.

Columbus also acquired a symphony orchestra in 1951. When conductor Evan Whallon arrived in 1955, he found Columbus "typical of American cities which have grown into enormous places, then want to add things like symphonies and art galleries . . . and find it takes an awful lot of salesmanship," he said in a 1970 *Citizen-Journal* interview. "In Europe, people just assume the arts are worthwhile. In America, you have to prove it. But the good thing about Columbus is that once you convince a few people that you have a good [thing] going, you can find people who'll really work hard to help."

In 1951, there was also another mayoral election in Columbus. Jim Rhodes felt he had latched onto a good job and wanted to hold on to it. Everyone must have agreed. "No one opposed me that year," he recalled.

The great exodus of Appalachian migrants was getting into full swing in the early '50s. When the coal boom that lasted from the turn of the century till the end of World War II finally played out, more than three million jobless people from Appalachian states headed north looking for jobs. Detroit, Youngstown, Akron and other places had more industrial work for unskilled workers than Columbus, which was primarily a white-collar city. But a surprising number of hill people from Kentucky, West Virginia and southern Ohio came up Route 23 into Columbus.

There were some plants in the south end of Columbus (the "port of entry") that hired new migrants. Many stayed in that area of the city with neighbors from their own background. Contrary to the stereotypes about "shiftless hillbillies," benchmark Columbus studies found Appalachians tended to be extremely industrious, hard workers, proud and highly independent. Within a decade, at least one-quarter of the city's population would be of Appalachian descent, some having arrived long before the exodus, the rest having gradually acclimated themselves to different jobs, life-styles and speech patterns until they became part of the midwestern culture. In the process, their customs became part of Columbus' life-style.

Rhodes left the mayor's office in January 1953 to become state auditor. His last actions included several more bond issues — principally for public recreation centers, for another 200 acres for the city's growing parks and recreation system, for a $4 million expansion of the sewage disposal plant and for the $17 million Hoover Dam project. Looking back on his three terms as mayor, Rhodes said — not boastfully but not bothering with false modesty either — "We worked it to perfection."

Increasing numbers of Columbus residents continued to move outward into the Franklin County suburbs and small villages. Between the end of World War II and the early 1960s, city growth exploded. The housing, construction and automobile industries, sluggish since the Great Depression, expanded rapidly when the war ended. Millions of Americans had postponed their dreams through the decade of hard times and conflict. Now they were eager to make their dreams materialize. Most younger Columbusites were lured to the suburbs by the promise of a brand-new house and a plot of grass they could call their own. This resulted in a whole new ring of suburban communities around the older city. Quality communities like Bexley and Upper Arlington retained their exclusivity but grew rapidly. The real growth was beyond the then-existing city limits. The strategy was not new. Suburban subdivision developments were built far enough beyond the city to benefit from low-priced land and low taxes. But they were still close enough to the city to benefit from the city services.

What was new, however, was the scale of growth. Up until this time, most subdivisions were small. No developer built more houses than he could sell in a reasonable time. (Prior to World War II, most subdivisions were only a few blocks in size.) But now the market for homes was fueled by the demands of returning veterans. Communities built hundreds of homes at a time. Entire villages came into being, such as Whitehall which had been little more than a crossroads on Route 40 east of Bexley, Berwick near Route 33 south of Bexley and Riverlea which had been an open area between Beechwold and Worthington.

The older residential neighborhoods beyond the downtown — such as Clintonville and the Hilltop — held stable. But as the new areas mushroomed, the downtown began to decay, even though the Metropolitan Committee worked valiantly to save the city with its comprehensive plan.

Bond issues — approved as the result of the Metropolitan Committee's work — eased the more pressing problems of physical services, health and education. But the inner city neighborhoods were not spared the coming of "the federal bulldozer." Federal, state and local planning agencies were convinced that the downtown areas of most major American cities were beyond repair. They adopted the strategy of totally clearing out slum areas and substituting totally new development. The first major example was the Goodale Redevelopment Project which virtually leveled Flytown and substituted the Thurber Village community of middle-class housing. By 1960, initial planning was under way for the Market-Mohawk Redevelopment Project to similarly level the area just east of downtown. The final word on these projects is still not in. But it is clear after 20 years that the beneficial values of urban redevelopment by clearance were sometimes outweighed by the human tragedy of forced removal and neighborhood disintegration.

The cold war was a hot subject during that era; and somewhere out there, sodded over or excavated for swimming pools — there still must be some of the bomb shelters for which people paid several thousand dollars.

After 1954, a feisty little 140-pound fast-talking Democrat named Maynard E. "Jack" Sensenbrenner moved into the mayor's office. He took one look at this "goin' and growin' city" and saw that, despite the overall increased population in Franklin County, the city itself was only 41.8 square miles, and "it took 120 years to get to that." Sensenbrenner figured the city better go and

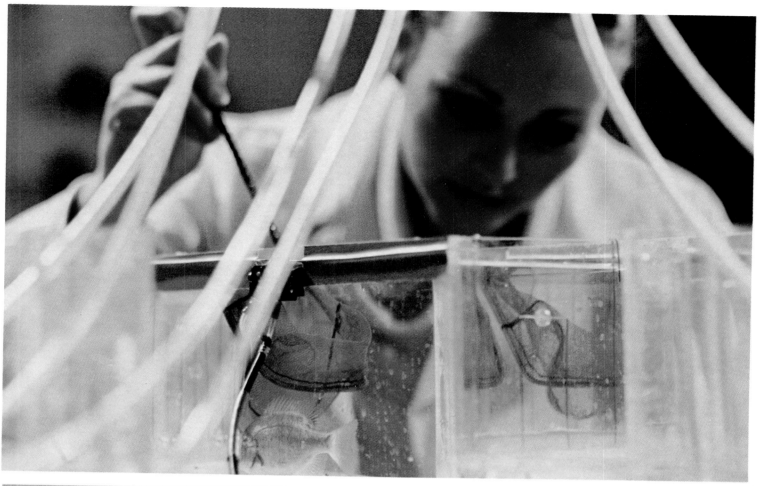

FOR SCIENCE: Research is in progress at the Battelle Memorial Institute's Columbus laboratories (top); visitors at the Center of Science and Industry (above) can explore the wonders of the universe in the planetarium (left).

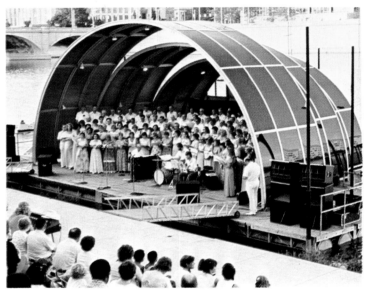

SOUND OF MUSIC: *The Columbus Symphony (top); downtown summer concerts staged in a floating bandshell on the Scioto River (above); Ohio University marching band member struts in front of city hall (right).*

AT THE ZOO: *Columbus Zoo director sitting down on the job (above); hulking gorilla people-watching (top inset); and youngster smiles tentatively in the embrace of a large snake (bottom inset).*

grow some more, so he followed the departing downtowners with the same persistent, optimistic spirit he showed when he spoke at a local country club right after taking office. "Ladies and gentlemen," he said, in all sincerity, "I can't tell you how happy I am to be here tonight, because I know if I hadn't been elected mayor, you never would have invited me."

Suburban officials did not exactly invite him out either, no matter how many times he got elected — three times, for the 14 years between 1954-1972 — but they needed the "dy-namic, tree-mendous All American City of Columbus" and its water and sewage services — unobtainable luxuries for most small suburbs with a near-nonexistent tax base. Bexley, Worthington and Upper Arlington could afford their own fire and police department and expensive school systems, but most could not. Sensenbrenner followed paths leading to new middle-class housing developments and small villages lapping out from the city in amoeba fashion, directionless and omnivorous. The areas were annexed through hardball tactics — "Come into the city, folks," he would grin, "or I might have to cut your water off, and you know how that hurts."

By 1972, under Sensenbrenner's policies, city boundaries had extended to most of today's 146 square miles. The city population then accounted for 471,316 of the 682,962 persons in Franklin County.

The nature of the industrial development was markedly changed. Prior to the war, civic and governmental leaders prided themselves on the diversified base of government, commerce and industry which provided for a more stable economy. World War II changed the industrial composition of the city. Large industry had not been lured to the city because civic leadership — and much of the population — were hostile toward organized labor.

In the late '40s and early '50s, General Motors and Westinghouse built large manufacturing facilities on the far west side of the city and employed thousands of workers. These companies were lured by the available manpower pool, a favorable tax and business climate and the availability of inexpensive land to develop their factories. Smaller industries could subcontract with a larger business. This made Columbus look more attractive to other large industries.

For a time, it appeared that Columbus was on the verge of another industrial transformation similar to the 1890s. As the migration of Appalachian and Ohio rural dwellers continued, Columbus seemed to be on the verge of becoming an industrial giant.

CHRISTOPHER COLUMBUS: Statues of the city's namesake stand in front of city hall (bottom right inset) and on the statehouse grounds (upper right inset); in earlier days, the statehouse statue stood in front of Saint Francis Hospital (below).

A ROSE IS A ROSE: A visit to the Park of Roses (inset) would not be complete without seeing the blush of the Columbus Rose (above).

But it did not happen. While Columbus needed the new industry to absorb its large work force, it continued to diversify. With the expansion of government in society after World War II and the growth of education, the increases in industrial employment were offset by growth in the other sectors. Research facilities like the Battelle Memorial Institute expanded, and other research and service firms were attracted, such as Chemical Abstracts. By the late 1960s, Columbus was as diversified as it had always been — the only real change being that organized labor was now a force to be dealt with in any conscientious program of civic betterment.

In 1955, Columbus Central High School's Howard "Hopalong" Cassidy became the second OSU football player to win the Heisman Trophy. All-Americans were a specialty of what was officially designated an All-American City" by *Look* magazine during Sensenbrenner's tenure, and Columbus was also designated headquarters of the American Rose Society, thanks to the Park of Roses the city installed at Whetstone Park. Both the parks and the recreation department — combined under the leadership of Mel Dodge — increased an already impressive amount of acreage and facilities. (The system is justifiably noted as one of the finest in the nation.)

At the Columbus Zoo, the city chalked up another world first. Staff experts succeeded in breeding and keeping alive the first baby gorilla ever born in captivity. "Colo" was born in 1958, as dainty as a little female gorilla could ever hope to be. Jack Sensenbrenner kept hoping the kid would be a boy, so they could name it after him — but shoot! Just so it was healthy, right?

When the mayor was not out making speeches, stalking suburban holdouts and promoting the city, he would frequent flea markets and auctions, picking up items for his collection of Columbus-related memorabilia. His entire office was lined wall-to-wall with such items as postcard views from the 1890s, stereopticon slides, commemorative plates and ashtrays, plaques, bowls, urns and *objects d'art* given by visiting dignitaries from other cities and countries.

Outside City Hall was the ultimate of those gifts — a giant (20 feet tall, 3.5 ton) bronze figure of Christopher Columbus, a gift from Genoa, Italy, home of the city's namesake. It was officially unveiled on Columbus Day, October 12, 1955, before approximately 100,000 spectators.

Jumpin' Jack Sensenbrenner wanted America to discover Columbus. He wanted it to be "the greatest city in the world" — and "at least a million strong" by 1970. What he forgot, as others had, is that no All-American city is an island unto itself.

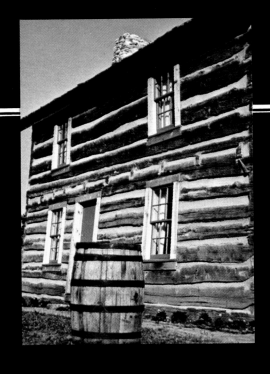

CHAPTER TEN

SOCIAL UNREST AND THE AMERICAN DREAM

1960-1980

Geometry in red and white reflected in one of the city's new office buildings.

ARCHITECTURAL HERITAGE: *The many faces of Columbus in the German brewing district (above) and village (left) and Renaissance restoration area (below).*

The American dream — to thousands of people in the late 1940s, it actually seemed possible. Aside from the Korean War in 1950, most middle-class people had been living in relative prosperity and comfort since 1948, watching the city's boundaries expand and its skyline rise. They retreated to the comfort of suburban homes complete with two-car garages, often a third car for teenagers, a small boat for summer outings and a camper or motor home for travel. On weekdays they drove past the inner city to the suburban white-collar heavens. Weekends they stopped or went to OSU football games or watched "Gunsmoke" on television. Adventure and violence were experienced vicariously.

Neat development of suburban Columbus.

In 1960, a chunky, golden-haired young man of 20, Jack Nicklaus — son of a Columbus pharmacist — was beginning a remarkable golf career. By 1963, the "Golden Bear" became the first person to surpass Bobby Jones' record of thirteen championship wins.

And there were other reasons to believe that the city was not on the verge of total abandonment to the suburbs. Many persons opposed the advent of federal clearance projects simply because they felt that their neighborhoods could be rehabilitated. They felt the result would not only be cheaper but a better neighborhood as well. Unfortunately few neighborhoods had both the housing and the people with means to prove their point. German Village was the exception. The old German community of the south end of Columbus, had seriously deteriorated, but its housing was still in structurally good condition. The neighborhood had not been cut up with new housing or strip shopping centers and it was roughly the same as it had been for decades. Because the houses were inexpensive, they could be bought individually and rehabilitated. In the late '50s, local residents began to restore the village.

The establishment of the German Village Commission in 1960 insured that the rehabilitation of the area would be consistent. The German Village Society, also founded in 1960, insured that the spirit of neighborhood — so essential to the survival of any community — would be retained. The German Village Society was founded in 1960. According to its booklet, *Wilkommen,* the non-profit organization's members "dedicated themselves to the preservation and restoration of the property in German Village." This included 1,700-1,800 structures in 223 acres which the city council declared a historic area.

The Society set out to retain "the community's charm and unique Old World atmosphere," to preserve it as "living history."

Skeptics said restoring the run-down old area — a slum by 1960 standards — would never work. But their skepticism was ill-founded. As renovation proceeded, prices for fully restored houses climbed from $20,000 to $30,000 and are still spiraling. (An unrestored house bought in 1971 for $16,000 recently was offered for sale for $80,000.) The restoration was a private effort — and it was successful. In the early days, it was considered slightly crazy. Today, this effort in urban neighborhood revitalizing is considered the pioneer movement. Six other restoration districts near downtown have now been organized.

In the meantime, the phrase "the displaced poor" was coined for the people who were living in the area before the restorations. A majority of them rented those homes from slum landlords. Most of these renters were blacks and Appalachian migrants living in the pocket between Route 23 (South High Street) and Parsons Avenue. As renovation progressed, landlords began selling the houses rapidly for high profits. The renters had to look for new cheap rentals. They moved into certain sections of the near west (bottoms) and north "short north" sides of the city — any area where landlords rented cheaply. Sometimes, the rent collection dates were worked around the time of month the Franklin County Welfare Department checks were sent out.

There were more poor people in Columbus than many suburban residents realized or cared to think about. But welfare caseworkers knew something of the worsening conditions. In *Columbus Monthly,* Pat Hoofstetter, a Franklin County Welfare Department caseworker since 1947, recalled conditions where she began work. One caseworker would do all the paperwork for 80 to 100 families a month. Most of those welfare recipients were embarrassed and ashamed. "They would break down and cry when they had to fill out an application," said Hoofstetter. "I tried very hard not to make them feel demeaned." Because the caseload was so much smaller then, she and fellow caseworkers made regular home visits. "There was personal bonding and a continuity. I came to know them well . . . their worries, their kids, their plans for the future. It was not even unusual for a funeral director to call and ask me to give a little eulogy for someone who had died from one of my families."

Those ties were possible, Hoofstetter felt, because

NIGHT ON THE TOWN: *The Ohio Theatre (above left) in detail (above right);*
supping in Max & Ermas (lower left) or in dining car coziness (lower right).

"family was still a strong premise then, and families helped each other out as a matter of ordinary pride." Welfare workers became part of those families, because "a lot of family support systems" began to disintegrate and "people didn't move as much then."

But sometime around 1960 or 1961, "we began to lose the clients, because we got so many federal regulations," said Hoofstetter. "Welfare was getting to be a much larger thing, just too much for local areas to handle." Within the next decade, the caseload per worker increased to as many as 350 families per month. And a vicious cycle began recurring for the displaced poor in all parts of town. When the welfare checks did not arrive on time and the poor could not pay their rent, they had to move to another place. By the time welfare department records recorded the address change, the next check arrived late, and the renter had to move again.

Still, Columbus, in the early '60s (as it had been throughout most of its history) was populated by a majority of middle-to upper-middle-class white-collar workers in government, business, universities, research offices and professional complexes. The Protestant work ethic predominated (as it still does), along with the pleasure of spending (savings set aside first) on personal amenities or amusements.

In 1961, Kenley Players Summer Theater was formed. It was the brainchild of John Kenley, an ageless theater professional who worked with the Shuberts on Broadway for many years.

In 1944, after the war, John Kenley decided "to use big Broadway, Hollywood and television stars in live shows," according to Joe Vispi, associate producer of Kenley Players. That was "in a little 400-seat theater he started at a place called Deer Lake Park, Pennsylvania, in the Pocono Mountains." He moved to a 1200-seat theater in Lakewood, Pennsylvania, where Joe Vispi, of Wilkes-Barre, Pennsylvania, first encountered Kenley. In interviews with Columbus Monthly, Vispi confessed to being hopelessly stage-struck "from the time I was a fourth-grader and I went to my first film and saw Bette Davis. I fell in love with her and that was that. All those gods and goddesses up there on that screen, bigger than life . . . that's what I wanted, to be with them."

In 1948, Vispi took pre-med at Pennsylvania State University, but he "hated . . . dissecting frogs," got "terribly ill and wound up in the college infirmary with shingles." His parents let him go into theater courses after that, and by his sophomore year, he was on the dean's list, "doing all the college shows."

That year a Hollywood studio began a search for an unknown actor to play Rudolph Valentino. One of Vispi's teachers submitted his photo, and he was called to Hollywood for tests. But Vispi lost out because "my eyelids were a bit too heavy, darlings, even though they did try to hold them up with patches for three days." However, he was signed as a contract player, as "a possible young James Mason," and he did bit parts in This Gun for Hire and Sea of Grass before he was released. "My timing was all wrong," Vispi said. "Just as I came along, urbane types were going out, and the new

stars were rough and ready types."

In 1949, enroute to Broadway to try his luck, Vispi and his wife Annie stopped in his hometown. They saw a newspaper ad for Kenley Players Lakewood Theater and went to see John Garfield do Golden Boy.

They met Kenley and were hired to work the rest of the summer at $25 a week — "$12.50 each," Vispi emphasized. When Kenley decided to establish a summer theater in Columbus in 1961, it was his then-trusted assistant Joe Vispi who was dispatched as producer, along with Annie to take charge of the box office.

At that time, most Columbusites had not seen anyone like Vispi — one of those "theater people," reed-slim, wearing designer sport jackets, dashingly tossed neck scarves and cravats and one of the first masculine shoulder handbags. It was a choice part, and Vispi performed it with camp and elán. Vispi was the best performer Kenley ever hired. Paul Lynde of Mount Vernon, Ohio, was the most popular box office attraction over the years and holder of most of the house records for attendance. But resident Joe Vispi — playing an eighteenth century court fop, redolent of cologne and decadence — was the first and most enduring attraction of the Kenley Players.

Another Columbus institution is (former astronaut) Ohio Senator John Glenn. He grew up in New Concord, Ohio, married his high school sweetheart Annie Castor and left Muskingum College when the World War II broke out. Since Glenn had always had an interest in flying, he went into the flying division of the Marine Corps. He flew 59 combat missions in F-4U Corsairs in the Marshall Islands campaign in the Pacific Theatre. After the war, he served as a flight instructor and took early training on jet airplanes. He had a "cool head and a keen eye." In Korea, he went into combat as a jet pilot in "Mig Alley" above the Yalu River, racked up 63 fighter bomber missions with the Marine Corps and 23 as an exchange pilot with the Air Force. On one occasion, he flew back with 300 bullet holes in his plane; on another, he was forced to glide 80 miles "dead stick" to base after using all his fuel to help another pilot in an air fight. In 1957, he became a test pilot — the most dangerous task any flier can undertake — and set a coast-to-coast record by flying an F8U Crusader from Los Angeles to New York in three hours, 23 minutes. Many times Glenn picked up the pieces of fellow test pilots whose experimental crafts (or split-second reflexes) had failed.

He was one of the "original seven Mercury Astronauts" chosen by NASA. On February 20, 1961, after 10 aborted launch schedules, John Glenn became the first American to orbit the earth. During the latter part of the orbit, a heat shield came loose. Sensing something wrong, Glenn deviated from ground control, went to manual control and diverted disaster.

Asked if he were afraid, Glenn has always answered in a light vein. "Sure. How do you think you'd feel sitting in something built by the lowest bidder on a government contract? But somebody had to bite the bullet and do it."

Glenn retired from the Marine Corps in 1965. He and

JACK SENSENBRENNER

Maynard E. "Jack" Sensenbrenner.

Maynard E. ("Jack") Sensenbrenner was mayor of Columbus longer than any single individual in the city's history. Once he was elected, there were people (especially Jack Sensenbrenner) who thought he might never leave. "I expect to run for mayor 50 terms," he exulted once. "Why should I quit when we're making real progress in this city? Why, it's DY-NAM-IC!"

"Dy-namic" was one of Sensenbrenner's favorite adjectives. A wiry little fellow, he only weighed "140 pounds with wet sponges on both feet, but I got the gift of gab" — not just gab, but a quality he called "Spizzerinctum". Roughly translated, that was a combination of guts and chutzpah, "1,000 times greater than enthusiasm!" That gift — and his unabashedly sentimental, old-fashioned flag-waving patriotism — made him the most colorful mayor the city ever experienced.

Sensenbrenner and his twin brother Marion were born in Circleville, Ohio, on September 18, 1902. As a child, he had his picture taken upon a jackass, and it was his fondness for that animal which led to his nickname, Jack. ("My friends leave off the rest.") Conceding he was known as an "ornery" boy, young Jack was so industrious that he "spent many a day picking peas for five cents a bucket. And my mother got the nickel," he would add hastily. (That story earned him the epithet "pea-pickin' mayor" during his first run for office.)

During the 1920s, Sensenbrenner left his hometown and went to the west coast. He worked as a hardware clerk, a ditch-digger in the oil fields of California, an ad salesman, a police reporter for the *Los Angeles*

Times, an extra in the 1926 film *Ben Hur* ("they paid me $5 a day to sit in the Coliseum") and in slack times, "the best Fuller Brush salesman on the west coast."

When his high school girlfriend, Mildred, joined him on the coast and they were married in 1927, he decided they should settle down in Columbus. They lived on the west side many years. There he continued his activities as "a practicing Boy Scout for over 50 years," served on the Ohio Civil Service Commission and owned a religious bookstore. He was also involved in community activities nearly 20 years, gaining a reputation as "Johnny on the Spot" when someone was needed to lead a Boy Scout troop, give an after-dinner speech at the Kiwanis Club or teach Sunday School classes.

One night in May 1953, he strolled into a meeting of the Franklin County Democratic Committee and — legend has it — said "The name is Sensenbrenner." He tilted his straw hat. "I want to run for Mayor. I hope you'll back me."

No Democrat had gained City Hall since 1932. He hit Columbus with a

brand of grass-roots, flag-waving, Bible-quoting politicking which has become a vanishing art form. He spoke to as many as eight to ten groups a night, sometimes at precinct meetings attended by no more than 25 persons, sometimes at neighborhood club outings, even at funeral homes where he would stop to visit the bereaved of persons whose obituaries he had clipped out of the morning paper. He would pump hands everywhere along the streets of Columbus, quote the Bible (referring to God as the "Great Scoutmaster"), practice not only Americanism but Boosterism, sincerely proclaiming Columbus "the goingest, growingest town ever!" And when all else failed, he would quote poems by Ella Wheeler Wilcox or Francis Willard. In the last month of the six-month campaign, he made over 180 speeches, promising to "sweep City Hall clean" and be the city's "most fightingest mayor ever."

In November 1953, he was elected mayor and continued to serve fourteen years — 1954-1960, 1964-1968 and 1968-1972. When he took office, he was the first Democrat to hold that position since Henry Worley in 1932.

Wherever he goes today, everyone still addresses M.E. "Jack" Sensenbrenner simply as "mayor". Seventy-eight now, he refuses to "head for Florida and be one of them old birds who play shuffleboard." Surrounded by wall-to-wall mementos of his colorful life and career, he asks only one favor of posterity. "I guess what I'd like people to say about me later is, 'Here was a guy who saw life and helped lift the level of the age he lived in. He didn't just eat, burp and go home!'"

FIRE FIGHTERS: *An antique fire engine on parade (above) and a Columbus fireman in the snow (inset).*

Annie decided to make Columbus home. When he was elected to the Senate in 1974, Glenn said, "This is no ego trip. I have already had more recognition in my life than anyone could want in 20 lifetimes. It wouldn't bother me a bit if nobody recognizes me on the street again. What I feel is not a desire for personal glory but a challenge to help make the world a better place for my kids and the ones to come."

In 1957, the late Fred Lazarus Sr. speculated to the Newcomen Society: "Let us assume that in the course of a millenium, our civilization has been surpassed and lies buried, like the seven cities of Troy. Let us picture to ourselves . . . some future archaeologist who, digging in the ruins . . . comes upon . . . remains of a department store! A department store would give our archaeologist material for a lifetime of well-founded conjecture . . . He could deduce, with reasonable accuracy, what was precious to us, what we considered necessary, the things we worked for, the fabric of our day-to-day lives. A department store is a living mirror of our civilization in which we see the constantly changing needs and wishes of our people."

That is a valid premise. If an archaeologist in the next century examined the Lazarus' downtown store of the '60s, he would find three-footed metal fire bowls with grill tops (altars for religious sacrifices?). On one floor, a sign with the legend would read "Boutique". There

would be women's garments with no sleeves and barely enough cloth to reach the knees, small round hats resembling flying saucers, and on white headshapes with no faces, headdresses of some type of hair, very high and round on top. Without a Rosetta stone for the 1960s, he would not know the display was fashioned after the bouffant-teased hairdos and pillbox hats made popular by First Lady Jacqueline Kennedy. He would not be able to picture people wandering in a daze on the streets outside that store in November 1963, tears coursing down most faces as they heard President John F. Kennedy had been shot. Kennedy once said there was "no town in the country where I get a warmer welcome, and fewer votes, than in Columbus, Ohio." But Columbus — with its national reputation for moderation and Republicanism — grieved openly for the next three days, while endless television sets broadcast nightmare pictures of Jacqueline Kennedy in her blood-stained suit, the coffin being carried from the airplane, the shooting of Lee Harvey Oswald and the funeral procession with the riderless white horse. The subsequent assassinations of Martin Luther King and Robert Kennedy were like further reels of horror movies run at the wrong speed. "Future shock" had set in.

Lyndon Johnson escalated the country's involvement in Vietnam, as did Richard Nixon. As the body count mounted in Vietnam, there was also blood in the streets

POWER TO THE PEOPLE: *Ohio State University student strike, May 1970 (above); People's Action Union demonstration at the Statehouse, 1978.*

at home. Dissension over the war, as well as the black civil-rights movement erupted in violence. Columbus reacted more moderately to those national events than many other cities its size. But the turbulence could not be kept outside the city.

On September 27, 1967, Mount Vernon Avenue — the main artery of Columbus' inner city — was the site of what newspapers called a "disturbance" rather than a riot.

A *Citizen-Journal* reporter walked down Mount Vernon the next day. It was nearly empty of people except for cruising policemen and workmen hammering plywood over broken windows. People hid inside their houses. "I don't know what all this trouble is about," said Ceatrice Garrison, a 56-year-old Monroe Street woman taking care of five grandchildren. (She had stayed awake all night, fearful.) "What I figure is, the people that are causing the racket must have come from somewhere else, like Dayton. The same people always causes rackets everywhere." Johnnie Mae Moore, young mother with a nine-month-old baby, had "strolled down to the store" the previous night. "All I know is a whole lot of folks were making fools of themselves out on Mount Vernon. My brother-in-law told me night before last there might be trouble. My father, he said, 'anyone [around] this house acting like a fool, you shoot first and ask questions later.' I don't know where the gun is, so [when] people

158

NEW CENTURIONS: *Columbus police force patrols on motorcycles, circa 1925 (above); a modern-day officer directs city traffic (inset).*

. . . knocked on the door, I wouldn't let nobody in."

Sam Keaton, an 81-year-old man with a ruffled three-inch shock of white hair, looked cheerful. "Why not? I've ducked everything that would have brought me down. I came out of a Georgia cotton patch at 19. You know who your friends are? Them dollars in the Huntington Bank. I keep my meat bag full and live independent. This trouble — I never thought it would happen here. I don't understand nothing without a cause, don't make sense."

A North Garfield Avenue woman, Mrs. Jackie Harris, was keeping seven children on $250-a-month welfare. Her living room was neat, filled with her children's art. Her eyes filled with tears when she talked. "There was a crowd, mostly youngsters . . . and this man with a microphone running around yelling 'Black Power!' But the people with those stores they ruined are kind to all of us. If you didn't have a dime, they'd wait. They won't have . . . money to build these stores back. People who demolish what little we [have] are no help."

On a streetcorner, young men, mostly in their 20s, clustered around the Cafe Society. They identified themselves, laughing, as "Rap Brown & Associates." "I'm not ashamed of what I am," Thomas Page, 24, said. "I'm proud of being a nigger. Not enough of us are proud."

Harold Williams, a 24-year-old Marine veteran, responded, "I've been out of the service two years now and not a decent job yet . . . . Rats in these houses climb right in bed with the babies . . . .White folks cringe when they hear the words black power, and they don't even understand what we mean. What we're talking about is the power of the dollar . . . the ability to do something, educate ourselves . . . not tearing down and destruction."

That night, a coalition of black and white leaders from all over the city walked those streets, going door to door, talking and urging moderation. The feared second night of violence did not come.

Although violence haunted the black community for the next several years, the city never experienced the nightmare confrontations of prolonged violence that plagued so many eastern cities. In July 1969, a very serious two-day riot prompted the calling out of the Ohio National Guard. But even in this confrontation, only one life was lost and damage was limited to a small area.

Troubles were minimal because of the reputation, power and influence of the Urban League which, in Columbus, argued against the forces of militancy and confrontation. Another factor was the spatial distribution of the black community. Since the end of World War II, the black community has been centralized on the near east side, but it had taken an ever-increasing share of areas which included single family houses on tree-lined streets.

FROM ARMORY TO ARTS: *The Ohio National Guard Armory, built in 1860, is now home for the Cultural Arts Center, its courtyard (right) and weaving area (left).*

Perhaps the most important reason was the feeling much of the black community had that progress was being made. With the passage of the Civil Rights Act of 1964, the federal government pledged increasingly large sums of money to assist in the social and cultural rehabilitation of inner cities. In the late '60s, many new organizations emerged to ease the plight of the poor. The Columbus Metropolitan Area Community Action Organization (CMACAO) and the Model Cities program contributed valuable services in the areas of health, education, public welfare, minority enterprise and neighborhood control of civic services. Supported and complemented by older groups like the NAACP, the Urban League, the East Central Citizens Organization, and the Mount Vernon District Improvement Association, many residents of the near east side felt that government and society were making preliminary efforts to solve the problems.

That same year, 1968, a burly figure of a man from Mechanicsburg, Ohio — within tobacco-spitting distance of Columbus — went to the Senate. William B. (Bart) Saxbe had been commuting to Columbus since 1947. The son of a Mechanicsburg cattle dealer, Saxbe was considered a "maverick" Republican. His honesty made him popular with the party and the voters and he was elected to the Ohio House of Representatives in 1947. His platform, just after World War II, was succinct — "I need the job." "Veterans were popular that year," he explained in a *Columbus Monthly* profile. Re-elected to

the Ohio House for three terms, he was Speaker of the House from 1953-54, was elected Attorney General of the State of Ohio in 1956, defeated in 1958 and re-elected in 1966. In 1968, after swearing he would never run for the U.S. Senate, "I had moments of lucidity," he ran and was elected. "I spent the first six months wondering how I got there and the next six months wondering how the rest of them got there." Saxbe was a severe critic of President Richard Nixon, but he wound up as Attorney General of the United States. Nixon needed someone, "independent" to shore up what was left of his reputation after the discovery of Watergate, and he could not have put in anyone more independent. Saxbe emerged as one of the few members of the Nixon cabinet not to go to jail.

In May 1970, four Kent State students were shot on campus in an anti-war demonstration. Violence broke out on campuses all across the country in the wake of that tragedy. Governor James A. Rhodes — who had sent the National Guard onto the Kent State campus — also urged Ohio State University officials to close the school on May 6 to stem the violence simmering in crowds of protestors. It was the first closing in OSU's history. But there was no bloodshed on campus.

As Columbus entered the 1970s, emotions were mixed. The Vietnam War dragged on. Campuses were still afire with protest of what had come to be called Mr. Nixon's War. Public acceptance of continued effort to improve the lots of minority Americans had cooled as

HISTORY LIVES: A blacksmith works in his shop at Ohio Village (left); the Ohio Historical Center (inset) includes a communication's exhibit (right).

more middle-class whites felt the poor were receiving too many tax dollars with too little return. In the neighborhoods occupied by those who had suffered the twin disasters of depression and war, America seemed to have "gone soft". To many, the presidential campaign of George Wallace made sense, and Wallace's American Independent Party did quite well in Ohio until he was wounded in 1972.

On the other hand, much of the local black community was also disillusioned. Militant leaders in the black community were less satisfied with minority responses to forceful change. Increasingly, they adopted a more pragmatic view which stressed separatism from the white community. Recognizing the increasing hostility of whites to programs for black uplift, the black community stressed less integration and cooperation and more social and cultural enhancement of the black community itself.

While the passions of the 1960s were cooling, life was going on in Columbus. An increasingly literate and sophisticated young America began to leave college and trade schools and move into the work force. They were different from their parents. Accustomed to economic stability, they generally were more open-minded on social issues, less reluctant to adapt to change and more interested in the intangible than the concrete, symbols of the good life. At least they thought they were. By the middle '70s, they were marrying and starting families. They were marrying later and often more on the basis of hardheaded planning than impulse. They were also divorcing more frequently. As the decade progressed and

the responsibilities of family life became apparent, many of their illusions about a new generation changed.

With increasing prices of energy much of the assumed nature of the good life — affordable cars, nice homes and easy entertainment — was replaced by the hard realities of galloping inflation, hard times and the growing realization that people really did have to work for a living. There were more working mothers and two-paycheck families. Purchase of material goods were often postponed because of dwindling disposable income. Suddenly the tangible symbols of success were no longer just symbols. In many cases, they were necessities.

To many Columbusites, the court ordered desegregation of the Columbus public schools and subsequent student busing programs were among the major challenges of the decade. Busing worked extremely well in Columbus. There was no violence, and the program produced favorable national publicity. Public school officials credited the whole community — business leaders, teachers, parents, clergy and administrators — for successfully achieving peaceful integration. However, the busing program has contributed to the general trend of movement to the suburbs by white middle class families.

Present-day white middle class households tend to have fewer children than did previous generations; thus the black student population is an increasing portion of the total enrollment. White families with school age children have left Columbus for the suburbs, but it is likely that the trend toward racially balanced metropolitan schools may someday affect suburban school districts as well.

161

FOR THE FUTURE: *Architectural renderings (facing page, top left and right) show sleek, clean lines of a new Port Columbus for the many planes that land and take off there. The Galbreath hotel and office complex (right) will be part of Capitol South (outlined above), a redevelopment area of downtown Columbus. Opening day ceremonies, autumn 1980, of the city's new convention center (below) were well attended.*

Tom Moody, mayor of Columbus.

COLUMBUS MAYORS

Jarvis Pike	1816-1817
John Kerr	1818-1819
Eli C. King	1820-1822
John Laughrey	1823
William T. Martin	1824-1826
James Robinson	1827
William Long	1827-1833
Philo H. Olmstead	1833
John Brooks	1834-
John Bailhache	1835
Warren Jenkins	1836-1837
Philo H. Olmstead	1838-1839
John G. Miller	1840-
Thomas Wood	1841
Abram I. McDowell	1842
Smithson E. Wright	1843-1844
Alexander Patton	1845
Augustus S. Decker	1846
Alexander Patton	1847-1849
Lorenzo English	1850-1861
Wray Thomas	1861-1864
James G. Bull	1865-1868
George W. Meeker	1869-1870
James G. Bull	1871-1874
John H. Heitman	1875-1878
Gilbert G. Collins	1879-1880
George S. Peters	1881-1882
Charles C. Walcutt	1883-1886
Philip H. Bruck	1887-1890
George J. Karb	1891-1894
Cotton H. Allen	1895-1896
Samuel L. Black	1897-1898
Samuel J. Swartz	1899-1900
John N. Hinkle	1901-1902
Robert H. Jeffrey	1903-1905
DeWitt C. Badger	1906-1907
Charles A. Bond	1908-1909
George S. Marshall	1910-1911
George J. Karb	1912-1919
James J. Thomas	1920-1931
Henry W. Worley	1932-1935
Myron B. Gessaman	1933-1939
Floyd F. Green	1940-1943
James A. Rhodes	1944-1953
Robert T. Oestreicher	1953
Maynard E. Sensenbrenner	1954-1959
W. Ralston Westlake	1960-1963
Maynard E. Sensenbrenner	1964-1971
Tom Moody	1972-Current

STATEHOUSE SQUARE: *Domed rotunda of the state office building (upper left); young visitor climbs a cannon on display (left).*

The resolution of this unequal situation is one of the key challenges of the 1980s.

Columbus also experienced a change in leadership as Republican Tom Moody defeated Maynard Sensenbrenner. Moody — much younger, more sophisticated and low-key than his rival — set the tone for much of Columbus in the 1970s. Moody's election signaled the simple fact that Columbus was now a new city, filled with people who were swayed less by party affiliation than by the qualifications of the person seeking the post. The same philosophy accounted for the election of Dr. John Rosemond to the city council in 1970 as well. Rosemond was the first black to be elected to the council in more than 50 years. And while his election signaled the increasing importance of the black community, the majority of his votes came from white voters.

The city was growing again. The downtown was transformed by such redevelopment projects of the 1960s as Market Mohawk, but until the 1970s the restoration of downtown was not fully implemented. Throughout the '60s, as slum clearance and redevelopment proceeded, more people moved to the suburbs which expanded in all directions. With the completion of the Outerbelt, the growth of little villages such as Hilliard, Dublin, Reynoldsburg and Grove City was phenomenal. It seemed, then, that there was no limit to continued metropolitan expansion, and this expansion was no longer limited to the middle class. Independent communities like Upper Arlington and Bexley continued to grow as well, while whole new exclusive subdivisions continued to be built.

But there was another movement developing — the return of the middle class to the city. By the mid-1970s, Columbus had six active restoration districts — The Driving Park and Olde Towne East in addition to the German Village, Victorian and Italian villages (on the north) and Hungarian Village (on the far south end). The middle-class moving into these districts faced many of the same problems that their predecessors in German Village had — reluctant bank financing, difficult restoration problems and the hostility of established residents to newcomers. The past ten years in the older districts of downtown have seen the first fundamental reversal of the principle that populations will separate by distance and class on the basis of available transportation, (a principle which has guided growth for the past 100 years).

The downtown is also on the verge of an urban revival. With the implementation of Section 1728 grants in the mid-'70s, Columbus began the process of rebuilding its downtown. In late 1980, the Ohio Center — a magnificent convention facility with hotel accommodations — opened on the site of the former Union Station. Near the Statehouse, the Capitol South Redevelopment Project was moving ahead. A four-block area south of the Statehouse was completely redeveloped, leaving such landmarks as the fully-restored Ohio Theatre. The opening of these two facilities alone will guarantee a new rebirth of nightlife as well as growth for the downtown. Complementing the Statehouse is the new

PARK PLACES: *Franklin Park Conservatory (top); July 4 dedication ceremonies of Bicentennial Park, 1976 (above).*

BancOhio Headquarters at Third and Broad. Across the square is the State Office Tower erected in 1974, and near the convention center is the new Nationwide Insurance Building completed in 1979.

The Ohio Center will be linked with Capitol South by the massive redevelopment and rehabilitation of High Street. This includes new landscaping and the narrowing of High Street from six lanes to two in order to install overhead walkways and malls along the street from the center to the courthouse. The civic center around City Hall will be expanded to include new office and parking facilities for city government. Bracketing the north end of the riverfront will be the new headquarters building of the American Electric Power Company. To the south, Bicentennial Park and the Arsenal Cultural Arts Center will be enhanced by residential condominiums on the riverfront.

In 1980, controlling interest in Buckeye International was purchased by Worthington Industries, a local steel fabrication company celebrating its 25th anniversary. Buckeye was the only one of the steel companies founded before 1900 which still remains. Worthington was founded by John H. McConnell in 1955 in his home with $600 borrowed on his car and $1800 savings. It is now a leading manufacturer of pressure cylinders.

WOODY HAYES

Hayes was born in Clifton, Ohio, in 1913. When his father became school superintendent of Newcomerstown, Ohio, Hayes told *Ohio Magazine* in an October 1978 profile, that he became, at an early age, part and parcel of "Noble County, the hilliest and least populated area of Ohio." It was home turf for his forebears, grandfather Isaac Hayes, who had "been orphaned at the battle of Antietam . . . in 1862, [was] put into several homes and . . . escaped and came into that area and ran into a beautiful German girl." That grandmother, Maria Hoffman, provided "the smarts in the family. There were some geniuses among them." Isaac and Maria Hoffman Hayes had twelve children, one of whom — Wayne Benton Hayes — married Effie Jane Hupp of that area. They had three children: Woody's late brother, Ike, once an All-American guard at Iowa State University, then a veterinarian; Mary Hayes North, a vaudeville actress who co-starred with George Jessel then teamed with her husband to write radio shows; and the baby, Wayne Woodrow Hayes, who was "favored by his mother."

Hayes opted, after five years in the Navy and commanding two ships, to get a master's degree in Educational Administration at OSU. He had already taught English and coached high school football at Mingo Junction and New

OSU's Woody Hayes

Philadelphia, Ohio. After his discharge, he coached three years at his alma mater (1935) Denison University, then two years at Miami University in Oxford before making his debut at Ohio State in 1951.

The coaching staff left behind by the resigned Wes Fesler was looking out the football office windows to get a glimpse

of the new man. Hayes arrived at the parking lot, pulled his car into a tight space (there aren't many other kinds) allotted for staff cars, and found he could not open either his left or right hand doors. He sat there for awhile, obviously in deep thought. The coaching staff watched. Hayes backed out, got behind his car's rear bumper and *pushed* it into the exact amount of allotted space. "What's odd about that?" he asks. "Worked, didn't it?"

Woody Hayes' coaching record ended in January 1979 with a remarkable total — during his 28 years at Ohio State alone — of 205 wins, 61 losses and ten ties — a winning percentage of .760.

Only two Big Ten coaches ever coached longer than Wayne Woodrow Hayes' 28 years — Amos Alonzo Stagg, with 41 years at Chicago, and Bob Zuppke at Illinois, for 29. Hayes ranks fourth among all major college coaches in terms of victories, led only by "Bear" Bryant (still coaching in Alabama) and the late Glenn "Pop" Warner and Amos Alonzo Stagg. Hayes used to theorize that "winning was damn near everything; without winning, there is no civilization." With his chin stuck out defiantly after being ousted from a profession where he'd done that first and foremost, despite controversy, he declared he'd been wrong to say that. "Winning," he concluded finally, "is *everything.*"

THE OLD AND NEW: *Mercy Hospital (below), Hawkes Hospital (bottom), a dissection class at Ohio Medical University circa 1890 (right) and Doctors Hospital (lower right).*

Preparing for the race, Marysville Balloon and Air Show.

R. David Thomas had built his Wendy's hamburger chain from one store in Columbus into a national and international organization, second only to McDonald's in size and influence. These two make up two sides of an important point about Columbus business. On one hand, the older established companies have adapted well to late twentieth-century business practices. On the other, Columbus has been fertile ground for developing small service and research-oriented industries.

Back in the 1950s, *Readers Digest* latched onto Columbus as a test city because its demographic, economic and social make-up was remarkably representative of America as a whole. Since the late 1950s, Columbus has been a test market by America's manufacturers for a little of everything. Some of the products tested, such as paper diapers with flexible gathers, have succeeded. Others — milk packaged in plastic bags — did not. But out of this test market experience, Columbus was selected by Warner Communications to be the test market for its latest innovation — interactive cable television. Begun in 1976, the QUBE system not only provides 30 channels of interference-free television, (including channels devoted exclusively to children, religion, sports and adult

movies), it permits the daring viewer to talk back via pushbuttons on a control box in his living room. Viewers have registered their opinions on new products, the merits of political candidates, and programming. But the high point came in mid-1980 when QUBE telecast a local semi-pro football game with the viewers calling the signals of the home team by remote control. (In a perhaps unrelated development, the home team folded shortly after the game.)

Columbus has produced some notable people. It has had some moments of tragedy and comedy. But all cities have such people and such moments. What makes Columbus different is that it is a state capital in the Midwest and sits strategically at that point where New England met the South on the beginning of the journey west to find America. For that reason, it became a crossroads of the people, ideas and innovations that have made Columbus what it is. It has resolutely avoided being dominated by any of them. It remains now, as it has always been, a city of symbols — of the state, the region, the city and the people who made it. Its fascination is that it is America in miniature. With all its faults and imperfections, it is still a pretty good place to live.

SIGNS OF THE TIMES

The trend of the '70s was reflected by items listed under a December 21, 1979, *Citizen-Journal* headline, "The '70s: Columbus Survives a Turbulent Decade."

• January, 1970. Dr. John Rosemond . . . sworn in as a city councilman, the first black man in this century elected to municipal office in a citywide election.

• April 29, 1970. Mayor M. E. Sensenbrenner declares an emergency in the Ohio State University area racked by student rioting. Ohio National Guardsmen move up North High Street with fixed bayonets to bring order. Meanwhile, Governor James Rhodes orders more than 3,700 guardsmen to Ohio highways to quiet the "open warfare" of a 29-day-old Teamster strike.

• November 3, 1970. Democrat John J. Gilligan edges out Republican Roger Cloud to become Ohio's 62nd governor.

• March 8, 1971. Racial tensions erupt . . . over alleged racism in Columbus public schools. The incident results in early closings and vandalism to several downtown stores.

• November 2, 1971. (Republican) Tom Moody, 41-year-old Republican dark-horse and former municipal court judge beats four-term incumbent M. E. Sensenbrenner to become Columbus's 44th mayor.

• April 4, 1972. Central Ohio Transit Authority agrees to buy Columbus Transit Company from Columbus & Southern Ohio Electric Co. for $5,436,335.

• May 12, 1972. Police and . . . up to 1,500 anti-war demonstrators clash violently, resulting in 68 arrests and $3,000 damage.

• January 24, 1973. James Rhodes . . . thwarted in attempt to run for a third term as Ohio governor when petitions are refused on constitutional grounds. Five months later, the Ohio Supreme Court rules Rhodes could serve a third term as governor

Don't walk on the ice.

without violating the constitution's ban on "two successive terms of four years."

• February 14, 1973. U.S. District Judge Joseph Kinneary strikes down Ohio's century-old abortion law. The first Ohio abortion is performed the next day and plans announced for an abortion clinic.

• June 14, 1973. Nationwide Insurance announces it will build a $150 million, 40-story office tower at Spring and High streets.

• November 2, 1974. James Rhodes wins his third four-year term as Ohio governor by defeating incumbent Democrat John J. Gilligan 1,485,977 to 1,475,799.

• January 6, 1975. Columbus teachers stay off jobs in the city's first teacher strike. Common Pleas Court orders teachers back into classrooms four days later.

• January 9, 1975. Franklin County charitable institutions awarded $89 million as Battelle Memorial Foundation's charity liability from 1929 to 1974, after a six-year legal battle.

• January 25, 1975. *Columbus Dispatch* publisher Edgar T. Wolfe, businessman Carlton S. Dargush Jr., Frederick W. LeVeque and two pilots killed when their airplane strikes a radio tower near Washington, D.C.

• December 2, 1975. Ohio State University tailback Archie Griffin becomes the first player ever to twice win the Heisman Trophy.

• January 17, 1977. Central Ohio records coldest day of the century . . . minus nineteen degrees. Temperatures do not rise above freezing and snow continually covers the ground from December 26.

• January 27, 1977. Rhodes declares natural gas crisis in face of severe weather warning for weekend. Columbus schools close Monday. 25,000 area workers expected to be laid off as production plants shut down.

• February 1, 1977. City schools plan to conserve energy by closing until March 7, launching nationally-praised "school without schools" program, with lessons broadcast by radio and television and classes held in homes.

• April 22, 1977. Hungry baseball fans ignore rain to turn out 15,721 strong for the first Columbus Clippers game as baseball returns to the old Jet Stadium, now refurbished and renamed Franklin County Stadium.

• January 26, 1978. A raging killer blizzard, the worst in U.S. history lambasts Ohio, packing gusting winds up to 80 mph. and -60° chill factor, crippling entire state. Schools, businesses and most activity throughout state are shut down.

• January 30, 1978. Electric crisis looms as stockpiled coal dwindles or freezes up and 54-day-old UMW strike crawls on.

• February 9, 1978. Governor Rhodes declares a state of emergency and asks President Carter to exempt Ohio utilities and industries from federal coal-burning regulations.

• August 12, 1978. Confusion reigns as Supreme Court Justice William Rehnquist stays the desegregation of Columbus schools.

• July 2, 1979. U.S. Supreme Court upholds system-wide desegregation plans for Columbus schools.

STATE UNIVERSITY: The "college in the corn field," circa 1900 (bottom facing page); University Hall (top facing page); The Oval (top); graduation day (right); Mirror Lake (above).

GOOD SPORTS: A young golfer rose to national prominence as a student at OSU. Columbus claims Jack Nicklaus (above) as a favorite son. The Columbus Magic on the soccer field (below left); OSU football team on home turf (below right); harness racing (bottom left) and motorcycle racing on ice (bottom right).

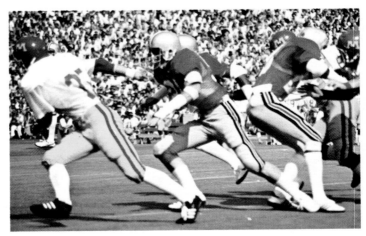

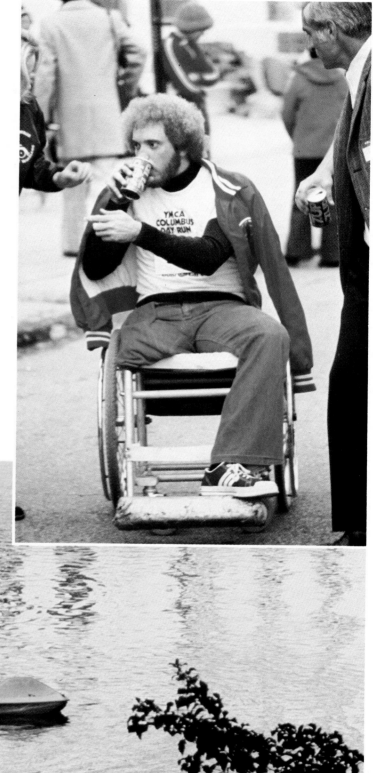

COLUMBUS OUTDOORS: *The Columbus Clippers draw baseball fans (above left); a participant takes a break at the YMCA's annual Columbus Day Run (above right); a paddleboat tour of downtown via the Scioto River (below).*

POPULATION BY DECADE IN "AMERICA'S CROSSROADS"

Prior to 1840, there was no official census recording Columbus' population separately from Franklin County. At that time, the county designation was assigned and counts were recorded for both the county and the city. Black people were counted separately from whites in the three census prior to 1840. The term "free colored" was used until the census of 1879 when it was changed to "colored."

In 1815, Columbus was officially incorporated as a borough. Approximately 700 residents were in the new city, and the official census of 1810 indicated the presence of 43 "free coloreds" in a population of slightly over 6,000 in Franklin County. 1820 (Columbus: 1,450 whites; 132 "free coloreds". Franklin County: 10,300. 1830 2,438 whites; 216 "males and females of African descent." Unofficial count for Columbus 2,435; Franklin County — 14,756. 1840 Unofficial count of both caucasians and blacks, approximately 6,048; Franklin County 24,880.

	Columbus	Franklin County
1850	17,882	42,909
1860	18,554	53,217
1870	31,274	63,524
1880	51,647	86,797
1890	88,150	124,087
1900	125,560	164,460
1910	181,511	222,567
1920	237,031	283,951
1930	290,564	361,055
1940	306,087	388,712
1950	375,901	503,410
1960	471,316	682,962
1970	539,677	833,249
1980	545,980	843,788

McKinley statue on Statehouse grounds.

PARTNERS
IN
PROGRESS

German Furniture Company, 1884.

A community is born when people gather together for their mutual benefit. They barter and trade services and skills. As they grow, demand increases. Others are hired to expand and provide more skills and services. More people move in because there are jobs and because of the services. The community becomes a town, a city.

Columbus began with entrepreneurs and businessmen who understood the process of growth and free enterprise. Their abilities made Columbus grow and prosper. Many of the city's leading businesses have lent their support and financial commitment to *Columbus: America's Crossroads*. They have provided their corporate histories which follow.

The crossroads of America were as vital to the economic development of Columbus yesterday as they continue to be today. Through Columbus's history, transportation — a factor second only to its early designation as the state capital — has played an influential role in the city's continued success. Columbus's early accessibility to the marketplace via the National Road and the arrival of the railroads in the 1850s were the first indications of the recurring role transportation would play.

In 1820 there was little indication that Columbus and Franklin County would one day dominate the mid-Ohio region. The county population grew from 10,300 people in 1820 to 86,882 in 1880. Columbus had become a miniature western metropolis with roads extending in all directions when the Columbus Board of Trade was founded in 1858. The Columbus & Xenia Railroad went into operation for the first time that year. Two other railroads — the Central Ohio and the Columbus, Cincinnati and Cleveland — were off the drawing boards. The city itself had grown from 6,408 in 1840 to 17,882 in 1850.

Before 1858, there had been no effort to attract new businesses and manufacturers to Columbus. By that year, the business community realized a need to alert the public to patronize local industries in order to stimulate local business growth. Proposed industries were being stolen away by other Ohio cities, and irate businessmen decided something had to be done.

Yet there were those who questioned the desirability of a political center being involved in any large industrial enterprise. Investment in industry still seemed like a great big risk to the folks in Columbus who primarily were involved in agricultural or commercial enterprises. Early business leaders such as Sullivant and Goodale had made their money in real estate. Still, Ridgeway, Gill (later to be president of the Board of Trade) and Hayden (another Board of Trade stalwart) all had made their fortunes in iron and steel.

Newspapers continuously promoted the business and industrial interests and planted the seeds of the idea for a Board of Trade. Finally, various forces

The Variety Store, 214 North High Street, in 1872.

culminated in the inevitable need for a united front in the business community.

The existence of a board of trade could influence those reluctant capitalists whose financial backing was necessary to maintain a labor market and create new industry. It could serve as a watchdog against fraud. (Flour in the markets of local millers was found short in weight. A liquor tax was eating into the profit of local businesses. Needed agricultural products were being grown locally but shipped out of state for extra profit.)

The first program of the board was largely educational. The method of operation was to pinpoint a business problem, do research and study and report back to the board which then took action. In 1858, those actions included beautifying city parks (specifically, removing hucksters and prostitutes from Goodale Park), endorsing several Columbus business colleges and sponsoring a celebration for the laying of the Atlantic cable.

Beginning in 1870, Columbus entered a period of accelerated economic growth. Three related factors contributed to this upsurge. The population began growing even more rapidly; by the year 1900, 125,560 people were living in Columbus. Expansion of the rail system made the resources and raw materials of southeastern Ohio readily available, providing wider markets and greater investment opportunities. Coal became the key to manufacturing growth from 1870 to 1900. Coal from southeastern Ohio permitted the rapid expansion of the railroad and provided an available source of energy. In turn, the growing mining communities of southeastern Ohio gave Columbus its first large market for manufactured goods.

The growth of industrial firms between 1870 and 1900 inevitably followed one of three paths of development. Many businesses were a continuation and

expansion of firms previously established when transportation facilities were limited. As better transportation facilities became available, these machine shops, mills and foundries had access to new raw materials and new markets.

A second group of firms emerged in this period based on the city's increased importance as a transportation center. These firms gave Columbus a national name as a manufacturing center. Carriage and wagon shops — coupled with the small supply shops that made seats, wheels, dashes and bent wood products — made the city a major carriage manufacturing center. By 1887, there were 18 companies employing 3,000 workers producing carriages in Columbus. Other local firms produced iron rails, railroad cars and railroad equipment.

A third group of firms established as a result of the vast store of raw materials in southeastern Ohio were the mining and manufacturing firms. In 1887, the Lechner Manufacturing Company (now the Jeffrey Manufacturing Company) began producing mining machinery and rotary drills for the coal industry. In addition, the city supported a large foundry industry which included Buckeye Steel Castings and the Columbus Steel Works.

The Civil War temporarily disrupted the Columbus Board of Trade, but by the following decade, the board was actively encouraging new firms to locate in Columbus — an activity that continues with the present-day Columbus Area Chamber of Commerce. But while other cities openly sponsored new firms in their respective cities, Columbus' approach was more restrained. The board believed that they "should extend every courtesy and encouragement to parties seeking a location in our city . . . but measures of contemplating financial aid are impracticable."

Despite its restrained approach, the board was quite successful in attracting new firms and in assisting the growth and development of existing firms. A. K. Raring Engineering Company (a manufacturer of engines, compressors and pumps) located in the city primarily through board efforts. By the 1890s, more than 900 factories in the city produced a wide variety of goods from mining equipment and carriages to jewelry and watches.

The early 1900s provided no new major stimulus to growth. Development was slow but stable. A minor depression between 1900 and 1914 further inhibited growth. But between 1900 and 1914, the Columbus Board of Trade (which changed its name to the Columbus Area Chamber of Commerce, on June 23, 1909) actively encouraged outside firms to locate in the city. The chamber also sought to establish a $1 million guarantee fund to financially assist new firms to relocate. At this time the chamber was publishing promotional material to help sell the city. But they wanted to ensure the city's economic stability by expressing an early growth policy. It assured its members that "great care [was] used in the selection of prospects and in making offers . . . the city does not want new plants which have not good prospects of success."

The efforts were successful. By 1914, the city had more than 800 manufacturing plants and was ranked among the top 40 industrial cities in the nation. Major factories included the foundries and furnaces of the Carnegie Steel Company, and U.S. Steel and the Columbus Iron and Steel Company. Other major Columbus firms were the Jeffrey Manufacturing Company, Kilbourne & Jacobs, Wolfe Brothers Shoe Company, Capital City Dairy Products, M.C. Lilley and Company, Peruna Drug Company, and the Columbus Buffy Company.

A significant element of growth from 1914 to 1920 was based on federal contracts and defense-related activities of World War I. A lasting influence was the construction of a major ($7 million) government depot. The Defense Construction Supply Center continues to be one of the area's major employers today. By the end of 1917, more than 50 local firms were engaged in the production of war materials.

The period between 1920 and 1940 was one of very slow growth and structural transformation. The Great Depression was perhaps the main cause of this slackened growth. Leading products at the end of the period were mining machinery, concrete mixing equipment, oilwell derricks, oilcloth, shoes and

The neighborhood in which Simon Lazarus set up business in 1851.

artificial teeth facings. The furnace industry expanded to include the Armstrong Furnace Company from London, Ohio, and the Midland Furnace Company. It was not until after the end of World War II that Columbus experienced expanding industrial growth. In 1941, the $14 million Curtiss-Wright aircraft plant was built in Columbus at government expense. The plant added a major new dimension to the city's manufacturing base. More importantly, the plant attracted many kinds of workers from other cities, towns and surrounding farms. At the outset, the firm employed only about 3,000, but at its peak employment rose to more than 25,000. Expansion and conversions of other plants to support the war effort also stimulated growth. So, for a second time the influence of the federal government directly and significantly affected the pattern of industrialization in Columbus.

Transportation was a second major factor affecting the location of industry in Columbus from 1900 to 1952. The coming of the automobile and the airplane provided new land and air routes. The focus of the auto industry a

scant 200 miles to the north, enabled Columbus to participate in its growth.

The third factor attracting new firms was a stable supply of semi-skilled labor. Generally, unions were not active in Columbus. Strikes were rare. Wages were generally low. The shoe industry and components of the auto industry expanded their operations partially because of the availability of a stable labor force.

With the conclusion of World War II, the surplus of labor, the availability of land and a good transportation network all served to attract new firms. Among these were the Ternstedt Division Plant (Fisher Body) of General Motors, a new Westinghouse Plant and the conversion of the Curtiss-Wright Plant by the North American Aviation Corporation.

In the 1950s and 1960s, Columbus experienced rapid and substantial growth in population and employment. Population growth in Franklin County increased 37.5 percent between 1950 and 1960 and 22 percent between 1960 and 1970 — easily exceeding national and statewide growths. Employment growth advanced in all sectors.

Wholesale row, circa 1910.

During the 1960s, the Chamber took on new responsibilities for the social and cultural well-being of the area. Some of these topics were controversial such as schools, open housing, police-community relationships, county and city taxes and public transit — concerns that have continued for the past 20 years. A new structural change occurred with the creation of Plan for Progress, a committee to help bring about equal job opportunities. Another Chamber group zeroed in on the Problems of the Inner City (POTIC). Recognizing the need for improved information, the Chamber also assumed responsibility for the Columbus Regional Information Service (CRIS) which compiles all types of business, cultural, educational and community information.

The Columbus Area Growth Foundation was formed in 1963 by the city of Columbus and Franklin County as a non-profit community improvement corporation. Through 1978, the CAGF had been instrumental in issuing more than $100 million worth of industrial revenue bonds for about 60 companies.

In 1965, the Chamber established the Forward Columbus Fund to channel business contributions into civic projects and ballot issues. From 1969 to 1979, money from this fund backed 32 city and school issues, 29 of which passed. Recent support from the Fund in 1980 won new income for the Central Ohio Transit

Authority (COTA) through voter approval of a county sales tax.

During the 1970s, the Chamber could point with pride to its role in Borden's decision to make Columbus its headquarters; its participation in the Far East International Trade Tour; the formation of the Columbus Careers Conference; the retention of North American Rockwell and the Downtown Area Committee's involvement in the effort to save the Ohio Theatre. Other major businesses attracted with the help of the Chamber during the 1970s were the J. C. Penney Distribution Center, Toledo Scale, Kal Kan Foods and the Equitable Life Insurance Company.

By 1977, a Chamber committee conceived a campaign to raise the self-esteem of Columbus residents about their home city. Its first purpose was to build up the visibility of Columbus both at home and nationally. The second purpose was to marshall all public and private resources to create a certain number of new jobs in the Columbus area. On January 1, 1978, the Central Ohio Economic Development Council was formed to carry out the promotional work called "Columbus, We're Making It Great" that would upgrade Columbus' image.

In 1979, the Chamber formed a new organization for those 1800 members who employ less than 100 people — CASE (Columbus Area Smaller Enterprises).

CASE's purpose is to approach topics from the perspective of the smaller business. Specific programs include education and training, legislative action, membership services and direct assistance.

By spring of 1979, the Chamber realized that the Columbus area's years of greatest numerical growth were over but that the area's most significant growth was yet to come. The Chamber felt that the economic growth potential of Central Ohio lay primarily with the balanced mix of companies already doing business in the Columbus area. The Chamber also decided that any efforts to attract new industry would be directed at the specific types of business likely to take advantage of the wealth of research and development facilities locally. A third priority was to stimulate the return of federal tax dollars to the Central Ohio area.

Specific community issues such as transportation, energy, education, voter registration and the quality of life continue to be the focus for local programs. Balanced with these are the range of special events held in honor of sports events and teams; the Chamber's participation in the Columbus Day U.S.A. Pageant; the annual clambake; luncheons with public officials and policy-makers; and the Chamber's affiliates including the Safety Council, the Sales Executives Club, the Treasurers Club, and the Columbus Area Leadership Program. Whatever the issue or concern of the membership, the Chamber will continue to be the catalyst for positive action and resolution.

Sources
Industrial Evolution of Columbus Ohio. Henry L. Hunker, Bureau of Business Research at Ohio State University, Columbus, Ohio, 1958.

Overall Economic Development Plan for the City of Columbus, Department of Development, City of Columbus.

"A History of Action by the Board of Directors of the Columbus Area Chamber of Commerce and its Predecessor The Columbus Board of Trade."

Anderson Concrete Corp.

Concrete firm a part of everyday life in central Ohio

The Omort truck and Jaeger drum mixer and carrying trailer used by Anderson Concrete in the late '20s.

W. E. Anderson, founder of Anderson Concrete Corp., got his start in the transportation field in the early 1900s with Cincinnati's Queen City Coal Co., hauling one ton of coal at a time by horse and wagon. In 1918, he helped haul the dirt to build the earthen dams after the Miami Valley floods.

The enterprising young Anderson soon found it profitable to haul aggregates to road building jobs in the summer. This prompted him to form the C&C Trucking Company in Cincinnati with his brother Archie and the Francis brothers.

In 1921, when American Aggregates Corp. bought a gravel plant in Columbus, Anderson founded W. E. Anderson & Son Trucking Company with his son Willis and hauled primarily for the large aggregate firm. In fact, one of the first jobs for the crew at Anderson's garage on Gift Street was hauling all the stone used to build Camp Willis during World War I, in the area known today as Upper Arlington.

During the late '20s, Anderson moved into the concrete field, delivering mixed concrete in dump trucks and operating out of new offices on Harmon Avenue.

Soon highschooler Ralph H. Anderson, son of W.E. Anderson and current chairman of the board of Anderson Concrete Corp. (he is now chairman of the board of Anderson Concrete Corp.) became a driver for his father. In 1933 he left his job as a school teacher in Jeffersonville, Ohio, to join his father full time. When Ralph's brothers, Bob and Eddie, joined the firm it became W. E. Anderson Sons Co.

In the early '30s, Anderson used the Blaw-Knox chain-driven agitator on White trucks and later the Omort truck with Jaeger drum mixers. Later in the '30s the firm was one of the first to use pneumatic tires; it also got its first orange power take-off truck, and today orange is the trademark of all Anderson trucks.

During World War II, under Ralph H. Anderson's leadership, the company worked primarily on government jobs. Anderson supplied all the ready mix concrete for the DCSC Army Depot in Columbus, one of the principal supply depots for the country during the war. Anderson also produced almost all of the concrete for Lockbourne Air Force Base (now Rickenbacker).

After the war, the company's wartime expertise boosted it into a period of tremendous growth. Anderson was soon building additional concrete plants to meet the growing demand for post-war housing, street paving and commercial projects.

Its largest commercial job came in the early '50s with the building of the Westinghouse plant. In 1952, the firm was one of the first in the country to equip its trucks with two-way radios, which greatly improved service, speed of deliveries and efficiency.

By 1954, the same year W. E. Anderson died, the increasing popularity of Anderson's ready mix concrete had persuaded Ralph H. Anderson to change the company name to Anderson Concrete Corp.

Anderson Concrete is responsible for many of the landmarks built during the last 20 years in central Ohio, including The Ohio Historical Society (a unique use of lightweight, high-strength concrete); Scioto Downs; the State Capitol underground parking garage; Busch Brewery; Ohio Center; Nationwide Plaza; Franklin County Courts complex; Lazarus parking garages and many projects at The Ohio State University.

The company also helped build Riverside Hospital, Port Columbus International Airport, the major shopping centers in Columbus, several Battelle buildings, the Columbus Water Plant, the Columbus Sewage Plant and the majority of the interstate bridges in Franklin County. Columbus Bituminous Concrete Corp., a separate company formed by Ralph H. Anderson in 1945, provided most of the asphalt for the interstate work.

Today, concrete is a part of everyday life in central Ohio as Anderson Concrete's 80 mixer trucks make deliveries from its 12 ready mix plants. Headquartered now on Frank Road, the influence of Anderson's founder is still felt as third-generation Andersons are actively involved in company management.

Ralph W. (Andy) Anderson is president, Richard Anderson is vice president and David is salesman and assistant secretary. Together they guide Anderson Concrete and its 200 employees, including a few fourth-generation Anderson teenagers, to even greater growth as the leading ready mix concrete producer in a growing central Ohio.

BancOhio Corporation

A tradition of security and progress

When Harry P. and Robert F. Wolfe walked into the Ohio Trust Company in 1907 to demonstrate their faith in the bank and the Columbus community by depositing money during a period of financial crisis, they could not have known they were taking the first steps toward establishing BancOhio National Bank, Ohio's largest statewide banking system.

The economic recession of that year shook the country, and Ohio's capital city felt the effects with the rest of the nation.

The brothers, in an effort to help restore the confidence of the bank's customers and discourage withdrawal of deposits, boldly deposited $100,000 (a huge amount in 1907). This act had the desired calming effect and Ohio Trust emerged unscathed from the recession. In addition, the brothers purchased a substantial interest in the stock in the bank, and thus began the progression of events that would lead to Ohio's first bank holding company, and later, the first and largest statewide banking system.

In 1919, Ohio's General Assembly passed legislation permitting banks chartered by the state to establish branch offices within a city or contiguous village.

During the next eight years, the bank, then called Citizens Trust and Savings Bank (following a merger with Citizens Savings Bank) put 11 new branches on the Columbus map.

In 1928, Citizens Trust merged with First National Bank, becoming First Citizens Trust Company. Shortly thereafter, the two brothers also purchased controlling shares of Ohio National Bank, another sound and profitable Columbus financial institution.

They soon discovered that, while running central Ohio's two most prosperous banks had advantages, there were also difficulties such as duplication, excessive manpower and differing managements.

The "umbrella" solution which would eventually minimize these problems was a holding company.

On September 19, 1929, BancOhio Corporation, the state's first bank holding company, was incorporated, creating a self-reliant, economical banking system. The next month shares in the new corporation were made available to the public.

In 1931, it was decided to merge the two BancOhio banks in order to create a bank with the strength afforded by the combined capital of the two institutions. In September, the *new* Ohio National Bank opened its doors with assets totaling $57 million.

During the 1930s, BancOhio began a program of acquisition which strengthened banking in central Ohio. In that depression era, the strength and stability of BancOhio Corporation helped keep the banks in the holding company family in sound condition and no BancOhio bank failed.

The 1930s and 1940s brought many changes in banking to accommodate hard times and changing attitudes about cash and credit.

For example, BancOhio banks were among the first to extend credit to consumers for automobiles, home appliances and home improvements — items previously considered outside the sphere of bank lending.

By the end of the 1950s, BancOhio had grown to a family of banks in more than 20 counties, including a new, state-chartered Ohio State Bank serving Franklin County. Ohio State Bank made history with its founding when it opened in one of the first shopping centers in America.

The '60s brought a number of new services including Master Charge and BancPlan Reserve, an automatic line of credit coupled to the customer's checking account.

During the 1970s, BancOhio continued its acquisition program by adding 18 banks to the holding company, bringing the total number of separate banks to 41.

In 1976, BancOhio opened its new headquarters in Columbus, the BancOhio National Plaza, giving the downtown area an attractive, contemporary landmark, and Robert G. Stevens became chairman, president and chief executive officer.

Stevens' task was to meld 41 banks into an efficient, effective and profitable organization capable of dealing with changes in social, political and economic forces in the country.

Under his guidance, BancOhio management made significant steps by expanding commercial lending, improving information systems and operations, creating a common identity, and adopting new approaches to organization and marketing.

In 1978, the Ohio General Assembly passed legislation which, in effect, would permit banks to operate statewide.

After careful consideration, BancOhio decided to merge 40 of its banks. Ohio State Bank of Columbus would operate as a separate bank to continue the multi-

As this photo, taken in the early '50s, shows, banking has changed its "look" over the years. The lobby of BancOhio's High-Town office in Columbus reflects a more opulent architectural era.

bank holding company's franchise with both a state and a national charter. The merger took place on June 29, 1979, and the successor — BancOhio National Bank — became the 31st largest bank in the United States and the largest in Ohio, with assets of more than $4.2 billion. Most of the tedious, expensive red tape required to service customers was eliminated. In addition, the new bank had a lending capacity of more than $25 million to a single customer, establishing an Ohio source for larger commercial customers.

BancOhio National Plaza, headquarters for BancOhio's offices across the state, opened in the Columbus downtown area in 1976. The six-tower building with glassed-in lobby area and shopping Galleria is a downtown landmark.

Today, BancOhio National Bank has twice as many offices as any other commercial bank in Ohio and covers the most rapidly growing areas of the state. Customer service is extended by the use of more than 90 AnytimeBank® machines and Bank365® automated teller machines located throughout the state. BancOhio is positioned to be one of the major regional banks in the United States.

BancOhio Corporation is owned by more than 15,000 shareholders who live in every one of Ohio's 88 counties, and in all states of the United States, as well as in several other nations. Its stock is traded over-the-counter and is quoted by NASDAQ.

® *AnytimeBank and Bank365 are service marks of BancOhio.*

Bank One

A history of looking toward the future

In 1863, while the United States struggled — divided against itself — one man attempted to bring order to the nation's otherwise fractionalized banking system.

The National Currency Act of 1863, developed by Secretary of the Treasury

City National Bank of Commerce, in the early 1930s.

Salmon Chase, had its roots in Ohio's banking law drafted by Alfred Kelley some 18 years before. It gave the stability necessary for an evolution of a powerful

Vault in the Commercial Bank, 1923.

national bank system.

Five years later, in 1868, the first of the BANK ONE ancestors appeared with an office at Long and High Streets. F.C. Session chartered Sessions and Company and one year later joined with J.A. Jeffrey and Orange Johnson to become the Commercial Bank. (Orange Johnson's house now stands preserved as a museum today, in Worthington, Ohio.) The year 1923 brought a move to new offices at Nine East Long Street, still in use today as a branch.

The second of BANK ONE's three ancestors was the City Deposit Bank. Organized in 1898 at Fifth Avenue and North High Street, the bank moved downtown to Gay and High Streets in 1900. That same year, City Deposit Bank received a new charter and with it a new name — City National Bank of Columbus.

The third and youngest of BANK ONE's genitors was the Bank of Commerce Company organized in 1900 by J.C. Campbell and located at Chestnut and High. In 1905 it became the National Bank of Commerce. In 1926 The National Bank of Commerce and City National Bank consolidated to form the City National Bank of Commerce.

Finally, in the depth of the Depression in 1929, the roots reaching back to 1868 joined to form the City National Bank and Trust Company with the merger of Commercial National Bank and City National Bank of Commerce.

In 1935, the bank had resources of $25 million and a new president, John H. McCoy. The new bank rapidly emerged as a primary banking force in Ohio's capital

city where its efforts were focused. By 1958, its resources reached $150 million and John G. McCoy had succeeded his father. The younger McCoy's tenure was to have a pronounced effect on banking across the nation. Ten years after he became president, John G. McCoy led the bank through a significant evolution. Horizons were pushed outward from Columbus to include the entire state when City National Bank and Farmers Bank in Mansfield joined to form First Banc Group of Ohio, Inc., a multi-bank holding company.

In late 1979, First Banc Group changed its name to the BANC ONE CORPORATION with each of its affiliate banks adopting the name of BANK ONE of its home city. Thus, City National Bank entered the decade of the 1980s as BANK ONE OF COLUMBUS. As 1980 began, the corporation could count 19 bank affiliates, 119 branches, a trust company and three non-bank affiliates, and two additional bank acquisitions pending.

Over the years of its existence, BANK ONE has etched a lengthy list of industry innovations into banking history.

1915 — it became the first bank in Columbus to offer trust services to its customer. Many years later, in 1973, BANC ONE received the first national charter ever given a trust company for its subsidiary now known as BANK ONE TRUST COMPANY.

1937 — the development of an installment loan program for consumers, one of the first in the country. Most bankers in 1937 limited their lending to businesses, feeling that the consumer posed far too great a risk. Today, of course, installment

loans make up a large percentage of the asset portfolio of almost every bank in the country.

1950 — construction of one of the country's first drive-in banks — at 1245 Olentangy River Road, which is still in operation today.

The computer age was dawning with the 1960s and BANK ONE moved into automation, building its first operations center. Today the bank does data processing for financial institutions in 25 states.

1966 — the first step toward creation of the nationwide bank credit card system with an agreement between Bank of America and City National Bank introducing the BankAmericard in Ohio, which up until then had been limited to California.

1967 — the development of a major online credit card processing network that today is the nation's second largest.

1970 — introduction of the first 24-hour cash dispensing machines in the country.

1972 — the first major installation of automatic total teller equipment using a debit card.

1980 — BANK ONE was the first in the nation to give consumers a 24- hour a day access to account information including balances, allowing them to pay bills from their own homes or businesses by linking a television set to the BANK ONE computer via an ordinary telephone.

There is little resemblance between today's national leader in electronic banking and the tiny banking office at the corner of Long and High in 1868. But just as a plant's roots determine its growth so will the history of the BANC ONE CORPORATION influence its future.

Banning & Pickett

Development with a difference signaled rapid success

A different approach to real estate development made Banning & Pickett one of Columbus' business success stories of the 1970s. Since the company's founding in 1969, its unique approach to total development of commercial sites and luxury office parks earned the firm the reputation as central Ohio's leading commercial developer.

James V. Pickett, whose background was in building and design, joined forces in 1969 with George W. Banning, a former real estate broker, to develop commercial real estate for investment purposes. Just one year later, in 1970, the firm established its unique approach — the development of investment real estate that would enhance the surrounding environment. And, through that approach, the Banning & Pickett philosophy of Development Management evolved.

According to Pickett, president of the firm, "Development Management involved a number of sequential events, all interrelated with another." A system of continual review and supervision was established for each Banning & Pickett project, enabling staff members to efficiently track the progress of each building.

"Most importantly," Pickett added, "Development Management enabled Banning & Pickett to establish an air of trust between ourselves and our clients."

By mid-decade, the company's emphasis had focused on the creation of luxury office parks. Most were located in suburban settings, although the company's first venture in 1980, One Capitol South, took the Banning & Pickett development touch downtown. All developments, from the award-winning Officescape 270 and the

The Cascade Corporate Center, in Worthington, is one of Banning & Pickett's most notable developments emphasizing preservation of the environment. A wooded, ravine setting along I-270 was chosen for the office park development, (above.) Banning & Pickett's award-winning Officescape 270, in Worthington, became home to businesses both large and small.

Cascade Corporate Center, both in Worthington, to the highly acclaimed $100 million MetroCenter in Dublin, reflected again the firm's basic goal — a luxury office setting could be melded into a natural environment with no sacrifice on the part of either.

In addition to the creation of luxury office and commercial space, Banning & Pickett came to represent a total service approach to leasing and client services. In keeping with the Development Management philosophy, Banning & Pickett's staff of professionals implemented the development process from beginning to end: from financial planning and forecasting to market research, land acquisition, project design, construction management and follow-up client services geared to individual tenants in each Banning & Pickett building.

Through its decade-long history, Banning & Pickett has operated under the belief that a quality development makes the best long-term investment. As the Banning & Pickett corporate philosophy reflects, tomorrow exists only for a company that has a continuing awareness of the present.

Battelle Memorial Institute

Using science and education to meet human needs

Aerial view in the early 1940s showing Battelle's original building and, behind it, the first of many other buildings that have been built in the ensuing years, (above.) Gordon Battelle, the founder of Battelle Memorial Institute, (inset.)

The history of Battelle Memorial Institute is the story of a man, of an idea and of an organization that grew out of the idea to become a pioneer in contract research and the world's largest independent research institute.

The man central to the history of the institute is Gordon Battelle. Gordon Battelle died in 1923, leaving a will which provided that the bulk of his estate be used to create "a Battelle Memorial Institute ... for the encouragement of creative research ... and the making of discoveries and inventions." The institute, to be governed by a self-perpetuating board of trustees, was to serve as a memorial to his family — pioneers in Ohio and in its early steel industry.

The Battelle board of trustees acquired a site of about 10 acres in Columbus on King Avenue adjacent to the Ohio State University and built the institute's original building, which was opened in October, 1929. To begin operations, the board chose a director — Dr. Horace W. Gillett, who was considered by his peers "The Dean of American Metallurgy". It was Dr. Gillett who determined that the work of the institute should initially be concerned primarily with metallurgy.

One of the most important events in the early history of the institute was the decision by Dr. Gillett in 1934 to ask the board of trustees to relieve him of administrative duties and to name Clyde E. Williams as director. During Williams' years as director — the title in his later years was President — capabilities and interests were extended far beyond materials technology to serve the changing research needs of industry, and through industry, the public.

One example of Battelle's efforts to broaden its capabilities was nuclear research. The institute became involved in the "Manhattan Project" of World War II because of its international reputation in the field of metallurgy and was asked to study the fabrication of the then almost unknown metal uranium. In the next decade, Battelle became one of the country's outstanding centers for nuclear research.

During this period, Battelle, with remarkable foresight, pursued the development of "xerography" — a development that would later have a far-reaching effect on Battelle and on the entire business world.

The postwar years were not only a period when Battelle expanded its range of research interests, but also a period when it established its presence outside the United States. It was in the early '50s that the institute built research centers in Frankfurt, Germany and Geneva, Switzerland. Thus, in 1957, at the time of Williams' retirement, the total worldwide Battelle staff stood at 3,100, and total annual research expenditures were just over $25 million.

Williams' retirement, and the appointment of his longtime associate Dr. B.D. Thomas, as president, coincided closely with a rather dramatic shift in science policy in the United States and elsewhere as the space age began. One important factor in the growth of the institute under Dr. Thomas' leadership was the U.S. Atomic Energy Commission's selection of Battelle in 1964 to operate the former Hanford Laboratory in Richland, Washington, with its staff of 2,000.

In the 1960s, with Dr. Thomas' leadership, the institute sought a broader approach to its mission than contract research and its traditional involvement in education. During this period, for example, Battelle embarked on a far-reaching program, known as the Battelle Institute Program. Funded by Battelle, the program provided support for a cadre of fellows conducting work of a basic or scholarly character.

Dr. Sherwood L. Fawcett, the fourth and current chief executive at Battelle, assumed the presidency in 1968. With his leadership, Battelle has continued to grow and diversify its activities. For example, total sponsored research revenues, which were $116 million in 1970, surpassed $360 million in 1979. And the staff total had climbed from 5,602 at the end of 1970 to about 7,200.

Having passed the half-century mark, the institute continues to be a dynamic world organization with strong roots in Columbus. "Battelle," as Dr. Fawcett has observed, "is a large organization with many facets and with a wide range of interests and activities. Its purpose, however, is simple and constant — the use of science, technology and education to meet human needs."

Big Bear Stores Company

Company built on innovative retailing concepts

In 1934, as the nation was beginning to recover from the Depression, an innovation in food retailing was introduced in Columbus when Wayne E. Brown opened the first self-service supermarket in central Ohio.

Brown leased a 70,000 square foot building on Lane Avenue near the Ohio State University campus that had failed as a dance hall and roller rink.

The name Big Bear was chosen because Brown felt it was catchy and easy for people, especially children, to remember.

More than 200,000 people visited the store during the first three days it was open and were amazed by the huge variety and low prices. Advertised specials such as coffee, 18 cents per pound, butter 24½ cents per pound and ham, 10 cents per pound were bargains even in 1934.

Big Bear was an instant success with consumers who liked the opportunity to select their own items and the convenience of one-stop shopping. A reputation for quality fruits, vegetables and the finest meats was quickly established that endures to this day.

Children enjoyed going to the store with their parents because a trained bear was caged near the entrance and did tricks for those who stopped to watch. After a

A typical combination Big Bear Supermarket-Harts Family Center.

few years, the bear was donated to the Columbus Zoo.

By February, 1935, the second Big Bear store opened at 2030 E. Main Street in an old piano factory.

The anniversary sale introduced even more innovations in the two stores. Departments included a restaurant, flower shop, bakery, soda fountain, pharmacy, appliances and a shoe repair service. Together, the stores provided a parking area for 3,000 cars in an era when few people could afford to drive.

Since most people in Columbus relied on streetcars for transportation and the Lane Avenue store was nearly a mile from High Street, a free bus ran from the store

to the trolley stop every 20 minutes.

By 1939, the company had four stores open and two under construction. Space for products was already a problem because Big Bear carried 30 brands of coffee, 22 brands of tea, 41 brands of dog food and 53 brands of bar soap.

Brown realized that he needed to sell a huge volume to defray the costs of offering such a wide variety at low prices. He used many unique promotions such as auctions and contests to bring customers to the store. Big Bear was one of the first companies to use radio advertising as a major part of a promotional program.

Expansion slowed during the war years, but the company again began growing in

The first Big Bear supermarket in Ohio opened in 1934 and is still in operation on Lane Avenue in Columbus, Ohio.

the late '40s and '50s. In 1947, the warehouse was opened at its present location at 770 W. Goodale Blvd. There were 11 Big Bear stores at that time and plans were announced to open 10 new stores by the end of 1949.

The company began to move into new fields of business. In 1948, Brown met with several other supermarket operators to form Topco Associates, Inc., the company that produces private label products under the Food Club, Top Frost and other labels.

The Buckeye Premium Stamp Company is a wholly owned subsidiary that was founded to offer stamps as a promotional premium to Big Bear shoppers.

Big Bear also operates the Betty Brown Bakery at 1550 N. High Street, which provides bread and other baked products for the supermarkets.

In 1963, the first Harts Family Center discount department store was opened in Bridgeport, Ohio. The company now operates 18 Harts stores with four in Columbus.

The company has always been an active supporter of local community projects including area sports events, Columbus Zoo, Shrine Circus and many events sponsored by local charitable groups.

Following Brown's death in 1976, Michael J. Knilans was elected president.

In January 1980, the company was operating 56 supermarkets and 18 Harts Family Centers in central and southern Ohio and northern West Virginia.

The philosophy of meeting the needs of today's customer and building new stores to reach out to new customers continues the tradition begun by Wayne Brown and Big Bear nearly a half century ago.

Big Drum, Inc.

Growth through innovation

During the summer of 1904, a young engineering student from Ohio State University visited the Louisiana Purchase Exposition in Saint Louis. The young man's name was Carl R. Taylor. That visit, and the events that occurred during his stay, determined the future of an individual's life and greatly influenced the history behind the Columbus-based Big Drum Corporation.

At the World's Fair that year, Carl Taylor observed Ernest A. Hamwi of Damascus, Syria, introducing a Persian food novelty known as a zalabia. This was a wafer-like pastry baked on a flat waffle iron and served with sugar or other sweets.

Hamwi's concession stand was next to an ice cream booth which served its product on dishes. On one hot day when demand for ice cream outstripped the supply of dishes, Hamwi offered a solution by rolling one of his thin wafers into the shape of a cone that could hold ice cream. Customer approval to this new novelty was instantaneous and the ice cream cone was born.

Intrigued with this phenomenon, the young Taylor returned to Columbus where he began developing some of the first cone producing machinery.

While attending mechanical engineering school, Taylor resided in the home of Werd W. Turnbull, owner of the Turnbull Machine Company and an individual who was equally fascinated with the rolled cone concept. About 1905, Taylor joined Turnbull's company. Working together, the two men developed a turntable-type machine for continuously baking sugar and flour wafers which could then be hand-rolled into cones. With this accomplishment, the Turnbull Machine Company began to produce both cone baking equipment and rolled sugar cones.

Big Drum's growth is demonstrated by the advances made over the years in engineering and machining technology. Shown above is one of its early machine shops assembling sugar cone baking equipment.

Despite their early success working together, Taylor and Turnbull had differing views on how to expand their business and about 1910 they parted ways. For health reasons, Turnbull went south, where he also thought the market for cones might be less seasonal. Carl Taylor moved to Cleveland and later, in 1913, incorporated the Cream Cone Machine Company. Producing cone baking machines as well as selling and distributing sugar cones, Cream Cone Machine Company prospered over the next several years as the ice cream cone became more and more popular.

During the '30s and early '40s another popular ice cream novelty known as the "Drumstick" was growing in popularity all over the country. As America's original "factory-made" chocolate nut sundae in a rolled sugar cone, the frozen Drumstick provided a large commercial market for sugar cone manufacturers like Cream Cone Machine Company. Their output, in particular, served a growing number of dairies making Drumsticks in the Midwest.

The Drumstick had its beginning in 1930 in Fort Worth, Texas. There, a young man named I.C. Parker conceived the idea of filling a rolled sugar cone with ice cream, dipping the whole affair in chocolate, and sprinkling the result with peanuts. His wife remarked that it looked like a chicken leg or "drumstick", and the names of this new product and a company to sell it were born.

In its early years of business the Drumstick Company consisted of I.C. Parker and his two brothers, "Stubby" and Bruce, who travelled the country selling and merchandising the Drumstick novelty. Through their efforts, it wasn't long before Drumsticks became a standard item for countless ice cream novelty manufacturers across America. As the demand for sugar cones expanded, the Cleveland-based Cream Cone Machine Company provided the source of cone baking equipment for many bakeries. During this time, a friendly business relationship developed between Carl Taylor and Stubby Parker, which contributed favorably to both of their companies.

However, the early '40s brought some unwelcome hardships to Cream Cone Machine Company. The war effort caused domestic shortages of both raw materials and laborers, severely curtailing the company's output. Upon Carl Taylor's death in 1944, the company was left in the hands of his family. In 1947, Carl Taylor's nephew, Robert T. Wise, became interested in the business as did "Stubby" Parker and his son, Thomas L., who had been associated with the Drumstick Company. They joined in purchasing the Taylor family interests.

In 1948, the newly reorganized Cream Cone Machine Company was moved to Columbus. In the years that followed, the company was able to support continued

Big Drum's modern manufacturing facility today produces fully automated cone baking machines as well as sophisticated packaging equipment for the specialized needs of diverse markets around the world.

growth of commercially produced Drumsticks and other cone novelties. Technological advancements reminiscent of Carl Taylor's innovations 50 years earlier opened new areas of opportunity as well. These included the development of fully-automated cone baking equipment as well as several automatic packaging systems used by dairy and non-dairy food processors for a variety of products. In 1962, operations had become so diverse

that it was decided the company should become a publicly-held corporation through the issue of stock shares. A new name, "Big Drum," was selected because it related to the Drumstick cone while not being explicitly tied to that one product.

In the years since, Chairman Robert T. Wise, President Thomas L. Parker and many skilled employees have guided Big Drum into the realm of international commerce. Today, in addition to producing millions of sugar cones annually, Big Drum is known worldwide for designing product concepts, packaging processes and merchandising programs for manufacturers producing a wide range of dessert and other specialty products. The company's growth, not unlike the Columbus community, is a result of its founders' ingenuity and perseverance. That unbridled imagination has evolved into a company philosophy which today is reflected in the proficiency and dedication of more than 400 employees. Their innovative spirit will serve to expand Big Drum Corporation and enrich the communities where they live for a long time to come.

Borden Inc.

Perseverance led company from condensed milk to diverse product

"I tried and failed; I tried again and again, and succeeded."

These words on the tombstone of Gail Borden, Jr. epitomize the philosophy of the founder of what is today Borden Inc., the diversified, chemical, foods and dairy concern with corporate administrative headquarters in Columbus.

The company's first product — sweetened, condensed milk — was only one of many inventions of a rugged individualist who tried his hand in many fields. As an inventor, Borden was particularly interested in condensing foodstuffs. One of his inventions, a product made of meat extract and flour which he called a "meat biscuit," went to California during the 1849 Gold Rush and won Borden a Gold Medal at the Great Council Exposition in London in 1851.

The impetus for condensing milk reportedly resulted from Borden's long sea voyage home, after he received the medal from Queen Victoria. Borden was affected by the sight of babies deprived of fresh milk because the cows on board were too seasick to be milked. He set out to discover a method of preserving milk. By 1853, he had a satisfactory product: pure, fresh milk with most of the water removed

Gail Borden, Jr.

Borden milk wagon of about 1896.

under vacuum at low temperature, and sugar added as a preservative.

Borden's process received a patent in 1856. That year, Borden set up his first factory at an abandoned carriage shop in Wolcottville, Connecticut, close to well-kept herds whose care he could monitor.

Gail Borden's first successful condensery was established in 1857 at Burrville, Connecticut.

He designed most of the machinery, ran the factory, and sold the milk himself from a pushcart on New York City streets. The public was slow to try Borden's revolutionary, new product, however, and the business failed.

With new financial backing, a new enterprise — called Gail Borden, Jr. and Company — was opened at Burrville, Conn., on May 11, 1857. It was renamed the New York Condensed Milk Company in 1858. The Civil War and the Union Army's supply needs spread Borden's name and the taste for his product far and wide, and the business prospered. Gail Borden died in 1874, and control passed to his sons.

The company began selling fluid milk in 1875 and in 1885 became the first to sell milk in bottles. In 1899, the company was reorganized as the Borden Condensed Milk Company and the first international operation was opened, in Canada.

The new century saw continued acquisitions and the start of milk pasteurization in 1911. In 1919, the name was shortened to The Borden Company, in recognition that the company was no longer tied to one product.

Geographic expansion continued through World War I and the postwar years, and in 1928 an organized program of product diversification was introduced. The diversification provided the nucleus of the later divisions by making the company a major force in ice cream, cheese, dried milk and casein.

The four divisions of Borden today — Foods, Chemical, Dairy & Services, and International — reflect the company's diversification. The present alignment was formalized in 1968 with another name change — to Borden Inc.

The Foods Division markets a wide variety of products including Cracker Jack, Wyler's, ReaLemon, Creamette, Wise, Buckeye, Guy's, Old London and Borden brands and the product line includes cheese, condensed milk, snack foods, sugar, jams and jellies and bouillon.

The Chemical Division, growing from milk-based casein glue operations, has made Borden one of the nation's largest and most diversified chemical companies. It currently markets thousands of products in four major product areas: agriculture; consumer products; adhesives, resins, films, tapes and inks; and petrochemicals and thermoplastics. The division is the largest producer of formaldehyde in the world. Under the Elmer's brand, it is also the foremost producer of household glues worldwide.

The Dairy & Services Division markets a full line of dairy products including milks, ice creams, cultured dairy products and frozen novelties. A fleet of Borden vehicles distributes products to homes, stores, warehouses, restaurants, schools, hospitals, industrial establishments and vending operations.

The International Division is responsible for distribution of all Borden products outside the United States, in more than 130 countries, and for manufacturing operations in almost 30 countries abroad.

Today, Borden Inc., with almost 300 plants around the world, remains a growing, dynamic company in line with its founder's ideals — looking for better ideas, trying and succeeding.

Buckeye Federal Savings and Loan Association

Savings and lending services from a community institution

In 1895, in Columbus, High Street had just been paved, the city's horse car service was extended, and the first waterworks system was installed. Everyone who possibly could, owned a buggy. Twenty-three establishments in Columbus were manufacturing a total of 20,000 horse-drawn vehicles each year.

The articles of incorporation for the new Buckeye State Building and Loan Company were issued on January 2nd. It was on January 4th, 1895 that nine

founding directors including John J. Schwartz, L. L. Rankin, and L. P. McCullough, each of whom later became president of the institution, joined in the organization of the original Buckeye State Building and Loan Company. The organizational meeting was held in Rankin's law office on the second floor of the Wesley Block Building, on the west side of High near Gay Street.

The directors thought big enough to provide a basic plan for 10,000 shares of

stock at $100 each, but issued only 511 shares to start. They also established a 50%-of-appraisal limit on real estate mortgage loans.

Most early loans were for less than $500 each and might total $5,000 to $7,000 per month. The loans were on both town and farm property. For the most part, the town property was located within the present inner-city and near northside areas.

The second president was founder and attorney L. L. Rankin, a builder. Out-

Changes have been made to the Buckeye Building savings lobby since this 1940 photograph, but it remains one of the most beautiful and impressive building lobbies in the Columbus downtown area.

growing his law office headquarters, he purchased land and built the first Rankin Building, an office for Buckeye at 22 West Gay Street, in March, 1899. Rankin meanwhile had bought the "Munich Cafe" building next door and, utilizing the two locations, he constructed the new, larger Rankin Building in 1911.

By 1912, when Buckeye moved into its new building, its assets had reached $5 million. And Buckeye grew from $5 million to almost $16 million in the next six years, to the time of Rankin's untimely death in 1918.

Less than a decade later, the association had grown to over 88,000 customers, once reporting 10,000 new accounts in a six month period. It was time for a new building.

A large 15-story building at 36 East Gay Street was proposed for the site of B. F. Keith's Theatre, a vaudeville house which had hosted the greatest vaudeville performers of the times. During its construction, the Buckeye Building was one of the most significant projects of the times, costing over one million dollars. The building housed a barber shop and beauty shop on the fifth floor as well as a large dining room with a modernly-equipped kitchen. Luxurious men's and ladies' restrooms equipped with shower baths and lockers were available for customer

and employee convenience. Within a few months after the Buckeye Building opened, 80% of the office space was rented on a long-term lease.

During the Depression, Buckeye, with a strong emergency cash reserve, remained the hub of home financing activity and emerged as the city's leading mortgage lender. Today, Buckeye Federal still remains the leader in mortgage lending with almost $900 million in outstanding loans.

After World War II, as people began building homes further away from the downtown area, Buckeye began building branch offices. The Association now has some 20 locations through central Ohio.

In 1949, the association converted to the mutual form of organization and adopted its current name. Today, as a federally-chartered stock company, Buckeye Federal is the largest savings and loan in central Ohio and one of the largest in the state with assets approaching $1 billion.

Buckeye Federal has continued to serve the community by making loans to finance the purchase, construction or improvement of residential and other real property, and by providing a safe, convenient sanctuary for the savings deposits of

A rendering of the Buckeye Building, circa 1929.

central Ohio families. It has contributed and will continue to contribute significantly to the vitality and life of the great Columbus and central Ohio community.

(Note: portions of the above are excerpted from retired Buckeye Federal President and Chairman William S. Guthrie's "Newcomen Address" delivered at the "1969 Columbus Dinner" of the Newcomen Society in North America, December 10, 1969.)

191

Buckeye International, Inc.

Portrait in steel painted with determination

Buckeye International — entering the 1980s as a healthy, diversified corporation with annual sales approaching $200 million began as a struggling manufacturer of cast iron goods in 1883. Lacking a well defined market for its products, the company hovered on the brink of failure for about a decade. Fortunately, management soon recognized the importance of what was then the growth industry of its day — railroads. And, in the 1890s, Buckeye started producing iron automatic couplers for railroad cars. As trains became longer and heavier, the company constructed an ultra-modern plant on South Parsons Avenue to manufacture the much stronger cast steel couplers.

By 1915, Buckeye had clearly emerged as a leader in the steel castings industry, and its plant was the largest of its type in the world — which position it has maintained to this day.

During World War I, the company turned to the production of gun forgings and billets for shells. With the return of the country to peaceful conditions, Buckeye once again became a prime supplier of steel castings for the nation's railroads. In the 1920s and 1930s, the firm joined with other companies and with Columbus' Battelle Memorial Institute to begin the manufacture of high tensile alloy steel castings. During World War II, the corporation converted its plant to the output of defense materials, in addition to railroad car parts. It has remained an important supplier of armor to this day.

In the past 20 years, new challenges have led Buckeye's management into additional fields. To counter the highly cyclical railroad market Buckeye's management moved into the production of industrial castings and castings for mass transit cars. Completely new fields were also entered — plastics, precision metal parts, and others. By the late 1970s Buckeye had become a diversified corporation quite different from what it had been just two decades before. Yet, continuity also characterized the corporation's evolution, as the Steel Division, with its expanded markets, capacity and service, continued to account for two-fifths of the company's sales.

Buckeye has played important roles in

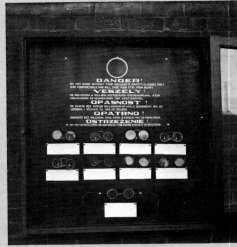

Multi-lingual Safety Bulletin, 1915

the social and cultural, as well as economic development of Columbus. From the earliest days to the present its management has, in particular, taken active parts in the work of philanthropic, civic and cultural organizations. In the opening years of the 20th century company

Open hearth operations, 1915

192

management helped form the Associated Charities of Columbus, and in the mid-1920s led in that body's reorganization as the Community Fund of Columbus and Franklin County. Other organizations — the YMCA, the YWCA, the South Side Settlement House, and various hospitals — received substantial support and volunteer services from Buckeye. During the Great Depression of the 1930s, at a time when most businesses were retrenching, Buckeye increased its contributions to philanthropic organizations. This support continued in the years after World War II and Buckeye's officers and staff have become increasingly involved in community and state affairs in recent years.

Buckeye's story is, then, one of success. Many factors — the nature of its management, its location, luck, and good community relations — insured Buckeye's survival and growth. Buckeye's success did not come easily, however; it was punctuated with missteps and difficulties. As Samuel P. Bush, one of Buckeye's early presidents, wrote his wife in 1908 — "We have had hard things to bear." Reflecting the determination of many of the company's officers, he continued, "But, surely we should not care to have our lives easy, for there would be no accomplishment, no development."

Geo. Byers Sons, Inc.

A family affair for four generations

Historically, America's great cities have been built by strong families who were schooled in our country's finest tradition of hard work ethics — "start at the bottom and work your way up." Possibly the saying, "The truest and noblest act of all is to work," is best exemplified by one of Columbus' oldest families — the Byers family.

George Byers brought his family to Columbus from near Chillicothe, Ohio, in 1898 to reestablish his livery and sales stable, The Blue Ribbon Stable. Moving with the current of the times, however, the stables gave way to automobiles. In 1918 Byers' sons recognized the opportunities before them and organized Geo. Byers Sons, Inc., an automobile dealership. Starting with just a few cars, the family put many, many hours of hard work into the business to make it grow. During those early years, the company sold Dixie Flyer, Rickenbacker Willys-Overland, Hudson-Essex and others. By 1929, the industry's manufacturers could not help but recognize the progress made by the Byers — who had attained annual sales of $5 million in just five short years.

The Byers brothers soon seized the opportunity to become DeSoto-Plymouth car and parts wholesaling distributors for Columbus and 23 central Ohio counties and, in 1940, added part of Indiana and Kentucky to their trade territory.

General Motors trucks were introduced in 1934 and, in 1955, Byers opened its all-new facility for its General Motors Truck Division at 1275 West Mound Street. Today, having grown to 23 acres of truck facility, Byers is General Motors Corporation's second largest truck sales and service facility. Two truck service buildings — larger than football fields — denote the family's involvement and commitment to this franchise.

The Hertz franchise for car and truck rentals was taken on by Byers in 1954 and

George Byers, Sr., in the early 1900s, enjoying a favorite past-time, (below.) One of Geo. Byers Sons, Inc.'s original Hertz licensees, at 100 North Front Street, (inset.)

now operates from three locations — car rental and lease at 100 North Front Street, Port Columbus with truck lease, and rental at 669 Sullivant Avenue.

Geo. Byers Sons, Inc. continued to grow and between 1955 and 1970, diversified into the worlds of real estate, financial institutions, insurance, parking garages and lots, and motels.

In the 1970s the family again recognized

quality and opportunity by accepting the Subaru motor car distributorship. The Subaru division has grown into a four-state area — Ohio, Michigan, Indiana and Kentucky — servicing 55 independent new car franchises with automobiles, parts, service and administrative assistance.

In 1957 the Import Division was organized. Today it is housed in a new modern facility at 401 North Hamilton Road with Volvo, Triumph and Subaru.

By the end of 1980, Byers will have delivered to its dealers and customers more than 300,000 automobiles and trucks — a phenomenal achievement.

With the talents and skills of many Byers family members present within the company, the growth and stability of the organization can best be described as — Geo. Byers Sons, Inc. — a family affair.

From its strong family ties, the tiny operation of the early '20s has grown into a dynasty of an all-family-owned and operated, diversified conglomerate whose sales totalled $100 million in 1979. It currently employs around 400.

The success of the Byers company was not achieved in one easy step — but in many steps, with family and employees working together, bringing up the next generation by the family philosophy of "start at the bottom and work up." Today the fourth Byers generation is a part of the family tradition.

Geo. W. Byers, Sr., is currently chairman of the board of the company, and Frank M. Byers, Sr., is president and chief executive. Vice presidents are Geo. Byers, Jr., Frank M. Byers, Jr., Geo. Byers III, Robert C. Byers, Don DuRivage and Jack Sugar; John A. Herzog is controller and treasurer.

Columbia Gas of Ohio, Inc.

For 75 years a warm spot in the heart of Ohio

The year was 1814 and Ohio was still a young state.

On a summer day that bore little other significance, a salt manufacturer drilling for brine in Noble County unearthed instead a gas pocket that shot a mixture of oil and water some 40 feet in the air.

Similar mixtures were encountered again and again.

To a flourishing salt industry, they became an annoyance. Oil ruined the brine and the gas that gushed it forth was considered completely useless.

It wasn't until a quarter century later — in 1838 — that natural gas was first put to work in Ohio by an ingenious Findlay resident.

His method — crude, but effective — was to place an inverted sugar kettle over a shallow well in the heart of the city to collect gas. Wood pipe carried this gas to the fireplace in his home, where he burned it from the muzzle of a gun for heating and cooking.

From these meager beginnings, natural gas slowly grew to be the dominant heating and processing fuel that it is today in Columbus and throughout Ohio.

Natural gas came to the city of Columbus for the first time on December 31, 1889. The first customer was the Columbus Club.

Initial service to the Columbus area came from a number of the small companies characteristic of the early days of natural gas — small companies that included Columbus Natural Gas and Fuel Company and Federal Gas and Fuel.

Operations of these small, local companies were predictably short-lived. Once local production peaked, the small firms often were unable to finance production elsewhere. While some went out of business, most were absorbed by larger

Four story office hugging the corner of Front and Long Streets has been a home of the gas company since 1927.

companies with access to more abundant resources.

Among the latter category was Ohio Fuel Corporation.

Under the leadership of George W. Crawford, a natural gas pioneer with an indefatigable drive to provide service to Ohio towns, Ohio Fuel had obtained the most promising gas producing territories in central and southern Ohio.

Crawford and Ohio Fuel stood in excellent position to take over local companies and one such acquisition included Federal Gas and Fuel in 1903.

While Crawford pursued the gas industry in central and southeastern Ohio, another pioneer was equally busy in the Cincinnati area.

Philip G. Gossler was among the first to recognize the potential for natural gas to become the primary source of energy for homes and industry.

An engineer by training, Gossler became chairman of the fledgling Columbia Gas and Electric Company in 1912. Energy hungry Cincinnati and adjoining towns were Columbia's initial service area.

During Gossler's first dozen years at the head of Columbia, the company's service area expansion carried it into central Ohio and included the acquisition in 1924 of Columbus gas distribution operations including those which had been acquired and later sold by Ohio Fuel and descendants of the old Columbus Natural Gas and Fuel Company.

The present Columbia Gas System, of which Columbia Gas of Ohio is a sub-

sidiary, was born in 1926 with the union of Gossler's Columbia Gas and Electric Company and the Ohio Fuel Corporation.

Gossler, who served at the helm until 1947, was convinced Columbia resources and properties would make routine household chores less tedious and increase production capacity on the industrial

Pipeline construction crew just outside of Columbus, in 1900 used tongs and wooden levers to install line.

front, strengthening communities it served. When the nation came around to the same conclusion, what would become one of the largest integrated energy systems in the world stood ready to serve.

The merger of Columbia and Ohio Fuel, which served contiguous areas, allowed

the two companies to pool gas supplies and accomplish economies in transmission through more direct routing.

By the time the nation first swung to gas in a big way just before World War II, Columbia had acquired and built a giant system of pipelines capable of delivering a fuel that had come to be recognized as clean, efficient and cheaper than oil and coal.

System realignments led to the formation of Columbia Gas of Ohio in 1964. Further realignment in the early 1970s stripped Columbia of Ohio of transmission activities, but made Columbus headquarters for one of the largest combined natural gas distribution networks in the nation.

Today the Front Street location, long a center of Columbia System operations — and its annex, the old Hanna Paint Building at 95 West Long St. — is corporate headquarters for seven Columbia Gas Distribution Companies. Together they serve nearly two million customers, more than half of whom are in Ohio.

Columbus office operations support a largely underground delivery system that includes 14 million feet of pipe buried under the streets of Columbus.

The massive system continues to deliver what Gossler knew and millions have learned is still Ohio's best energy value.

The Columbus Citizen-Journal

Pioneer paper still a leader in a pioneer city

Historian Edwin Emery called them "low priced . . . small in size, but well written and tightly edited; hard-hitting in both news and editorial page coverage of the local scene."

He was talking about the newspapers Edward W. Scripps founded near the turn of the century. The description still fits, especially at the *Columbus Citizen-Journal.*

The Citizen-Journal, more often called simply "C-J" by loyal readers, traces its roots to the *Columbus Citizen,* one of the first newspapers added to what later became world famous as the Scripps-Howard Newspapers concern.

Scripps made his name in American journalism as a champion of the common man. He wanted his newspapers to educate citizens who could not afford formal schooling. He insisted that his writers use clear and simple language in their news stories. And he insisted on a price anyone could afford: In those days, it was one penny per copy.

This was the longtime home of the Columbus Citizen *before it became the* Citizen-Journal *and moved to new quarters.*

It was therefore only natural that the *Columbus Citizen* caught Scripps' eye just after the turn of the century.

Founded March 1, 1899, the *Citizen* was a penny paper like Scripps' other Ohio publications in Cleveland and Cincinnati.

It had enjoyed success from the day its

first eight-page issue rolled off the presses at 210 South High Street. Within months, the *Citizen* outgrew its original quarters and moved to the ground floor of 208 South High Street inside the same building. The firm moved again in 1900, this time to bigger offices in the Mithoff Building at 47 East State Street.

All this rapid expansion and popular acclaim brought it national attention.

Scripps liked what he heard about the *Citizen* enough to pay a personal visit. He also liked what he saw.

He bought controlling interest in 1904 and made a front-page prediction that proved he was among the first to see what the city of Columbus would become by the time the end of the new century drew near:

"The 'Scripps people,' as they are sometimes familiarly called, do not select a city to be represented therein except upon the fullest investigation and absolute proof that there is a flourishing community,

The old composing room at the Columbus Citizen was populated by line-casting machines and their operators. However, "hot metal" has been replaced by "cold type" and the C-J's composing room today is dramatically different.

with a great future in prospect.

"This is the firm conviction of the Scripps-Rae League (as Scripps-Howard Newspapers was then known) regarding the city of Columbus."

The *Citizen* continued its pioneering under its new ownership. It had all the big stories — and the big people — of the day:

— The 1910 street car strike which paralyzed the city and almost paralyzed the *Citizen* news staff. The paper hired extra reporters to keep up with the fistfights and dynamited street cars.

— The 1913 flood, one of the city's worst disasters. Rain which began falling in mid-March broke the levy and a wall of water swept the west side, trapping thousands in their homes.

— *Citizen* reporter James "Jimmy" Fusco, who scored a scoop so dramatic it seemed better suited to a movie script than a news column. Assigned to cover the unsolved slaying of an Ohio State University coed in the late 1920s, Fusco's digging uncovered clues which led to an OSU professor who was later tried, convicted and executed for murder.

— *Citizen* Editor Robert S. Brown, who decided he should do more than just supervise the reporting of World War II. He enlisted in the U.S. Army as a captain, and had risen to lieutenant colonel by 1944 when he was killed in a plane crash in the Pacific.

In the meantime, the *Citizen* had long ago outgrown and abandoned its East State Street home. The Scripps organization built a new building at 34 North Third Street in 1910, and had to enlarge it and add a third floor by 1925.

The newspaper added a Sunday edition in 1938 but the next major change did not come until November of 1959, when the *Citizen* became the *Citizen-Journal* so well known to Columbus readers today.

The *Citizen*, an evening paper since its birth, took over the morning slot vacated by the failing *Ohio State Journal*. Thus the *Citizen* became the *Citizen-Journal*.

The new C-J moved to its present home at 34 South Third Street, where it contracted with the Dispatch Printing Co. for mechanical and business functions.

Once again publishing six days each week, the paper continued under the same proven, distinguished and award-winning Scripps-Howard leadership and ownership.

Still non-partisan and independent, the C-J today gives readers the advantages of the Scripps-Howard state and national wires, United Press International and the New York Times Service, as well as the skills of its own highly-trained staff.

It offers the same tightly edited and well written news pages which won E. W. Scripps his world fame.

And its price has increased only 14 cents in 81 years — still a bargain anyone can afford.

The Columbus Show Case Company

Eighty-five years later the dream lives on

From the turn of one century to within years of the advent of another is a long time to hold on to a dream. As The Columbus Show Case Company marked its 85th anniversary in 1980, celebrating its founding in 1895, the dream of building quality, handcrafted showcases still shone clear and true.

Founded and headquartered in Columbus for those 85 years, The Columbus Show Case Company has always been a family organization, on both management and production levels. The company's physical facilities grew many times since the firm's founding, and the present manufacturing location at 850 West Fifth Avenue is augmented by a second manufacturing site in Bellevue, Ohio. The Bellevue plant's emphasis on producing metal cases and fixtures was a carryover from the 1960s when Columbus Show Case purchased the Imperial Equipment Company in Sandusky.

The Aschinger family has been active in the company since W.F. Aschinger joined the firm in 1898. He worked his way up through the manufacturing and managerial ranks, becoming a director at age 28. Today, son Carl J. Aschinger, Sr., and grandson Carl J. Aschinger, Jr., hold the titles of chairman and president, respectively.

The Columbus Show Case Company has grown to one of the largest store fixture manufacturers in the United States. Its two plants occupy more than 300,000 square feet and produce thousands of units each year.

In the 1970s, the company organization was divided into food and store equipment merchandising, with sales and marketing responsibilities assigned to both.

Food merchandising provided display equipment for supermarkets, bakeries and other food related markets. The company's heritage as the nation's oldest and largest manufacturer of bakery display equipment made this area of merchandis-

The Columbus Show Case Company moved to its present location at 850 West Fifth Avenue in 1922. With office and plant expansions, facilities here grew to total more than 250,000 square feet.

From its first location on West Naghten Street to this building on North Grant Avenue (1907), The Columbus Show Case Company enjoyed a steady growth as the need for hand-crafted, quality store fixtures expanded along with a booming retail industry.

ing an historical as well as profitable one.

Store equipment merchandising has traditionally encompassed several types of retail outlets including department stores, mass merchandisers, catalog showrooms, drugstore, photo, jewelry, office supply and book stores. Satisfied clients have included Lazarus, Saks Fifth Avenue and Lord & Taylor as well as mass merchan-

disers such as K mart.

Today, there are likely to be more Columbus Show Case display units in a larger variety of stores than those of any other manufacturer.

Throughout the years, The Columbus Show Case Company's dedication to quality craftsmanship never wavered. Today's Columbus Show Case Company offers a wide range of products to meet a wide range of merchandising needs; professional assistance in marketing and store design; and, most importantly, a genuine concern for the customer.

Columbus and Southern Ohio Electric Company

From street cars to electricity: a century of service

Edison's incandescent light bulb was still a dream when the forerunner of the Columbus and Southern Ohio Electric Company began operations in 1863. The need for public transportation in Colum-

bus was growing, and the Columbus Railroad Company began operating that year with the first horse-drawn street car on an unpaved High Street.

The Columbus Electric Light and Power

Company wasn't incorporated until 20 years later, when it was given a contract by the city "for lighting the streets and public places." In 1903, the operations of these two companies came together under the new Columbus Railway and Light Company.

As a new energy source, electricity was often viewed with hesitation and mistrust. Many hotels and public buildings posted signs to assure people that electricity was indeed safe. As public acceptance of electricity grew, Columbus began finding new uses for it. In 1890, the city had its first electrically powered street car, and after the turn of the century, the arches built across High Street in 1888 were changed from gas to electric illumination.

Increased emphasis was being placed on service to residential customers. Homes were being wired for electricity — "the ser-vant that takes no holidays" — and people were being urged to "work by wire — cheap, convenient."

Between 1887 and 1908, seven companies began providing electric and heating service to various parts of the city. It wasn't until 1915 that all of the street car, electric and heating companies were consolidated under the Columbus Railway, Power and Light Company.

During this time, electricity was generated by plants located in the city.

The Spring Street generating station, which operated from 1890 to 1929, was originally built to power electric street cars. Later it was expanded to provide power for street lights and other electric service.

The Spring Street generating station, located a few blocks west of the Ohio Penitentiary, operated from 1890 until 1929. Smaller generating stations operated on the south side of Broad Street at the west end of the Scioto bridge and on the northeast corner of Gay and Third streets.

These stations would later be replaced by generating stations built away from the city in order to be near the source of their fuel — coal.

The demand for electricity continued to grow. In 1931, 94,133 Columbus customers used nearly 213.5 million kilowatt hours of electricity. At that time, the average residential customer paid about a nickel per kilowatt hour.

In the meantime, the consolidation and incorporation of small electric companies was taking place in southern Ohio, forming the Southern Ohio Electric Company. On May 13, 1937, the Columbus Railway, Power and Light Company merged with the Southern Ohio Electric Company to become the Columbus and Southern Ohio Electric Company. This merging process included 20 street railway firms, 29 electric companies, five electric and heating companies, three electric and railway enterprises, an ice and coal company, a waterworks and an artificial gas plant.

Electricity became even more important in the years ahead as new appliances were introduced and business and industry found new ways to put it to work. C&SOE met this demand by adding to the Picway generating station, located just south of the Franklin County line near Rt. 23, and by building the Poston generating station in Athens County, completed in 1951. In 1959, the Conesville generating station in Coshocton County was dedicated.

Transportation began to play less of a role in the company's history. The era of the street car came to an end on September 4, 1948, when the Neil Avenue/Main Street line made its last run. The following year, the transportation system was transferred to a wholly-owned subsidiary, the Columbus Transit System.

Street cars were replaced by electric trolley cars. But in 1965, the last trolley car left the streets of Columbus and electricity ceased to play a direct part in city transit. In 1973, after 110 years of providing transportation service to central Ohio, the Columbus Transit System was sold to the Central Ohio Transit Authority (COTA).

Today Columbus and Southern is committed to providing electric service and growing with the communities it serves. The company enters the 1980s serving nearly two million people in 25 counties. From its horse-drawn beginnings, C&SOE has grown up through service to people.

In 1895, line crews used specially equipped horse-drawn carriages to build and maintain electric lines.

The Dispatch Printing Company

Policy of Independent news presentation endures into second century

On June 28, 1971, 10 Columbus men — printers, publishers and editors — formed The Dispatch Printing Company. They had $900 in working capital and a commitment to independent presentation of the news.

Three days later, the first issue of *The Daily Dispatch* rolled off a rented press — a six column, four-page paper sold to its initial 800 subscribers for three cents a copy.

An Ohioan, U.S. Grant, occupied the White House, and Rutherford B. Hayes, a future president, held the governor's office in the 10-year-old Statehouse in Columbus. Ground had been broken for the Ohio Agricultural and Mechanical College which was to become mammoth Ohio State University.

Within the young city of 32,000 and the farming, mining and industrial areas of surrounding counties, patterns of growth and healthy diversity were being set which *The Dispatch* would reflect, promote and support through 11 decades.

In less than two months, the fledgling newspaper exceeded the combined circulation of its two politically-partisan competitors. From then on, as Columbus became a major midwest center of government, education, industry and retail trade, *The Dispatch* continued to be the dominant newspaper voice of the area.

Through changes in ownership and downtown location, expansion and technological advance, the name of the paper and its commitment to independence and service remained constant.

In mid-1874, the founders sold the paper to Capt. John H. Putnam and Dr. G.A. Doren. They sold the paper two years later to two printers, Capt. L.D. Myers and William D. Brickell.

Myers, after being appointed Columbus postmaster, sold to Brickell in 1882.

With a steady circulation increase, additions in staff and equipment, *The Dispatch* outgrew its first home at 26 North High Street. In 1895, it moved to the northeast corner of Gay and High Streets, put new perfecting presses and its first six linotype machines into operation, and celebrated with a 72-page edition on April 10.

Four years later, Brickell bought the *Sunday News* and issued *The Dispatch's* first Sunday edition.

In 1903, J.J. Gill, a Steubenville congressman with senatorial ambitions, bought *The Dispatch* from Brickell. In 1905, he sold the paper for $275,000 to a broker representing brother Harry P. and

Home of The Dispatch since 1925, now a full block deep, is at 34 South 3rd Street, across from Statehouse Square. (1980 photo)

Fed by 1,700-pound rolls of newsprint from the reel room below it, one of the four mammoth Dispatch presses, center level, runs at a normal speed of 2,000 feet per minute and prints about 60,000 copies an hour. On the top level, webs of paper are manipulated to assemble pages and sections in proper sequence. The Dispatch uses 55,000 tons of newsprint and 1,750,000 pounds of ink a year. (1980 photo)

Robert F. Wolfe, owners of Wolfe Bros. Shoe Co and since 1902, of *The Ohio State Journal*.

On April 9, 1907, *The Dispatch* survived a disastrous fire without missing an edition and used rented quarters and salvaged equipment until the plant was rebuilt. Arson was suspected, in retaliation for the paper's disclosures of graft in City Hall.

The Dispatch moved in 1925 to 34 South 3rd Street, to a building now grown to a full block's depth between 3rd and 4th Streets.

On November 8, 1959, the merger of *The Columbus Citizen* and *Ohio State Journal* was announced, and the first edition of the new morning *Columbus-Citizen Journal* appeared the next day. It is published in *The Dispatch* building with news content controlled and produced by the Scripps-Howard Company and *The Dispatch* providing all other production services by contract.

Modernized to the publishing standards of the computer age, *The Dispatch* employs 1,400 persons to serve more than 200,000 daily and 340,000 Sunday subscribers.

Through 85 years as its publisher, the Wolfe family has maintained the paper's original precepts, and adhered to a favorite motto of H.P. and R.F. Wolfe:

"If it's good for Columbus, it's good for *The Dispatch*."

From a 1907 campaign against corrupt streetpaving contractors to a recent probe of state mental health programs, *The Dispatch* has kept a watchful editorial eye on officialdom and the public good.

Through Dispatch Charities, it has distributed more than $1 million among worthy programs and institutions.

Dollar Savings Association

A diversified savings association geared toward future growth

Columbus in the 1890s was a good place for a business to begin. The soil was fertile and the years to come would offer growth and expansion opportunities yet unimagined.

So it was that on May 4, 1894, the Globe Building and Loan Association was established. Thirteen years later, in January 1907, Globe became Midland Savings Company and opened offices on South High Street. In May of 1907 the Dollar Building and Loan Company was incorporated as a state chartered stock institution and opened its doors at 198 South High Street.

The company experienced a great many changes in the years that followed, including a merger, in 1915, with Midland Savings Company and a move, in July 1923, to 38 West Gay Street.

In 1926, Dollar's board of directors persuaded Harold C. Gockenbach, Sr. to leave his post as Franklin County Clerk of Courts and become managing director of Dollar Building and Loan. Gockenbach's tenure was a period of important change and substantial growth for the firm.

In September 1933, traditional credit sources for homebuilders were drying up. Building and loan associations were springing up all over the country, however, due to the passage by Congress of the Home Owners Loan Act. Dollar, by this time well established as a building and loan, joined the Federal Home Loan Bank and converted to a federal savings and loan association in March 1936. Its name was changed to Dollar Federal Savings and Loan Association.

In May 1936, Dollar took further action to protect its depositors by having all accounts insured by the Federal Savings and Loan Insurance Corporation (FSLIC).

By the end of World War II, Dollar Federal had grown to $2.5 million in assets and was gearing up for the post-war housing boom and rapid expansion.

In 1946 a young teller — H.C. Gockenbach, Jr. — began his career with the company. Today he is chairman of the board.

With its assets steadily climbing, Dollar was ready, in 1955, to introduce another facility. Its second office was opened in March, 1955 at Olentangy River Road and West Third Avenue. The downtown office was moved, in 1957, to the corner of Gay and High Streets where it still serves as the firm's main office.

In 1947, Dollar's assets were $4,768,000.

The site of Dollar Savings' main office at Gay and High Street, as it appeared in 1900.

By 1957, assets had grown to $27,724,000 — a 481 percent increase in 10 years compared with an average increase for all Columbus associations of 209 percent. Ten years later, in 1967, the firm's assets had climbed to $67,300,776 — a 142 percent increase. Total assets were near $400 million in December 1979.

A temporary Dollar office was opened in Hilliard in July 1959 and finished as a permanent facility in 1960. Then, also in 1960, the Gay Street office was expanded to four floors; marble facing was applied to the exterior and the addition of bronze eagles gave the building a fresh, distinguished appearance.

Innovative customer services were introduced during the 1960s — including interest paid on Christmas club accounts, open-end certificate passbooks, and daily compounding of interest.

Twice in the '60s Dollar was the recipient of the George Washington Honor Medal from the Freedoms Foundation of Valley Forge, Pennsylvania. The first award, in 1963, was for a program in economics education conducted by newspaper advertising and printed materials. The second award was received for publishing "Dollar Hollar," a monthly newsletter on Americanism, and "My American Heritage Date Book," a series of historical facts about the United States which has since become a 12-month calendar and is distributed free.

The 1970s marked a period of rapid expansion and growth in buildings and assets by the firm. Sunbury Savings and Loan was acquired in December 1970 and became a full service branch of Dollar Federal. Later, additional new offices were opened in Reynoldsburg, Pickerington, German Village and the Eastmoor-Bexley areas — enabling the firm to better serve the financial needs of a growing Columbus.

Dollar Financial, Inc., a subsidiary of Dollar Savings, was formed in 1975 to give the savings association a wider range of services in the fields of property management and lending.

The year 1973 saw another name change and conversion to a state chartered institution. Dollar Federal Savings and Loan was now known as Dollar Savings Association. By 1979, the firm had 12 full service branch offices operating in Central Ohio and plans were underway for the construction of two more offices in 1980.

Today, Dollar Savings operates as a total family financial center, a widely-diversified savings and loan geared to future growth and changing financial demands.

By branching out into areas such as land development, consumer lending and counseling, remodeling services and loan sales, the company hopes to modify the traditional savings and loan structure into a more competitive financial organization better suited for future challanges.

Ebco Manufacturing Company

A thirst for success led to satisfying the world's thirst

At almost any moment of any day, thirsty people somewhere in the world are likely to be quenching their thirst from a made-in-Columbus Oasis water cooler, the major product of Ebco Manufacturing Company.

Ebco was formed in 1935 by a group of investors, headed by A. R. Benua, who purchased the D. A. Ebinger Sanitary Manufacturing Company.

Ebinger, incorporated in 1910, made a number of plumbing and appliance products and by 1913 was in the water cooler business with a line of "EBCO" iced water coolers and beer coolers. It helped design the first electric water cooler in 1924 and subsequently manufactured them for most of the big-name water cooler marketers of those days: Frigidaire, General Electric, Norge, Copeland, Kelvinator and others.

But its many products for many markets brought Ebinger to bankruptcy and the entry of Mr. Benua in 1935 to the presidency and leadership of the new company, Ebco Manufacturing Company.

Benua, who had many years of experience in metal manufacturing and management as owner of Triumph Brass Company, gradually molded the new company into a capable and profitable business operation by concentrating on the production of electric water coolers.

The now-famous Oasis brand name was introduced early in 1941 with the plan to establish a national network of plumbing and electrical wholesaler distribution. World War II quickly brought this distribution plan to a halt, and what production was permitted during the war years was limited to supplying military installations and defense plants.

After the war, water cooler sales increased steadily and the product line was augmented in 1949 with the introduction

This advertisement, circa 1930, illustrates the water cooler designs of that era.

of a line of portable dehumidifiers. Manufacturing space inadequacies and inefficiencies at its 401 West Town Street plant, however, became a limiting factor on the company's growth potential.

This led Benua to start plans for a new plant facility that would bear his personal design for the production of water coolers and dehumidifiers, as well as special amenities for the comfort and safety of employees.

His dream was realized in 1955 when the company moved into its new plant at 265 North Hamilton Road. Benua's foresight in design was confirmed by the naming of the facility as one of the ten best plants of that year. At the time, it was one of the few in the country that was air-conditioned throughout the entire factory production area. Additions over the intervening years have almost doubled its size.

As its domestic distribution and sales increased, Ebco turned to international markets for further expansion. The company's products are now distributed in more than 120 foreign countries, and export sales represent an important part of its business.

The U. S. Department of Commerce has twice recognized Ebco's excellence in export sales, with the "E" Award in 1963 and the "E Star" Award in 1971 for continued excellence.

Pride in being one of the first, as well as the largest, manufacturers of water coolers and in being the oldest continuous manufacturer of dehumidifiers led to the creation of a museum of its history at its Hamilton Road headquarters. Memorabilia from its earliest days are on display, including twelve vintage water coolers and dehumidifiers.

A. R. Benua died in 1963. Louis Benua, who succeeded his father as president in that year, comments, "Dad put this place together . . . got it started and on its way. He made it easier for us who followed."

Under Louis Benua's leadership, Ebco has continued to prosper. Unit sales in 1979 were well over three times the sales in the year he became president. Benua family members who have assisted him in management were, first, his brother, the late Tom, Sr., and, currently, his wife Bettie and nephew Tom, Jr.

While new products and new markets

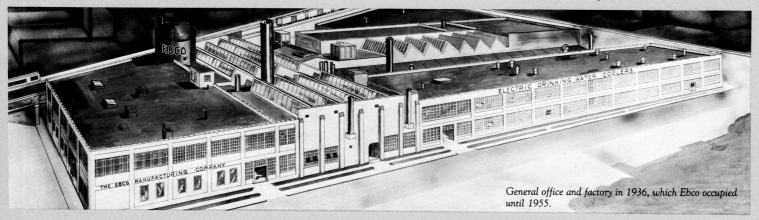

General office and factory in 1936, which Ebco occupied until 1955.

have contributed to this sound growth record, Benua attributes much of his success to the continuation of traditions established by his father — quality products manufactured and marketed by quality people. He has every expectation that the Benua family will continue to direct the privately-held company in the years ahead.

Franklin Federal Savings and Loan Association

90 years serving central Ohio

In the late 1800s, the south portion of the city Columbus became populated predominantly with first and second generation German settlers. From this background, a group of local merchants and businessmen met to discuss the feasibility of organizing a savings institution to serve this rapidly-growing area. These men recognized an obvious need, and saw the opportunity to support and benefit their local community.

On April 25, 1890, a charter evolved from this congenial meeting of friends and from the State of Ohio for Franklin Loan and Savings Company through a limited stock issue. Eleven directors were elected to the company including the mayor of Columbus, Phil H. Bruck, and Henry Pausch, treasurer of Franklin County. Also on the first board of directors were J.L. Trauger, J.P. Bliss, Fred J. Immel, Henry Kropp, P.J. Magly, Charles Frank, Charles A. Deibel, Phil Schmitt, and Peter Baker. A local grocer, Henry Kropp, volunteered the rear portion of his store at 345 South High Street for the site of the newly-formed company.

The assets of the company grew, and, by 1900, it became necessary to move into more adequate quarters. A rented storeroom was procured at the northwest corner of Mound and High Streets. These new quarters were large enough to accommodate a manager and two tellers, and the company began full-time operation. Not long after settling into the new quarters, the company faced its first crisis — a $35,000 shortage in the vault cash. The directors of the company personally replaced the missing funds to protect the integrity and solvency of the young company.

On September 1, 1920, with assets of $3.6 million, the Franklin Loan and Savings Company moved into its new six-floor building at Main and High Streets, the present location of the main office. The location and size of this new office was designed to serve the company for many years to come.

The company continued to grow and prosper and reached assets of $8.5 million before the onset of the Great Depression in the early '30s. It would be several years before the company would again reach

The main office of Franklin Federal at the corner of Main and High Streets in 1949.

Walter C. Kropp (left) and one of the original founders. Henry Kropp (right), surveying the new office quarters during the early 1920s.

that benchmark. During those trying economic times, Franklin continued normal operations when many other financial institutions faltered or failed. With the advent of the new financial regulations promulgated by the federal government, Franklin Loan and Savings was able to meet the requirements and, in 1935, converted to a federally-chartered association. At this time, the name of the company was changed to Franklin Federal Savings and Loan Association, and insurance of accounts up to $5,000 was immediately available.

Two landmarks have been associated with Franklin Federal. From 1936 until the mid-'50s, a large, three-sided, decorative clock which chimed every hour on the hour dominated the front of the building. This fostered the expression that

Franklin Federal was located "at the chimes." In 1940, a large neon sign was erected as part of the Association's 50th anniversary celebration, and this sign remains a distinct part of the modern-day Columbus skyline.

It was necessary to expand again and, in 1958, this was accomplished by a substantial addition, complete renovation, and provisions for parking. These improvements were quickly followed, in 1963, by the association's first branch office on Livingston Avenue, which was to serve the many families who had migrated in an easterly direction. Since that time, a total of nine branch sites have opened to serve Franklin and the surrounding counties, including two sites served by a totally self-contained mobile unit — the first in the Midwest.

Franklin Federal Savings and Loan Association has profited from capable management since it was organized in 1890. Throughout the institution's 90-year history, direct ties to the founders have existed and only four chief executive officers have served — Henry Kropp, Walter C. Kropp, Fred C. Kaiser, and Walter H. Kropp.

Franklin Federal has soundly and responsibly met the financial needs of its customers, and the fact that it still serves the children and grandchildren of many of its earlier customers speaks well of the respect and integrity in which the association is held.

With assets of $190 million today, Franklin Federal has played an important role in the growth of Columbus, and will continue to share in its future.

Franklin University

Spirit of its founding major ingredient in university's growth

If there is one main theme threading through the fabric of Franklin University's 78-year history, it is the university's primary concern for the individual student. "Since its beginning, Franklin has pioneered in meeting the needs of people who have the ambition to earn their education after working hours and at other unusual times," said Frederick J. Bunte, appointed president in 1978. Franklin set the pace in Columbus by being the first institution of higher learning to initiate 7 a.m. or "early bird" classes for the convenience of the student. Today the university operates on a seven-day basis, with "early bird" morning, evening, midnight, Saturday and Sunday afternoon classes.

Just as important, Franklin also has shown its concern for the individual student by making teaching its central mission. It strives to strike a balance between academic theories and their practical applications in the business, government and technical worlds.

Franklin was not "founded" in the usual sense, but arose as a response after a group of young people began meeting at the Columbus Young Men's Christian Association in 1890 to discuss the current and moral issues of the day. In 1902, the foundation for the university was established by the creation of an educational division of the Columbus YMCA called the "School of Commerce."

The illiteracy rate in Columbus was high in the early 1900s so the primary emphasis was placed on teaching the

Franklin's first building, above, was erected in 1969 and is one of four buildings that today comprise an 11-acre campus. The university has always been known for offering many of its courses during the evening hours.

basics of reading and writing. During those early years, students worked during the day and pursued their education at night, a concept in contrast to traditional education of that time. Other firsts were introduced to the educational scene of Columbus from 1903 through 1931 — night law school and a cooperative day school where students could attend classes a half day and work the remaining part. Women were admitted to the "School of Commerce" in 1917.

In 1923, the entire "School of Commerce" was reorganized as a separate branch of the YMCA and ten years later the name "Franklin University" was adopted. Franklin separated from the YMCA in 1964 and became incorporated under Ohio law as a non-profit, independent educational institution governed by its own board of trustees. To meet the demands of a burgeoning enrollment, Franklin's first building was erected in 1969.

Today the university comprises an eleven-acre campus and is the largest four-year private university in central Ohio and the fourth largest in the state. Its pioneering spirit and concern for the individual student still exist in what Dr. Bunte calls the "non-traditional delivery system of education." The university was the first in central Ohio to offer classes from midnight to 3 a.m. at Columbus business and industrial locations. In 1977, one of the few undergraduate degree programs in public administration in the country — and presently the only one in Ohio — was instituted. Franklin inaugurated Sunday afternoon classes in 1979.

Other developments include the creation of a division of continuing and management education to administer workshops, company training programs and courses on cable television. Through an affiliation with the Mt. Carmel School of Nursing, Franklin offers prerequisite courses in science and liberal arts to students who pursue their major studies at Mt. Carmel. The two institutions are committed to developing an articulated bachelor of science degree in nursing.

Franklin's highly motivated students, whose average age is 27, are not preparing for life: they are living it. They see their degree as a tool for upward mobility and they are willing to make great sacrifices to get it. Many are employed full-time and many have families.

Students are given a "real world" education by full-time professors and adjunct faculty members who are in active practice as certified public accountants, business executives, attorneys, engineers, scientists, sales professionals, and government officials. Bachelor's and associate degrees are offered in business administration, public administration and engineering technology.

With a 32 percent increase in enrollment in the past five years, trustees in 1979 launched a major $4 million "Commitment to Excellence" capital expansion program. Plans included the construction, in 1980, of a library-classroom building. In planning for its future growth, university trustees and administrators chose to keep the university in the downtown location.

"Since its inception in 1902," stated a recent editorial in one of Columbus' daily newspapers, "Franklin has been a major part of the Columbus educational community. It merits public support in recognition of its continuing excellence and for its continuing support of its individual students."

John W. Galbreath & Co.

Faith in the future rewarded

They were the worst of times.

John W. Galbreath was 32 in 1929 — and literally broke. Certainly, his situation was common enough, and in these circumstances Galbreath's disappearance into the darkness of the Depression would have gone virtually unnoticed.

An original, though extremely risky, idea propelled Galbreath from the financial depths. Believing property to be universally undervalued, Galbreath knew small amounts of financial leverage could be used to free foreclosed properties from banks and other lending institutions.

Low interest rates, long paybacks and Galbreath's intense belief in the national recovery were the catalysts that attracted unencumbered property owners to invest.

More than 7,000 real estate transactions later, his dogged faith in the American economic system's inherent strength had paid off — years later, not one of the mortgages Galbreath held had gone into default.

It was a beginning. But even before another decade had concluded, insight into the hopes of the American worker would also be rewarded.

In 1941 John W. Galbreath was asked if he wanted to buy a town — McDonald, Ohio. Many giant corporations traditionally owned "company towns." Miners and millworkers were only tenants in run-down houses.

With corporate paternalism dying, and workers resisting their employer's efforts to sell the homes, Galbreath dove into the project. A massive capital infusion was ar-

With John W. Galbreath at the controls and Peter B. Ruffin looking on, ground is broken for New York's Mobil Building, a 1955 joint venture.

ranged, and with solid corporate backing McDonald underwent an unprecedented renovation — everything from indoor plumbing to street paving was brought in.

The decision was right. Workers wanted to own their homes because home ownership was a source of pride. Most important, home ownership created a personal bond between workers and the American economy, something they had never had before.

In the end, all 292 homes were sold to their former tenants. And McDonald was no longer a "company town."

With Galbreath leading the way in 16 states, the decade saw the end of "company towns" across the country. Social conscience and innovation had again been rewarded.

In the 1950s there was a different stimulus. A healthy economy was generating an expanding housing market. Complete, new communities were required, and innovative mass-housing became the Galbreaths' next challenge.

Encouraged and supported by industrial giants like U.S. Steel, John W. Galbreath & Co. jumped head-first into the residential development market. From Pennsylvania to Arizona total communities were created — usually from scratch.

Also in the early '50s, the Galbreath Organization grew in another direction. John W. Galbreath & Co., in tandem with the Galbreath-Ruffin Corporation, began developing, arranging financing, managing, and leasing high-rise office buildings.

Initially, there was a starting point — 525 Wm. Penn Place — Pittsburgh.

Then, national expansion . . . New York's — Mobil Building . . . San Francisco's — One Market Plaza . . . Chicago's — Montgomery Ward Plaza . . . Cleveland's — Erieview Tower . . . Columbus Center . . . and by the late '70s the Galbreath Organization had developed millions of square feet of prestige office space.

With Galbreath Organization projects

Ninety-nine 20-story condominiums form the core of Mei Foo Sun Chuen, the world's largest privately-financed residential complex, another Galbreath Organization project.

the combination of Oriental and American know-how.

Blending commercial, retail and public uses has evolved in other ways in the United States. Under Daniel M. Galbreath's leadership, projects such as Cincinnati's Fountain Square South and Columbus' Ohio Center are showing new ways to most effectively utilize valuable urban land through mixed-use development.

The Galbreath reputation for excellence, however, hasn't been restricted to real estate development.

Thoroughbred racing has long held a special appeal for the Galbreaths. And they have parlayed a modest stake into international acclaim. Horses from the Galbreaths' Darby Dan Farms have been the only winners of both England's celebrated Epsom Derby and the Kentucky Derby.

The Pittsburgh Pirates, another Galbreath enterprise, have produced excitement for millions. And with players like Willie Stargell and the late Roberto Clemente displaying a penchant for pennants, the Pirates have brought a special pride to the Galbreaths.

Even with all the success, the awards and accumulated accolades of half a century of building progress, John W. Galbreath & Co. has continued to remember the most elementary detail . . . never lose faith in tomorrow.

literally spanning the continental United States, international work was only a short, logical step away.

Mei Foo Sun Chuen, completed in 1978 at Kowloon, Hong Kong, is one example.

With 80,000 residents living around a vital commercial core, this development is the world's largest privately-financed residential community. Success in this redevelopment of scarce land came about through

Hanna Chemical Coatings Corporation

Nearly a century of progress with Columbus

The Hanna name first appeared on the Columbus paint manufacturing scene in 1886 — when J.B. and Clarence Hanna joined a company organized to produce paint products. It was called The Orr, Hanna, Abbot Company.

The Orr, Hanna, Abbot Company association was short-lived. The company was reorganized and incorporated two years later — on December 24, 1888 — as the Hanna Paint Company. Officially, this was the founding of today's Hanna Chemical Coatings Corporation. Between then and now, however, Hanna patterns of progress and growth have wrought many corporate changes.

Less than 25 years after its founding, Hanna Company production and sales activity were bursting the seams of the tiny East Long Street facility.

Walter S. Hanna became a leading central Ohio varnish-maker. As J.B. and Clarence presided over a growing paint business, younger brother Walter S. Hanna began cooking varnishes in a sprawling Columbus paint facility adja-

Jay S. Hanna, president.

cent to the Ohio Penitentiary. Hanna Paint was reinforced by Walter Hanna's lacquer and varnish products. By 1893 the company had found the path to Columbus' substantial buggy-making and furniture-manufacturing industries.

Following Clarence Hanna's death in 1908, J.B. Hanna guided the company to a respected position among the country's top paint manufacturers. Company sales representatives pounded beats far from the home office. Warehouse operations were established, therefore, in Kentucky, Indiana and in Cleveland, Ohio.

By the time J.B. Hanna retired in 1928, Hanna paint was enjoying wide distribution and acceptance in eight states. J.B. Hanna's ill health forced him to take a less active role, and he was succeeded in the presidency by Robert P. Hanna Sr.

Company leadership became a cooperative effort between Robert Hanna and Executive Vice President Charles W. Gardner. Gardner's qualifications made him an excellent leadership candidate in the paint manufacturing industry. In 1937, Robert Hanna died at 47 years of age, and Hanna's veteran executive, Charles Gardner, became president. His death less than two years later led to the naming of Walter Moore — Hanna's production chief — as president.

205

Hanna's son, Jay, who stepped in as president upon his father's death. The 36-year-old man had started tending the varnish fires and cooking pots 40 hours a week while he was a junior at Columbus Academy a few years before. He had performed nearly every chore the paint manufacturing plant had to offer, had gone on to manage the Birmingham operation, and — at age 32 — had become a vice president in Columbus.

Less than eight months later, the corporate anatomy underwent dramatic change. Hanna merged with the Columbus Varnish Company and Walter Hanna Sr. became president.

The late Walter S. Hanna Jr., was a man of small stature, driving energy and keen wit. When he assumed leadership of what was then known as the Hanna Paint Manufacturing Company, America was about to become an active World War II participant.

With V-J Day and the end of the war, Hanna's reconversion to peace-time production was quick and effective. So also was Hanna's readjustment to the competitive atmosphere of the paint marketplace.

The Columbus Varnish Company was redesignated Hanna Industrial Finishes — a division — soon after Hanna acquired the Sipes Company of Pittsburgh, Pennsylvania.

In 1951 the American Paint Manufacturing Company of Birmingham, Alabama became a Hanna property. Four years later, in 1954, DL Paint Company of Dallas, Texas joined Hanna's corporate family. That same year, the company moved Columbus operations from its downtown location to the present site.

In the mid-'50s, Hanna went international with the acquisition of an affiliate in Beirut, Lebanon.

By the time the '60s rolled around, Hanna products were being applied on metal siding material and roll goods for dozens of other products, before it was fed into harsh shaping and perforating machines. The corporate identity was changed to Hanna Chemical Coatings Corporation. Those years were probably the most exciting the company will ever know.

Walter Hanna was a dynamic man who made things happen. The company lost the influence of this leader upon his death in late November 1974.

Well trained in the business through an early association with the firm was Walter

Hanna's management team — Jay Hanna, president, Albert F. Dorton, executive vice president, Lorenzo D. Sheets, treasurer, Robert Torba, vice president of manufacturing, and Timothy Keller, controller — approaches the 1980s with the same spirit of service and dedication that has characterized its progress since 1886, nearly 100 years ago.

Hanna is a leader in the manufacture of chemical coatings. Its marketing area coil coating industry which includes predesigned, metal building, appliances, aluminum siding, mufflers, and steel lockers. Metal decorating includes can coatings, collapsible tube coatings and various protective coatings for the interior and exterior of sanitary containers. General industrial finishes include post painted products such as farm machinery, earth moving and construction equipment, air conditioners, water heaters, vacuum sweepers and other related products.

Hanna has developed many unique coatings for the coating industry such as high solids and water reducible baking enamels to meet the new governmental regulations for the 1980s.

Harper Engraving and Printing Company

Nearly one hundred years of quality engraving and printing

Charles Harper arrived in Columbus from New Philadelphia, Ohio sometime around the end of the nineteenth century and set up a small tea and spice business in the downtown area of Columbus. Towards the early 1890s he acquired a small hand-operated embossing press to produce engraved monogrammed social stationery for the ladies who frequented his shop.

In the early 1900s Harper abandoned the tea and spice business and decided to become a full-time stationer. He moved his operation, which now included four embossing presses, to 98 North Fourth Street — an old private residence. By 1923 he had expanded to ten presses and was

The home and staff of Harper Engraving in 1927.

probably one of the largest engraving stationers in the Midwest.

While this attempt at product line expansion had no relation to salt and pepper, he found the engraving business to be both unique and much in demand.

He added printing equipment and office supplies to his line and was a leading designer of newspaper mastheads.

The unique thing about Harper's success was his marketing approach. Daily circulars were sent to all parts of the country to solicit orders from lawyers and businesses.

While the scale of the operation is larger today, it still embodies the same principle that Charles Harper established years ago.

The business moved again in 1926 to 283 East Spring Street and remained there until the spring of 1980.

During the years since Harper's death in 1943, the company has taken a more specialized position in the graphic arts field. While many of his direct selling techniques are still used for soliciting stationery orders from out-of-state customers, the company now maintains its own sales force covering a wide geographical marketing area. The one engraving press which Harper started with has grown to 16, and the offset and letter-press printing fuctions today account for more than half the total sales of the company.

What was once six people in an old residence on North Fourth Street is now 37,000 square feet and 56 employees at 2626 Fisher Road. The firm's customer list includes many local as well as national and international companies, and law firms in virtually every state and some foreign countries. The product line includes all types of stationery, business cards, financial and business forms as well as a variety of office supplies.

As Harper Engraving and Printing Company moves toward its first hundred years of continued operation, Mr. Harper's motto is as important today as it was almost 90 years ago — "at Harper's, quality is a word we understand."

Highlights for Children, Inc.

Steadfast in its dedication to "Fun with a purpose"

Early in 1946 Dr. Garry Cleveland Myers, at the age of 62, and his wife Caroline Clark Myers left their professional careers to found *Highlights for Children*, which was to become the world's most honored children's publication. They decided that the editorial and business offices should be completely

separate, and as editor and managing editor, Dr. and Mrs. Myers established an office in Honesdale, Pennsylvania, near Mrs. Myers' family home.

World War II had ended a few months earlier, and it was difficult to find suitable paper for the new venture. The Heer Printing Company was able to provide suf-

ficient paper and the necessary printing skill, and that was the determining factor in locating the business and publication office in Columbus. Space was rented on the third floor at 37 East Long Street in a room designed as Heaton Music Company's recital hall. In June 1946, 23,000 copies of the first issue of *Highlights for*

HIGHLIGHTS
FOR CHILDREN

fun WITH A PURPOSE

The first issue of Highlights for Children was published in June, 1946.

In 1921 the new home of The Zanerian College of Penmanship was built at 612 North Park Street facing Goodale Park.

Children were published.

The early years were tenuous as circulation grew slowly. In 1951 Garry C. Myers Jr. was persuaded to leave his career as an aeronautical engineer and come to Columbus to assist with the business management. Through his innovations the company became financially sound. His wife, Mary, while raising a growing family, established an office at home and, with the help of neighbors, compiled lists of elementary schools to which were mailed introductory subscription offers for students, and lists of physicians and dentists who were urged to subscribe for their waiting rooms. Garry Myers Jr. was elected president in 1954.

Circulation was 125,000 in 1956 when Richard H. Bell joined the company as sales director to build a representative sales force. By 1960 the new team had built circulation to 500,000, and the offices on Long Street were overcrowded. A modern home office was constructed at 2300 West Fifth Avenue, and in May Dr. and Mrs. Myers dedicated the new building — as each issue of *Highlights for Children* is dedicated — ". . . to helping children grow in basic skills and knowledge, in creativeness, in ability to think and reason, in sensitivity to others, in high ideals and worthy ways of living —

for *children* are the world's most important people." That summer *Children's Activities*, a magazine with which Dr. Myers had been associated as editor from 1934 to 1946, was purchased and in September was incorporated into *Highlights for Children*.

Tragedy struck on December 16, 1960, when Garry and Mary Myers and Cyril G. Ewart, all officers and directors of the company, were killed in an airplane collision over New York City. Richard Bell, then a vice president, had built the sales force to more than 800 representatives nationwide, and under his leadership as acting president *Highlights* began to rebuild its management staff. He was elected president in January, 1963, when circulation passed 750,000. That September, prominent author and educator Dr. Walter B. Barbe joined the editorial staff.

At the age of 87 Dr. Garry C. Myers died on July 19, 1971, a few weeks after the publication of *Highlights for Children's* 25th Anniversary Issue. At that time many educators were discovering what Dr. and Mrs. Myers had known all along — that children begin to think, to reason and to learn at a very early age, which was why *Highlights for Children* had consistently provided editorial content to stimulate all

children between the ages of two and twelve. Caroline Myers died nine years later on July 3, 1980.

Circulation had passed one million when in May, 1972 Highlights purchased The Zaner-Bloser Company located at 612 North Park Street, marking its entry into textbook publishing. Richard Bell was elected its president while continuing as president of Highlights.

In 1888 C.P. Zaner founded The Zanerian College of Penmanship in Columbus, and in 1891 E.W. Bloser became his partner. Both were master penmen. In addition to teaching they marketed handwriting texts for schools and business colleges and a patented finger-fitting pen. After Zaner's death in 1918, Bloser incorporated the company and began to publish a series of texts known as *The Zaner Method of Handwriting* which was promoted to schools by graduates of The Zanerian College. Bloser died in 1929, and was succeeded as president by his son, Robert E. Bloser. A younger son, Parker Zaner Bloser, himself a master penman, became secretary-treasurer and authored succeeding series of handwriting texts.

In 1975 Zaner-Bloser published its latest textbook series, *Creative Growth With Handwriting*, with Dr. Walter Barbe as its chief author. That series, and its 1979 Second Edition, attained 85 percent of the handwriting textbook market nationwide. In 1980 the *Zaner-Bloser Kindergarten Program: Foundations for Formal Learning* was introduced.

As *Highlights for Children's* circulation neared 1.3 million in 1980, Richard Bell was elected chairman of the board and chief executive officer of the corporation and to continue as president and chief operating officer of Zaner-Bloser. Garry C. Myers III, who had served on the board since his grandfather's death in 1971 and in its employ since 1975, was elected president and chief operating officer of the Magazine Division of Highlights for Children, Inc.

Columbus has been an ideal home for Highlights and the principal source of its efficient and talented employees.

The Huntington National Bank

Innovation and confidence marked success of Columbus' oldest bank

To understand the early history of industry and commerce in Ohio, you must understand there was a problem with money. The problem was — there wasn't any!

So the settlers used substitutes. A buck deerskin was worth one dollar and a mink skin only 12½¢ — because it didn't wear well!

But making change was a problem.

Eventually each bank made its own currency. But some was worth more than others so people became careful of the "money" they accepted.

In 1863, the federal government passed

The Huntington National Bank maintains its head-quarters today at Broad and High Streets where it has been all of its 114 years.

the National Currency Act making currency issued by the federal government the only legal currency.

Meanwhile, Pelatiah Webster Huntington was learning to be a banker. As an employee of the Exchange Branch of The State Bank of Ohio, he vowed to open his own bank. In 1865, when the Exchange Bank closed its doors, "P.W." was 26 years old and the time was right.

On January 2, 1866, P.W. Huntington and Company opened at the northwest corner of Broad and High Streets with "P.W." as president. This was the beginning of a banking tradition that was to be enriched by succeeding generations of Huntingtons.

The bank prospered under "P.W.'s"

leadership. In 1878, he built a five-story brick "skyscraper" on the southwest corner of Broad and High and moved the bank across the street. As the tallest building in town, it housed the weather bureau.

The mergers in 1923 with the State Savings Bank and the Hayden-Clinton Bank gave The Huntington its first savings department. This was an innovation for the bank which had always been industrial and commercial oriented.

By 1924, the bank had outgrown the "skyscraper" and moved to its present location at 17 South High Street, in the center of downtown Columbus and opposite the State Capitol.

The main office remains there today with one of the most distinctive banking rooms in the nation. The three-story high ceiling and many other details of the unique and beautiful room were designed in 1924 by the renowned Tiffany. The people at The Huntington take particular pride in the careful preservation of this historical heritage.

In 1966, changes in state banking regulations spearheaded the formation of Huntington Bancshares Incorporated. The Columbus-based bank holding company, with more than 6000 shareholders and a statewide organization of 15 affiliated banks was to replace the once family-owned bank.

In the years following, The Huntington offered many innovative and exclusive banking services to its central Ohio customers. In 1973, it led the nation and the world with the first free-standing, fully self-service banking office called the Huntington Handy-Bank. This 24-hour facility was acclaimed by the world press for its unique contribution to the banking industry and brought bankers from most major countries to study the concept.

Meanwhile, plans were underway to consolidate the 15 affiliated banks of Huntington Bancshares into one

statewide bank. This was formally completed on December 31, 1979 with the organization of The Huntington National Bank with resources of more than $2.5 billion.

Planning for the statewide bank started in 1974 when the name "Huntington" was adopted by all the banks and the process of unifying services and operations began.

The course that "P.W." had set more than 114 years ago enabled The Huntington to make a great contribution to the growth and security of Columbus and Ohio. As the bank enters the 1980s, The Huntington will continue to be responsive to the needs of the communities it serves.

The Huntington National Bank, with more than 100 offices in the state and strong leadership at the helm, is looking forward with confidence to its future as an important regional bank in the United States.

In 1878, The Huntington built its own five-story "skyscraper", known as the tallest building in town, at the southwest corner of Broad and High Streets.

The Kroger Co.

Hard work and perseverance are its formula for success in retail foods

When 23-year-old Barney Kroger started his own grocery store in 1883, little did he realize what that one business would someday encompass.

Kroger's experience in business and his lifelong association with hard work began when he quit school at age 13 to go to work and help the family. Farm labor, door-to-door sales and eventually the management of a small grocery store laid

the groundwork for Bernard H. Kroger's personal investment in the grocery business in Cincinnati. It was an investment which, by the time of his death in 1938, would make him a giant in the food store chain industry.

The first Kroger store in Columbus opened in March 1907 at 494 North High Street. By 1909, nine Kroger stores were operating in Columbus and the firm had

its own warehouse at 208 West Broad Street. Barney Kroger bought wholesale groceries in large quantities, even carloads. He would then run large ads in the newspaper and realize quick profit from the customers who trusted his merchandise and responded to his advertising. The food was good and the prices were right. In the friendly competitive spirit which prevailed in that era, even com-

In 1904 Kroger became the first grocery store to combine meat and groceries under one roof.

Fresh bread was offered in Kroger stores around the turn of the century. Kroger was the first to operate bakeries and supplied fresh bread to all its own stores.

petitors bought wholesale at the Kroger warehouse.

The Kroger firm experienced rapid growth in the next several years, much of it due to the acquisition of other grocery operations. In 1916 the company acquired eight more stores from "Ohio Grocery and Baking," and much of its advertising was accomplished through the use of the yellow service wagons drawn by donkey teams. Byron A. Redman, who became branch manager of the Columbus division in 1929, was a driver of one of those wagons.

Twelve more stores were acquired in 1917 — from Tamian Brothers — and in 1926 Kroger's Columbus division moved its headquarters to 457 Cleveland Avenue.

A year later, the firm purchased a packing plant regarded as one of the most modern in the industry. It processed 3,000 hogs per week, 250 cattle, 100 lambs and 75 calves.

In its last year of acquisition, 1928, Kroger bought 31 stores from Piggly Wiggly.

By 1936 the Columbus division operated some 300 stores — in Columbus, Springfield, Zanesville, Newark, Mansfield, Athens, Lancaster, Marion and Portsmouth. That same year the Cookie and Cracker Bakery was added to the Cleveland Avenue operation.

In the 20 to 30 years which followed, the grocery store industry underwent major innovations and evolutionized from the mom-and-pop store-on-every-corner concept to the larger, more centrally located supermarket concept. By the year 1956, Kroger operated 62 stores, many of which embodied the new concept. That same year, the office and warehouse facilities were moved to 4450 Poth Road.

The company opened its meat fabricating and distribution plant in 1967. Five years later, its first Superstores were introduced in Reynoldsburg and

Worthington. Much larger in size than their forerunners, the Superstores offered consumers complete variety with more than 15,000 different products. Specialty shops such as delicatessens, in-store bakeries, floral and wine shops, international foods, fresh seafood, bulk produce, were key features that contributed to their acceptance and instant success.

Combination stores were a further extension of Superstores and the first Kroger Sav-On was opened in Westerville in 1977. Larger still than the Superstore, the Sav-On occupies 56,000 square feet and features "one-stop shopping" at its finest. Not only does the Sav-On have all the features of Superstores but it also sells appliances, hardware, housewares, toys, audio and video equipment and offers a full-line pharmacy and in-store restaurant.

Today Kroger is the number one food chain in Columbus — operating 28 stores in Franklin County — and the number two food chain in the world. Its marketing area's general offices are conveniently located in East Columbus along with a large warehouse distribution facility (more than 441,000 square feet), and meat fabricating and distribution plant (more than 78,000 square feet). The Columbus marketing area currently operates 97 Kroger stores in Ohio and West Virginia.

The Columbus distribution center assembles 12½ million pounds of groceries, frozen food and produce per week. Its dock transfers another 10 million pounds of product that originates in other Kroger facilities such as milk, bread, Kroger manufactured products, nonfoods, and cookies. It services 85 stores and dispatches 1,000 loads per week. To sum up the activities of the distribution center — there is a load leaving the gate every 10 minutes around the clock and the 72 Kroger tractors travel an average of 140,000 miles per week.

Approximately 800,000 loaves of bread are produced each week by the Kroger bakery. Not to mention approximately 96,000 boxes of Kroger saltines each week, all accomplished by 700 bakery employees.

Kroger's Tamarack Dairy opened in July, 1978 and currently processes approximately 900,000 gallons of milk per week. Sixty percent of its milk comes from local Ohio farmers, through a co-op.

Kroger's Columbus meat plant fabricates and ships more than 114 million pounds of meat annually and services over 127 Kroger stores, shipping approximately 85 semi-loads of product to Kroger stores weekly.

The stubborn, uncompromising, confident Barney Kroger would be pleased today to see that his early struggles and ongoing persistence have built a chain of quality, respected food stores.

Those stores are a tribute to his initiative and hard work.

Lane Aviation Corporation

Barnstorming biplanes to modern biz planes

Lane Aviation's 55-year-old background actually began in 1925 when its founder, Foster Lane, first flew in a Jenny airplane. Later, as a pilot, Lane started a barnstorming venture from town to town, flying passengers out of hayfields, flying a Waco 9 and a five passenger Standard J-1. Both were fabric covered with water-cooled engines. Added attractions were wing walkers and parachute jumpers.

During the Depression of 1934 and just married, Foster and Ruth Lane decided to start a fixed base flying service somewhere in the midwest. They selected Columbus, Ohio, with a population of 315,000 and its nearly new Port Columbus Airport. The equipment: a biplane, a desk, and a telephone.

Passenger flights moved from hayfields to the airport. There was flight instruction and sometimes rush trips to Detroit, Cleveland, Chicago, and Louisville and even smaller towns without airports where the pilot landed the airplane in the nearest pasture. Passengers wore helmets and goggles and the control tower used a hand held red or green light gun to direct the traffic.

Airplanes improved and cockpits became cabin airplanes. Lane Aviation flew Taylor Cubs, Taylorcrafts, Darts, Culvers, and Staggerwing Beechcrafts. Self starters were added and it was no longer necessary to hand prop the propeller to start the engine.

By 1940 World War II was being fought in Europe and Lane Aviation had been selected to participate in an emergency government civilian training program (CPT). Lane started flying in July of 1940 and one and a half years later, after the attack on Pearl Harbor in Dec. 1941, war was declared. CPT became WTS (War Training Service). The U.S. Navy took possession of Port Columbus Airport; Lane moved to Don Scott Field, which was under construction, and managed it for the duration of the war, training WTS Navy Cadets. During the period between 1942 and 1945, Lane trained 1,053 Navy Cadets.

The war over, the firm re-leased the Transworld Hangar I and on April 3, 1946, moved back to Port Columbus Airport. Dealerships were signed with Taylorcraft, Republic See Bee Amphibian, North American Navion, and Cessna. Post war sales boomed. Many business firms began to buy airplanes and use them for business trips. Columbus became an important air hub city.

In 1956 the city started construction on a new administration building on the northwest corner of the original airport property. At the same time Lane Aviation built two hangars just west of the new terminal area. This (1956 to 1979) was the beginning of a 23-year period of construction and of acquiring buildings which resulted in five hangars and office buildings, an air freight building, and shop and parts departments.

The original Lane emergency flights have grown into a business charter service with a fleet of airplanes flying the eastern half of the U.S. and Canada and with a 46-year-old air safety record.

Many people have contributed to the growth and development of LAC over its 46-year history, including officers who grew up with the business, such as Robert Varner, LAC's president who has been with the company for 40 years; Thomas L. Johnston, executive vice president, with LAC for 25 years; George Bubalo, vice president with the firm for 23 years. Second generation Donna Lane Earl has assumed management of corporate affairs. Foster A. Lane is working chairman and there are 112 employees in Lane Aviation's various professional divisions.

Foster Lane's Jenny airplane was only the beginning.

Foster Lane and 1928 model Waco biplane in front of the Lane Aviation hangars.

Lazarus

A one-room venture that grew and grew and grew

The Lazarus department store, an integral part of the community and "flagship" of Federated Department Stores, Inc., traces its roots to 1851 when Simon Lazarus opened a one-room men's clothing store in an inside room at the corner of Town and High Streets — within "walking distance" for everyone who lived in the village that was then Columbus.

In the 1860s the store's growth was spurred by the availability of ready-made men's clothing through the invention of the sewing machine. Mass manufacture of Civil War uniforms provided the necessary expertise for the manufacture of ready-made civilian men's clothing after War's end.

In the mid 1870s, Fred Lazarus, Sr., and Ralph Lazarus joined their father in business, sharing his firm views on customer service and fairness. After their father's death in 1879, Fred and Ralph expanded the store to the north and south. Ralph wrote the store's advertising which talked of "one low price" and "strictly one-price store" — highly unusual because most stores then engaged in bargaining with customers.

A clock tower and a new store front were added early in the 1890s. The store had its own electric light plant and a steam whistle which blew weather signals three times daily. After the turn of the century, women began to accept ready-to-wear fashions as replacements for the custom products of dressmakers. Accordingly, a new store across Town and High Streets was built, and women's and girls' apparel was added to the store's inventory.

On August 19, 1909, a moving escalator stairway, the Niagara Soda Fountain and an aviary of chirping canaries awaited customers.

By 1920, apparel business had expanded and such things as cameras, records and yard goods became important new merchandise areas, necessitating the addition of a building on High Street to the north. By 1926 home furnishings and electrical appliances were introduced in Lazarus stores. The addition of size and figure specialization in the apparel industry prompted the addition of Lazarus' Town and Front building and the opening of its first size-specialization area — for juniors.

By 1940, shorter work hours gave new significance to leisure and hobby goods. Foreseeing this, Lazarus opened its State Street building to house such merchandise

Lazarus store about 1900, showing the Clock Tower. Lazarus was then a one-floor store, stretching through several buildings, and offering mens' and boys' wear and shoes for the family, (above). One of the series of newspaper ads which announced the new six-story store of 1909. Others stressed Lazarus value standards, the confidence customers could continue to have in Lazarus quality goods, and the courtesy of Lazarus associates, (inset.)

and initiated horizontal stocking by which stocks were conveniently adjacent to merchandise displayed.

Lazarus opened the first unit of its Bulk Service Buildings in 1946 to more efficiently handle large quantities of merchandise and, in 1947, the first of four downtown garages opened. In 1960, a major High Street addition was completed.

With the spreading of the community, the first Lazarus branch store opened in 1962 in what was to become the Westland shopping center, followed by the Northland store in 1964 and the Eastland store in 1966. Then came a regional store in Mansfield, the Kingsdale store in suburban Columbus, the second regional store in Lima, the Home Store East, and the first Lazarus Budget Capri store. Even with expansion and remodeling in recent years, no Lazarus store has ever been closed to the public because of construction.

The early 1970s brought the opening of two Lazarus stores in Indianapolis, Indiana and, in 1978, a third facility opened

there, along with two more Capri stores in Columbus.

A fourth Indianapolis store opened in 1980 and Lazarus' continuing expansion plans also include a store in Huntington, West Virginia in 1981 and an Evansville, Indiana, store in Fall 1982.

Charles Y. Lazarus, present chairman of the company, reflects that his ancestors were men of vision but probably never envisioned more and more Lazarus stores serving hundreds of thousands of people. "But the need was there, the need will continue to grow, and we're proud that our stores are as contemporary as, and in some cases, even more advanced than the finest department stores in the world. Lazarus offers the things people need and want. But the store was founded on — and thrives on — principles of service and giving the customer more than just necessities."

Lazarus can take credit for several "firsts" in the department store industry: first to install escalators, first to install a door that's simply a curtain of air, first with size selection, first with horizontal merchandising and the first store in the country to be completely air-conditioned.

In 1916, when a driverless electric car roared across the street and into a Lazarus plate glass window, a sign was quickly installed proclaiming "everything new comes to Lazarus first." "It's as true today as it was then," says Mr. Charles.

Lennox Industries Inc.

Innovation fostered expansion to worldwide operations

Eastern Division sales and manufacturing headquarters were established in Columbus in 1941 at 1711 Olentangy River Road. When this photo was taken, circa 1962, Lennox facilities consisted of the group of buildings at right center. Lennox purchased the adjacent buildings on the left several years later.

Since its beginning in the 1890s in Marshalltown, Iowa, Lennox has grown from a locally owned and operated furnace company to an international corporation ranking among the top three producers of sophisticated heating and air conditioning equipment. In the United States, Lennox operations are geographically divided among five divisions. Lennox Eastern Division manufacturing and sales headquarters, at 1711 Olentangy River Road, were established in 1941 to accommodate Lennox' growing eastern markets.

The historical development of Lennox began unfolding in 1904 when D.W. Norris, a young newspaper editor and publisher, purchased the Lennox Furnace Company from David Lennox, a mechanical genius who felt uncomfortable in the furnace business and wanted to sell out. As president of the new firm, Norris was instrumental in developing technology that moved Lennox from simple coal-burning gravity furnaces to sophisticated forced-air gas and oil furnaces. As a result, Lennox' market expanded to the eastern seaboard.

Initially, Lennox-Columbus manufactured primarily coal-fired furnaces in a relatively small factory of 100,000 square feet. Oil and gas burning equipment comprised only a small portion of furnaces

produced in the Columbus plant. As Lennox grew and heating and air conditioning technology matured, new facilities were built to provide nearly one million square feet of office and factory space for more than 1,000 employees.

Although growth and change have highlighted Lennox' long history, the company remains a family-owned corporation and retains its direct-to-dealer method of merchandising which has played an important part in the company's success.

Succeeding D.W. Norris in 1949 was his son, John W. Norris, Sr., who added residential air conditioning to the growing Lennox product line in 1952. Following his retirement in 1971, Ray C. Robbins, the first non-family member chief executive officer, ushered Lennox into the exciting new age of solar energy. Lennox solar collectors have proved to be the most efficient yet produced. It was during Robbins' administration that Lennox corporate headquarters and its research and development laboratory were relocated to the Dallas, Texas area from Marshalltown. Today, John Norris, Jr., the third generation of Norris leadership, is at the helm as Lennox continues to develop high efficiency products that make the best use of the world's scarce

energy supplies.

Lennox-Columbus began under the leadership of General Manager Don Kinnan, who became president of the Armstrong Furnace Company which was under Lennox ownership then. There were several interim general managers until 1948 when Gordon Rieley, who has served as president of the Columbus Chamber of Commerce, began his 15 year term. Ray Turnbull succeeded Rieley in 1963 as group vice president and general manager.

Under Turnbull's leadership, Lennox-Columbus manufactures state-of-the-art air conditioning and heat pump equipment for residential and small commercial buildings. Large multizone units for rooftop applications, a concept pioneered at Lennox during the mid-1960s, also are produced here for installation on commercial and institutional structures such as hospitals, schools and office facilities.

As Lennox continues to develop heating and air conditioning products of the highest quality and efficiency, experience gained since the turn of the century will help provide the technology to do so. As one of the largest Lennox factory/sales headquarters, Lennox-Columbus remains a conscientious organization dedicated to the future of the city of Columbus.

Liebert Corporation

Refrigeration mechanic's dream is now "First . . . and growing"

The beginning was hardly glamorous. Ralph C. Liebert, refrigeration mechanic, had grown restless, and was ready for a change. In 1946 he loaded his family and tool box into his well-used station wagon. Armed with only a small refrigeration franchise and a $600 loan, they made the short drive from Cincinnati to Columbus — the first step in the evolvement of today's $60 million Liebert Corporation.

Settled in Columbus, Ralph Liebert was filled with optimism and new hope as he began his own business — Capitol Refrigeration, headquartered in downtown Columbus at 963 North High. Always innovating, Liebert soon developed and installed the world's first large industrial heat pump. Later, in more spacious quarters at 500 Dana Avenue, he was responsible for the early efforts in freeze-dried foods and coffee.

As Capitol Refrigeration grew Liebert explored new horizons and challenges that involved all phases of commercial air conditioning. The challenge to improve the computer room environment was the greatest of all. Computing speeds and capacities were constantly increasing and the net result — larger, more concentrated heat loads — now exceeded the capabilities of conventional air conditioning. Furthermore, answers to problems of humidity and air flow and cleanliness, so critical to these systems, simply did not exist.

Ralph Liebert grew increasingly frustrated, tired of the limitations imposed by these unsuitable technologies. His penchant for learning and innovative thinking was rewarded within six months, however, when he finalized the design of the first computer room environmental control system.

By 1965 Liebert Corporation had been born. With the first prototype system complete, Liebert approached IBM. Impressed, the larger corporation leased booth space to the fledgling corporation at the World Computer Conference. Not only was that first system sold directly from the floor to General Motors, but the first year's production schedule was taken back to Columbus.

The year was 1967. Disaster struck Liebert Corporation. Fire completely destroyed both building and inventory. In temporary headquarters, eight employees restored business within three weeks, and in 1968 the first new Liebert plant

The first Liebert facility, in 1946, at 963 North High Street (Above.) The Liebert Corporation headquarters in 1980, at 1050 Dearborn Drive (Inset.)

was constructed on Huntley Road for 38 employees.

By 1970, as shipments quadrupled, a company research and development team was formed to initiate the air conditioning industry's first line of solid state temperature and humidity controls.

The 75 employees were making sales records a way of life by 1971 as Liebert entered the international marketplace. Within a few years these efforts were rewarded with the "E Award" by the President of the United States. The award signified extraordinary accomplishments in the area of export marketing.

Production levels continued to soar. In 1975 the staff of 160 moved into yet another new facility constructed on Dearborn Drive. Diversification appeared to be the key to the future, so one year later the Special Products Division was formed to explore new markets for the advanced technology that had made Liebert so successful.

Most notable in a variety of early projects was the contract to furnish the equipment for the olympic bobsled run at Lake Placid. Then, the immediate acceptance of a self-contained energy package

for supermarkets, another Liebert first, gave the firm national identity.

Meanwhile, the sales of computer room environmental systems continued an upward spiral, now internationally as well as domestically, and in 1978 another 130,000 square feet of production area was added.

Another chapter in the Liebert story began in 1979 and incorporated more diversification, once again in a totally new direction. As computer power requirements became increasingly critical, the quality of commercial power steadily declined — a serious void, another need. The solution was the formation of a subsidiary company. Conditioned Power Corporation was to develop and produce the world's first self-contained computer power system. The new opportunity for growth necessitated the addition in 1980 of 150,000 square feet to Liebert's facilities.

Today a Liebert team totalling 750 continues to write the company's story — and the future is as unlimited as ever. Plans are now being finalized to develop a 42-acre Liebert Center. With an annual growth rate averaging 36 percent, chances are very good that Liebert will retain its motto — "First . . . and growing."

The McElroy-Minister Company

The insurance Professionals — providing service with integrity and experience

As the Industrial Revolution spread to Columbus in the 1870s, the ingenuity and enterprise of men like Harvey Bancroft helped to create a new protective business — insurance — to keep pace with the transformation and growth of the educational, professional, business, and industrial worlds. He realized — and based his business on the premise — that insurance was indispensible to the growth of free enterprise. Thus, insurance became more important — as did Bancroft's services.

In 1875, at 71 North High Street, "H. BANCROFT — GENERAL FIRE INSURANCE" came into being because fire was the one thing most feared by property owners. As the city of Columbus expanded, however, the insurance industry had to meet the changing needs of its business community. When Frank McElroy joined the firm in 1883, the concept of a "fire agency" disappeared, and "BANCROFT-McELROY" was established with new headquarters at 85 North High Street.

The newly formed Bancroft-McElroy agency let it be known that it had broadened coverage to include "cyclone, plate glass, steam boilers, and surety bonds." In addition, burglary coverages were becoming necessary in the growing city. And at the turn of the century, automobiles began to change the lifestyle in Columbus — which created the need for types of insurance coverages never dreamed of before, such as collision and theft. Bancroft-McElroy was able to meet the need.

In the early part of the 1900s, legal disputes between management and labor began in order to determine management responsibility for medical expense and loss of income resulting from industrial accidents. "Employer's liability" was demanded; and these policies were written by Bancroft-McElroy. This need was short-lived, however, because of the passage of the Workman's Compensation Act of 1915.

In 1911, having bought out Mr. Bancroft, Frank McElroy renamed his agency "F. C. McELROY & COMPANY", and moved its headquarters to 79 East State Street. Harry T. Minister, who became an employee in 1915, later acquired an interest in the ownership.

In 1934, the company was renamed "McELROY-MINISTER," and in that

Above, Bancroft-McElroy sales force, circa 1907-1911, at 85 North High Street. The McElroy-Minister Company today, 141 East Town Street, (inset.)

same year, Robert McClure joined the organization. Austin McElroy, who had joined his father Frank in 1907, succeeded him upon his death in 1942; today he is Chairman Emeritus. H. Thorp Minister, Jr. became a member in 1949.

In the '50s, "all-risk" coverage became popular. In a most unusual request — which demonstrates its "total service" concept to provide creative, specialized service in total management of personal and business insurance — The McElroy-Minister Company was requested to furnish "all-risk" coverage on a submarine being shipped over land.

Even more exciting and spectacular was the harnessing of nuclear energy in electric power plants in the 1960s. The McElroy-Minister Company issued the first insurance anywhere in the world for liability coverage on a nuclear reactor.

More than 50 Ohio colleges and universities are clients receiving assistance for student health insurance, employee benefits, property and casualty, tax deferred annuities, and retirement plans. In addition, there are hospitals, banks, trade associations, schools, retailers, wholesalers, contractors, manufacturers, and thousands of individuals and families whose personal insurance accounts form the foundation of The McElroy-Minister

Company.

In 1960, John C. Glandon and Hugh M. Hadley became associated with McElroy-Minister. In 1965, Richard P. Banks joined the firm.

The year 1975 marked the 100th anniversary of the company. In addition to making a grant to The Columbus Foundation in recognition of that special occasion, the management of the company instituted an employee stock ownership plan. Under this plan, all employees who are aged 25 or older become shareholders of the company after being employed by the company for one year.

H. Thorp Minister, Jr., is currently chairman of the board of The McElroy-Minister Company, John C. Glandon is president, Richard P. Banks is executive vice president, Hugh M. Hadley is senior vice president and Hall B. Liles and George S. McElroy, Jr., are vice presidents.

The McElroy-Minister Company today is a company which maintains a close touch with all major insurance markets ... that participates in educational programs offered by appropriate trade associations, professional societies and management groups ... and a company which has learned the quality of service which it offers its clients is far more important than size; that service by its professionals in the insurance field is the key to its past, present, and future growth with Columbus.

The Midland Mutual Life Insurance Company

Company became a true "pearl" in the industry

Following the Civil War, hundreds of small assessment life insurance associations were formed, frequently by irresponsible promoters and, worse still, by more than a few dishonest promoters. Up until the early 1900s, abuses in the insurance industry ran rampant.

In addition, millions of dollars in life insurance premiums were drained each year from Ohio and paid to companies in other states. There the money was invested in various questionable securities under lax investment laws. Only a modest amount came back to Ohio — in the form of death benefits and matured endowments.

It remained for a body of public-spirited men who were concerned about these abuses to create a Columbus-based life insurance company in which the people of Ohio would have absolute confidence.

On August 31, 1905, 18 incorporators met to organize The Midland Mutual Life Insurance Company. Their names read like a "Who's Who" in Columbus of that day. Two should be singled out because they were to preside over the affairs of the company. Dr. William Oxley Thompson, president of The Ohio State University, was among the foremost educators of his time. An ordained minister, he also was an authority on financial and economic matters. Thompson served as The Midland's first president from 1905 until 1925. Upon his retirement, he was succeeded by H. B. Arnold, a leading attorney of the state, who served as president until his death in 1933.

The company charter was written by The Honorable Arthur I. Vorys, Superintendent of Insurance, with the assistance of H. B. Arnold, then counsel for the company.

The Midland founders would have preferred to charter a mutual life insurance company. However, the laws of

Dr. William Oxley Thompson was the first president of The Midland, 1906-1925, while also president of The Ohio State University.

Ohio at that time did not, nor do they yet, permit the incorporation of a mutual company. Of necessity, therefore, The Midland was started as a stock company. It is obvious, however, from the restrictions which the Articles of Incorporation placed on the stock, that the founders were paving the way for a mutual company. The Articles provided for 3,000 shares of $100 par value capital stock with dividends limited to $10 per share per year, and with the right of recall by the company at $200 per share.

The company was incorporated on September 30, 1905, and commenced business on July 2, 1906.

Over the years, the possibility of retiring the stock and converting the company into a "true mutual" had been thoroughly discussed. But the fact was, except for the modest $30,000 annual dividend, the company was in effect being operated as a mutual company. The mutualization procedures were rather complex, and the stockholders, who were in large part the founders or their heirs, believed that the policyholders were more than amply protected. They saw no urgent reason for conversion.

On three occasions between 1915 and 1955 the Midland stockholders received overtures regarding mutualization from other interests. In January, 1915, Thompson discussed in a letter to stockholders a scheme by a group of promoters to combine The Midland with nine other companies. The second overture came in 1927 when certain parties in Chicago threatened to "take over" the company.

The third and final attempt to buy The Midland arose in the spring of 1955. It was accompanied by much publicity and ultimately led to the mutualization of the company. It occurred when another Columbus life insurance company expressed an interest in acquiring the firm. Since the other company was a stock company, a merger was entirely logical from their vantage point. Conversely, had one been a Midland officer, director, employee or heir of a founder, one might have done everything in one's power to prevent such a merger and, therefore, would have supported a plan for mutualization.

Midland officers were approached by the other company regarding the possibility of merging the two companies. The stockholders as a group could sell their shares for $3 million or alternatively redeem their stock at $200 per share for the total sum of $600,000. They were being asked to give up $2.4 million and also to forego any future dividends. This was the sacrifice the stockholders were called upon to make if the idealistic charter provisions were to be carried out. They made that sacrifice.

On December 8, 1955, a meeting of the policyholders was held under the direction of the Superintendent of Insurance. The plan of mutualization was adopted overwhelmingly with a 92 percent affirmative vote.

After the fulfillment of a number of other legal requirements, a special meeting of stockholders was held on December 26, 1956, at which amended Articles of Incorporation and a new Code of Regulations were adopted. The stock was then retired.

The man who led The Midland up until its period of mutualization was its third president, George W. Steinman, who served the company for more than 44 years. A member of the bar, he joined The Midland in 1912 and served as president from 1933 until 1954. Steinman was elevated to chairman in 1954 and was succeeded as president and chief executive officer by Chester O. Sullivan, who presided over the company until 1967. Sullivan, an actuary by profession, had more than 47 years of active service with the company.

The Midland moved into its new 22-story home office building at 250 East Broad Street in 1970.

In 1967, James B. McIntosh succeeded Sullivan as the fifth president of The Midland. During his tenure as president,

the 22-story Midland Building was constructed, a successful group department was developed and an aggressive investment policy was adopted. The McIntosh era saw a reaffirmation of the company's accent on quality — quality people, quality product and quality service.

On January 1, 1980, McIntosh became chairman and Gerald E. Mayo became the firm's sixth president.

Today, The Midland is one of about 1,800 life insurance companies in the United States. It is a large company, with $360 million in assets and $3 billion of insurance in force. At the same time, it is a small company when compared with the giants of the industry.

When plans for construction of the new home office building were announced in June, 1968, the proposed building was alluded to as "The Pearl of the Midwest." And today, whether The Midland is considered a big company or a small company, its fundamental objective continues to be building a jewel of a company — a true "Pearl of the Midwest."

Motorists Mutual Insurance Company

Service and innovation mark company's first half-century

On the eve of the 1928 national election, 25 Ohio businessmen gathered at the Alms Hotel in Cincinnati. They had come to hear Carl N. Crispin discuss his plan for the formation of a new insurance company — a company that would stress prompt, fair claim service, yet give lower rates through economy of operation.

Crispin's work as Ohio's director of the Sesquicentennial Celebration, plus chamber of commerce and insurance experience, eminently qualified him for the venture. He had discussed his plan with then Ohio Governor, Vic Donahey, who felt such a company was needed and suggested further discussion with former Ohio Insurance Commissioner, Judge Harry L. Conn. This contact led to the Cincinnati meeting and to the approval of his plan.

Motorists Mutual became a company on November 28, 1928. Initially offering only automobile insurance, it began operations three days later with $15,000 capital borrowed under guarantee notes from the Motorists Insurance Agency, a corporation formed for the dual purpose of financing and promoting the mutual company. Heading the fledgling company was President Vic Donahey, whose term as governor was to end in early January. Carl

Motorists Mutual home office complex, 1980.

Crispin was named secretary and general manager, with the responsibility of directing all activities.

It was hardly a propitious time to start a new company. Within a year, the stock market collapsed, heralding the worst depression in the country's history. But an air of optimism prevailed at Motorists,

and the company's steady growth throughout the Depression was in marked contrast to the many firms who were forced to close their doors.

The company first gave notice of its future role as an insurance innovator in 1938 when it pioneered a new insurance coverage. Known today as "Medical Payments," it has subsequently been adopted by all casualty companies. Other pioneering efforts followed, most notably "Unsatisfied Judgment" (now known as Uninsured Motorists) in 1954 and the Anniversary Policies, a trend-setting series of policies incorporating new concepts in rating and deductibles, in 1978.

World War II, which began as the '30s ended, did more to restrict Motorists Mutual's growth than had the Depression. But, despite a slowing and then a shutdown of civilian automobile production, 1942 proved to be the most profitable in the company's brief history, and growth continued throughout the war.

The first major change in the company's management occurred in 1946, with the death of Vic Donahey, founding president and director. Donahey, who, during his tenure as Motorists' president had served a term in the United States Senate, was succeeded by Carl Crispin.

Having previously expanded into Pennsylvania, Indiana, Michigan, Kentucky, and West Virginia, Motorists Mutual became an all-lines company in 1955 with the passage of the Ohio Multiple Line Law. This permitted the addition of fire and allied lines to the company's casualty coverages and added impetus to postwar expansion.

Motorists had its third president in 1958 as James W. Huffman succeeded Carl

Motorists Mutual management in 1980 included, left to right: Chairman of the Board-President Cameron E. Williams, Senior Vice President J. Robert Keltner, Executive Vice President-Treasurer Lloyd G. Wright, and Secretary Lester L. Foust.

Crispin to that position, when the latter became chairman of the board. A former United States Senator, Huffman had been associated with the company since 1946.

If the '50s were a time of expansion for Motorists, the '60s can best be characterized as a time of diversification, as a variety of new coverages were made available to the insuring public. Motorists Life, a subsidiary company whose organization had been coordinated by Cameron E. Williams, was incorporated in 1965 and issued its first policy in 1967. This was the first of several subsidiaries, the rest of which followed in 1971.

Vic Donahey, son of Motorists Mutual's first chief executive, became president in 1969 as James Huffman was named chairman of the board. Ground was broken the following year and, in 1973 a new 21-story home office building pierced the Columbus skyline.

Cameron Williams, whose association with Motorists began as an agent in 1940, succeeded Vic Donahey as president in 1974 as the latter became chairman of the board. Williams assumed the additional title of board chairman in 1977. Under his leadership the company has celebrated its 50th Anniversary and has moved into the '80s with new strength and vitality — structured to meet the challenges of the future and the opportunities of today.

The Nationwide Organization

"We have a strong bond of progress with Columbus . . ."

"We are proud to have grown up with this community for more than half a century," General Chairman Dean W. Jeffers told a civic leadership audience about the $5 billion Nationwide organization. "We have a strong bond of progress with Columbus that has existed from our beginning."

"The story of that beginning," Jeffers went on, "is refreshing to retell in these days when people who could do for themselves will so often turn to government and others to solve their problems."

In the mid-1920s, a small group of Ohio farmers rebelled against their auto insurance rates. They were angry because their rates were as high as those for city drivers, who had more accidents than they did. When they couldn't get existing insurance companies to change this, they decided to start their own.

They needed capital so the Ohio Farm Bureau Federation put up $10,000 in bonds. State law required 100 pledged

Early home office: an old converted mansion at 620 East Broad Street.

Nationwide's founders had to convince conservative-minded farmers they should pledge to buy insurance from a company that didn't yet exist.

policies before the Farm Bureau Mutual Automobile Insurance Company could be licensed. The determined farmers obtained $1,000. Their first policy, full coverage on a 1924 Ford (list price: $580), was issued April 14, 1926.

At the outset, Farm Bureau Insurance sold only auto coverages and only to rural Ohioans. But the idea of quality auto insurance at lower rates was so appealing that people in towns and cities and in other states soon sought the company's services. Expansion into other states was begun within two years; services were extended to city people in the early 1930s.

World War II interrupted the territorial expansion in 1943 but it resumed again in 1952. Along the way, Farm Bureau Insurance outgrew its name and, in 1955, it was changed to Nationwide.

Farm Bureau Insurance became a multiple-line insurer in the 1930s, well before the concept caught on throughout the insurance industry. A mutual fire insurance company was organized in 1934. The following year, the American Insurance Union, a struggling life insurer that would be built into an industry leader, was acquired.

(A legacy of the American Insurance Union is the downtown Columbus LeVeque Tower, formerly known as the AIU Building.)

Heart of the Nationwide organization of more than 45 companies today is the five insurance companies bearing its name: Nationwide Mutual, Nationwide Mutual Fire, Nationwide Life, Nationwide General and Nationwide Property and Casualty — which together comprise one of the largest insurance organizations in the United States.

Nationwide also is engaged in varied enterprises including radio and television communications, real estate development, consumer finance and mutual funds, a diversification begun in 1946.

A third major segment of the organization is a leading financial services holding company, Nationwide Corporation, which started operations in 1955.

And Nationwide is multi-national today, with reinsurance business in some 30 countries, and auto, fire and life insurance subsidiaries in West Germany.

The late Murray D. Lincoln, a founder of Nationwide, headed its operations for the first 38 years. He was succeeded as president in 1964 by Bowman Doss. In 1969, George H. Dunlap was elected general chairman and chief executive officer. In 1972, President Dean Jeffers succeeded Dunlap as general chairman, John E. Fisher was elected president of the Nationwide Insurance Companies, John L. Marakas president of Nationwide Corporation, and Charles W. Fullerton president of Affiliated Companies.

Farm Bureau Insurance started its operations in 1926 in a rented fourth-floor room at 199 East Gay Street in downtown Columbus. It outgrew that site and another at 620 East Broad Street within ten years. The home office from 1936 to 1978 was at 246 North High Street, a facility which had to be tripled in size during the period. In 1976 the organization began to move into its present international headquarters, One Nationwide Plaza. The building, highlighted by a 40-story office tower, was completed and dedicated in 1978. It is the centerpiece of the largest privately backed redevelopment effort in the history of Columbus.

"Nationwide is proud to have grown up with its home community," says General Chairman Jeffers, "and we are tremendously excited about the future. There is no better place I know for a family or business to call home than Columbus, Ohio."

The Neil House

Continuing a long tradition of service and hospitality

To recount the history of the Neil House is to trace the political and social history of Columbus and of much of the state of Ohio. For the Neil House, in one of its five existences, has been around almost as long as the city and state.

A look backward into history shows the establishment of William Neil's Tavern ". . . across the High Street from the State House" to be a significant step in the community's emergence from the severity of frontier life.

Starting with his original tavern in 1822, William Neil served the public and prospered. He built a larger establishment — the first to be known as the "Neil House" — in 1839.

On the night of November 9, 1860, at the time Abraham Lincoln was being elected president, the second of William Neil's hotels burned to the ground.

A third Neil House was built and opened in the fall of 1862, the first truly modern hotel in the city. It was built at the then fantastic cost of $100,000.

The fourth Neil House, the one we know today, was built in 1925 at a cost of more than $4 million.

With each succeeding enlargement and modernization, the Neil House has fur-

THE NEIL HOUSE, COLUMBUS, OHIO'S
FAMOUS AND HISTORICAL HOSTELRY
LOCATED IN THE CENTER OF THE
COMMERCIAL AND THEATRICAL DISTRICT,
EUROPEAN PLAN.
BEN H. HARMON, GEN'L MGR.
State Capitol Grounds and McKinley Monument.

The Neil House in its early days, mid-1800s, across the street from the State House (Above.) The Neil House, today (Below.)

thered the memory of the original tavern keeper who set up business at 41 South High Street so long ago.

The third Neil House, which immediately preceded the present establishment at 41 South High Street, was as colorful as the era in which it existed. Its celebrated bar was a focus of the state's political life.

In the days when affairs of state were considered the exclusive concern of men, a gentleman's rendezvous — as luxurious and genteel as The Neil House bar — was a natural, if unofficial, forum of partisan debate second only to the legislative chambers across the street.

From the beginning of the Neil House establishment — 39 years before the present Capitol was completed — governors, their cabinets, legislators and all concerned with Ohio's early and later govern-ment, pursued the course of their official business into its parlors, corridors and public rooms.

The registers of The Neil House list the names of 14 presidents of the United States, including Andrew Jackson, William Henry Harrison, Abraham Lincoln, U.S. Grant, Rutherford B. Hayes, James A. Garfield, Chester A. Arthur, Grover Cleveland, William McKinley, Benjamin Harrison, William Howard Taft, Theodore Roosevelt, Woodrow Wilson and Warren G. Harding. Every president since that time has been one of its guests.

Outside politics and the worlds of science, the arts and theater, The Neil House has entertained a dazzling array of the great and the famous.

Guests who have enjoyed its hospitality down through the years include Charles Dickens and Oscar Wilde of the literary world, Jenny Lind, Adelina Patti, the great Henry Clay, Gen. Winfield Scott, Gen. Phil Sheridan, Adm. David G. Farragut, Horace Greeley, Louis Kossuth, Carl Schurz, Daniel Webster, the great Shakespearean stars Julia Marlowe and E. H. Southern, and so on through more than a century's array of the brilliant figures of American public life.

Many famous artists and musicians have performed for Neil House patrons. The famous Meyer Davis, impressario of dance music whose bands served the elite affairs of New York and Washington, once supplied an orchestra for dinner dancers of the hotel.

The Neil House of 1980 remains a favored residence and meeting place of politicians — and it attracts the city's social sophisticates and entertainment seekers.

The Hotel Investment Company, Inc., a Columbus-owned corproation, took over the reigns of management on midnight, March 31, 1968. Since that time, Columbus' oldest hotel has returned to its lofty position among the leading hotels of Ohio and the nation.

The Neil House today continues the close and warm identification with the city it serves — a special tradition which links it closely with the community.

The Ohio Bell Telephone Company

Columbus said "hello" to phone a century ago

Dr. Alexander Graham Bell's invention was still widely regarded as an amusing electrical gadget when the first telephone office opened in Columbus on January 1, 1879.

The tiny office at 9 East Long Street was the second in Ohio, following Cincinnati's office by four months. Actually, the first two telephones in

Columbus had been in operation since July 12, 1877 — only 99 days after Charles Williams, Jr., builder of Bell's hand phones, installed the first telephone line in the world at Boston, Massachusetts.

The Brown Brothers, Columbus title abstractors, used the new gadgets to communicate between their main office at 37 North 3rd Street and the branch office a mile away, near the Courthouse. Their yelling between offices was the city's first telephone conversation.

Columbusites were amazed and intrigued by the mysterious invention, and 1,500 persons jammed the city's Opera House on December 6, 1877, to hear a professor lecture on the marvels of the telephone. They listened enthralled as a black boxlike instrument began to emit music — all the way from Chicago, 300 miles away.

In the autumn of 1878, during the Ohio State Fair, the Electric Supply Co. rigged a telephone line from its downtown office via Long Street to the fairgrounds, then located at Franklin Park. Fairgoers waited for as long as two hours to make a test call for a nickel.

Seeing this popularity, George H. Twiss and Francis C. Sessions soon formed a

Ohio Bell consolidated many of its offices in Columbus in 1973 when some 2,000 employees moved into its new headquarters at East Gay and North Fourth streets downtown.

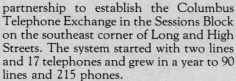

partnership to establish the Columbus Telephone Exchange in the Sessions Block on the southeast corner of Long and High Streets. The system started with two lines and 17 telephones and grew in a year to 90 lines and 215 phones.

The first phones were one-piece combination receivers and transmitters, and required considerable dexterity from those who used them. To speak, the flat end of the instrument was held to the mouth. To hear, it had to be shifted to the ear.

Early phone service was far from efficient, and sometimes operators and customers clashed. When aggravated customers began cursing into the instrument, the young male operators would respond in kind. Owners soon realized that public relations were deteriorating and they recruited a young lady to add some decorum to the service.

Alice Belle Hodgkins, 16, and just out of high school, consented to take the job on trial. In October, 1879, she became the first female telephone operator in Columbus and one of the first in the country.

About this same time, William Bresnahan, hired as a night operator, showed that not all boys will be brash. He was so polite that he raised his hat when answering ladies on the telephone.

By the early 1880s telephone use was becoming common. In 1881, Columbus had more than 500 phones installed, and lines were extended to Westerville, Worthington, and other neighboring villages. And by April, 1883, connections were made with distant cities including Dayton, Newark and Williamsport, and the next year toll lines were extended to Mansfield, Chillicothe, Greenville and Zanesville.

Public pay stations appeared in May, 1880, and subscribers to telephone service could make pay phone calls for five cents, while all others were charged a dime.

Columbus operators in 1908 handled long distance calls individually in this office, but today the most sophisticated electronic switching equipment can place up to 550,000 toll calls per hour.

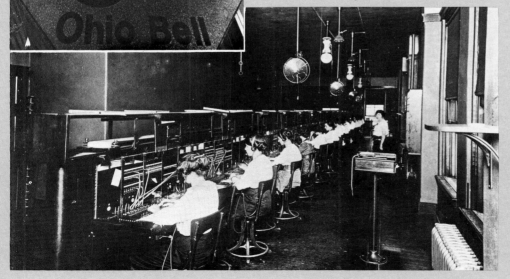

Emergency communications in those days left a great deal to be desired. The first fire alarm involving the telephone occurred in February, 1880, when the operator on duty — informed by phone of a fire — opened the window and yelled across the street to firemen in the old Ruggery Building.

Six months after its formal beginning, the Columbus Telephone Exchange was bought on July 13, 1879 by Charles W. Ross, chief operator of the Western Union Telegraph Co. In April, 1880, when Western Union withdrew from the telephone field, Ross and his associates organized the Columbus Telephone Co. and took over the exchange.

Two years later it was acquired by Midland Telephone Co., then in 1883 by Central Union Telephone Co., and on December 31, 1920, by The Ohio Bell Telephone Co.

Since then, telephone facilities in Columbus have been modernized many times. For example, in 1933 Ohio Bell converted its entire local system to allow customers to dial their own local telephone calls.

Compared with the 17 original phones, the Columbus system now serves more than 800,000 telephones, of which about 600,000 are residential and the remainder are business.

Statewide, Ohio Bell has grown into a company providing communications to five million telephones. The company's 2.5 million customers made about nine billion local calls in its centennial year and more than 500 million long distance calls.

In 1968 Ohio Bell's second electronic switching system (ESS) was installed in Columbus. Today, more than one-third of the business and residence customers of Ohio Bell are served with similar computerized systems.

ESS provided a historic improvement in call-switching capabilities. Its "memory" features made available Custom Calling options such as Call Waiting, Call Transfer and Three-Way Calling.

Recent years also have seen development of Touch-Tone® or pushbutton service, computerized handling of long distance calls and the introduction of international direct dialing.

A new dimension to long distance calling was added in 1978 when Ohio Bell installed its first "super switcher" in Columbus. This electronic wizard is capable of switching 550,000 toll calls per hour — about 150 per second — or five times as many as the old electromechanical equipment.

Headquarters for much of this sophisticated equipment and for some 2,000 of Ohio Bell's employees in Columbus is an eye-pleasing 26-story building occupied in 1973. The structure is one of the dominant features of a growing Columbus skyline.

The Ohio Company

Investment firm was instrumental in Columbus' development

From a small bond department in an early Columbus bank to the second largest investment banking firm headquartered outside New York City, The Ohio Company has been a story of growth. The firm presently has offices in a ten-state area with equity capital in excess of $25 million.

The story began in 1907 when two brothers and partners — Robert F. Wolfe and Harry P. Wolfe — came to the rescue of The Ohio Trust Company of Columbus, which was about to close its doors. This was the start of their involvement in the Columbus financial community.

Through a series of acquisitions and mergers of several Columbus banks and the resulting integration of their bond departments, BancOhio's Securities Company emerged in late 1929. Twelve years later the name would be changed to The Ohio Company.

During these years of rapid growth and expansion for the firm, what is now downtown Columbus was itself rapidly developing. The small bond department that Robert and Harry Wolfe started, under the direction of John A. Kelley, was actively involved in the city's growth. What is now known as the LeVeque Lincoln Tower was the largest of the firm's real estate underwritings. The Palace Theatre, the Capital City Products Company and the first ramp garage in Columbus were a few of the financings handled by the securities firm.

Since its inception, The Ohio Company's prime function has been to generate capital enabling corporations to expand and communities to meet the demand for public services. An underwriting firm's growth is directly proportional to its performance in helping other entities to grow.

As a pioneer in preparing and marketing issues for which neither legal precedent nor underwriting procedures had previously been established, The Ohio Company has earned a reputation as an innovator in the field of public finance.

The firm played a key role in the financing of the Ohio Turnpike in the early 1950s by assisting in the preparation of necessary legislation and by serving as financial advisors for the Ohio Turnpike Commission.

Another Ohio Company "first" involved the issuance of the City of Columbus' off-street parking mortgage revenue bonds. The proposed issue — the first of its kind in Ohio — weathered two test suits in The Ohio Supreme Court before legality was established and the bonds were marketed.

In more recent years, The Ohio Company was actively involved in the financ-

Riverside Methodist Hospital was expanded in 1974 and in 1980 with funds raised by The Ohio Company through the issuance of First Mortgage Hospital Revenue Bonds.

ing of the Underground Parking facility beneath the Ohio Statehouse grounds, continuing to aid in Columbus' development.

Health care is another crucial area where the firm has become deeply involved in the needs of communities. The many capital financing programs put together by The Ohio Company have brought new hospital service to towns and cities of every size.

As important as helping communities grow is the task of helping corporations grow. An organization may need funds to expand facilities, purchase new equipment or develop a new process or product. Whatever the reason, The Ohio Company has been involved in helping them achieve their goals.

Under President Ewing T. Boles (1936-1963) the corporate finance area was intensively developed and expanded to include areas outside Ohio.

Two more recent success stories — Wendy's International, Inc. and Worthington Industries, Inc. — are examples of companies that have turned to The Ohio Company for financial planning assistance.

In addition to assisting companies acquire capital through the sale of securities, The Ohio Company offers services and assistance in negotiation of acquisitions and mergers.

Big Bear Stores Company, Big Drum, Inc., Bob Evans Farms, Inc., Brodhead-Garrett Co., Buckeye International, Inc., Columbus & Southern Ohio Electric Company and Schottenstein Stores Corp. are a few of The Ohio Company's prestigious clientele.

On the other side of The Ohio Company's investment coin is its aid to private investors. The opportunity for growth is provided by the firm through quality investments in municipal issues and in corporation stocks. The company's sales force is intensively trained to match available investments with the financial objectives of clients.

When Edgar S. Noland succeeded to the presidency in the 1960s the services of The Ohio Company to corporations, communities and private investors was expanded to include states contiguous to Ohio.

Under President Donald C. Fanta (1971-present) this out-of-state growth has become pronounced, expanding to the entire Eastern United States.

Kobacker Store, Inc. built new corporate headquarters and warehouse facility in 1977 through the issuance of $4.2 million in Industrial Development Revenue Bonds by The Ohio Company. The facility created 300 jobs for Columbus residents.

The Ohio State University

"... Striving to fill the need demanded by a better civilization"

Columbus was a city of 35,000 when the first 24 students arrived at the Ohio Agricultural and Mechanical College north of town.

The date was September 17, 1873. The college, renamed The Ohio State University five years later, had been chartered by the Ohio legislature in 1870, but the work of getting under way was beset by delays.

When the seven-member faculty met its first classes, the main campus building, University Hall, was still unfinished. Doors had not been hung, and the sound of carpenters' hammers echoed for months after college opened. Yet despite these and other hardships, the new college was on its way. Later enrollment brought the first year's attendance to 50 students. The growth has continued, except for periods of war and depression, to the present enrollment of nearly 58,000.

Along with this has come a like development of its service and research functions. Today Ohio State stands among the nation's largest comprehensive universities, the state's leading center for graduate and professional study.

Even before instruction began, a controversy arose over the scope of courses to be taught. A "narrow gauge" camp held that the college should teach only agriculture and the mechanical arts, while a "broad gauge" group favored a wider program. The latter prevailed in 1871 largely through the efforts of Joseph Sullivant, a Columbus member of the board of trustees.

An early duty of the trustees naturally was the selection of the first president. In 1873 they chose Edward O. Orton, Sr., then president of Antioch College. He served eight years, resigning the presidency to continue as faculty member and state geologist.

The ninth and current president, Dr. Harold L. Enarson, was appointed in 1972. He had been president of Cleveland State University and succeeded Emeritus President Novice G. Fawcett in the Ohio State post.

With its founding, Ohio State became one of the nation's 72 land-grant universities, a fact that influenced its development in important ways. A federal act signed by President Lincoln in 1862 had given land to the states, including Ohio, to be sold for the financial support of colleges. This landmark legislation served to extend the benefits of higher education beyond the needs of the privileged few.

President Orton (center), a geologist, conducts a field trip, 1888.

University Hall, completed in 1873. Was replaced in 1976.

During the past 110 years, the spirit of the Land-Grant Act has helped guide Ohio State's growth in enrollment, its academic offerings and its research.

Some milestones in the university's history:

— Enrollment topped 1,000 for the first time in 1897. It passed 10,000 in 1923 and 50,000 in 1970.

— The first six graduates received diplomas in 1878. Since then the university has conferred more than 280,000 degrees and has more than 223,000 living alumni throughout the world.

— At the outset, the university laid plans for 10 academic departments; its first six colleges were organized formally in 1896. Today Ohio State has 17 colleges, within them 132 instructional units, through which 6,900 courses are offered.

— The university's Research Foundation was organized in 1934. Research investigations now take place in more than 125 fields, with annual awards for this work and other sponsored programs totaling more than $63 million.

— The first legislative appropriation of funds for the university — $4,500 — came in 1877. With a current budget totaling some $468 million annually (about a third

223

provided by state appropriations), Ohio State has an obviously significant impact on the economy of the Columbus area.

These changes — and many others still under way — have paralleled a century's explosion of knowledge and a broadening vision of the role that higher education is called upon to play.

And these changes portray a university, in the words of the fifth president, William Oxley Thompson, "striving to fill the need demanded by a better civilization."

The Palmer-Donavin Manufacturing Co.

Expansion and diversification result of foresight and planning

From macaroni to tinware and sheet metal to building materials — including heating and air conditioning equipment, and fireplaces. That, in a nutshell, represents the 73-year history of The Palmer-Donavin Manufacturing Company.

Being a small jobber in the horse-and-buggy days of Columbus was only the beginning of seven decades of steady growth for the company. Today, Palmer Donavin is a large wholesaler serving most of Ohio.

It was in 1907 that Fred L. Palmer sold a macaroni factory and became a prime manufacturer of tinware and sheet metal products. Associated with Palmer was John Donavin, who, unfortunately, passed away shortly after World War I.

During the early 1900s, the company sold its products to hardware stores and farm supply stores in the Columbus area. Merchandise was delivered by horse-drawn wagons, and many of the deliveries were personally made by Fred Palmer.

Back then, little did Messrs. Palmer and Donavin dream that 73 years later The Palmer-Donavin Manufacturing Company would be serving building construction and remodeling material dealers throughout most of the state. They could not have imagined that the company would step into the 1980s as a distributor handling the lines of well-known manufacturers such as Armstrong Cork, Celotex, Alcoa and Rheem. Nor could the founders have envisioned that their limited number of tinware and sheet metal items manufactured at the start of the business would eventually become more than 10,000 items stocked in three warehouses by one of the largest distributors in central Ohio.

Originally the company made pots and pans, jar caps and wash boilers. These products were sold to the hardware dealers and general farm stores in a small area now known as metropolitan Columbus.

The first offices and manufacturing facilities of The Palmer-Donavin Manufacturing Company were at 78 East First Avenue. The firm maintained that location until August, 1940 when there was a disastrous fire. It then moved to 225 North Front Street, formerly occupied by

Palmer-Donavin Manufacturing Company

the E. E. Shedd Wholesale Grocery Company.

The Depression of the '30s did not slow the growth of Palmer-Donavin. In 1932 the corporation foresaw the need for expansion to meet future markets and a branch distribution warehouse was opened in Lima, Ohio to serve dealers in that part of the state.

The manufacture of sheet metal and tinware was discontinued at the start of World War II due to difficulty in obtaining tin from England. The tin shortage, plus the fire in 1940 which completely destroyed all manufacturing equipment, resulted in the company becoming a wholesaler.

Not only did Palmer-Donavin enjoy growth as a wholesaler, but when World War II ended, management had the foresight to seek the need for a central location. Realizing that existing traffic flow patterns would change rapidly with the construction of freeways, five acres were purchased in early 1947 from what was known as the Twin Rivers Golf Course. A new building was constructed at what is now known as 750 Twin Rivers Drive. The address was originally 575 Olentangy River Road. But as progress was made with interstate highways in the area, a separate road became necessary.

This was the first acquisition at the site, which later became a prime location. It is

now referred to as the "Golden Finger" with WBNS-TV, the Coca-Cola Company and the main U.S. Post Office as neighbors of the corporation.

Despite changes in distribution patterns and technology, the current president, Robert J. Woodward, has great confidence in the free enterprise system. He feels there will always be a need for the independent wholesaler. So expansion of the existing warehouses has become a necessity in order to handle the increasing flow of traffic created by the company's dependable service to present customers — lumber yards, home centers, home improvement contractors, heating and air conditioning contractors, stove shops, industrial and commercial accounts.

Quality has always been a concern of Palmer-Donavin — whether the products were made by the company's own facilities or purchased from other manufacturers. Many changes have been made in products since the firm was organized back in 1907. And with today's energy crisis there is a new series of products designed for the building material industry so the home owner can enjoy more comfort yet reduce operating costs.

Today, Palmer-Donavin takes great pride in providing employment for approximately 90 employees — compared to ten when the firm was organized in 1907. The original sales force of two, using horse-drawn wagons, has now grown to 15 sales people and a fleet of 10 modern trucks. The original market area has expanded from the city of Columbus itself to serving the entire state — with further expansion into additional markets planned.

In today's computer age where customers are sometimes identified by numbers, The Palmer-Donavin Manufacturing Company continues to treat each customer as an individual and maintains a personal one-to-one relationship.

Ranco Incorporated

Since 1913, making devices that make decisions

A young man right out of college — an ambitious, intelligent fellow by the name of E.C. Raney — was working in 1908 for a coal-mining company in eastern Ohio. There, in his position overseeing electrical systems and equipment, the later founder of Ranco encountered and solved the first of many control-related problems. In this initial case, the problem was electrical — the annoying and dangerous condition that resulted when an underground short circuit caused a circuit breaker above ground to trip open. The solution, as Raney invented it, was safer and infinitely more efficient than anything then in use — and he called it an *automatic reclosing* circuit breaker, because it opened and closed in response to load conditions. Raney's device was so advanced that variations of his first invention are still used today.

Following this development, E.C. Raney went to work perfecting and patenting, doing his later testing at the engineering laboratory of Ohio State University. In 1913, after trying unsuccessfully to sell his patent to several major electrical firms, Raney organized a new company to manufacture and market this device. The Automatic Reclosing Circuit Breaker Company (ARCB Co.) was founded.

Success came gradually for the young firm, which was first located above a livery stable at West Mound and Wall Streets — and later, on a site now occupied by Columbus City Hall. Eventually, as the automatic reclosing circuit breaker came into great demand, it was specified for extensive use in coal mines, in steel mills, and on interurban railways. Some of ARCB Co.'s biggest customers, in fact, were the very corporations that turned down Raney's patent just a few years earlier. The company prospered along with the growing nation, throughout the years of World War I and into the '20s.

Times change and along with them product demands change, and the late '20s found a declining market for Raney's breaker. At the same time, however, new developments were taking place that held great opportunity, and Raney and company were fortunately in a position to take advantage.

Mechanical refrigeration was coming into its own but was in need of simpler, more reliable and more compact controls to become commercially feasible. Prompt-ed by a friend's suggestion, Raney went to the drawing board and developed the necessary refrigeration controls, the first step in a new and promising direction. Raney's control, known later by the shortened trade name "Ranco," became so widely known and respected that in 1936 the firm took on the name of its products and became Ranco Incorporated.

Beginning with its venture into the refrigeration business, the company steadily became the leading developer and supplier of devices controlling temperature, pressure and electric current. Another major step which shortly followed was its entry into the automotive market, in this instance as the inventor of the automatic temperature control for the Nash Weather Eye, a completely new car heater system.

The early '40s saw a drastic change in Ranco's production, as the requirements of war were felt and answered by American industry. Ranco began manufacturing altitude controls, pressure gauges, thermoswitches and binoculars for the war effort, and was honored with the coveted Army and Navy "E" Award for its accomplishments.

Third "home" of Ranco, at Sixth and Indianola Avenues. A steel addition was later built adjacent to this structure to accommodate increased business.

Original plant of Automatic Reclosing Circuit Breaker Company, predecessor of Ranco Inc. Factory occupied rear portion of second floor until 1917.

After the war, the company resumed production of refrigeration and heater controls, while initiating expansion into other related areas such as devices for the control of humidity, time sequencing and fluid flow. The growth of air conditioning led to Ranco's development of many controls for this market, including the reversing valve which made possible the increasingly-popular heat pump. Still later came humidifier and dehumidifier controls and — as the need for pollution abatement began to be felt nationally — automotive emission controls.

As the company's product line grew, so too did its area of operations. Beginning in 1950 with the opening of a manufacturing facility in the United Kingdom, Ranco has enjoyed substantial growth overseas. Its products are manufactured in eight countries and sold in virtually every country in the world.

Most recently, Ranco has entered boldly into the emerging field of electronic controls, an area of technological opportunity as promising as reclosing circuit breakers were in 1913, and refrigeration controls were in 1928. As new markets and new demands evolve, Ranco continues to evolve with them.

RAX Systems, Inc.

Innovators who pioneered the fast food restaurant industry

RAX Systems, Inc. headquarters, at 1169 Dublin.

RAX Systems, Inc. is a new name for an established fast food company headquartered in Columbus.

Since its founding by J. Patrick Ross in 1963 — under the name of Restaurant Administration Corporation (RAC) — the company has owned and operated a variety of restaurant enterprises. Starting with one Burger Chef store in Wheeling, West Virginia, the firm's growth was soon evident through its additional Burger Chef restaurants in Ohio, Kentucky, Pennsylvania and West Virginia. Alternative food concepts were pioneered by RAC in these geographical areas.

RAC continued to broaden its expertise over the next several years by owning and operating Ponderosa Steak Houses, Patriot Steak Houses, Wendy's Old Fashioned Hamburger Restaurants and JAX Roast Beef. From 1968 through 1977, RAC built more than 99 restaurants and managed a total of 195 stores.

Eventually, the success of JAX Roast Beef Restaurants convinced the company to sell its other enterprises, focusing attention on the roast beef business.

The first JAX unit opened in Springfield, Ohio in 1967. In 1969, General Foods purchased the concept, converting the name to RIX Roast Beef. When General Foods later abandoned RIX, Restaurant Administration Corporation converted its 10 franchise units back to JAX.

In 1976, a brand new look was created for the JAX stores. This new restaurant image and the operational changes it incorporated were highly regarded and

RAX Systems, Inc. general offices at 1169 Dublin Road.

widely accepted by other individuals in the fast food industry. From this encouragement, it was decided to franchise JAX nationwide.

In 1977, JAX was changed to RAX (a more suitable trademark for registration) and in 1978, the first franchise unit opened. The corporate headquarters changed from Restaurant Administration Corporation to RAX Systems, Inc. and is currently developing company-owned RAX units in Ohio, West Virginia, Delaware, Pennsylvania, Kentucky, Indiana and Washington.

The 100th RAX in the system opened in 1979, with franchise units spanning the country, coast to coast.

The three years between 1977 and 1980 — when RAX Systems, Inc. was formed and franchising began — form the key to the company's success. Sales in 1980 approximate $60 million for RAX and its franchise operation — double the 1979 figure.

The innovations instituted by the industry leader have proved to be successful and stand as a promise for the future.

Roman Catholic Diocese of Columbus

Keeping alive the spirit of toleration

In 1833, two non-Catholic families were prompted to donate the property on which would later be constructed the first Catholic church in Columbus. Otis, Phoebe, Samuel and Margaret Crosby and Nathaniel and Catharine Medbury, desiring to promote religion and toleration, donated Lot 761 — on the corner of East Rich and South Fifth Streets — where Holy Cross church now stands.

As Columbus grew, so did the Catholic Church, keeping pace all through the years with the city's expansion and development and continuing the spirit of toleration evidenced in 1833.

A few Catholic families, most of German descent, resided in the Columbus area in the early 1800s. They became the first worshippers of St. Remigius (later, Holy Cross), built in 1838, and their children attended the first Catholic school, begun in 1843 — two years before the tax-supported public school system. The Sisters of Notre Dame de Namur, the first nuns to take charge of a Columbus parish school, arrived in 1855.

By 1868, when Columbus became the See city of a newly established diocese, there were three Catholic parishes in the city — Holy Cross (formerly St. Remigius), St. Patrick's (1854) and St. Mary's (1868) — with the present St. Joseph's Cathedral parish in formation. Sylvester Horton Rosecrans, a convert to Catholicism and brother of General William Stark Rosecrans of Civil War fame, became the first bishop.

The new diocese embraced the southeast quarter of the state and included Perry County, where the first Catholic church was dedicated in 1818.

The first statistical report of the new diocese as given in 1869 listed 41 churches

St. Joseph, Columbus, Ohio observed its centennial in 1978.

The Most Rev. Edward J. Herrmann, D.D., Bishop of Columbus.

and 23 chapels and stations serving 40,000 Catholics, with only 43 priests for the whole area. In Columbus itself, 1,020 students were enrolled in four parish schools. The Franciscan Sisters operated St. Francis hospital, the Good Shepherd Sisters had come to care for wayward youth, and the Dominican Sisters had moved their academy for girls from Somerset to St. Mary of the Springs (now Ohio Dominican College in Columbus).

Bishop Rosecrans' task was to organize the new diocese and to build the cathedral. It took 10 years to complete the great Gothic structure, with dedication taking place on October 20, 1878. The tireless bishop died the evening of the following day.

Other chief shepherds of the diocese included the scholarly John A. Watterson (1880-1900), Henry Moeller (1900-1903), afterwards archbishop of Cincinnati, James J. Hartley (1904-1944), who led the diocese through a long period of building and expansion, Michael J. Ready (1944-1957), Clarence J. Issenmann (1957-1964), John J. Carberry (1965-1968), later Cardinal Archbishop of St. Louis, and Clarence E. Elwell (1968-1973). The present Bishop, Edward J. Hermann, was installed in 1973. Edward G. Hettinger, now retired, became auxiliary bishop in 1941. The second auxiliary bishop, George A. Fulcher, was ordained in 1976.

Today there are 255 priests active in the diocese, with a Catholic population of 210,000. There are 43 parishes in the city of Columbus and six more in the county. Catholic schools have multiplied with the growth of Ohio's capital city and during Bishop Ready's time several regional Catholic high schools were built.

Other significant events in the history of the diocese include, in 1911, the hosting of the first convention of the Catholic Press Association of America — a meeting which was the foundation of the Association; the establishment in 1944 of the diocese of Steubenville, a move which took 13 counties from the diocese of Columbus and added several counties from the archdiocese of Cincinnati; and the joining by the Columbus Catholic Diocese in 1967 with the local Council of Churches in the founding of the Metropolitan Church Board.

Also noteworthy is the Pontifical College Josephinum, which is located just north of Columbus and is the only seminary in the western hemisphere directly under the jurisdiction of the Pope in Rome.

The Catholic Conference of Ohio, was established in 1945, with offices in Columbus. It brings together representatives of the six Latin Rite and the one Byzantine Rite dioceses of Ohio and coordinates on a state level all policies of the Catholic Church pertaining to Catholic education, hospitals, charities and social action. Its other areas of concern include legislation, the Catholic press, liturgy and the Councils of Catholic men and women in each diocese.

A communications department, sponsored by all the dioceses of the state, works with radio and television through its Columbus offices.

And the Ecumenical Commission of the Roman Catholic Diocese of Columbus keeps alive the spirit of toleration present at its founding in 1833.

Ross Laboratories
Division of Abbott Laboratories

Simple beginnings bring leadership in nutrition

When two men met in a Columbus night school accounting class at the turn of the century, it was the start of a business relationship which would bring Ross Laboratories nutritional products to millions of persons.

The history of Ross Laboratories, now a division of Abbott Laboratories, a worldwide health-care manufacturer, dates back to 1903. That year, Harry C. Moores, a Columbus-area farmer, and Stanley M. Ross, a clerk in a local department store, turned their new friendship into a business alliance, beginning the Moores and Ross Milk Company.

The dairy operations, including a stable of horses to draw milk wagons, were located at the corner of Long and Ninth streets, just blocks from the now bustling heart of downtown Columbus. The pre-dawn clip-clop of the horse-drawn milk wagons on the brick streets of early Columbus was a common sound as residents awoke to find fresh dairy products on their doorsteps.

Times changed and, with the advent of the horseless carriage on the Columbus scene, Moores and Ross adapted motorized vehicles to their delivery fleet. Harry Moores invented the first stand-up milk truck to aid in the speedy delivery of dairy products, a concept used in delivery trucks today. The now widely-used wire-bottom milk carrier was also a result of the founders' business ingenuity and progress. And, they delivered the milk in sterilized glass bottles rather than ladling it into pails, as was the custom of the day.

The dairy operations prospered but that part of the business enterprise is now history. The glass milk bottles carrying the raised letters spelling Moores and Ross are now collectors' items, for the dairy portion

The first of the company's motorized milk trucks.

of the business was sold in the mid 1920s.

Harry Moores and Stanley Ross had identified a new business interest, one which would bring a nutritious milk-based formula to infants. In turn, they named the company M&R Dietetic Laboratories and moved to the former Franklin Brewery building on Cleveland Avenue. Only the last vestige of that building remains among the company's modern buildings on Cleveland Avenue.

Franklin Infant Food, the forerunner of the market-leading *Similac* Infant Formula, was introduced in 1925. The initial formula was based on the laboratory work of Columbus milk chemist Alfred Bosworth, who participated in pioneering research in infant formula at the Boston Floating Hospital.

The original *Similac*, so named by an editor of the *Journal of the American Medical Association*, was prepared as a powder to be reliquefied at home with boiled water.

The company, during World War II, was given six Armed Forces E Awards for supplying dried milk and ice cream concentrates to service personnel. It was the only milk products company to receive such recognition.

The post-war years brought numerous advances to infant feeding. While the breast milk of healthy mothers remains the best form of nutrition for infants, the company worked to pioneer new formulas for those whose mothers were either unable or elected not to breastfeed. *Similac* Concentrated Liquid, introduced in 1951, made home formula preparation simpler.

The horses knew the way as the milk wagon went on appointed rounds.

And, in 1959, the company established another milestone in infant feeding when it introduced an iron-fortified formula, *Similac* with Iron. The year 1966 brought the introduction of *Isomil* Soy Protein Formula for infants allergic to cow milk.

M&R Dietetics in 1964 merged with Abbott Laboratories, becoming the Ross Laboratories division of the worldwide health care organization. While Columbus remains headquarters for the Ross division, Abbott corporate headquarters are North Chicago, Illinois.

With the merger, Ross received responsibility for the marketing of pediatric and maternal pharmaceuticals. Answering a need for improved nutritional health for patients recovering from disease or surgery, Ross in the 1970s researched and developed a full line of adult medical nutritional products. The *Ensure* line of products, offering many different formulations for specific nutritional needs, is used as either total or supplemental nutrition.

Ross Laboratories today is known throughout the United States for its nutritional products and research. The division also provides educational conferences, publications and service aids in the area of nutrition to the medical profession. Providing its products through an ethical marketing program, Ross seeks to assist medical professionals to better help their patients.

Ross, with plants in Columbus, Sturgis, Michigan and Altavista, Virginia, has offered employment to thousands of Columbus-area persons. As it progresses into the future, its goal will remain much as it was in 1903 — working through the private enterprise system to the benefit of the consumer.

The Thomas W. Ruff and Company

Accent on excellence provides basis for company success and growth

When Tom Ruff opened his new office furniture business in 1936, he had but one goal — to be the very best in his dealings with customers, suppliers, and employees. This simple but demanding goal continues to be the basis of the Thomas W. Ruff and Company's philosophy and has propelled the business into one of the nation's largest office and commercial furniture dealerships.

Ruff drew on his business experiences as an office equipment buyer for Railway Power and Light and then as sales manager for an office furniture manufacturer, in emphasizing the value of service to the customer and how important employee attitudes are in providing that service. Not once during the hard years to follow did he lose this accent on excellence.

World War II eliminated new sales and forced Ruff to close his showroom at 20 North Fourth Street. Contacts with customers were maintained, however, and Ruff continued in business by personally servicing his customers' furniture and equipment. After the war, new

When Tom Ruff started his company in 1936, office needs were relatively simple, requiring mostly functional placement of desks and chairs.

Today, Thomas W. Ruff & Company designs total office interiors to meet modern office needs of space, privacy and efficiency.

showrooms and offices were opened at 110 South Fourth and the business prospered. But the Korean War curtailed shipments again. Although sales were made by allocation, Ruff was able to stay in business and even managed to expand his staff to eight.

Tom Ruff died in 1953 and one of his employees, Jack Gorman, was appointed manager. Gorman later purchased the company from the Ruff family and maintained Ruff's original goal of excellence. (In 1979, Gorman's employees honored his leadership by establishing a Jack Gorman Scholarship Fund at Columbus' Franklin University. The fund was set up entirely from employee donations.)

By 1954 capacity had caught up with demand and increased competition dictated innovations in office styling. Simple office layouts were giving way to more sophisticated and more practical designs. Ruff and Company quickly recognized the trend and, in 1957, pioneered the establishment of total in-house services, including design, carpet, drapery, delivery, and installation departments. (When the first high-rise office building since World War II was built in 1958 — The Electric Company — Thomas W. Ruff and Company was ready, supplying furniture, carpet and draperies.)

Recession and corporate austerity programs in 1958 prompted the company's diversification into the hotel/motel, institutional and educational furnishings market. Expertise was gained in office logistics, interior design, and installation techniques from contracts with such industry giants as Holiday Inn, Hilton, Howard Johnsons, and various university and medical complexes. This attentiveness to changing times and needs helped the employee-owned company grow steadily through the years to a position of prominence within the office furniture industry.

In 1959 the business recorded its first million dollar sale when Western Electric selected Thomas W. Ruff and Company as its office furniture supplier. A look at the Columbus skyline illustrates others who supported this trust. Ruff was the major office furnisher of the State Office Tower, Nationwide Plaza, the Borden and Motorist Insurance buildings, BancOhio, Ashland Chemical complex, Ohio School Employees Retirement System, and Ross Laboratories. Other Columbus and national accounts are a who's who of commerce and industry.

In 1963 the company moved to its present location at 1114 Dublin Road with additional service and warehouse locations at 1019 and 1051 West Goodale Boulevard. Two years later, Thomas W. Ruff established an Employee Pension Plan Trust and Profit Sharing Trust. The latter was converted to an employee stock ownership trust in 1975 and is recognized as outstanding for any business and unparalleled in the office furniture industry.

In order to better serve its national accounts, Ruff opened complete office, showroom and warehouse facilities in Orlando, Florida in 1974. (A new facility in Miami will be completed and opened in November 1980.) Combined, all locations service customers in the Southwest and Middle Atlantic states. Sales of 25 million are projected for 1980 and all 150 employees in are involved in extensive programs, preparing for new growth in the office furniture industry. Radically changing office environments dictated by efficiency, energy, electronic data processing, and space utilization offer Thomas W. Ruff & Company a challenging future.

Active involvement in civic and service organizations continues a tradition begun by Tom Ruff. A foundation established in his memory supports charitable and educational groups in Columbus and Orlando. Numerous civic and national awards, including Geyer Awards for design and installation, emphasize the success that resulted from one man's initial commitment. As the Thomas W. Ruff and Company approaches its golden anniversary, the goal of its founder remains consistent — to be the very best.

Ruscilli Construction Company

From concept to lockset . . . building Columbus for 35 years

Begun with pride . . . nourished by tradition . . . directed with confidence . . . Ruscilli Construction Company today is in its third generation of single family ownership.

Founded in 1945 by Louis G. Ruscilli, Jr., a young serviceman newly returned from the armed forces, the company's first construction projects centered about

New corporate home of Ruscilli Construction Co., Inc., in ArlingGate Business Park.

World War II's durable Quonset hut. A short time later Ruscilli was joined in the new company by his father, Louis Ruscilli, Sr., who had been concrete foreman during construction of the Ohio State University football stadium in the 1920s.

Quonset huts and concrete work quickly became the young company's trademarks. The post-war building boom provided long hours of work even as it created a critical shortage of building materials. Balancing a customer's timetable and budget against the availability of labor and materials was a constant struggle. Against considerable odds, Ruscilli Construction acquired the reputation of a "can-do" company.

In 1947, Ruscilli Construction became associated with Armco Steel Corporation and Armco Pre-Engineered Building Systems. By 1980, when the company was named Armco's Dealer of the Year for the second consecutive year, Ruscilli was the nation's second oldest Armco Systems contractor, and third in total steel sales volume internationally.

With the arrival in the company of the third generation of Ruscillis in 1966, the firm entered a new phase of growth and expansion. When Louis "Jack" Ruscilli joined the company as a salesman, annual volume amounted to $600,000. Today, as general manager and chief executive officer, Mr. Ruscilli directs a company whose construction volume totals $20 million.

While there are many reasons for the company's dramatic increase in sales volume, none has been more important to its success than its pioneering of Design and Build services . . . total in-house capabilities for performing all phases of the construction process, from conceptual drawings to finished building.

Design and Build services, as developed by Jack Ruscilli, means a customer can, if he chooses, initiate and complete the total building process with one company, one contact, one contract for maximum efficiency and economy. Ruscilli calls this service "single source responsibility".

Through Ruscilli Construction Company and its affiliated companies, Ruscilli Realty and Ruscilli Investment, a prospec-tive customer can receive assistance with site selection and land use planning; total design capability for building and plant layout; help in selecting the best and most cost-efficient building materials; accurate and comprehensive cost projection and construction scheduling of both standard and conventional building systems; and total job construction of all phases of the project.

For companies seeking to locate in one of mid-Ohio's most prestigious corporate/industrial parks, Ruscilli has developed ArlingGate Business Park . . . 200 acres adjacent to Columbus' I-270 outerbelt. Additionally, two other parks are under development, totaling 275 acres. In 1977, corporate headquarters moved to ArlingGate where the company is presently involved in $9 million in construction within the Park.

Has single source responsibility done what Ruscilli intended for company and customer alike? Indeed it has, as a few figures will quickly document. As the 1980s began, Ruscilli Construction Company had already completed more than 10 million square feet of finished construction, achieving a 45% market penetration in central Ohio according to MBMA con-

Ruscilli on the job: building a modern 90,000 square foot multi-story office and research development project for Sherex Chemical Co., Inc., subsidiary of Schering AG, West Germany.

World War II's Quonset hut in civilian dress (1949): Ruscilli's early construction projects centered about peacetime applications of the durable wartime hut.

struction statistics. The more than 1.1 million square feet built in 1979 continued the 20% or better annual growth which the company experienced over the last decade. In the words of the company motto: "From concept to lockset, Ruscilli builds it better."

Ruscilli has designed and built just about every type of building required by one of America's fastest growing metropolitan areas: office buildings, manufacturing and chemical processing plants, freight terminals, auto dealerships, retail stores, schools and dormitories, ice rinks, tennis courts and aircraft hangers. Even a Shrine Mosque, for which Ruscilli received the Metal Building Systems Industry's 1979 Building of the Year Award.

So great an involvement in central Ohio's growth and development was to bring yet another third generation Ruscilli into the company. Upon graduation from college in 1969, Robert A. Ruscilli joined the family business. Today, as vice president and superintendent of manpower, he shares responsibility with his father, Louis, Jr., for supervising and controlling the company's many construction projects.

And since controlling construction includes maintaining control of construction supply costs, Ruscilli is constantly seeking ways to improve this vital client service. Today, an in-house computer keeps cost-estimating and job pricing up to the minute. In addition, the Ruscilli computer provides an audit trail and documentation for better and more complete cost accounting.

A family tradition of pride and a commitment to excellence began Ruscilli Construction Company. The skills and dedication of Ruscilli employees renew that commitment every day, on the job.

Ruscilli Construction Company . . . building a new way into the '80s.

SCOA Industries Inc.

Shoe retailer found perfect fit with general merchandising

The Northland Gallenkamp store reflects the modern presentation of merchandise by the national chain.

In 1920, a newly-incorporated shoe retailer established home offices in Columbus and began business with a store in Marion, Ohio and a leased footwear department in the former Boston Department Store on North High Street. A year later, the firm had six retail outlets. It was an inauspicious beginning for a company that was to become one of the largest corporations headquartered in Columbus — SCOA Industries Inc.

SCOA was founded as The Schiff Company, changed its name to Shoe Corporation of America in 1946 and adopted its present name in 1969. Robert Schiff, along with other family members, founded the company after working several years as an employee and part owner of shoe stores in Ohio, Illinois and Indiana. A Lithuanian immigrant, he possessed a natural talent for the shoe business. He developed merchandising concepts and expansion strategies to build a solid company that survived the Great Depression and paid consecutive quarterly dividends from 1929 to the present.

Schiff Shoe stores spread through central Ohio, then statewide and then into neighboring states. Meanwhile, the company pioneered the concept of operating leased shoe departments in stores such as the Boston Department Store. The relatively new way of doing business provided the means for SCOA to grow faster with less capital invested than by opening only its own stores.

SCOA's growth was further accelerated through acquisitions of other shoe retailers. The company has followed strict criteria for an acquisition candidate, the most important being that the candidate must be profitable and that its managers remain to operate the business after the acquisition. The philosophy worked well. So well that before World War II SCOA had become a major footwear retailer in the Midwest.

Following World War II, SCOA entered footwear manufacturing. Although SCOA became a major manufacturer in the American footwear industry, during the 1970 decade the company began phasing out shoe manufacturing to focus all its attention on retailing. By 1980, only two SCOA factories in Maine were producing footwear.

In the 1950s, Gallenkamp shoe stores became a part of the growing SCOA organization. Gallenkamp then was a chain of stores on the West Coast with the heaviest concentration in California. The acquisition established SCOA as a national footwear retailer and increased its status in the industry.

During the late 1970s, SCOA changed the name of its company-owned shoe stores to Gallenkamp and for the first time advertised the chain in national media. By then SCOA was ranked among the top half dozen shoe retailers in the country. In 1980, the company launched a chain of Duet self-service shoe stores in Louisiana, opening another avenue for growth in the footwear business.

To service its widespread and expanding footwear business, SCOA built a 160,000-square-foot distribution center in 1952 on Innis Road and three years later added 80,000 square feet. In recent years, the facility was completely automated and expanded to 340,000 square feet to make it one of the largest and most modern of its kind in the American footwear industry. The distribution center serves retail outlets from the East Coast to the Rocky Mountains, shipping more than 20 million pairs of shoes annually. Another smaller distribution center in Reno, Nevada serves the western states.

In 1960, SCOA began a diversification program into general merchandising which was to result in greater growth than the company experienced in its entire history. In that year the company acquired The Dry Goods promotional department store in downtown Wilmington, Delaware. This was followed in 1964, by the acquisition of the seven-unit Hills Department Store chain in the Youngstown area. The next year the Kelly & Cohen chain of 12 major appliance stores headquartered in Pittsburgh was added to the growing general merchandising group. And then in 1967 the Rudnick Company, operator of leased domestics departments, was acquired. The Dry Goods has expanded to four units in Delaware and New Jersey, Kelly & Cohen to 43 units in five states, Rudnick to 84 leased domestics departments, and Hills to 81 stores operating in 11 mid-central states. Hills is now a leading regional discount department store chain and SCOA's most profitable and fastest growing division.

General merchandising has grown to be the most important part of SCOA's operations. In 1979, general merchandising business represented 71 percent of sales and 76 percent of profits.

Herbert H. Schiff, son of founder Robert Schiff, has served as chairman, president and chief executive since 1968, the period during which SCOA has experienced its greatest growth.

A New York Stock Exchange listed company, SCOA has come a long way from the two retail footwear units that began business in Ohio in 1920. The company's sales are approaching an annual rate of one billion dollars.

SCOA's first retail outlets were Schiff Shoe stores in Ohio.

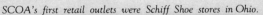

Schoedinger Funeral Service

125 years under same family operation and ownership

George J. Schoedinger (right) poses in front of his establishment at 11 West State Street in 1905.

Philip Schoedinger's horse-drawn hearse with glass sides is shown in front of his South High Street location in this circa 1865 photograph.

In 1855, Columbus was a small town of 14,000 people. Houses in the capital city weren't numbered. Instead, addresses of citizens were listed in the directory as: "south side of Broad between third and fourth." The first recorded funeral had been conducted just 43 years previous.

Thousands of businesses have been established, flourished and moved on in the 125 years since 1855. In fact, the 1980 directory of Columbus shows only two firms still operating under the same name as existed back in 1855, and only one still under the same family ownership and management. That company is the Schoedinger Funeral Service.

Philip Schoedinger, the founder, was born in Bayern, Germany in August, 1825. When he was four years old, his family emigrated to America and settled in tiny Columbus.

As was traditional with craftsmen of his day, Philip Schoedinger served his apprenticeship years in cabinetmaking, studying the art of woodcraft. Later he formed a partnership with a Mr. Brown in cabinetmaking. The firm of Schoedinger and Brown operated at 102 S. High Street.

Expanding with the bustling capital city, the partners added to their furniture business with the manufacture of looking glasses and mattresses. Adjunct to the new business was the undertaking department. "And having provided themselves with a new and beautiful hearse," Schoedinger declared in a Columbus paper advertisement, "to be ready at all times punctually and promptly in attendance at funerals."

Schoedinger and Brown flourished until 1865, when Schoedinger devoted his entire interest to the funeral business. He opened his new establishment at 11 West State Street and remained until 1919. And, a curious location it must have seemed at the time, for the most characteristic features of the block were three saloons and the brick residence of county commissioner William Wall, at the corner of State and Front.

Philip Schoedinger died at his residence in May, 1880. His son, George J. Schoedinger, assumed control of the business and was later joined by his brother, J. Albert. In 1905, the business became known as George J. Schoedinger and Bro. On display in their new location at 17 West State, was a selection of caskets in cedar, mahogany, rosewood, walnut, some even copper-lined.

In 1912, there was a new addition to the firm's stables at the corner of Chapel and Wall Street. It was central Ohio's first automobile hearse — the Great Eagle — and was proudly attended to by Ferdinand P. and George R. Schoedinger, sons of George J., then serving in the family business.

The year 1919 marked the completion of a Columbus landmark, as well as the new home of the Schoedinger Funeral Service. A new chapel was opened at 229 East State Street, the site of the converted home of famous Columbus physician Dr. Starling Loving.

The funeral chapel was the first built in Columbus and one of the earliest in America of such magnitude. The bell tower has become a Columbus landmark, but the bell itself has only chimed once in more than 50 years. On that occasion, a waggish emloyee told a new man that he was to ring it each morning at 5 a.m. After his initial performance, the bell rope was hidden.

After the passing of George J. in 1916, his two sons, Ferdinand P. and George R., together with J. Albert Schoedinger, continued the business under the name of Schoedinger & Co. In 1933, George R.'s sons, Robert S. and John F. Schoedinger, also entered into the family business.

As Columbus grew, Schoedinger neighborhood chapels were constructed throughout the community. A Hilltop chapel was opened on West Broad in 1950. In 1961, a Northwest chapel was opened in Upper Arlington, and another in Linden on Cleveland Avenue. A Grove City chapel was added in 1967 and another on the far east side in 1969. The seventh chapel opened on Karl Road in northeast Columbus in 1980.

Today, under the leadership of Robert S., John F. and his sons David S. and John A. Schoedinger, the company is represented in nearly every civic, philanthropic and cultural activity in Columbus and the descendants of the founding father remain committed to the care, comfort and concern of the many central Ohio families which they serve. Since 1855, people in Columbus have come to recognize Schoedinger as a name worthy of their trust.

M/I Schottenstein Companies, Inc.

Company's success a parallel to development of metropolitan Columbus

The story of the success of M/I Schottenstein Companies, Inc. began in 1961 when two cousins, Melvin and Irving Schottenstein, — united in their belief in the growth potential of central Ohio — pioneered quality apartment construction.

Both men believed in the necessity of distinguished design and recreational amenities for apartment areas. The Wyandotte Communities were among the first to offer its residents swimming, tennis and leisure activity areas.

Wyandotte Communities' construction coincided with the apartment boom that swept the Midwest in the 1960s, and its marketing and management quickly earned a reputation for success. The Schottensteins carried the concept into successful ventures: Wyandotte East, Wyandotte North, Eastland Cascades, Bexley House, Heritage in Columbus, Countrybrook North and Wyandotte South in Indianapolis. In all, the apartment developments totaled some 3,000 apartments and townhouses. Since inception, the properties have maintained excellent occupancy standards and are today managed by M/I Management — a division of the main company.

In 1970, in a joint venture with the W. Lyman Case Co. and Connecticut General Insurance Corporation, M/I Schottenstein Companies started the planned community development of the 600-acre Little Turtle property. Through the Columbus City Council the partners pioneered the Planned Unit Development Zoning classification — which grants developers greater flexibility in land use within a large parcel of ground. In four years, 450 condominium homes — surrounding a Pete Dye Golf Course — were built and sold at Little Turtle.

In 1975, in a joint venture with the Indiana National Bank, M/I Schottenstein affiliates began Beckett Ridge, an 1800-acre planned community north of Cincinnati. The Beckett Ridge Community offers condominiums, patio houses, single family detached houses and custom lots in a country club setting.

In 1976, believing that Americans continue to aspire to home ownership, the two partners created a new division of their company — M/I Homes. The firm entered the single family market in many locations simultaneously. Its aim — to create a niche in the market between the production and the custom builder, offering a wide variety of floor plans — was

Apartment Development, EASTLAND CASCADES, 1969

Melvin Schottenstein, left, and Irving Schottenstein, 1980

accomplished through the use of large scale construction techniques which afford many choices to the buyer.

In 1979, M/I Homes closed more than 300 housing contracts, becoming the second largest builder of single family houses in the area. M/I Homes continues to expand the number of home designs of-

234

fered and currently has building projects under way in Westerville, Gahanna, Reynoldsburg, Worthington, Dublin, Hilliard, Powell, and Columbus.

M/I Schottenstein today is a diversified services real estate company involved in all phases of the real estate business including land development, home building, property management, general contracting, brokerage and home sales. The product and communities that bear its name are widely recognized for their quality and distinction, and the company has been the recipient of numerous awards and commendations. Among them are First Honor Award/Architects' Society of Ohio, American Institute of Architects' National Home for Better Living Award in cooperation with *House & Home*, American Wood Council Design for Better Living Award, Columbus City Beautiful Award, *Better Homes and* *Gardens* and Armstrong Cork Company Concept Home, National Association of Home Builders and *Better Homes and Gardens* Decade '70 Award, and other Architectural Design & Planning Awards.

For nearly 20 years, the M/I Schottenstein Companies have built upon the two partners' belief in the growth potential of central Ohio. The growth of the company has closely paralleled the exciting modern growth of the area which is its home.

The Setterlin Company

Approaching one billion dollars worth of construction in central Ohio

The Setterlin Company was founded in 1935 although its history was rooted back in 1895 when young Robert Setterlin left his Boliver, Ohio home to become an apprentice carpenter.

While practicing his craft over the next four decades, Setterlin progressed from carpenter to part owner of a small construction company. Construction contracts became difficult to obtain during the Depression. In 1935, however, Setterlin took advantage of an opportunity to buy out his partners — to own a family type business that would involve his sons and future generations.

After obtaining several contracts to build schools in the surrounding communities, "Bob" Setterlin asked his oldest son, Ralph, to join him as partner. Ralph, who received his degree in Civil Engineering in 1929 from The Ohio State University, left a secure position with the federal government as a design engineer on the Hoover Dam in Colorado. He brought with him a wealth of experience in concrete construction methods.

As the nation slowly regained its strength prior to World War II, the young company quickly established its reputation in the central Ohio area as a leader in the construction industry. With the advent of war, the company concentrated its efforts on defense-related projects, performing the design and construction of numerous local industrial facilities such as the Lennox Industries complex. Today this concept is known in the industry as the Design/Build approach.

Following the war, in 1945, Robert W. Setterlin, Jr. joined the firm. "Bob" Jr. had received his degree in civil engineering from The Ohio State University in 1940, and had served as a captain in the Corps of Engineers during World War II. With the addition of another "Setterlin" the firm continued to experience rapid growth.

Robert Setterlin Sr. and his son Ralph, open the first office.

All during this growing era the Setterlins felt strongly that it was very important to maintain a personal day-to-day involvement, including daily job site visits to every project, in order to insure adherence to schedule, maintenance of budgeted costs and to provide the quality workmanship which is now a Setterlin trademark.

With the decision to keep their market area in central Ohio, it quickly became apparent that further growth must come from offering clients a broad range of expertise in construction capabilities. The firm's portfolio grew to include a broad range of projects such as distribution centers, housing developments, warehouses, industrial waste facilities, parking garages, high rise office buildings, hospitals, truck terminals, banking and research facilities and remodeling/ rehabilitation projects.

The company's background of public works projects continued and includes many Columbus landmarks — The Ohio Historical Center, Franklin County Hall of Justice, Franklin County Jail, State School for the Deaf and more than 30 major buildings at The Ohio State University and Capital University.

In the '50s and '60s new construction techniques such as pre-cast concrete, lift slab floors, pre-stressed and post-tensioned concrete evolved and were being designed into many new projects. The Settlerlin Company became recognized for its leadership in providing the construction knowledge and techniques to accomplish these concepts.

In the early '60s, after military service, Ralph Setterlin Jr., an architectural graduate of The Ohio State University, joined the firm. He was followed in the early '70s by Robert Setterlin III, after his military service, and Jim Setterlin, graduates of The Ohio State University and Bluffton College, respectively.

With the third generation, the com-

The Franklin County Hall of Justice and Jail Complex, a Columbus landmark and a Setterlin Company project.

One of The Setterlin Company's first projects, a school in Rushsylvania, Ohio, in 1936.

pany's name was changed to The Setterlin Company and a new generation of growth including construction management, turnkey, fast track, and design/build projects was undertaken. To meet the needs of an expanding list of clients, land development, feasibility studies, budget consultation, and other related services became a part of the firm's diverse capabilities.

Diverse capabilities and flexible management approaches were utilized to complete many major projects like the Grange Mutual Companies' new home office, an 11-story contemporary office bulding, and The Limited Stores National Headquarters and Distribution Center, housing more than 500,000 square feet of "state of the art" distribution systems.

Ralph Setterlin Sr. reflecting on the company's growth, recently stated — "We have grown because of the outstanding professional engineers, estimators, superintendents, and staff associated with our company. As we approach one billion dollars' worth of buildings in central Ohio that are meeting the needs of our clients, I feel proud of what I see. And I don't have to drive very far either — we've built all over town."

The Sherman R. Smoot Company, Inc.

Built on belief that quality work exemplifies man's dignity

The Sherman R. Smoot Company was founded in Charleston, West Virginia in 1946, on a bricklayer's dream and a total investment of $300. Dreams do come true. At least they did for Sherman Smoot. What began as a one-man masonry operation more than 30 years ago, is now a major management and general construction firm, nationally recognized for quality workmanship.

Perhaps symbolic of the dedication and high ideals on which the Smoot Company built its reputation is the very first major masonry project handled by the fledgling business — St. Anthony's Catholic Church in Charleston, West Virginia. The project was completed in 1954.

Columbus became the home of the Smoot Company in 1956. The city's larger metropolitan area provided opportunities for greater growth and a positive environment in which this promising black-owned company could build a place for itself. During the period of the 1950s and 1960s, the firm experienced steady growth. Its first projects in Columbus were the East Side Y.M.C.A. building and

McGuffey School. Among contracts during this era, Smoot felt a special commitment to Sawyer Manor and the Bolivar Arms, the first projects to provide optimum housing for minorities in which a minority construction firm was involved.

The Smoot Company soon began to service large retail and commercial masonry contracts such as the Lazarus and Sears Northland stores.

School and hospital projects followed. Bexley High School and Worthington's Perry Middle School, as well as schools in East Liverpool, Ohio and Brook County, West Virginia, all carry the quality stamp of Smoot masonry.

Buildings for higher education like the striking House of Studies on the Ohio Dominican College campus and the Ohio State University's Lincoln and Morrill Towers, School of Journalism and Biological Science buildings were all important masonry contracts in the history of this growing organization.

Projects for private business and industry were to play an important role in the building of the Smoot Company. The

Anheuser-Busch Brewery, St. Anthony's Hospital, and a series of major power generating plants for American Electric Power all were milestones of achievement for the young company.

Assisting in the development and management of the company during the late '50s and '60s was Lewis R. Smoot Sr., who joined his father in the family business in 1958. In 1963 the corporate headquarters were established at 907 North 23rd Street in Columbus, the company's current location.

In the early 1970s, the Sherman R. Smoot Company moved to broaden its activities, expanding its scope to general contracting and construction management. Smoot's past experience and expertise in all phases of construction made the expansion a logical move, and today about 75 percent of the firm's business involves general contracts. These contracts have spanned the gamut of facilities for education, recreation, health, energy production and aviation. Recent Columbus-area projects in which Smoot has been especially pleased to participate

include the Ohio State University's Mershon Auditorium music addition; the Centrum, first phase of the Capital South redevelopment program; and the Alum Creek Recreation and Camping facilities. The company is proud of its achievements, bringing to the owners of these facilities projects that will stand to exemplify the high quality of construction for which the Smoot Company has become known.

In September 1979, Smoot opened regional offices in Washington, D.C. The District of Columbia Court House; the National Air and Space Museum; the Mobil Oil Complex, Fairfax, Virginia and the U.S. Department of Health, Education and Welfare Social Security Head-

As a young bricklayer, Sherman R. Smoot built a solid business foundation on quality workmanship. Today the Smoot Company executes projects such as the District of Columbia Court House and the Mobil Oil Complex in Fairfax, Virginia, with the same dedication and skill.

quarters in Baltimore, Maryland, are all nationally important projects for which The Sherman R. Smoot Company was chosen.

During the first 34 years of his company's operation, founder Sherman Smoot fulfilled the duties of company president and chairman of the board. In 1980, Lewis Smoot was named to the presidency of the company while his father continued as company chairman.

The Smoots credit their company's success to management experience and

insistence on high quality workmanship. Smoot's supervisory staff averages 20 years in length of employment with the company, providing the stability and experience which produce quality results on time and on budget.

The Sherman R. Smoot Construction Company is the solid reality of a dream come true — a success story built on hard work and high ideals. Behind that success, the by-word of the company's founder continues to operate. "Pride in workmanship is still the rule within the Smoot Company," says President Lewis Smoot. "We also have genuine pride in the Columbus community, and in our great nation, and we are grateful for the opportunity it has afforded our company."

State Auto Mutual Insurance/
Columbus Mutual Life Insurance

Partners dedicated to the practice of the Golden Rule

Robert S. (Bob) Pein was disturbed and angry about the auto insurance industry as it functioned in 1921. Rates were largely based on whatever the traffic would bear and claim service could be a frustrating experience. He was determined to do something about it.

The result was the establishment of the first casualty company headquartered in Columbus — today's State Automobile Mutual Insurance Company, flagship company of the State Auto Group, which also includes another, even longer established Columbus-based firm, The Columbus Mutual Life Insurance Company.

Undaunted by a post-war depression,

Headquarters of The Columbus Mutual Life Insurance Company.

237

A tradition in central Ohio is State Auto's annual home office Christmas display featuring this nativity scene in front of the east wing.

Pein borrowed $30,000 and hired three employees to start an automobile insurance company based on his philosophy of "sure insurance at lowest cost."

"Service" was his keynote. To that end he committed State Auto to the independent agent system as promising the best service to policyholders. Insisting on fast — even immediate — claim service, he broke with tradition by hiring company adjusters to expedite payment of claims. He pioneered another precedent by making auto insurance available on an installment payment plan.

Less than 10 years later, at the outset of the Great Depression when the nation's economic picture was bleakest, Bob Pein's courage and confidence surfaced again. Instead of retrenching, he chose to build an impressive new home office building in 1930 at East Broad and Washington, the present site of the State Auto Group headquarters.

With the advent of World War II, however, and civilian car production cut off and gas rationing imposed, the auto insurance outlook was anything but propitious.

Still, through prudent but progressive underwriting (even bicycle coverage) State Auto posted asset gains each year.

Following the war, State Auto surged forward. With a change in the Ohio law in 1955, the firm promptly amended its corporate charter to become a fully diversified, multiple-line property and casualty company. Aided by its new product diversification the company continued its geographical expansion and innovated new procedures for more efficient service to its agents and policyholders. During the 1950s, another five stories were added to the home office.

Another significant step was consummated in 1962 when The Columbus Mutual Life Insurance Company joined the State Auto Group. One of the top 10 percent of all United States Life carriers at that time, Columbus Mutual, like State Auto, was committed to the independent agent system.

The founders of the two companies were men of equal dedication to the uplifting of the industry, making the two companies extraordinarily suited running mates.

Unlike State Auto's strapping Bob Pein, Columbus Mutual's first president in 1906, Channing Webster Brandon, was small in stature, but the two were both giants in convictions and character. Brandon's iron determination and crusader's zeal never wavered in designing a life insurance company dedicated to providing "the best insurance for the least money" and "a square deal to the agent." He applied the Golden Rule to agents and policyholders alike, just as Pein did 15 years later in founding State Auto.

Seven succeeding presidents maintained and built on Brandon's commitments, generating many practices that were to become the standards of the industry.

In 1942, a new home office building was completed at East Broad and Sixth Street, its present location.

Since 1968, when Ralph E. Waldo assumed the presidency, Columbus Mutual Life has risen to the top 8 percent of the more than 1,700 life insurance companies, with more than three billion dollars of insurance in force.

Paul Gingher followed Pein as president of State Auto in 1956. Now chairman of the board and chief executive officer, Gingher's successor as president was Ned E. Neutzling. More recently, George D. Massar became State Auto's fourth president when Neutzling retired in 1977.

Other members of the State Auto Group include Southern Home Insurance Company, headquartered in Greer, South Carolina, and Columbus Security Life Insurance Company, activated in 1978 to add still another dimension to the multiple line offerings of State Auto independent agents. In 1979, the State Auto Group had combined premium writings of more than $285 million and at year end the combined assets of the Group exceeded $770 million.

State Savings

Savings "better than money in the bank" idea pays off

What is today the largest state-chartered savings association headquartered in central Ohio was, in 1945, a floundering savings and loan with little optimism for future growth. Calvin Reese purchased Fidelity Savings & Loan at the suggestion of regulators who were considering closing the company. Reese changed the name of the association to State Savings and immediately set to work to get it on firm footing. The company's assets were approximately $400,000 and, out of 21 companies in Franklin County, it ranked 20th in size. Today, State Savings has the strongest capital base of all the central Ohio state-chartered savings associations.

The company was to experience many changes in its growth over the next few years, beginning with its purchase of control — under the direction of Reese's brother Everett — of North High Savings, a somewhat larger association. Later, after

The opening of the Worthington office in 1970 revived company branching.

the death of State Savings' founder, Calvin Reese, North High Savings President Dick Riley and State Savings' Everett Reese, merged the two companies. The 1955 merger produced a company with $11 million in assets.

John G. Lambert was president and Everett Reese was chairman of the newly-merged State Savings Company. Webb Vorys, attorney for the merger, served as director. Other local citizens also played key roles in developing the new company, including Directors Sam Davis, Ralph Riley, J. N. Meeks and Paul Herbert (later Chief Justice of the Supreme Court).

The merged company had two offices and a new branch located at Graceland. Allan B. McFarland, employed as a teller after working his way through Ohio State University, was asked to transfer to the Graceland office. McFarland's hopes to be manager were temporarily dampened when he was asked simply to "help out" in the new office. Still, he saw the position in a positive light and considered it "a tremendous opportunity."

McFarland remained at Graceland for more than 15 years, leaving as State Savings president in 1968. His years of experience observing, working with and talking to the saving public were an asset to the character of the company in the years which followed.

McFarland noticed that when the savings public came to State Savings, they wanted to talk to people with management responsibility. Borrowers, on the other hand, wanted to talk to management people who could quickly respond to their questions. McFarland, who remains as president of the association today, concluded that State Savings should keep management people working with the public — not sitting in headquarters offices. He determined to keep overhead expenses low so the saver could be paid more on his investment, and he personally

66 E. Broad St. was, for years, the main office for State Savings.

went door-to-door with Tom Davis and Gib Reese, handing out dime savers and meeting the public.

Paying more for savings and branching more produced superior growth for State Savings. Capital, which had increased somewhat above the average rate for local savings institutions, was still not adequate. Profitability until 1965 remained below national levels and, partly because of capital constraints, branching slowed.

After the Westerville office opened in 1964, no new offices were opened for more than five years.

David E. Reese, a young bank officer from Citibank in New York, had a lot to do with the next phase of State Savings' development. His idea resulted in top management alignment in the early 1970s and this same group produced more than a decade of record capital and asset growth. McFarland was named president, Donald B. Shackelford was named chairman and David E. Reese became executive vice president. This stabilized the State Savings top management team during a decade when other larger local financial institutions experienced top management turnover.

The opening of the Worthington office in 1970 marked a revival of branching. Recruiting efforts were expanded. Overhead remained low and payments to savers remained above the S&L industry and banking industry average. Profits reached high performance levels and the earlier capital squeeze gave way to capital strength.

During the decade of the 1970s, net worth grew at an average rate of 21.5% per year — exceeding the rate of performance of Bank of America, Morgan Guaranty and other major banks. Even the far-off *New York Times* took notice by saying that, "The State Savings and Loan Association of Columbus, Ohio, is a notably sound, well-run operation." State Savings began pioneering urban redevelopment through the American Home Foundation.

By 1980, the association — which held 205th place in Franklin County at the end of World War II — ranked second in central Ohio and 16th in the state. And, when it reached the half billion dollar mark in assets, State Savings headlined an ad saying "Thanks" — to the many savers who had helped.

Suburban Motor Freight, Inc.

Responsibility of corporate citizenship important to company growth

Since its founding by James Ralph Riley in 1915, Suburban Motor Freight has provided valuable transport service to carry the nation's goods to the marketplace. For decades, the company has ranked among the top 100 of 16,000 trucking companies in America.

It all started with a shipment of eggs from Washington Court House to Columbus, Ohio, a distance of only 39 miles. Today, the Suburban shipping network includes 18 terminals in Ohio, Indiana, Illinois, Michigan and West Virginia. The firm's headquarters are located in Columbus at 1100 King Avenue and more than 750 persons are employed throughout its shipping system.

In 1980 Suburban shipped more than

one billion pounds of commercial and industrial goods for its customers in the Central States area. Suburban also has accredited accommodations for interline shipments to 40 other states and Canada.

James Ralph Riley, the company's president and chief executive officer, is recognized as a leading midwestern businessman who is active in a variety of

The Suburban staff of drivers assembled for this 1935 portrait in front of the company's terminal at 888 Goodale Boulevard. This is the truck that started it all back in 1915, a solid tire transporter that Mr. Riley used to establish Suburban service with regular shipments between Columbus and Newark, Ohio.

professional, educational and civic organizations.

Riley is a major contributor to the activities and interests of the trucking industry. His name is inscribed in the Truck Transportation Hall of Honor, and he is a founding member of the American Society for Traffic and Transportation. For 20 years he lectured on traffic transportation management at the Ohio State University.

Riley personally delivered one of the first shipments for the fledgling transport company — one washing machine to Newark, Ohio. The trip took three hours from Columbus in an old solid tire truck and paid 50 cents.

The first delivery outside Ohio went to Detroit in April, 1929. The company shipped 125 pounds of paper for 75 cents round trip!

Born and raised on a small farm in Utica, Ohio, near Columbus, Riley enlisted in the U.S. Army Corps of Engineers during World War I. Following his discharge, he earned his way through Ohio State University and is a member of Beta Gamma Sigma, honorary economics and finance fraternity; Alpha Zeta, professional agriculture fraternity; and Delta Sigma Pi, commerce fraternity. He also holds the honorary degree of Doctor of Laws from Otterbein College. Riley was 1967 chairman of the board of the Colum-

bus Area Chamber of Commerce, and has served as co-chairman of the Chamber's Safety Council.

He is past chairman of the Boy Scouts of America and past president of the Columbus Kiwanis. He has served as chairman of the board of trustees for Riverside Methodist Hospital and as a trustee for Otterbein College, Methodist Theological School, the Center of Science and Industry, and Citizen's Research, among many others.

He has also served as Director of Corco, Inc. in Worthington and State Savings in Columbus. Riley is emeritus chairman of the Development Committee for Greater Columbus.

Riley founded the Columbus Boychoir, presently in Princeton, New Jersey, and helped to establish the Columbus Town Meeting of the Air. He is listed in *Who's Who in the Midwest.*

A former chairman of the YMCA National Council and past chairman of the

YMCA International Management Seminar, he has addressed industrialists both at home and abroad. He was chairman of the 1963 U.S. delegation to the International Management Seminar.

The modern Suburban equipment fleet includes more than 350 city and highway tractors and 700 trailers. Suburban drivers have rolled up millions of accident-free miles. At the 1979 annual Safety Awards Banquet, 124 Columbus city and highway drivers were honored for 1149 years and more than 82 million cumulative miles of driving without a preventable accident.

This outstanding performance has been evident in National Truck Roadeo championships as well, where Suburban drivers have competed successfully for more than 20 years. At the 1979 National Roadeo, a Suburban driver earned a first place victory and was presented with the industry's most prestigious award as the driver who best exemplifies excellence and professionalism in trucking.

The Union Fork and Hoe Company

Conservative, yet consistent . . . the keystones of growth.

March 1982 will mark the 75th anniversary for The Union Fork and Hoe Company, one of the leaders in the manufacturing of hand tools and implements for the lawn and garden, farm, industrial and construction industries. The company's general line of nearly 450 items includes forks, hoes, shovels, rakes, snow tools, cutting and striking tools marketed internationally under the registered trademarks of Green Thumb, Flex-Beam, Yard 'N Garden, Farm King, Trail Blazer, Razor-Back, and Atlas.

The company today is the result of the disciplined business philosophies of the founder, George B. Durell. In 1907, Durell purchased and merged the U.S. Hoe and Tool Company of Columbus, Ohio, with the Continental Tool Company of Frankfort, New York, to form The Union Fork and Hoe Company.

In the first shop, dirt floors were common, stoves heated the work areas, oil lamps shed dim light and had to be moved from place to place as needed. The work day was 10 hours, and wages were 10¢ an hour. At that time, one could rent a very good house in Columbus for $5 a month.

In 1919, Edward Durell, son of G. B., went to work at Union. He was named president in 1934. Edward Durell told his employees, "How you budget the 168 hours in a week will probably determine what success you will attain." He attributes the continued growth of Union to the loyal and intelligent Union employees. Pride was the hallmark of success . . . a pride in honest workmanship and high quality products.

Edward Durell's fascination with history also contributed to Union's growth. His quests to collect and analyze old farm tools began in the 1930s. He studied how and why they were made and used and the results of his studies played a big part in the progress of the company, finding their way into the engineering of many of Union's products.

For the first 30 years, Union's product line was very basic — forks, hoes, repair handles, and rakes. In 1937, the Razor-Back shovel was introduced, the first major change for a broader product line. In 1962, Union added solid shank and wide blade shovels and steel and aluminum scoops.

The Durells' love of history and a sense of commitment to the community has dominated Union's outlook, highlighted by the family's dedication in 1964 of the

Union Fork & Hoe sample truck of the 1940s, traveling nationwide introducing Union tools to hardware dealers.

The Durell Street of Yesteryear at the Columbus Center of Science and Industry (COSI).

Durell Street of Yesteryear at Columbus' Center of Science and Industry (COSI). On the Street of Yesteryear, one can travel back in time to the shops of the blacksmith and mud streets era, furnishings and equipment intact. Ten years later, in 1974, the Farm Museum, a collection of pioneer farm tools and a complete pioneer kitchen and shed, was added to the COSI exhibit.

The company facilities were utilized during World War II for the manufacture of bayonets and standby jigs and fixtures for the manufacture of planes.

In 1965, Union's first warehouse was opened in the heart of Los Angeles, California. Each year the volume of tools handled through the Los Angeles warehouse continues to grow.

Across the years, sawmills have been strategically located near ash forests in nearby states to supply Union with the high quality ash necessary for the making of handles for Union tools.

The year 1966 saw the Union product line expand again to include post hole diggers, augers, wheelbarrows, snow shovels and pushers.

In 1968, G. Britton Durell II, Edward's son and grandson of the founder, was elected president of Union. During his tenure, the business has continued to grow and prosper. By 1972, striking tools were added to the firm's inventory of products, and by 1979, cutting tools joined the product catalog.

Throughout its history, Union Fork and Hoe's activities have been founded upon philosophies first deliniated by George B. Durell and then kept alive by succeeding generations of Durells.

According to the Durells, the two major ingredients of a successful manager are the ability to budget time and to lead other people. Their time is budgeted in five categories — family, business, community, church, and political affairs — followed by rest and recreation. This rather uncomplicated philosophy has always permeated the company to establish an environment in which pride and quality can contribute to conservative and consistent growth.

United Way of Franklin County

Voluntary support of human services carries on an American tradition

Deeply rooted in American democracy is the tradition of neighbor helping neighbor. From our earliest day as a nation, people have joined together in volunteer efforts to meet human needs in their communities.

Today, nothing better exemplifies this spirit than the United Way, with its emphasis on voluntary human services funded by voluntary contributions which are raised through a combined campaign.

In Columbus, the history of what is now United Way can be traced to 1885 when the first steps were taken toward creating a more unified system of charities. That year saw the formation of the Society for Organized Charities. Designed to "prevent overlapping and duplication," it was the city's first united community planning group and information agency.

The society operated as such until 1899 when it was reorganized into the Associated Charities of Columbus. This new organization gave each charitable group a voice in community fund-raising and planning decisions. It also began to consider the problems posed by numerous voluntary fund-raising appeals. But the actual development of a combined fund-raising campaign was still more than 20 years away.

America's entry into World War I gave new momentum to the process. Columbus became the second city in the nation to organize a War Chest and its efforts included the coordination of various charity drives. Then, in 1923, the major step was taken. A new group was formed — the Columbus Community Fund — to conduct a combined fund raising campaign for 28 human service agencies.

The Community Fund's campaign was called appropriately "One Campaign For All" and its chairman, the Reverend E.F. Chauncey, Rector of Trinity Episcopal Church, termed it a "crusade." Allied in support of the crusade were leading members of the Columbus business, industrial and education communities: Albert M. Miller, S.P. Bush, Simon Lazarus, Gerald Fenton, B. Gwinn Huntington, Austin McElroy, Fred Lazarus, Jr., William Oxley Thompson and Edward Orton.

The public responded enthusiastically to the new approach. The Community Fund's 1923 campaign had a goal of $488,425. It raised $600,769. The following year, the campaign listed 29,220 voluntary contributors, compared to the

In 1923, five years after this picture was taken, the District Nursing Service joined in the first combined campaign of the Columbus Community Fund. Now known as the Community Health and Nursing Service, it remains an important member agency in the United Way system.

"She's not heavy — she's a friend." This scene at Gladden Community House captures the spirit of neighbor helping neighbor today.

former maximum of 7,000 individuals who had previously contributed to Community Fund agencies in independent campaigns.

The combined campaign worked in Columbus, and it has continued to work ever since that successful beginning in 1923. From that year until 1940, the Community Fund continued its annual campaigns, and voluntary giving to fund human services steadily increased. With the outbreak of World War II, the fund became the War Chest, an echo of 1918, and when the War Chest was demobilized in 1946, what had been the Community

Fund became the Community Chest.

Since then, there have been other name changes — to United Appeals of Franklin County in 1951, then to the singular, the United Appeal, and finally, in 1972, to the United Way, a change designed to conform to the national trend. But the purpose has remained the same: to fund human services through voluntary contributions raised in annual campaigns conducted by community volunteers. And this approach is based on the strong conviction that private, voluntary agencies offer the most efficient means of providing these services at the community level.

Today, United Way of Franklin County continues to build on this record of more than 50 years of volunteer effort. In 1979, the United Way campaign raised more than $10,000,000 in voluntary contributions — the highest total in local history — to help fund 74 member agencies which provide services throughout the year to thousands of people.

These services respond to a wide range of human needs. They include health and rehabilitation programs, services for families and children, programs of recreation and character-building and neighborhood services. United Way agencies touch the lives of young people, the elderly and everyone in between. In the process, they help build a stronger community.

What is most important is that these services are an expression of community concern and volunteer effort. Through the United Way, the people of Columbus and Franklin County are carrying on the American tradition of neighbor helping neighbor.

WBNS TV Inc.

Broadcasting giant started with 15 watts of power

Jonathan Winters talks with Ray Rose, host of WBNS TV's "Gamboree," (1953) as the Frank LaRue Orchestra and guests look on.

For central Ohioans, the call letters WBNS TV are synonymous with a powerhouse broadcaster and news-gathering giant. That's the way it is today. But few persons know or recall that this same industry leader had its beginnings in a small electrical shop on west 10th Avenue in downtown Columbus, 56 years ago.

Started by C. A. Entrekin in 1924, WCAH as it was known then, transmitted radio signals with only 15 watts of power, and then for just a few hours each day. Mrs. Entrekin's living room was the studio, and the programming consisted of talks and her talents on the piano.

In the fall of 1933, after several technical advances, the station climbed out of its infancy and was purchased by the Wolfe family, who then changed the call letters to WBNS.

But in a few years radio was destined to give way to yet another step forward by science — television — and on January 28, 1948, application was made to the FCC for a license to operate WBNS Television on Channel 10.

As Casey Stengel's New York Yankees battled it out with Burt Shotton's Brooklyn Dodgers, WBNS Television inaugurated its regular programming with coverage of the 1949 World Series.

How to use the new invention was still an experimental notion with the people who ran the TV stations as well as the people who watched the sets back in those early days. This was the reason why WBNS TV didn't sign on until 3 o'clock in the afternoon at first. That was the time movie theaters opened, and certainly it was thought, no one would be watching anything before then.

Yet, if the beginning steps for Channel 10 were halting and deliberate, the next

few years, and in fact the decades since, have been packed with innovation, accomplishment, style and advancement.

The 1950s saw a burgeoning of new programming that covered the spectrum of tastes and keyed to local interests: "Look to Lazarus" was a half-hour daily daytime show that featured new products, celebrity guests, and a different set each day; "Homemaker's Hobnob" with co-hosts Jean Shea and Tom Gleba that filled an hour in the mornings with talk and music featuring Bob Marvin (later to star as Flippo the Clown) as vocalist, and Walter Knick on piano; all of the Cleveland Browns games were filmed and edited down to a half-hour program once a week; and "Haft's Wrestling" aired every Thursday from 10 to 11:30 p.m. with Marty DeVictor and a live remote from ringside in Memorial Hall, now the home of COSI.

Although still in its early stages, the technology of television was not content to grow modestly. This time is leapt forward and landed in a pool of color! For with the coming of October, 1950, WBNS TV became the first television station in central Ohio to broadcast in color with the Saturday afternoon football games from CBS.

But it didn't stop there. In 1955, the antenna height was increased from 595 feet to 839 feet. In 1957 its visual power was increased to 316,000 watts, a far cry from the 24,300 watts the station orginally radiated just eight years earlier. Both the changes in antenna and power pushed the Channel 10 signal to a radius of 65 miles in all directions.

March of 1962 saw the first color film origination from WBNS TV, and later that year, the first videotape origination was aired when a Douglas Edwards CBS

newscast was recorded at 7 p.m. from a live network feed, and played back later.

The first color picture to come live from a WBNS TV studio featured Flippo The Clown in 1967 as host of his early afternoon movie. Interestingly, color TV posed even a problem for the "King of the Clowns" as he was known then, for now his gray-and-white clown suit for black and white broadcasts had to be retired in favor of a red, white, and blue outfit.

Personalities quickly made their marks with viewers and soon were identified with Channel 10 as closely as the programs that surrounded them.

From very early days in the station's history, the name Chet Long meant news — not just the facts of the day's happenings, but the strength of his character and the credibility he generated in viewers' thoughts. He endorsed very few things publicly, for his preference for a product or service meant unquestioned acceptance by many.

Popular star and comedian Jonathan Winters found his way to WBNS TV in the early 1950s as a staff announcer. His talent and humor were quickly exported to New York where his career rocket took off, but not before his antics on the staff of Channel 10 went down in the station's own book of records.

Other names will be remembered — Irwin Johnson, Pat Wilson, Ray Rose, Edwina Zanes, Aunt Fran, Lucy and her Toyshop. And programs will be remembered — Columbus Town Meeting, Lucky Pup, Homemaker's Exchange . . . and more.

But the latest chapters in 10TV's history are taking shape in a streamlined, professional, full-service approach to broadcasting. In 1975, WBNS TV aired its first electronic live news picture from the state fairgrounds. And in October of 1979, Eyewitness News shot its first live picture from SkyCam, the station's owned and operated Bell JetRanger III helicopter available on a 24 hour basis.

The years to come bode with exciting changes, and WBNS 10TV has demonstrated its presence will be there at the forefront.

Early newscar and studio building in 1956.

Wendy's Old Fashioned Hamburgers

A hamburger chain built on "Quality"

"Does America need another hamburger chain?" This was the question being asked as R. David Thomas opened the doors to his first Wendy's Old Fashioned Hamburgers restaurant at 257 East Broad Street in downtown Columbus on November 15, 1969.

At that time, many food industry experts and some skeptical observers had commented that the fast food growth curve had peaked during the late 1960s, and that the rapid expansion of the industry was over. But this skepticism did not take into account the determination of R. David Thomas, often described as the "David after the hamburger Goliaths." He believed he had found a combination of food products to satisfy a distinctive market of consumers who wanted a better product.

Incorporating "Quality Is Our Recipe" as his company's philosophy, Thomas opened several Wendy's restaurants in the Columbus area during the following two years. He standardized the image building design and added some innovative techniques, which included the "Pick-Up Window" for fast service and customer convenience. The result was wide public acceptance, as sales began to grow for the company that prepared hamburgers with fresh (never frozen), 100 percent ground beef, 256 different ways by using a combination of eight condiments. In addition to its cooked-to-order hamburgers, which were available in three sizes: Single, ¼ lb., Double, ½ lb., and Triple, ¾ lb., the Wendy's menu also included rich and meaty chili, french fries, beverages, and Frosty dairy dessert.

On August 17, 1972, the company began franchising its quality food, quick service concept and granted its first Wendy's Old Fashioned Hamburgers franchise, which was later opened in Indianapolis, Indiana. During December of that year it established the Wendy's Management Institute (WMI) to train personnel for franchised and company-owned market areas.

The company's growth continued with the 100th Wendy's restaurant opening on June 25, 1975, in Louisville, Kentucky. Later during 1975 the company's stock "went public" and was first traded on the over-the-counter market (WNDY). By now the young company had attracted national interest and acclaim and approximately eighteen months later (December 15, 1976) the 500th Wendy's restaurant was opened in Toronto, Ontario, Canada.

The company reached a corporate milestone on March 21, 1978, in Spring-

Wendy's Old Fashioned Hamburgers

field, Tennessee, with the opening of its 1,000th Wendy's restaurant. In only eight years and four months, Wendy's had established its chain of 1,000 stores in operation. Never before had this accomplishment been achieved in the food industry in such a short period of time.

To understand Wendy's rapid growth and how it happened, you have to understand R. David Thomas, who is a strong advocate of the free enterprise system, and an impatient man with a goal "to be the best!" He has modestly described himself as "just a person who likes good hamburgers," but this does not accurately portray his vast knowledge of the food industry, nor his marketing foresight.

In the span of a little over 10 years, Wendy's Old Fashioned Hamburgers had grown from one man's dream into a chain of nearly 2,000 restaurants, which employed more than 75,000 full and part-time people, and with annual sales exceeding $1 billion dollars.

Today, there are Wendy's Old Fashioned Hamburgers restaurants in 49 states, Canada, and Puerto Rico, as well as stores in Japan and in European markets. While the basic company concept and philosophy has remained unchanged, the company has expanded its menu to offer a salad bar to broaden its market appeal.

R. David Thomas, chairman of the board and founder, Wendy's International, Inc.

White Castle System

Grandaddy of fast food chains alive and well in Columbus

In the world of fast-food razzmatazz, the White Castle System prospers in a quiet yet determined fashion. Founded in Wichita, Kansas in 1921, the company began with the "flattening of the hamburger" by Walt Anderson. It was E. W. "Billy" Ingram, however, who made the company into a regional chain. He was also generally credited with founding the fast-food industry.

As Ingram reminisced years later, "In 1930, one could ride all day without seeing a hamburger stand. In other cities, we could not find places specializing in the sale of hamburger sandwiches; we created our competition as we went."

The forefather of the unique White Castle hamburger was a tasteless carnival-type item, a meatball which sat on a grille for an indefinite time and was plopped into a cold bun. But Anderson flattened and pressed chopped onions into the patty, cooked it quickly at a high heat, and warmed the bun by placing it atop the cooking pattie. "Fix one the way you like them" soon became a standard order.

Billy Ingram was the real estate man sought by Anderson to help him lease a location for the business. The owner refused but finally agreed to lease to Ingram. And so began the partnership. Ingram selected "White" to emphasize cleanliness and "Castle" to denote respectability. In those days, the closest thing to a hamburger stand in prohibitionist Kansas was usually a front for a bootlegger. Anderson later sold his interest to Ingram.

Columbus restaurant operations began in 1929 with six locations. The first — at 49 South Front Street — was soon displaced by the original State Office Building. Of the original six establishments, two — at Broad and Central and at Arcadia and High — are still in operation, although their original buildings have long since been replaced. Another 1929 unit — at Fourth and Long — recently celebrated its 51st anniversary. Twelve of the little white buildings with the medieval flair are well known to many long-time Columbusites.

Columbus was then an all-day train ride from New York rather than an hour's flight, so Ingram sought a more central home office. Columbus met that qualification and was an ideal city in which to live and work. Ingram recognized these factors — not to mention his passionate enjoyment of Big Ten Football. In 1934 he moved corporate headquarters to 555

West Goodale, bringing his fledgling paper cap and steel fabrication operations from other cities at the same time.

In an industry where a cheerleading "Grow, for Growth's sake" is close to the norm, White Castle chooses a planned growth rate of 10-15 new units yearly. Generally conservative, the company prefers new units to be financed from current operating revenues.

About half the profits go to employees through a profit-sharing plan founded in 1949. The Pension Plan (1943), a firm "from the ranks" promotion policy, generous insurance, vacation, annual cash bonus, and similar benefits make up one of the most broad packages in the industry, and one where the basic package described above is applied to every employee.

The "promotion from within" policy has been equally applied to two more generations of the owning family, with years spent learning operations at the customer/employee level being a prerequisite for moving into management.

World War II nearly wiped out the hamburger business. With little product to sell and fewer available staff, White Castles dropped in number from 130 to only 80. E. W. (Edgar) Ingram, Jr., the second generation of management, noted the problem: "If we are to competitively face the future, we must actively begin to get ready for it now!"

He concentrated on replacing the lost units with larger, more modern stores (160 today), along with support facilities: nine

Wichita No. 4, the First White Castle, in 1921.

First White Castle in Columbus, 49 South Front Street. October, 1929.

regional office/warehouse sites and two special-product bakeries (Evendale, Ohio and Carteret, New Jersey) producing their very proprietary open-textured bun.

This period of controlled growth and renovation took White Castle into the '80s with a sales-per-unit average that is second in the industry, and second by a relatively small amount.

The manufacturing arm, too, received attention. Porcelain Steel Buildings Company (originally an in-house supplier of restaurant equipment), evolved into a complete steel fabrication arm with a long list of outside customers. A paper cap manufacturing plant (Lin-n-Look) in New Orleans was acquired.

Today, 555 West Goodale houses the restaurant division headquarters, PSB and its steel fabrication and electrostatic painting operations, the Lin-n-Look sales operation, and the developing White Castle I Company — a new venture to license overseas hamburger operations. Here, too, are the broadened support facilities — purchasing, real estate, research, engineering and construction, accounting (with data links from store to regional office to home office in Columbus), advertising, insurance and benefits, personnel, and other administrative services.

E. W. "Bill" Ingram III, president and chief executive officer sums it up — "My grandfather and father parlayed a borrowed $700 into a business that grosses over $150 million annually, and employs over 6,000 people. And they achieved this with a modestly-priced sandwich." (The 1980 price is 24-26¢, about half the industry norm.) "This growth is an example of what can result from a free enterprise system, unfettered by overregulation!"

The W.W. Williams Company

Heavy equipment distributor retains spirit of family business

The current headquarters of The W.W. Williams Company is a 17,000 square foot facility which houses the firm's word processing, data processing, accounting services and executive offices.

One of the nation's oldest and largest heavy equipment distributors — The W.W. WILLIAMS CO. — traces its history back to the energy, determination and vision of its founder, William Wallace Williams Sr. In the nearly 70 years since the company was founded, it has grown from a small supplier of steam shovels to a modern, multi-million-dollar distributor of construction, industrial and mining equipment employing more than 700 people in six states. Yet, W.W. Williams has retained the pioneering spirit of the family business begun in 1912.

William Sr., a former salesman for The Koehring Company, began his company as a distributor of Koehring concrete mixers. In 1915, he leased the company's first service facility, a forerunner of the reliable parts and service back-up which has become synonymous with the Williams name. The company was incorporated a year later by William Sr., president and general manager; his brother, Walter S. Williams, vice president, and three others.

In 1920 W.W. Williams moved its service facilities from the rented shop at 43 East Spring Street to 835 West Goodale Boulevard, site of the company's administrative office today. Additional office space was added in 1923. In the same year J. Clare Williams, eldest son of the founder, joined the company, which expanded with branches in Cleveland, Dayton, Cincinnati and Toledo.

In the years that followed, the great Depression hit hard at the young company and forced it to close its fledgling branch offices. W.W. Williams Sr., died in 1931, and a year later his wife, Rose, was installed as chairman of the board, an office she held for 28 years. J. Clare was elected president, serving in that capacity until 1963, and his brother, W. Wallace Jr., became vice president. Though financial difficulties persisted throughout the 1930s, the unswerving dedication and sound business sense of Mrs. Williams Sr. helped the company to survive, rebuild, and acquire new accounts and employees.

In 1934 the company — already distributing Iowa Manufacturing sand, gravel and crushing equipment — added Austin Western road graders to its lines. In 1936, Williams began to distribute International Harvester crawler tractors and tractor loaders. That relationship continued until 1955, when the company began its exclusive association with the Euclid Division (now TEREX) of General Motors.

The beginning of a new decade brought a new start for W.W. Williams. The company adopted pension, health, accident, and bonus plans to award key employees for performance. In the first expansion in more than a decade, a new Cleveland

The W.W. Williams Company's original building was home for the company's executive offices as well as its Columbus division offices, warehouse and shop. It was replaced in 1967 with the current headquarters facility.

office was built. Later it was replaced with a modern building, one of Williams' current 19 branch facilities, each housing its own parts, service and sales departments. Williams also continued to expand its equipment lines, in time supplying everything for the construction, industrial and mining markets.

In 1963, David F. Williams, grandson of the founder, became the company's third generation president. Rapid growth and financial gains followed, along with a modernized accounting system, computerization, expansion into Tennessee, Florida and western Pennsylvania, and diversification. In 1968, the company went public with the issuance of common stock, and is now listed with NASDAQ and traded on the OTC market.

Today W.W. Williams consists of four divisions: the Construction Equipment Division — a franchised distributor of heavy construction, industrial and mining equipment throughout Ohio, western Pennsylvania, Tennessee and Florida; Atlantic Power Systems — a distributor of diesel engines, transmissions and generator sets for the Detroit Diesel Allison Division of General Motors, in South Carolina and Georgia; Tri-W Equipment Rental — which rents small and medium sized equipment of a short-term basis from offices in Ohio, Pennsylvania, and Florida; and Will-Air — offering air charter freight and passenger service and serving as the fixed base operator at Columbus' Bolton Field.

The growth of W.W. Williams has paralleled the evolution of the construction industry. From the steam shovels of 1912 to huge hydraulic excavators of the present day, W.W. Williams has always represented the finest manufacturers in the industry. Iowa Manufacturing, the TEREX and Detroit Diesel Allison Divisions of General Motors, The Koehring Company, Galion Manufacturing, Ingersoll-Rand and many other manufacturers have shared in the growth of the company W.W. Williams Sr. founded almost 70 years ago.

Worthington Industries, Inc.

Growth through quality and service since 1955

Like his father and many other relatives, John H. McConnell was raised in the steel industry environment and worked in the mills near Weirton, West Virginia in his younger years. He served his country in the U.S. Navy, went to college and returned to the steel industry as a salesman. During this time, young McConnell realized the tremendous opportunity that existed for a firm that could position itself between the integrated steel producers and the hundreds of service centers in the country, to offer customers the advantages of both.

The young entrepreneur started his business, The Worthington Steel Company, in rented space on the east side of Columbus in 1955. Initial capital was a $600 bank loan collateralized by McConnell's family automobile.

During the first year of operation, three employees processed 1,000 tons of steel and realized approximately $340,000 in sales. Today, Worthington is recognized as one of the nation's fastest growing companies and a leader in four businesses with annual sales of over $400 million.

McConnell attributes the company's dynamic growth to concentrating on what he considers the fundamentals of good business practice. "We have not tried to be the biggest but rather the best," the firm's founder explains. "We have specialized in areas where we can do a superior job. Every aspect of our operation has been oriented toward helping our customers find a better, more economical way of producing their products. As a result, we have established excellent reputations for quality and service in the industries we serve. Second, we have practiced the philosophy of treating our employees, customers and suppliers the way we like to be treated. This approach has developed a unique *esprit de corps* within the company and invaluable outside relationships."

Worthington Industries is recognized nationally for its innovative motivational programs and excellent employee relations. In addition to deferred profit sharing, the company pays cash profit sharing quarterly, an incentive which is a significant part of each employee's total compensation and creates a very profit-conscious attitude. "Production workers are paid on a salary plan rather than an hourly basis, and this along with other benefits," says McConnell, "is designed to recognize each employee as a valuable part of the Worthington team."

Worthington's first plant in 1959.

Corporate headquarters and manufacturing facilities Columbus, Ohio.

Worthington's growth has also been aided by aggressive expansion and diversification. In 1959 the company purchased two acres of land on the north side of Columbus and built a 16,000 square foot plant. Business prospered — the plant was expanded several times and a second facility was acquired in Louisville, Kentucky.

The firm's first step toward diversification was its entrance into the pressure cylinder field in 1971. Management saw an opportunity to apply its metal working know-how to the production of cylinders used with such products as outdoor gas barbecue grills and camping equipment. To reflect its new diversity, the name Worthington Industries was adopted with The Worthington Steel Company and Worthington Cylinders becoming its primary operating entities.

The '70s were an exciting and explosive growth period for Worthington. The metal processing operations were geographically expanded via the purchases of facilities in Chicago, Illinois; Rock Hill, South Carolina and Baltimore, Maryland. A modern technical service laboratory was built in Columbus for the use of the company's engineering staff. New production capabilities were added such as annealing and pickling of flat rolled steel. Columbus operations were doubled in size and consolidated on one large tract of land adjacent to Interstates 270 and 71 on the far north side of the city. Worthington Cylinders plant was significantly expanded to accommodate its growth from a fledgling operation when acquired to its position as the industry leader. In 1978, a second major diversification step took place with the purchase of U-Brand Corporation, Ashland, Ohio, a leader in the field of malleable iron and plastic pipe fittings. During the '70s, total company sales grew from $21 million annually to $278 million.

The year 1980 marked two important events. Worthington made its most sizeable acquisition ever with the purchase of Buckeye International, Inc., one of the largest steel castings firms in the country, and the company celebrated the 25th anniversary of its founding. In that relatively short span of years, Worthington Industries established a track record matched by very few companies regardless of industry. And, in the words of Chairman McConnell, the company "barely scratched the surface" of its potential growth. "In the years ahead we will expand our business into many other areas of the country," predicts McConnell; "however, Columbus will remain the heart of our operations. This has been a great city in which to build a business."

CONCLUSION

by Betty Garrett

In 1969, when the venerable Deshler Hotel (then at the northwest corner of Broad and High) was razed this letter was found in its cornerstone box.

Columbus, Ohio
August Second, 1915

TO THE OWNER OF THIS PROPERTY WHEN THIS BOX IS OPENED —

It may seem a foolish thing for me to write a letter to a person who is probably not yet born and who will not be able to read the letter for over seventy-five years, but I wish to express my keen regret of the fact that it is impossible for me to be with you when you read the letter, not that I care to live that long — as I am sixty-two years old now, — but I would like to stand with you, when I place this box, so as to be able to see some of the wonderful changes that will take place and know about the surprising developments that will be made in art, science and mechanics, and the wonderful advance in real knowledge. How I regret that I cannot know what you will know and see what you will see, for I am sure the people in this world will continue to advance as they always have and you should be very glad that you are living in the twenty-first century instead of the twentieth century. When I compare conditions that exist in this city today, with those that existed one hundred years ago, as shown in my grandmother's letters, [Betsy Green Deshler, See Chapter I], it is simply impossible to realize what conditions will be in your time. I doubt very much if you will really be any happier than we are, or my grandmother was, but you will know so much more and things that will be simple to you, would be wonderful to us. I wonder how far you will develop the use of electricity; to what point aerial navigation will be practically used; how wonderful will be your system of transportation, the development of heat, power and light! I wonder what your form of government will be, for surely it will change from what it is now,; whether you will have wars and panics, sickness and poverty as we have! I hope not, and I believe these things are not entirely eradicated, they will be greatly minimized. I wonder how you will live and what you will talk about; whether you will drink beer and whiskey and smoke tobacco.

I am enclosing a manual of The Columbus Club. I wonder whether your men will assemble at any place like that — play cards, pool, billiards and take a social drink or two or three!

I want to tell you what I think will become of this property. I believe our Trust, a copy of which I am placing in this box, will expire by limitation in about 65 years from now. No doubt, the property will be sold by the parties who will then own it, some of whom are as yet unborn, and the money divided among them. The property will then have been in our family more than one hundred and sixty years.

The building I am now erecting is considered by our best architects, engineers and builders, as being the very best construction that we know of today. No one knows how long it will stand and probably no one ever will know, because it will become obsolete before it becomes insecure. Within seventy-five years you will tear it down, no doubt, and erect a structure that will be relatively as fitting to Columbus as you know it, as this house is to Columbus as I know it. How I would like to see that building! My idea is that by that time, Columbus' immediate environment will contain a population of one million people. The house I am building is appropriate for a city of about 500,000; we have a population now of 210,000.

Although I cannot be with you when you read this letter, I can imagine the sympathetic smile that will come over your face as you say, 'That poor old man, how far he was behind in the times.' But there is one thing you will not know that I will know — I know now where you will be when you take this letter out of the box, but you will not know where I am at that time, and possibly I may have progressed much further than you will have done.

I hope you will enjoy building your house as much as I have enjoyed building the one you are destroying. I hope it will be successfully used and I would request that you place a letter in your cornerstone to be read by the person who destroys your building to erect a better one, and place a copy of my grandmother's letters with it, as he will know more than either of us and may be interested in reading ancient history.

With my kindest regards and very best wishes, I remain, Yours very sincerely and regretfully,

John G. Deshler.

In 1915 the Deshler Block was leveled and the Deshler Hotel built.

Columbus, Ohio
1980
TO JOHN G. DESHLER, WHEREVER HE MAY BE:

Mr. Deshler, dear, wise friend from the past, and next-of-historical kin, please accept this sincere and regretful answer to your letter from a world you never thought would write to you.

The building you anticipated would be razed in 1990 was demolished 11 years ago. Most of the events you anticipated were merely in a greater hurry than your otherwise astute calculations about time. There is no cornerstone for this letter because, right now, the site which your family owned 160 years is a parking lot for automobiles . . . which is as fitting to the Columbus we know today as your hotel was to the Columbus you knew. But by 1990, when the 75 years you mentioned will have passed, it is quite likely that there will be another structure suitable to a city of about one million people.

While taking for granted — but wasting — the wonderful developments in heat, transportation and energy you anticipated, those of us in 1980 not only still drink beer and whiskey and smoke tobacco, play cards, pool and billiards but openly engage in some leisure pastimes which were practiced but not spoken about in "polite company" in 1915. The Columbus Club still stands, and remains a place where only men assemble. In 1980, that social segregation of the sexes is a rare anachronism, though. Sickness and poverty, wars and panics have certainly not been eradicated. Medical science has greatly minimized the effects of disease, beyond what even your acute vision might have imagined.

Poverty has been mitigated somewhat by laws and is not left strictly to the vagaries of individual charity. Government is far larger in proportion to the population than what you knew, but no more or less efficient than the democracy you had. People always think it is worse in the time they are living than what anyone else has known. Panics can and do occur in the national marketplace. In the 1930s, America endured a Depression more severe than any experienced prior to your time. You will probably not be surprised to learn that Columbus weathered the crisis better than most cities, however.

As for war, there have been two worldwide bloodbaths since your letter was written. Since 1945, a destructive — but potentially useful — energy source inherent in atoms has, to

date, kept the world from unrestricted warfare. It has not eliminated it and never will. All these problems arise from factors in human nature, which has never changed, and — barring some kind of apocalyptic miracle unimaginable to any of us — never will. Therefore, you are correct in assuming that we are no more, or less, happy than you and your grandmother before you were. Like you, we think the most wonderful things are yet to come and forget that the moment one is living (and often complaining about) precious, since it is the only thing which can be counted on until the moment which follows it.

Because of that, dear friend from the past, your letter is cause for a smile of empathy, not sympathy. You were certainly not "behind the times;" you were uncannily ahead of it in your predictions about what would happen in Columbus by 1980, and no doubt, by 1990. If you were also correct that you "may have progressed much farther" than we have, then history — and time itself — are not one-way progressions from the past to the future.

That would mean that you know what we are doing far more surely than we can surmise what you and your contemporaries did. If so, we may meet someday.

It would be interesting, Mr. Deshler, if we could all climb to the top of that hill where Lucas Sullivant went in 1823, just before his death, to look down at Columbus and imagine what will be happening there 100 years from now. And while the people of that time are taking their turn, we can finally have a good talk about what happened to all of us in our respective times.

It would be quite a gathering, John G. Deshler, you and Lucas Sullivant . . . and your grandparents, David and Betsy Green Deshler . . . Lida Rose McCabe and the gambler John Young and Orris Parrish and Lyne Starling; Simon Lazarus and Amelia Bloomer, Alice Keyes Strickler, Tod Galloway and Madam Metcalfe and William Dean Howells . . . Francis Sessions, "Cump" Sherman and Francis Dana Gage . . . Dr. S.B. Hartman, Frederick Schumacher and O. Henry . . . Robert Wolfe, Mary Agnes Fisher Thurber, Eddie Rickenbacker, Clara Reynolds and Ted Lewis . . . George Karb, Millicent Easter and Howard Thurston . . . James Thurber, Eileen McKenney and the Get-Ready Man . . .

All, sleeping on the hill, but rested and ready to learn more about Columbus — all the things which have never been written into the history books, besides themselves.

Index

Bibliography

Books

Architecture: Columbus. Columbus: The Foundation of the Columbus Chapter, American Institute of Architects, 1976.

Bernstein, Burton. *Thurber: A Biography.* New York: Dodd, Mead and Co., 1975.

Bode, Carl; Howard, Leon and Wright; Louis, B., eds. *American Literature,* Vol. III: "The Last Part of the Nineteenth Century." New York: Washington Square Press, 1966.

Brondfield, Jerry. *Woody Hayes and the 100-Yard War.* New York: Random House, 1974.

Bryant, Captain Donald H., ed. *History of Columbus Division of Police 1816-1974.* Columbus: Police Athletic League, 1974.

Columbus Area Social Profile. Columbus: Academy for Contemporary Problems, 1974.

Columbus Dispatch. Columbus Dispatch Centennial Library Edition, 1912.

Condon, George E. *Yesterday's Columbus: A Pictorial History of Ohio's Capital.* Miami, Florida: E.A. Seemann Publishers, Inc., 1977.

Dickens, Charles. *American Notes.* n.p., 1842.

Frary, I.T. *Ohio in Homespun and Calico.* Richmond, Virginia: Garrett and Massie, Inc., 1942.

Gill, Brendan. *Here at the New Yorker.* New York: Random House, 1975.

Harden, Michael. *Passage to America: Life of Salvatore Presutti.* Columbus, Ohio: Lawhead Press, 1975.

Hayes, Woody. *You Win with People.* Columbus, Ohio: Typographic Printing Co., 1973.

Hofstadter, Richard. *The Age of Reform.* New York: Vintage Books, 1955.

Hofstadter, Richard. *Great Issues in American History,* Vol. II. New York: Vintage Books, 1958.

Holbrook, Stewart H. *The Golden Age of Quackery.* New York: MacMillan, 1959.

Hooper, Osman Castle. *History of the City of Columbus, Ohio.* Columbus-Cleveland: The Memorial Publishing Company, 1920.

Hunker, Henry L. *Industrial Evolution of Columbus, Ohio.* Columbus, Ohio: Ohio State University, 1958.

Keys, Tom. *The Battling Buckeyes.* Columbus, Ohio: Education Associates, 1975.

Kolb, Charles B. *Helping Up the Man Who is Down: Or Seven Years in the Slums.* Columbus, Ohio: n.p., 1910.

Lee, Alfred Emory. *History of the City of Columbus.* 2 vols. New York and Chicago: Munsell and Company, 1892.

McCabe, Lida Rose. *Don't You Remember.* Columbus, Ohio: A.H. Smythe, 1884.

Marks, Mary Louise. *Negroes in Columbus.* Columbus, Ohio: Ohio State University Press, 1928.

Martin, Anna Mae. *Columbus: The Buckeye Capital.* Columbus, Ohio: Charles E. Merrrill Books, Inc., 1952.

Monkkonen, Eric H. *The Dangerous Class: Crime and Poverty in Columbus, Ohio 1860-1885.* Cambridge, Mass.: Harvard University Press, 1975.

Osborne, Harold, ed. *The Oxford Companion to Art.* Oxford: Clarendon Press, 1970.

Perry, Dick. *Ohio: A Personal Portrait of the 17th State.* Garden City, New York: Doubleday, 1969.

Pollard, James E. *History of the Ohio State University.* Columbus: Ohio State University Press, 1952.

Richardson, Lyon N.; Orians H. George; Brown, Herbert R., eds. *The Heritage of American Literature.* Vol. II New York: Ginn and Co., 1951.

Rippley, LaVern. *The Columbus Germans.* Baltimore: J.H. Furst Company, 1968.

Shedd, Carlos. *Tales of Old Columbus.* [Columbus]: n.p., n.d.

Sheridan, Philip. *Those Wonderful Old Downtown Theaters.* Columbus, Ohio: n.p., 1978.

Studer, Jacob Henry. *Columbus, Ohio.* [Columbus]: n.p., 1873.

Sullivant, Joseph. *Genealogy and Family Memorial.* Columbus: Ohio State Journal Book Rooms, 1874.

The Governors of Ohio. Columbus: The Ohio Historical Society, 1969.

Throckmorton, Robert J., ed. *Columbus, Ohio, Division of Fire.* Columbus. Ohio: Department of Safety, Division of Fire, 1976.

Thurber, James. *My Life and Hard Times.* New York and London: Harper & Brothers, 1933.

Thurber, James. *The Thurber Album.* New York: Simon and Schuster, 1952.

Thurber, James, *Thurber Country.* New York: Simon and Schuster, 1953.
NOTE: All Thurber material reprinted courtesy of Mrs. James Thurber.

Trade Unions of Columbus: Their History. Biographical Sketches. Columbus: n.p., 1895.

White, Ruth Young, ed. *We Too Built Columbus.* Columbus, Ohio: Stoneman Press, 1936.

Women of Ohio. Ohio Yearbook. Martha Kinney Cooper Ohioana Library. Columbus: n.p., 1973.

Interviews

Chenoweth, Doral
Harden, Michael
Hayes, Woody
Janowicz, Vic
Jauchius, Dean
La Nata, Lt. Anthony
Lazarus, Charles
Lazarus Jr., Robert
Reynolds, Clara
Rhodes, James
Wolfe, Preston

Ohio Historical Society Oral History Interview with George de Nucci.
"Memories of Old Columbus," unpublished interview with Alice Strickler Keyes.
Columbus Historical Calendar, Volunteers of America, 1980.

Other Sources

"Columbus and Franklin County, Past and Present." Columbus: Franklin County Historical Society, 1972.

Illustrated Guide to Columbus. Columbus, Ohio: Columbus Street Railway Company, 1899. (booklet)

Lentz, Edward R. "Rationalization and Reform: The Columbus Urban League 1942-1962." Ohio State University, 1969. (thesis)

The following newspapers were consulted extensively for use in this project:

Columbus Citizen
Columbus Citizen-Journal
Columbus Dispatch
Columbus Dispatch Sunday Magazine
Columbus Monthly
New York Times
Ohio Magazine
Ohio State Journal

Ohio State University Annual Reports "Wilkommen." German Village Society, n.d., n.p. (pamphlet)

Acknowledgements

The publishers are indebted to a number of people, who by their interest and commitment, have contributed to this portrait of Ohio's capital city. A special thanks to Sam Roshon, Public Library of Columbus and Franklin County.

To the volunteer leadership and professional staff of the Columbus Area Chamber of Commerce, Frank Wobst, chairman; John W. Kessler, immediate past chairman; Alfred S. Dietzel, president; and Marjory Pizzuti, vice president of public affairs, who supervised this project.

Others on the Chamber staff who contributed to the book include Billie Schmalz, Tanya Straker, Cathi DeVoe, Grace Juliano, Mary Buck, Mary Nesbitt and Ann Joyce.

Also, Bob Zimmer, Bob O'Brien, Dave Barker, Betty Rogers and Margie Goldberg. We are also indebted to Chris Shama, Karen Darrington, Wendy Wall and Cindy Pogue for their special attention to sense of direction.

To Dr. Michael Devine, formerly of the Ohio Historical Society, now of the Greater Cincinnati Consortium of Colleges and Universities, for his guidance and text authentication.

To William Kight, William Greffin and Jerry Merrell who contributed their talents and advice. Of course, we are indebted to Dave Lucas from the city of Columbus, who contributed marvelous photographs and lent helpful advice.

To Jerry Pizzuti and Judy Moore of Holiday Rent-a-Car Systems of Columbus for their fine, professional services.

To the professional staff of Ohio State University for their contributions of campus photographs and support toward this community project.

Mac and Jean McAlester, along with Don and Marge McCoy, provided fine Columbus hospitality and it was appreciated.

Others who contributed to the book's success were: Marie Flagg, Paula Sullivan, Missy Kruse, Wally King, Leslie Erwin, Caroline Johnson, Mike Hollifield and CHP staff members: Barbara Jameson, Pat Briggs, Nine LeMaire, Nancy Coats and Linda Logsdon.

Photograph credits

Battelle Columbus Laboratories: 145 upper center

Barsotti, John: 116.

Brubaker/Brandt Incorporated Architects: 162 upper right & left.

Capitol South: 163 upper right & left.

Center of Science & Industry: 4/5, 145 lower.

City of Columbus, Department of Development: 163 lower.

Columbus Dispatch: 123, 126, 156.

Columbus Mayors Office: 164 upper right.

Crain, Doug: 172 upper center.

Greffin, Bill: 152 upper right, 175.

Hamill, Larry: 9, 148 upper right, 162 lower, 170 lower, 176 upper center.

Lucas, David E.: 12/13, 32, 145 inset, 146/147 all, 148 right insets, 149 all, 150/151 152 upper left, 153, 154 all, 157 all, 158 lower left, 159 inset, 160 all, 161 all, 164 upper & lower, 165 all, 166 top, 167 center right, 168/169 all, 171 top and lower left, 172 lower right & left, center right & left, 173 all, 174 all.

National Archives: 102 upper center.

New York Public Library: 39 bottom.

Ohio Historical Society: 2/3, 6/7, 8, 10, 11, 12 upper, 14/15 all, 16, 17 all, 18, 19, 20, 21, 22, 23, 24, 25 all, 26, 28 all, 30/31 all, 33, 34 all, 35, 36, 37, 38 all, 39, 40, 41, 42 all, 43, 44 all, 46 all, 47, 48 all, 50, 51, 52, 53, 54 all, 55 all, 56 all, 57, 58 all, 59, 60/61 all, 62/63 all, 64/65 all, 65, 66/67 all, 68/69 all, 70/71 all, 72/73 all, 74/75 all, 76/77 all, 78/79 all, 80/81 all, 82/83 all, 84/85 all, 86/87 all, 88/89 all, 90/91 all, 92/93 all, 94, 95 all, 96 all, 98/99 all, 100/101 all, 103, 104/105, 106, 108, 110/111 all, 112/113, 114/115 all, 117, 118/119 all, 120/121 all, 122 center, 122, 123, 125 all, 126, 127, 128/129 all, 130 all, 132/133, 134/135, 136, 139, 140, 141, 143, 148 left, 159, 160/161, 167, 170 upper, 177, 178/179, 180, 250, 252, 255, 256.

Ohio State University: 158 upper center, 166 bottom, 171 lower right.

Ohio State University Department of Photography: 122 left.

Olentangy Management Company: 152 lower.

James Thurber excerpts

Union Station, 1916.

Concept and design by Continental Heritage Press, Inc., Tulsa
Printed and bound by Walsworth Publishing, Marceline, Missouri
Type is Goudy Old Style
Text sheets are Warrenflo by S. D. Warren Company
Endleaves are Multicolor Antique
Cover is Kingston by Holliston Mills